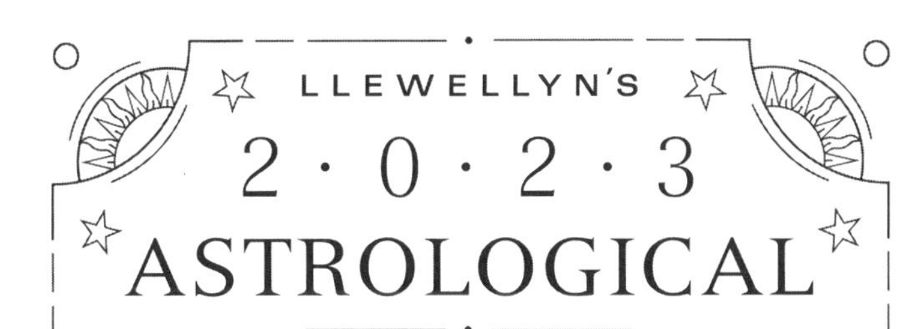

LLEWELLYN'S

2·0·2·3 ASTROLOGICAL

POCKET PLANNER

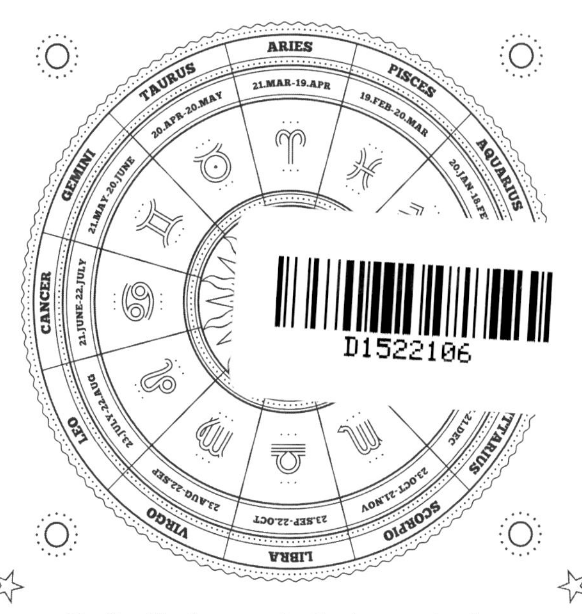

Daily Ephemeris & Aspectarian

2022–2024

ISBN-13: 978-0-7387-6390-3

Cover design by Shannon McKuhen
Edited by Hanna Grimson

A special thanks to Beth Rosato for astrological proofreading.

Published by
LLEWELLYN WORLDWIDE LTD.
2143 Wooddale Drive
Woodbury, MN 55125-2989
www.llewellyn.com

Printed in the United States of America

Table of Contents

Mercury Retrograde 2023

	DATE	**ET**	PT			DATE	**ET**	PT
Mercury Retrograde	12/29/22	**4:32 am**	1:32 am	—	Mercury Direct	1/18	**8:12 am**	5:12 am
Mercury Retrograde	4/21	**4:35 am**	1:35 am	—	Mercury Direct	5/14	**11:17 pm**	8:17 pm
Mercury Retrograde	8/23	**3:59 pm**	12:59 pm	—	Mercury Direct	9/15	**4:21 pm**	1:21 pm
Mercury Retrograde	12/12		11:09 pm	—	Mercury Direct	1/1/24	**10:08 pm**	7:08 pm
Mercury Retrograde	12/13	**2:09 am**		—	Mercury Direct	1/1/24	**10:08 pm**	7:08 pm

Moon Void-of-Course 2023

Times are listed in Eastern time in this table only. All other information in the *Pocket Planner* is listed in both Eastern time and Pacific time. Refer to "Time Zone Conversions" on page 8 for changing to other time zones. Note: All times are corrected for Daylight Saving Time.

JANUARY

Last Aspect		Moon Enters New Sign		
Date	Time	Date	Sign	Time
2	5:16 pm	2	♊	9:44 pm
4	7:08 pm	5	♋	9:15 am
7	5:23 pm	7	♌	9:40 pm
9	8:52 pm	10	♍	10:15 am
12	6:06 pm	12	♎	9:56 pm
15	3:40 am	15	♏	7:08 am
17	9:27 am	17	♐	12:33 pm
19	5:09 am	19	♑	2:11 pm
21	10:52 am	21	♒	1:29 pm
23	5:19 am	23	♓	12:36 pm
25	11:12 am	25	♈	1:48 pm
27	4:01 pm	27	♉	6:42 pm
30	12:52 am	30	♊	3:35 am

FEBRUARY

Last Aspect		Moon Enters New Sign		
Date	Time	Date	Sign	Time
1	6:58 am	1	♋	3:11 pm
4	1:19 am	4	♌	3:48 am
6	9:15 am	6	♍	4:14 pm
9	1:40 am	9	♎	3:47 am
11	11:41 am	11	♏	1:34 pm
13	6:52 pm	13	♐	8:31 pm
15	8:06 pm	16	♑	12:00 am
17	11:18 pm	18	♒	12:35 am
19	9:00 pm	19	♓	11:56 pm
21	11:06 pm	22	♈	12:14 am
24	2:22 am	24	♉	3:29 am
26	9:42 am	26	♊	10:48 am
28	8:07 pm	28	♋	9:40 pm

MARCH

Last Aspect		Moon Enters New Sign		
Date	Time	Date	Sign	Time
3	9:22 am	3	♌	10:16 am
5	10:18 pm	5	♍	10:38 pm
8	9:07 am	8	♎	9:44 am
10	6:37 pm	10	♏	7:06 pm
13	2:58 am	13	♐	3:21 am
15	4:50 am	15	♑	8:06 am
17	10:14 am	17	♒	10:25 am
19	6:33 am	19	♓	11:12 am
21	11:58 am	21	♈	12:01 pm
23	1:13 pm	23	♉	2:42 pm
25	12:19 pm	25	♊	8:42 pm
27	9:39 pm	28	♋	6:22 am
30	9:45 am	30	♌	6:31 pm

Moon Void-of-Course 2023 (cont.)

APRIL

Last Aspect Date	Last Aspect Time	Moon Enters New Sign Date	Sign	Time
2	2:03 am	2	♍	6:57 am
4	9:50 am	4	♎	5:51 pm
6	8:43 am	7	♏	2:29 am
9	5:09 am	9	♐	8:57 am
11	6:48 am	11	♑	1:33 pm
13	10:14 am	13	♒	4:42 pm
15	11:16 am	15	♓	6:57 pm
17	2:57 pm	17	♈	9:09 pm
20	12:13 am	20	♉	12:30 am
21	11:41 pm	22	♊	6:11 am
24	8:15 am	24	♋	2:58 pm
26	7:41 pm	27	♌	2:30 am
29	6:53 am	29	♍	2:59 pm

MAY

Last Aspect Date	Last Aspect Time	Moon Enters New Sign Date	Sign	Time
1	7:53 pm	2	♎	2:09 am
4	5:17 am	4	♏	10:32 am
6	10:38 am	6	♐	4:04 pm
8	4:28 pm	8	♑	7:33 pm
10	7:52 pm	10	♒	10:05 pm
12	11:15 pm	13	♓	12:39 am
14	10:56 pm	15	♈	3:56 am
17	5:10 am	17	♉	8:28 am
19	1:51 pm	19	♊	2:48 pm
21	6:12 pm	21	♋	11:28 pm
24	5:12 am	24	♌	10:35 am
26	2:38 am	26	♍	11:05 pm
29	5:46 am	29	♎	10:51 am
31	10:53 am	31	♏	7:45 pm

JUNE

Last Aspect Date	Last Aspect Time	Moon Enters New Sign Date	Sign	Time
2	8:51 pm	3	♐	1:03 am
4	11:24 pm	5	♑	3:31 am
7	12:40 am	7	♒	4:42 am
9	12:24 am	9	♓	6:14 am
11	9:20 am	11	♈	9:20 am
13	2:27 pm	13	♉	2:31 pm
15	9:36 pm	15	♊	9:46 pm
18	2:24 am	18	♋	6:58 am
20	5:43 pm	20	♌	6:04 pm
22	1:01 pm	23	♍	6:35 am
25	6:24 pm	25	♎	6:57 pm
28	4:19 am	28	♏	4:55 am
30	10:20 am	30	♐	10:59 am

JULY

Last Aspect Date	Last Aspect Time	Moon Enters New Sign Date	Sign	Time
2	9:33 am	2	♑	1:20 pm
4	12:45 pm	4	♒	1:30 pm
6	9:42 am	6	♓	1:33 pm
8	2:22 pm	8	♈	3:19 pm
10	7:11 pm	10	♉	7:55 pm
13	2:11 am	13	♊	3:26 am
15	8:35 am	15	♋	1:13 pm
17	11:06 pm	18	♌	12:39 am
20	10:08 am	20	♍	1:13 pm
23	12:06 am	23	♎	1:54 am
25	11:05 am	25	♏	12:55 pm
27	6:36 pm	27	♐	8:24 pm
29	7:51 pm	29	♑	11:44 pm
31	10:13 pm	31	♒	11:58 pm

AUGUST

Last Aspect Date	Last Aspect Time	Moon Enters New Sign Date	Sign	Time
2	5:15 pm	2	♓	11:05 pm
4	9:21 pm	4	♈	11:19 pm
7	12:13 am	7	♉	2:25 am
9	6:39 am	9	♊	9:05 am
11	1:27 pm	11	♋	6:52 pm
14	3:46 am	14	♌	6:36 am
16	5:38 am	16	♍	7:14 pm
19	4:51 am	19	♎	7:53 am
21	4:31 pm	21	♏	7:22 pm
24	1:10 am	24	♐	4:07 am
26	7:56 am	27	♑	9:05 am
28	7:49 am	28	♒	10:32 am
29	11:04 pm	30	♓	9:56 am

SEPTEMBER

Last Aspect Date	Last Aspect Time	Moon Enters New Sign Date	Sign	Time
1	6:36 am	1	♈	9:25 am
3	7:57 am	3	♉	11:00 am
5	12:46 pm	5	♊	4:07 pm
7	6:22 pm	8	♋	1:00 am
10	8:47 am	10	♌	12:36 pm
12	11:06 am	13	♍	1:18 am
15	9:49 am	15	♎	1:44 pm
17	9:06 pm	18	♏	12:58 am
20	6:21 am	20	♐	10:06 am
22	3:32 pm	22	♑	4:20 pm
24	4:05 pm	24	♒	7:29 pm
26	8:38 am	26	♓	8:18 pm
28	4:58 pm	28	♈	8:17 pm
30	5:50 pm	30	♉	9:18 pm

OCTOBER

Last Aspect Date	Last Aspect Time	Moon Enters New Sign Date	Sign	Time
2	9:20 pm	3	♊	1:03 pm
5	2:34 am	5	♋	8:32 am
7	3:12 pm	7	♌	7:24 pm
10	5:37 am	10	♍	8:02 am
12	4:10 pm	12	♎	8:22 pm
15	3:01 am	15	♏	7:04 am
17	11:44 am	17	♐	3:36 pm
19	3:02 pm	19	♑	9:55 pm
22	2:00 am	22	♒	2:06 am
23	3:04 pm	24	♓	4:33 am
26	2:39 am	26	♈	6:02 am
28	4:20 am	28	♉	7:44 am
30	7:36 am	30	♊	11:08 am

NOVEMBER

Last Aspect Date	Last Aspect Time	Moon Enters New Sign Date	Sign	Time
1	8:36 am	1	♋	5:30 pm
3	11:28 pm	4	♌	3:21 am
6	2:25 am	6	♍	2:39 pm
8	11:55 pm	9	♎	3:08 am
11	10:05 am	11	♏	1:39 pm
13	6:03 pm	13	♐	9:23 pm
15	5:57 pm	16	♑	2:41 am
18	3:27 am	18	♒	6:28 am
20	5:50 am	20	♓	9:29 am
22	10:10 am	22	♈	12:19 pm
24	12:40 pm	24	♉	3:29 pm
26	4:52 pm	26	♊	7:40 pm
28	8:03 pm	29	♋	1:54 am

DECEMBER

Last Aspect Date	Last Aspect Time	Moon Enters New Sign Date	Sign	Time
1	8:07 am	1	♌	11:00 am
3	9:11 pm	3	♍	10:50 pm
6	8:50 am	6	♎	11:35 am
8	8:05 pm	8	♏	10:35 pm
11	3:57 am	11	♐	6:11 am
13	1:48 am	13	♑	10:31 am
15	11:04 am	15	♒	12:56 pm
17	7:04 am	17	♓	2:58 pm
19	4:03 pm	19	♈	5:47 pm
21	9:47 pm	21	♉	9:50 pm
24	1:40 am	24	♊	3:15 am
26	2:55 am	26	♋	10:15 am
28	5:57 pm	28	♌	7:23 pm
31	12:18 am	31	♍	6:53 am

How to Use the *Pocket Planner*

by Leslie Nielsen

This handy guide contains information that can be most valuable to you as you plan your daily activities. As you read through the first few pages, you can start to get a feel for how well organized this guide is.

Read the Symbol Key on the next page, which is rather like astrological shorthand. The characteristics of the planets can give you direction in planning your strategies. Much like traffic signs that signal "go," "stop," or even "caution," you can determine for yourself the most propitious time to get things done.

You'll find tables that show the dates when Mercury is retrograde (℞) or direct (D). Because Mercury deals with the exchange of information, a retrograde Mercury makes miscommunication more noticeable.

There's also a section dedicated to the times when the Moon is void-of-course (V/C). These are generally poor times to conduct business because activities begun during these times usually end badly or fail to get started. If you make an appointment during a void-of-course, you might save yourself a lot of aggravation by confirming the time and date later. The Moon is only void-of-course for 7 percent of the time when business is usually conducted during a normal workday (that is, 8:00 am to 5:00 pm). Sometimes, by waiting a matter of minutes or a few hours until the Moon has left the void-of-course phase, you have a much better chance to make action move more smoothly. Moon voids can also be used successfully to do routine activities or inner work, such as dream therapy or personal contemplation.

You'll find Moon phases, as well as each of the Moon's entries into a new sign. Times are expressed in Eastern time (in bold type) and Pacific time (in regular type). The New Moon time is generally best for beginning new activities, as the Moon is increasing in light and can offer the element of growth to our endeavors. When the Moon is Full, its illumination is greatest and we can see the results of our efforts. When it moves from the Full stage back to the New stage, it can best be used to reflect on our projects. If necessary, we can make corrections at the New Moon.

The section of "Planetary Stations" on page 9 will give you the times when the planets are changing signs or direction, thereby affording us opportunities for new starts.

The ephemeris in the back of your *Pocket Planner* can be very helpful to you. As you start to work with the ephemeris, you may notice that not all planets seem to be comfortable in every sign. Think of the planets as actors and the signs as the costumes they wear. Sometimes, costumes just itch. If you find this to be so for a certain time period, you may choose to delay your plans for a time or be more creative with the energies at hand.

As you turn to the daily pages, you'll find information about the Moon's sign, phase, and the time it changes phase. You'll find icons indicating the best days to plant and fish. Also, you will find times and dates when the planets and asteroids change signs and go either retrograde or direct, major holidays, a three-month calendar, and room to record your appointments.

This guide is a powerful tool. Make the most of it!

Symbol Key

Planets:	☉ Sun	⚳ Ceres	♄ Saturn
	☽ Moon	⚴ Pallas	⚷ Chiron
	☿ Mercury	⚵ Juno	♅ Uranus
	♀ Venus	⚶ Vesta	♆ Neptune
	♂ Mars	♃ Jupiter	♇ Pluto
Signs:	♈ Aries	♌ Leo	♐ Sagittarius
	♉ Taurus	♍ Virgo	♑ Capricorn
	♊ Gemini	♎ Libra	♒ Aquarius
	♋ Cancer	♏ Scorpio	♓ Pisces
Aspects:	☌ Conjunction (0°)	⚺ Semisextile (30°)	⚹ Sextile (60°)
	□ Square (90°)	△ Trine (120°)	
	⚻ Quincunx (150°)	☍ Opposition (180°)	
Motion:	℞ Retrograde	D Direct	
Best Days for Planting:		**Best Days for Fishing:**	

World Map of Time Zones

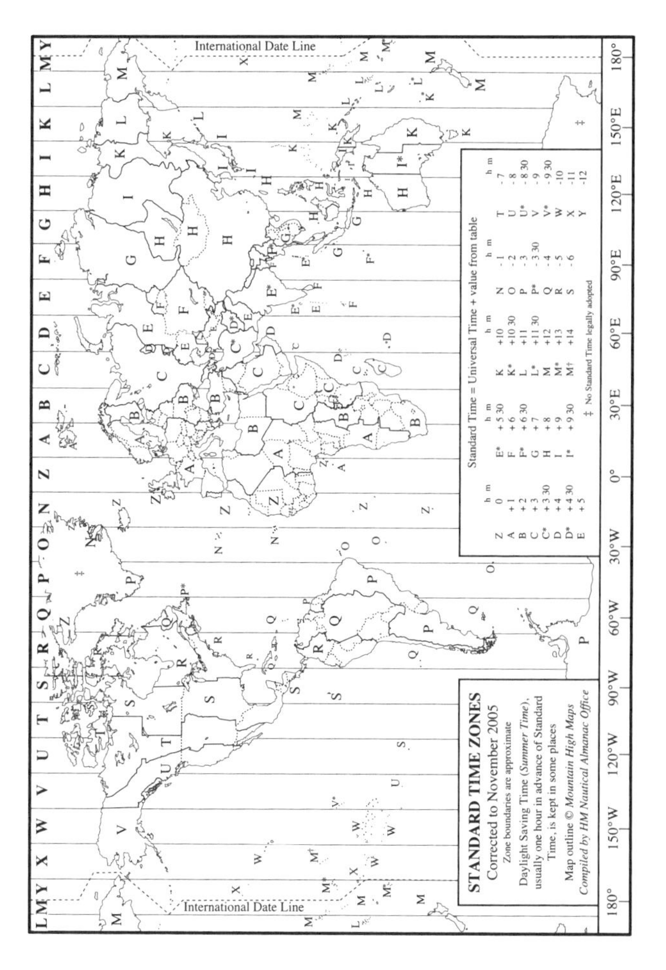

International Date Line
STANDARD TIME ZONES
Corrected to November 2005
Zone boundaries are approximate
Daylight Saving Time (Summer Time), usually one hour in advance of Standard Time, is kept in some places
Map outline © Mountain High Maps
Compiled by HM Nautical Almanac Office
Standard Time = Universal Time + value from table
Z 0; A +1; B +2; C +3; C* +3 30; D +4; D* +4 30; E +5
E* +5 30; F +6; F* +6 30; G +7; H +8; I +9; I* +9 30
K +10; K* +10 30; L +11; L* +11 30; M +12; M* +13; M† +14
N -1; O -2; P -3; P* -3 30; Q -4; R -5; S -6
T -7; U -8; U* -8 30; V -9; V* -9 30; W -10; X -11; Y -12
‡ No Standard Time legally adopted
180° 150°W 120°W 90°W 60°W 30°W 0° 30°E 60°E 90°E 120°E 150°E 180°

Time Zone Conversions

World Time Zones

Compared to Eastern Standard Time

( ) From Map
(S) CST/Subtract 1 hour
(R) EST
(Q) Add 1 hour
(P) Add 2 hours
(O) Add 3 hours
(N) Add 4 hours
(Z) Add 5 hours
(T) MST/Subtract 2 hours
(U) PST/Subtract 3 hours
(V) Subtract 4 hours
(W) Subtract 5 hours
(X) Subtract 6 hours
(Y) Subtract 7 hours
(A) Add 6 hours
(B) Add 7 hours
(C) Add 8 hours
(D) Add 9 hours
(E) Add 10 hours
(F) Add 11 hours
(G) Add 12 hours
(H) Add 13 hours
(I) Add 14 hours
(K) Add 15 hours
(L) Add 16 hours
(M) Add 17 hours
(C*) Add 8.5 hours
(D*) Add 9.5 hours
(E*) Add 10.5 hours
(F*) Add 11.5 hours
(I*) Add 14.5 hours
(K*) Add 15.5 hours
(L*) Add 16.5 hours
(M*) Add 18 hours
(P*) Add 2.5 hours
(U*) Subtract 3.5 hours
(V*) Subtract 4.5 hours

World Map of Time Zones is supplied by HM Nautical Almanac Office © Center for the Central Laboratory of the Research Councils. Note: This is not an official map. Countries change their time zones as they wish.

Planetary Stations for 2023

	JAN	FEB	MAR	APR	MAY	JUN	JUL	AUG	SEP	OCT	NOV	DEC
☿	-1/18			4/21–5/14				8/23–9/15				12/13–
♀								7/22–9/3				
♂	-1/12											
♃											9/4–12/30	
♄								6/17–11/4				
♅	-1/22									8/28–1/27/24		
♆									6/30–12/6			
♇							5/1–10/10					
⚷									7/23–12/26			
⚳			2/3–5/6									
⚴	-2/16											
⚵												
⚶												11/2–2/8/24

26 Monday

1st ♒

☽ v/c	**1:19 pm**	10:19 am
☽ enters ♓		11:34 pm

Kwanzaa begins

27 Tuesday

1st ♒

☽ enters ♓	**2:34 am**	

28 Wednesday

1st ♓

☽ v/c		10:21 pm

29 Thursday

1st ♓

☽ v/c	**1:21 am**	
☿ ℞	**4:32 am**	1:32 am
☽ enters ♈	**5:36 am**	2:36 am
2nd Quarter	**8:21 pm**	5:21 pm

Mercury retrograde until 1/18

Eastern time in bold type
Pacific time in medium type

30 Friday

2nd ♈

31 Saturday

2nd ♈

☽ v/c **7:44 am** 4:44 am

☽ enters ♉ **12:08 pm** 9:08 am

New Year's Eve

1 Sunday

2nd ♉

Kwanzaa ends • New Year's Day

December 2022

S	M	T	W	T	F	S
				1	2	3
4	5	6	7	8	9	10
11	12	13	14	15	16	17
18	19	20	21	22	23	24
25	26	27	28	29	30	31

January 2023

S	M	T	W	T	F	S
1	2	3	4	5	6	7
8	9	10	11	12	13	14
15	16	17	18	19	20	21
22	23	24	25	26	27	28
29	30	31				

February 2023

S	M	T	W	T	F	S
			1	2	3	4
5	6	7	8	9	10	11
12	13	14	15	16	17	18
19	20	21	22	23	24	25
26	27	28				

2 Monday

2nd ♉

☽ v/c	**5:16 pm**	2:16 pm
♀ enters ♒	**9:09 pm**	6:09 pm
☽ enters ♊	**9:44 pm**	6:44 pm

3 Tuesday

2nd ♊

4 Wednesday

2nd ♊

☽ v/c	**7:08 pm**	4:08 pm

5 Thursday

2nd ♊

☽ enters ♋	**9:15 am**	6:15 am

Eastern time in bold type
Pacific time in medium type

6 Friday

2nd ♋
Full Moon **6:08 pm** 3:08 pm

7 Saturday

3rd ♋
☽ v/c **5:23 pm** 2:23 pm
☽ enters ♌ **9:40 pm** 6:40 pm

8 Sunday

3rd ♌

December 2022

S	M	T	W	T	F	S
				1	2	3
4	5	6	7	8	9	10
11	12	13	14	15	16	17
18	19	20	21	22	23	24
25	26	27	28	29	30	31

January 2023

S	M	T	W	T	F	S
1	2	3	4	5	6	7
8	9	10	11	12	13	14
15	16	17	18	19	20	21
22	23	24	25	26	27	28
29	30	31				

February 2023

S	M	T	W	T	F	S
			1	2	3	4
5	6	7	8	9	10	11
12	13	14	15	16	17	18
19	20	21	22	23	24	25
26	27	28				

9 Monday

3rd ♌

☽ v/c	**8:52 pm**	5:52 pm

10 Tuesday

3rd ♌

☽ enters ♍	**10:15 am**	7:15 am

11 Wednesday

3rd ♍

12 Thursday

3rd ♍

♂ D	**3:56 pm**	12:56 pm
☽ v/c	**6:06 pm**	3:06 pm
☽ enters ♎	**9:56 pm**	6:56 pm
⚵ enters ♈		10:30 pm

Eastern time in bold type
Pacific time in medium type

13 Friday

3rd ♎
⚵ enters ♈ **1:30 am**

14 Saturday

3rd ♎
4th Quarter **9:10 pm** 6:10 pm

15 Sunday

4th ♎
☽ v/c **3:40 am** 12:40 am

☽ enters ♏ **7:08 am** 4:08 am

December 2022

S	M	T	W	T	F	S
				1	2	3
4	5	6	7	8	9	10
11	12	13	14	15	16	17
18	19	20	21	22	23	24
25	26	27	28	29	30	31

January 2023

S	M	T	W	T	F	S
1	2	3	4	5	6	7
8	9	10	11	12	13	14
15	16	17	18	19	20	21
22	23	24	25	26	27	28
29	30	31				

February 2023

S	M	T	W	T	F	S
			1	2	3	4
5	6	7	8	9	10	11
12	13	14	15	16	17	18
19	20	21	22	23	24	25
26	27	28				

Eastern time in bold type
Pacific time in medium type

16 Monday

4th ♏

Martin Luther King Jr. Day

17 Tuesday

4th ♏
☽ v/c **9:27 am** 6:27 am
☽ enters ♐ **12:33 pm** 9:33 am

18 Wednesday

4th ♐
☿ D **8:12 am** 5:12 am

19 Thursday

4th ♐
☽ v/c **5:09 am** 2:09 am
☽ enters ♑ **2:11 pm** 11:11 am

Eastern time in bold type
Pacific time in medium type

20 Friday

4th ♑
☉ enters ♒ **3:30 am** 12:30 am

Sun enters Aquarius

21 Saturday

4th ♑
☽ v/c **10:52 am** 7:52 am
☽ enters ♒ **1:29 pm** 10:29 am
New Moon **3:53 pm** 12:53 pm

22 Sunday

1st ♒
♅ D **5:59 pm** 2:59 pm

Lunar New Year (Rabbit)

December 2022

S	M	T	W	T	F	S
				1	2	3
4	5	6	7	8	9	10
11	12	13	14	15	16	17
18	19	20	21	22	23	24
25	26	27	28	29	30	31

January 2023

S	M	T	W	T	F	S
1	2	3	4	5	6	7
8	9	10	11	12	13	14
15	16	17	18	19	20	21
22	23	24	25	26	27	28
29	30	31				

February 2023

S	M	T	W	T	F	S
			1	2	3	4
5	6	7	8	9	10	11
12	13	14	15	16	17	18
19	20	21	22	23	24	25
26	27	28				

23 Monday

1st ♒

☽ v/c **5:19 am** 2:19 am

☽ enters ♓ **12:36 pm** 9:36 am

24 Tuesday

1st ♓

25 Wednesday

1st ♓

☽ v/c **11:12 am** 8:12 am

☽ enters ♈ **1:48 pm** 10:48 am

26 Thursday

1st ♈

♀ enters ♓ **9:33 pm** 6:33 pm

27 Friday

1st ♈

☽ v/c	**4:01 pm**	1:01 pm
☽ enters ♉	**6:42 pm**	3:42 pm

28 Saturday

1st ♉

2nd Quarter **10:19 am** 7:19 am

29 Sunday

2nd ♉

☽ v/c 9:52 pm

December 2022

S	M	T	W	T	F	S
				1	2	3
4	5	6	7	8	9	10
11	12	13	14	15	16	17
18	19	20	21	22	23	24
25	26	27	28	29	30	31

January 2023

S	M	T	W	T	F	S
1	2	3	4	5	6	7
8	9	10	11	12	13	14
15	16	17	18	19	20	21
22	23	24	25	26	27	28
29	30	31				

February 2023

S	M	T	W	T	F	S
			1	2	3	4
5	6	7	8	9	10	11
12	13	14	15	16	17	18
19	20	21	22	23	24	25
26	27	28				

Eastern time in bold type
Pacific time in medium type

30 Monday

2nd ♉
☽ v/c **12:52 am**
☽ enters ♊ **3:35 am** 12:35 am

31 Tuesday

2nd ♊

1 Wednesday

2nd ♊
☽ v/c **6:58 am** 3:58 am
☽ enters ♋ **3:11 pm** 12:11 pm

2 Thursday

2nd ♋

Imbolc • Groundhog Day

Eastern time in bold type
Pacific time in medium type

3 Friday

2nd ♋
⚳ ℞ **2:13 pm** 11:13 am
☽ v/c 10:19 pm

4 Saturday

2nd ♋
☽ v/c **1:19 am**
☽ enters ♌ **3:48 am** 12:48 am

5 Sunday

2nd ♌
Full Moon **1:29 pm** 10:29 am

January 2023

S	M	T	W	T	F	S
1	2	3	4	5	6	7
8	9	10	11	12	13	14
15	16	17	18	19	20	21
22	23	24	25	26	27	28
29	30	31				

February 2023

S	M	T	W	T	F	S
			1	2	3	4
5	6	7	8	9	10	11
12	13	14	15	16	17	18
19	20	21	22	23	24	25
26	27	28				

March 2023

S	M	T	W	T	F	S
			1	2	3	4
5	6	7	8	9	10	11
12	13	14	15	16	17	18
19	20	21	22	23	24	25
26	27	28	29	30	31	

Eastern time in bold type
Pacific time in medium type

6 Monday

3rd ♌
☽ v/c **9:15 am** 6:15 am
☽ enters ♍ **4:14 pm** 1:14 pm

7 Tuesday

3rd ♍
⚳ enters ♈ **11:47 pm** 8:47 pm

8 Wednesday

3rd ♍
☽ v/c 10:40 pm

9 Thursday

3rd ♍
☽ v/c **1:40 am**
☽ enters ♎ **3:47 am** 12:47 am

Eastern time in bold type
Pacific time in medium type

10 Friday

3rd ♎

11 Saturday

3rd ♎

☿ enters ♒	**6:22 am**	3:22 am
☽ v/c	**11:41 am**	8:41 am
☽ enters ♏	**1:34 pm**	10:34 am

12 Sunday

3rd ♏

January 2023						
S	M	T	W	T	F	S
1	2	3	4	5	6	7
8	9	10	11	12	13	14
15	16	17	18	19	20	21
22	23	24	25	26	27	28
29	30	31				

February 2023						
S	M	T	W	T	F	S
			1	2	3	4
5	6	7	8	9	10	11
12	13	14	15	16	17	18
19	20	21	22	23	24	25
26	27	28				

March 2023						
S	M	T	W	T	F	S
			1	2	3	4
5	6	7	8	9	10	11
12	13	14	15	16	17	18
19	20	21	22	23	24	25
26	27	28	29	30	31	

13 Monday

3rd ♏

4th Quarter	**11:01 am**	8:01 am
☽ v/c	**6:52 pm**	3:52 pm
☽ enters ♐	**8:31 pm**	5:31 pm

14 Tuesday

4th ♐

Valentine's Day

15 Wednesday

4th ♐

☽ v/c	**8:06 pm**	5:06 pm
☽ enters ♑		9:00 pm

16 Thursday

4th ♑

☽ enters ♑	**12:00 am**	
⚴ D	**9:26 am**	6:26 am

Eastern time in bold type
Pacific time in medium type

17 Friday

4th ♑
☽ v/c **11:18 pm** 8:18 pm
☽ enters ♒ 9:35 pm

18 Saturday

4th ♑
☽ enters ♒ **12:35 am**
☉ enters ♓ **5:34 pm** 2:34 pm

Sun enters Pisces

19 Sunday

4th ♒
☽ v/c **9:00 pm** 6:00 pm
☽ enters ♓ **11:56 pm** 8:56 pm
New Moon 11:06 pm
♀ enters ♈ 11:56 pm

January 2023

S	M	T	W	T	F	S
1	2	3	4	5	6	7
8	9	10	11	12	13	14
15	16	17	18	19	20	21
22	23	24	25	26	27	28
29	30	31				

February 2023

S	M	T	W	T	F	S
			1	2	3	4
5	6	7	8	9	10	11
12	13	14	15	16	17	18
19	20	21	22	23	24	25
26	27	28				

March 2023

S	M	T	W	T	F	S
			1	2	3	4
5	6	7	8	9	10	11
12	13	14	15	16	17	18
19	20	21	22	23	24	25
26	27	28	29	30	31	

20 Monday

4th ♓
New Moon **2:06 am**
♀ enters ♈ **2:56 am**

Presidents' Day

21 Tuesday

1st ♓
☽ v/c **11:06 pm** 8:06 pm
☽ enters ♈ 9:14 pm

Mardi Gras (Fat Tuesday)

22 Wednesday

1st ♓
☽ enters ♈ **12:14 am**

Ash Wednesday

23 Thursday

1st ♈
☽ v/c 11:22 pm

Eastern time in bold type
Pacific time in medium type

24 Friday

1st ♈
☽ v/c **2:22 am**
☽ enters ♉ **3:29 am** 12:29 am

25 Saturday

1st ♉

26 Sunday

1st ♉
☽ v/c **9:42 am** 6:42 am
☽ enters ♊ **10:48 am** 7:48 am

January 2023

S	M	T	W	T	F	S
1	2	3	4	5	6	7
8	9	10	11	12	13	14
15	16	17	18	19	20	21
22	23	24	25	26	27	28
29	30	31				

February 2023

S	M	T	W	T	F	S
			1	2	3	4
5	6	7	8	9	10	11
12	13	14	15	16	17	18
19	20	21	22	23	24	25
26	27	28				

March 2023

S	M	T	W	T	F	S
			1	2	3	4
5	6	7	8	9	10	11
12	13	14	15	16	17	18
19	20	21	22	23	24	25
26	27	28	29	30	31	

Eastern time in bold type
Pacific time in medium type

27 Monday

1st ♊
2nd Quarter **3:06 am** 12:06 am

28 Tuesday

2nd ♊
☽ v/c **8:07 pm** 5:07 pm
☽ enters ♋ **9:40 pm** 6:40 pm

1 Wednesday

2nd ♋

2 Thursday

2nd ♋
☿ enters ♓ **5:52 pm** 2:52 pm

Eastern time in bold type
Pacific time in medium type

3 Friday

2nd ♋

☽ v/c	**9:22 am**	6:22 am
☽ enters ♌	**10:16 am**	7:16 am

4 Saturday

2nd ♌

5 Sunday

2nd ♌

☽ v/c	**10:18 pm**	7:18 pm
☽ enters ♍	**10:38 pm**	7:38 pm

February 2023

S	M	T	W	T	F	S
			1	2	3	4
5	6	7	8	9	10	11
12	13	14	15	16	17	18
19	20	21	22	23	24	25
26	27	28				

March 2023

S	M	T	W	T	F	S
			1	2	3	4
5	6	7	8	9	10	11
12	13	14	15	16	17	18
19	20	21	22	23	24	25
26	27	28	29	30	31	

April 2023

S	M	T	W	T	F	S
						1
2	3	4	5	6	7	8
9	10	11	12	13	14	15
16	17	18	19	20	21	22
23	24	25	26	27	28	29
30						

Eastern time in bold type
Pacific time in medium type

6 Monday

2nd ♍

Purim begins at sundown

7 Tuesday

2nd ♍

Full Moon **7:40 am** 4:40 am
♄ enters ♓ **8:35 am** 5:35 am

8 Wednesday

3rd ♍

☽ v/c **9:07 am** 6:07 am
☽ enters ♎ **9:44 am** 6:44 am

9 Thursday

3rd ♎

Eastern time in bold type
Pacific time in medium type

10 Friday

3rd ♎

☽ v/c	**6:37 pm**	3:37 pm
☽ enters ♏	**7:06 pm**	4:06 pm

11 Saturday

3rd ♏

⚵ enters ♉	**11:15 am**	8:15 am

12 Sunday

3rd ♏

☽ v/c		11:58 pm

Daylight Saving Time begins at 2 am

February 2023

S	M	T	W	T	F	S
			1	2	3	4
5	6	7	8	9	10	11
12	13	14	15	16	17	18
19	20	21	22	23	24	25
26	27	28				

March 2023

S	M	T	W	T	F	S
			1	2	3	4
5	6	7	8	9	10	11
12	13	14	15	16	17	18
19	20	21	22	23	24	25
26	27	28	29	30	31	

April 2023

S	M	T	W	T	F	S
						1
2	3	4	5	6	7	8
9	10	11	12	13	14	15
16	17	18	19	20	21	22
23	24	25	26	27	28	29
30						

Eastern time in bold type
Pacific time in medium type

13 Monday

3rd ♏
☽ v/c **2:58 am**
☽ enters ♐ **3:21 am** 12:21 am

14 Tuesday

3rd ♐
4th Quarter **10:08 pm** 7:08 pm

15 Wednesday

4th ♐
☽ v/c **4:50 am** 1:50 am
☽ enters ♑ **8:06 am** 5:06 am

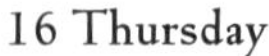

16 Thursday

4th ♑
♀ enters ♉ **6:34 pm** 3:34 pm

17 Friday

4th ♑
☽ v/c **10:14 am** 7:14 am
☽ enters ♒ **10:25 am** 7:25 am

St. Patrick's Day

18 Saturday

4th ♒
☿ enters ♈ 9:24 pm

19 Sunday

4th ♒
☿ enters ♈ **12:24 am**
☽ v/c **6:33 am** 3:33 am
☽ enters ♓ **11:12 am** 8:12 am

February 2023

S	M	T	W	T	F	S
			1	2	3	4
5	6	7	8	9	10	11
12	13	14	15	16	17	18
19	20	21	22	23	24	25
26	27	28				

March 2023

S	M	T	W	T	F	S
			1	2	3	4
5	6	7	8	9	10	11
12	13	14	15	16	17	18
19	20	21	22	23	24	25
26	27	28	29	30	31	

April 2023

S	M	T	W	T	F	S
						1
2	3	4	5	6	7	8
9	10	11	12	13	14	15
16	17	18	19	20	21	22
23	24	25	26	27	28	29
30						

Eastern time in bold type
Pacific time in medium type

20 Monday

4th ♓
☉ enters ♈ **5:24 pm** 2:24 pm

Int'l Astrology Day
Sun enters Aries • Ostara • Spring Equinox • 5:24 pm EDT/2:24 pm PDT

21 Tuesday

4th ♓
☽ v/c **11:58 am** 8:58 am
☽ enters ♈ **12:01 pm** 9:01 am
New Moon **1:23 pm** 10:23 am

22 Wednesday

1st ♈
⚳ enters ♍ **11:38 pm** 8:38 pm

Ramadan begins at sundown

23 Thursday

1st ♈
♇ enters ♒ **8:13 am** 5:13 am
☽ v/c **1:13 pm** 10:13 am
☽ enters ♉ **2:42 pm** 11:42 am

Eastern time in bold type
Pacific time in medium type

24 Friday

1st ♉

25 Saturday

1st ♉

♂ enters ♋	**7:45 am**	4:45 am
☽ v/c	**12:19 pm**	9:19 am
☽ enters ♊	**8:42 pm**	5:42 pm

26 Sunday

1st ♊

February 2023

S	M	T	W	T	F	S
			1	2	3	4
5	6	7	8	9	10	11
12	13	14	15	16	17	18
19	20	21	22	23	24	25
26	27	28				

March 2023

S	M	T	W	T	F	S
			1	2	3	4
5	6	7	8	9	10	11
12	13	14	15	16	17	18
19	20	21	22	23	24	25
26	27	28	29	30	31	

April 2023

S	M	T	W	T	F	S
						1
2	3	4	5	6	7	8
9	10	11	12	13	14	15
16	17	18	19	20	21	22
23	24	25	26	27	28	29
30						

Eastern time in bold type
Pacific time in medium type

27 Monday

1st ♊
☽ v/c **9:39 pm** 6:39 pm

28 Tuesday

1st ♊
☽ enters ♋ **6:22 am** 3:22 am
2nd Quarter **10:32 pm** 7:32 pm

29 Wednesday

2nd ♋

30 Thursday

2nd ♋
☽ v/c **9:45 am** 6:45 am
☽ enters ♌ **6:31 pm** 3:31 pm

31 Friday

2nd ♌

1 Saturday

2nd ♌
☽ v/c 11:03 pm

April Fools' Day (All Fools' Day—Pagan)

2 Sunday

2nd ♌
☽ v/c **2:03 am**
☽ enters ♍ **6:57 am** 3:57 am

Palm Sunday

March 2023

S	M	T	W	T	F	S
			1	2	3	4
5	6	7	8	9	10	11
12	13	14	15	16	17	18
19	20	21	22	23	24	25
26	27	28	29	30	31	

April 2023

S	M	T	W	T	F	S
						1
2	3	4	5	6	7	8
9	10	11	12	13	14	15
16	17	18	19	20	21	22
23	24	25	26	27	28	29
30						

May 2023

S	M	T	W	T	F	S
	1	2	3	4	5	6
7	8	9	10	11	12	13
14	15	16	17	18	19	20
21	22	23	24	25	26	27
28	29	30	31			

3 Monday

2nd ♍
☿ enters ♉ **12:22 pm** 9:22 am

4 Tuesday

2nd ♍
☽ v/c **9:50 am** 6:50 am
☽ enters ♎ **5:51 pm** 2:51 pm

5 Wednesday

2nd ♎
Full Moon 9:34 pm

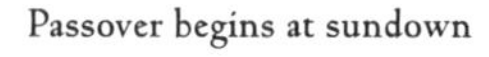
Passover begins at sundown

6 Thursday

2nd ♎
Full Moon **12:34 am**
☽ v/c **8:43 am** 5:43 am
☽ enters ♏ 11:29 pm

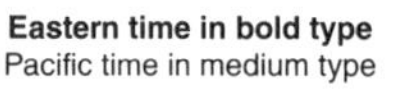
Eastern time in bold type
Pacific time in medium type

7 Friday

3rd ♎
☽ enters ♏ **2:29 am**

Good Friday

8 Saturday

3rd ♏

9 Sunday

3rd ♏

☽ v/c	**5:09 am**	2:09 am
☽ enters ♐	**8:57 am**	5:57 am

Easter

March 2023

S	M	T	W	T	F	S
			1	2	3	4
5	6	7	8	9	10	11
12	13	14	15	16	17	18
19	20	21	22	23	24	25
26	27	28	29	30	31	

April 2023

S	M	T	W	T	F	S
						1
2	3	4	5	6	7	8
9	10	11	12	13	14	15
16	17	18	19	20	21	22
23	24	25	26	27	28	29
30						

May 2023

S	M	T	W	T	F	S
	1	2	3	4	5	6
7	8	9	10	11	12	13
14	15	16	17	18	19	20
21	22	23	24	25	26	27
28	29	30	31			

10 Monday

3rd ♐
♀ enters ♊ 9:47 pm

11 Tuesday

3rd ♐
♀ enters ♊ **12:47 am**
☽ v/c **6:48 am** 3:48 am
☽ enters ♑ **1:33 pm** 10:33 am

12 Wednesday

3rd ♑

13 Thursday

3rd ♑
4th Quarter **5:11 am** 2:11 am
☽ v/c **10:14 am** 7:14 am
☽ enters ♒ **4:42 pm** 1:42 pm

Passover ends

Eastern time in bold type
Pacific time in medium type

14 Friday

4th ♒

Orthodox Good Friday

15 Saturday

4th ♒

☽ v/c	**11:16 am**	8:16 am
⚶ enters ♉	**1:01 pm**	10:01 am
☽ enters ♓	**6:57 pm**	3:57 pm

16 Sunday

4th ♓

Orthodox Easter

March 2023

S	M	T	W	T	F	S
			1	2	3	4
5	6	7	8	9	10	11
12	13	14	15	16	17	18
19	20	21	22	23	24	25
26	27	28	29	30	31	

April 2023

S	M	T	W	T	F	S
						1
2	3	4	5	6	7	8
9	10	11	12	13	14	15
16	17	18	19	20	21	22
23	24	25	26	27	28	29
30						

May 2023

S	M	T	W	T	F	S
	1	2	3	4	5	6
7	8	9	10	11	12	13
14	15	16	17	18	19	20
21	22	23	24	25	26	27
28	29	30	31			

17 Monday

4th ♓
☽ v/c **2:57 pm** 11:57 am
☽ enters ♈ **9:09 pm** 6:09 pm

18 Tuesday

4th ♈

19 Wednesday

4th ♈
☽ v/c 9:13 pm
New Moon 9:13 pm
☽ enters ♉ 9:30 pm

20 Thursday

4th ♈
☽ v/c **12:13 am**
New Moon **12:13 am**
☽ enters ♉ **12:30 am**
☉ enters ♉ **4:14 am** 1:14 am

Sun enters Taurus • Solar Eclipse 29° ♈ 50'

Eastern time in bold type
Pacific time in medium type

21 Friday

1st ♉
☿ ℞ **4:35 am** 1:35 am
☽ v/c **11:41 pm** 8:41 pm

Ramadan ends • Mercury retrograde until 5/14

22 Saturday

1st ♉
☽ enters ♊ **6:11 am** 3:11 am

Earth Day

23 Sunday

1st ♊

March 2023

S	M	T	W	T	F	S
			1	2	3	4
5	6	7	8	9	10	11
12	13	14	15	16	17	18
19	20	21	22	23	24	25
26	27	28	29	30	31	

April 2023

S	M	T	W	T	F	S
						1
2	3	4	5	6	7	8
9	10	11	12	13	14	15
16	17	18	19	20	21	22
23	24	25	26	27	28	29
30						

May 2023

S	M	T	W	T	F	S
	1	2	3	4	5	6
7	8	9	10	11	12	13
14	15	16	17	18	19	20
21	22	23	24	25	26	27
28	29	30	31			

Eastern time in bold type
Pacific time in medium type

24 Monday

1st ♊
☽ v/c **8:15 am** 5:15 am
☽ enters ♋ **2:58 pm** 11:58 am

25 Tuesday

1st ♋

26 Wednesday

1st ♋
☽ v/c **7:41 pm** 4:41 pm
☽ enters ♌ 11:30 pm

27 Thursday

1st ♋
☽ enters ♌ **2:30 am**
2nd Quarter **5:20 pm** 2:20 pm

28 Friday

2nd ♌

29 Saturday

2nd ♌
☽ v/c **6:53 am** 3:53 am
☽ enters ♍ **2:59 pm** 11:59 am

30 Sunday

2nd ♍

March 2023

S	M	T	W	T	F	S
			1	2	3	4
5	6	7	8	9	10	11
12	13	14	15	16	17	18
19	20	21	22	23	24	25
26	27	28	29	30	31	

April 2023

S	M	T	W	T	F	S
						1
2	3	4	5	6	7	8
9	10	11	12	13	14	15
16	17	18	19	20	21	22
23	24	25	26	27	28	29
30						

May 2023

S	M	T	W	T	F	S
	1	2	3	4	5	6
7	8	9	10	11	12	13
14	15	16	17	18	19	20
21	22	23	24	25	26	27
28	29	30	31			

1 Monday

2nd ♍
♇ ℞ **1:09 pm** 10:09 am
☽ v/c **7:53 pm** 4:53 pm
⚵ enters ♊ 9:50 pm
☽ enters ♎ 11:09 pm

Beltane

2 Tuesday

2nd ♍
⚵ enters ♊ **12:50 am**
☽ enters ♎ **2:09 am**
♀ enters ♌ **1:03 pm** 10:03 am

3 Wednesday

2nd ♎

4 Thursday

2nd ♎
☽ v/c **5:17 am** 2:17 am
☽ enters ♏ **10:32 am** 7:32 am

Eastern time in bold type
Pacific time in medium type

5 Friday

2nd ♏
Full Moon **1:34 pm** 10:34 am

Cinco de Mayo • Lunar Eclipse 14° ♏ 58'

6 Saturday

3rd ♏
☽ v/c **10:38 am** 7:38 am
♇ D **3:24 pm** 12:24 pm
☽ enters ♐ **4:04 pm** 1:04 pm

7 Sunday

3rd ♐
♀ enters ♋ **10:25 am** 7:25 am

April 2023

S	M	T	W	T	F	S
						1
2	3	4	5	6	7	8
9	10	11	12	13	14	15
16	17	18	19	20	21	22
23	24	25	26	27	28	29
30						

May 2023

S	M	T	W	T	F	S
	1	2	3	4	5	6
7	8	9	10	11	12	13
14	15	16	17	18	19	20
21	22	23	24	25	26	27
28	29	30	31			

June 2023

S	M	T	W	T	F	S
				1	2	3
4	5	6	7	8	9	10
11	12	13	14	15	16	17
18	19	20	21	22	23	24
25	26	27	28	29	30	

8 Monday

3rd ♐

☽ v/c	**4:28 pm**	1:28 pm
☽ enters ♑	**7:33 pm**	4:33 pm

9 Tuesday

3rd ♑

10 Wednesday

3rd ♑

☽ v/c	**7:52 pm**	4:52 pm
☽ enters ♒	**10:05 pm**	7:05 pm

11 Thursday

3rd ♒

Eastern time in bold type
Pacific time in medium type

12 Friday

3rd ≈

4th Quarter	**10:28 am**	7:28 am
☽ v/c	**11:15 pm**	8:15 pm
☽ enters ♓		9:39 pm

13 Saturday

4th ≈

☽ enters ♓ **12:39 am**

14 Sunday

4th ♓

☽ v/c	**10:56 pm**	7:56 pm
☿ D	**11:17 pm**	8:17 pm

Mother's Day

April 2023

S	M	T	W	T	F	S
						1
2	3	4	5	6	7	8
9	10	11	12	13	14	15
16	17	18	19	20	21	22
23	24	25	26	27	28	29
30						

May 2023

S	M	T	W	T	F	S
	1	2	3	4	5	6
7	8	9	10	11	12	13
14	15	16	17	18	19	20
21	22	23	24	25	26	27
28	29	30	31			

June 2023

S	M	T	W	T	F	S
				1	2	3
4	5	6	7	8	9	10
11	12	13	14	15	16	17
18	19	20	21	22	23	24
25	26	27	28	29	30	

Eastern time in bold type
Pacific time in medium type

15 Monday

4th ♓

☽ enters ♈ **3:56 am** 12:56 am

16 Tuesday

4th ♈

♃ enters ♉ **1:20 pm** 10:20 am

17 Wednesday

4th ♈

☽ v/c **5:10 am** 2:10 am

☽ enters ♉ **8:28 am** 5:28 am

18 Thursday

4th ♉

Eastern time in bold type

Pacific time in medium type

19 Friday

4th ♉

New Moon	**11:53 am**	8:53 am
☽ v/c	**1:51 pm**	10:51 am
☽ enters ♊	**2:48 pm**	11:48 am

20 Saturday

1st ♊

♂ enters ♌	**11:31 am**	8:31 am

21 Sunday

1st ♊

☉ enters ♊	**3:09 am**	12:09 am
☽ v/c	**6:12 pm**	3:12 pm
☽ enters ♋	**11:28 pm**	8:28 pm

Sun enters Gemini

April 2023

S	M	T	W	T	F	S
						1
2	3	4	5	6	7	8
9	10	11	12	13	14	15
16	17	18	19	20	21	22
23	24	25	26	27	28	29
30						

May 2023

S	M	T	W	T	F	S
	1	2	3	4	5	6
7	8	9	10	11	12	13
14	15	16	17	18	19	20
21	22	23	24	25	26	27
28	29	30	31			

June 2023

S	M	T	W	T	F	S
				1	2	3
4	5	6	7	8	9	10
11	12	13	14	15	16	17
18	19	20	21	22	23	24
25	26	27	28	29	30	

Eastern time in bold type
Pacific time in medium type

22 Monday

1st ♋

23 Tuesday

1st ♋

24 Wednesday

1st ♋

☽ v/c	**5:12 am**	2:12 am
☽ enters ♌	**10:35 am**	7:35 am

25 Thursday

1st ♌

☽ v/c		11:38 pm

Shavuot begins at sundown

Eastern time in bold type
Pacific time in medium type

26 Friday

1st ♌
☽ v/c **2:38 am**
☽ enters ♍ **11:05 pm** 8:05 pm

27 Saturday

1st ♍
2nd Quarter **11:22 am** 8:22 am

28 Sunday

2nd ♍

April 2023

S	M	T	W	T	F	S
						1
2	3	4	5	6	7	8
9	10	11	12	13	14	15
16	17	18	19	20	21	22
23	24	25	26	27	28	29
30						

May 2023

S	M	T	W	T	F	S
	1	2	3	4	5	6
7	8	9	10	11	12	13
14	15	16	17	18	19	20
21	22	23	24	25	26	27
28	29	30	31			

June 2023

S	M	T	W	T	F	S
				1	2	3
4	5	6	7	8	9	10
11	12	13	14	15	16	17
18	19	20	21	22	23	24
25	26	27	28	29	30	

Eastern time in bold type
Pacific time in medium type

29 Monday

2nd ♍
☽ v/c **5:46 am** 2:46 am
☽ enters ♎ **10:51 am** 7:51 am

Memorial Day

30 Tuesday

2nd ♎

31 Wednesday

2nd ♎
☽ v/c **10:53 am** 7:53 am
☽ enters ♏ **7:45 pm** 4:45 pm

1 Thursday

2nd ♏

Eastern time in bold type
Pacific time in medium type

2 Friday

2nd ♏
☽ v/c **8:51 pm** 5:51 pm
☽ enters ♐ 10:03 pm

3 Saturday

2nd ♏
☽ enters ♐ **1:03 am**
Full Moon **11:42 pm** 8:42 pm

4 Sunday

3rd ♐
☽ v/c **11:24 pm** 8:24 pm

May 2023

S	M	T	W	T	F	S
	1	2	3	4	5	6
7	8	9	10	11	12	13
14	15	16	17	18	19	20
21	22	23	24	25	26	27
28	29	30	31			

June 2023

S	M	T	W	T	F	S
				1	2	3
4	5	6	7	8	9	10
11	12	13	14	15	16	17
18	19	20	21	22	23	24
25	26	27	28	29	30	

July 2023

S	M	T	W	T	F	S
						1
2	3	4	5	6	7	8
9	10	11	12	13	14	15
16	17	18	19	20	21	22
23	24	25	26	27	28	29
30	31					

Eastern time in bold type
Pacific time in medium type

5 Monday

3rd ♐
☽ enters ♑ **3:31 am** 12:31 am
♀ enters ♌ **9:46 am** 6:46 am

6 Tuesday

3rd ♑
☽ v/c 9:40 pm

7 Wednesday

3rd ♑
☽ v/c **12:40 am**
☽ enters ♒ **4:42 am** 1:42 am

8 Thursday

3rd ♒
☽ v/c 9:24 pm

Eastern time in bold type
Pacific time in medium type

9 Friday

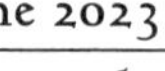

3rd ♒
☽ v/c **12:24 am**
☽ enters ♓ **6:14 am** 3:14 am

10 Saturday

3rd ♓
4th Quarter **3:31 pm** 12:31 pm

11 Sunday

4th ♓
♇ enters ♑ **5:47 am** 2:47 am
☿ enters ♊ **6:27 am** 3:27 am
☽ v/c **9:20 am** 6:20 am
☽ enters ♈ **9:20 am** 6:20 am

May 2023

S	M	T	W	T	F	S
	1	2	3	4	5	6
7	8	9	10	11	12	13
14	15	16	17	18	19	20
21	22	23	24	25	26	27
28	29	30	31			

June 2023

S	M	T	W	T	F	S
				1	2	3
4	5	6	7	8	9	10
11	12	13	14	15	16	17
18	19	20	21	22	23	24
25	26	27	28	29	30	

July 2023

S	M	T	W	T	F	S
						1
2	3	4	5	6	7	8
9	10	11	12	13	14	15
16	17	18	19	20	21	22
23	24	25	26	27	28	29
30	31					

Eastern time in bold type
Pacific time in medium type

12 Monday
4th ♈

13 Tuesday
4th ♈
☽ v/c **2:27 pm** 11:27 am
☽ enters ♉ **2:31 pm** 11:31 am

14 Wednesday

4th ♉

Flag Day

15 Thursday

4th ♉
☽ v/c **9:36 pm** 6:36 pm
☽ enters ♊ **9:46 pm** 6:46 pm

16 Friday

4th ♊

17 Saturday

4th ♊

♄ ℞	**1:27 pm**	10:27 am
New Moon		9:37 pm
☽ v/c		11:24 pm

18 Sunday

4th ♊

New Moon	**12:37 am**	
☽ v/c	**2:24 am**	
☽ enters ♋	**6:58 am**	3:58 am

Father's Day

May 2023

S	M	T	W	T	F	S
	1	2	3	4	5	6
7	8	9	10	11	12	13
14	15	16	17	18	19	20
21	22	23	24	25	26	27
28	29	30	31			

June 2023

S	M	T	W	T	F	S
				1	2	3
4	5	6	7	8	9	10
11	12	13	14	15	16	17
18	19	20	21	22	23	24
25	26	27	28	29	30	

July 2023

S	M	T	W	T	F	S
						1
2	3	4	5	6	7	8
9	10	11	12	13	14	15
16	17	18	19	20	21	22
23	24	25	26	27	28	29
30	31					

19 Monday

1st ♋

Juneteenth

20 Tuesday

1st ♋

☽ v/c	**5:43 pm**	2:43 pm
☽ enters ♌	**6:04 pm**	3:04 pm

21 Wednesday

1st ♌

⚳ enters ♎	**7:30 am**	4:30 am
☉ enters ♋	**10:58 am**	7:58 am

Sun enters Cancer • Litha • Summer Solstice • 10:58 am EDT/7:58 am PDT

22 Thursday

1st ♌

⚵ enters ♋	**7:40 am**	4:40 am
☽ v/c	**1:01 pm**	10:01 am
⚶ enters ♊	**3:17 pm**	12:17 pm

Eastern time in bold type
Pacific time in medium type

23 Friday

1st ♌
☽ enters ♍ **6:35 am** 3:35 am

24 Saturday

1st ♍

25 Sunday

1st ♍
☽ v/c **6:24 pm** 3:24 pm
☽ enters ♎ **6:57 pm** 3:57 pm

May 2023

S	M	T	W	T	F	S
	1	2	3	4	5	6
7	8	9	10	11	12	13
14	15	16	17	18	19	20
21	22	23	24	25	26	27
28	29	30	31			

June 2023

S	M	T	W	T	F	S
				1	2	3
4	5	6	7	8	9	10
11	12	13	14	15	16	17
18	19	20	21	22	23	24
25	26	27	28	29	30	

July 2023

S	M	T	W	T	F	S
						1
2	3	4	5	6	7	8
9	10	11	12	13	14	15
16	17	18	19	20	21	22
23	24	25	26	27	28	29
30	31					

Eastern time in bold type
Pacific time in medium type

26 Monday

1st ♎
2nd Quarter **3:50 am** 12:50 am
☿ enters ♋ **8:24 pm** 5:24 pm

27 Tuesday

2nd ♎

28 Wednesday

2nd ♎
☽ v/c **4:19 am** 1:19 am
☽ enters ♏ **4:55 am** 1:55 am

29 Thursday

2nd ♏

Eastern time in bold type
Pacific time in medium type

30 Friday

2nd ♏

☽ v/c	**10:20 am**	7:20 am
☽ enters ♐	**10:59 am**	7:59 am
♆ ℞	**5:07 pm**	2:07 pm

1 Saturday

2nd ♐

2 Sunday

2nd ♐

☽ v/c	**9:33 am**	6:33 am
☽ enters ♑	**1:20 pm**	10:20 am

June 2023

S	M	T	W	T	F	S
				1	2	3
4	5	6	7	8	9	10
11	12	13	14	15	16	17
18	19	20	21	22	23	24
25	26	27	28	29	30	

July 2023

S	M	T	W	T	F	S
						1
2	3	4	5	6	7	8
9	10	11	12	13	14	15
16	17	18	19	20	21	22
23	24	25	26	27	28	29
30	31					

August 2023

S	M	T	W	T	F	S
		1	2	3	4	5
6	7	8	9	10	11	12
13	14	15	16	17	18	19
20	21	22	23	24	25	26
27	28	29	30	31		

Eastern time in bold type
Pacific time in medium type

3 Monday

2nd ♑
Full Moon **7:39 am** 4:39 am

4 Tuesday

3rd ♑
☽ v/c **12:45 pm** 9:45 am
☽ enters ♒ **1:30 pm** 10:30 am

Independence Day

5 Wednesday

3rd ♒

6 Thursday

3rd ♒
☽ v/c **9:42 am** 6:42 am
☽ enters ♓ **1:33 pm** 10:33 am

Eastern time in bold type
Pacific time in medium type

7 Friday

3rd ♓

8 Saturday

3rd ♓

☽ v/c	**2:22 pm**	11:22 am
☽ enters ♈	**3:19 pm**	12:19 pm

9 Sunday

3rd ♈

4th Quarter	**9:48 pm**	6:48 pm
♀ enters ♍		11:55 pm

June 2023

S	M	T	W	T	F	S
				1	2	3
4	5	6	7	8	9	10
11	12	13	14	15	16	17
18	19	20	21	22	23	24
25	26	27	28	29	30	

July 2023

S	M	T	W	T	F	S
						1
2	3	4	5	6	7	8
9	10	11	12	13	14	15
16	17	18	19	20	21	22
23	24	25	26	27	28	29
30	31					

August 2023

S	M	T	W	T	F	S
		1	2	3	4	5
6	7	8	9	10	11	12
13	14	15	16	17	18	19
20	21	22	23	24	25	26
27	28	29	30	31		

Eastern time in bold type
Pacific time in medium type

10 Monday

4th ♈

♀ enters ♍	**2:55 am**	
♂ enters ♍	**7:40 am**	4:40 am
☽ v/c	**7:11 pm**	4:11 pm
☽ enters ♉	**7:55 pm**	4:55 pm
☿ enters ♌		9:11 pm

11 Tuesday

4th ♉

☿ enters ♌	**12:11 am**

12 Wednesday

4th ♉

☽ v/c		11:11 pm

13 Thursday

4th ♉

☽ v/c	**2:11 am**	
☽ enters ♊	**3:26 am**	12:26 am

Eastern time in bold type
Pacific time in medium type

14 Friday

4th ♊

15 Saturday

4th ♊

☽ v/c **8:35 am** 5:35 am

☽ enters ♋ **1:13 pm** 10:13 am

16 Sunday

4th ♋

June 2023						
S	M	T	W	T	F	S
				1	2	3
4	5	6	7	8	9	10
11	12	13	14	15	16	17
18	19	20	21	22	23	24
25	26	27	28	29	30	

July 2023						
S	M	T	W	T	F	S
						1
2	3	4	5	6	7	8
9	10	11	12	13	14	15
16	17	18	19	20	21	22
23	24	25	26	27	28	29
30	31					

August 2023						
S	M	T	W	T	F	S
		1	2	3	4	5
6	7	8	9	10	11	12
13	14	15	16	17	18	19
20	21	22	23	24	25	26
27	28	29	30	31		

Eastern time in bold type
Pacific time in medium type

17 Monday

4th ♋

New Moon	**2:32 pm**	11:32 am
☽ v/c	**11:06 pm**	8:06 pm
☽ enters ♌		9:39 pm

18 Tuesday

1st ♋

☽ enters ♌ **12:39 am**

Islamic New Year begins at sundown

19 Wednesday

1st ♌

20 Thursday

1st ♌

☽ v/c	**10:08 am**	7:08 am
☽ enters ♍	**1:13 pm**	10:13 am

Eastern time in bold type
Pacific time in medium type

21 Friday

1st ♍

22 Saturday

1st ♍

♀ ℞	**9:33 pm**	6:33 pm
☉ enters ♌	**9:50 pm**	6:50 pm
☽ v/c		9:06 pm
☽ enters ♎		10:54 pm

Sun enters Leo

23 Sunday

1st ♍

☽ v/c	**12:06 am**	
☽ enters ♎	**1:54 am**	
⚷ ℞	**8:42 am**	5:42 am

June 2023

S	M	T	W	T	F	S
				1	2	3
4	5	6	7	8	9	10
11	12	13	14	15	16	17
18	19	20	21	22	23	24
25	26	27	28	29	30	

July 2023

S	M	T	W	T	F	S
						1
2	3	4	5	6	7	8
9	10	11	12	13	14	15
16	17	18	19	20	21	22
23	24	25	26	27	28	29
30	31					

August 2023

S	M	T	W	T	F	S
		1	2	3	4	5
6	7	8	9	10	11	12
13	14	15	16	17	18	19
20	21	22	23	24	25	26
27	28	29	30	31		

Eastern time in bold type
Pacific time in medium type

24 Monday

1st ♎

25 Tuesday

1st ♎

☽ v/c	**11:05 am**	8:05 am
☽ enters ♏	**12:55 pm**	9:55 am
2nd Quarter	**6:07 pm**	3:07 pm

26 Wednesday

2nd ♏

27 Thursday

2nd ♏

☽ v/c	**6:36 pm**	3:36 pm
☽ enters ♐	**8:24 pm**	5:24 pm

28 Friday

2nd ♐
☿ enters ♍ **5:31 pm** 2:31 pm

29 Saturday

2nd ♐
☽ v/c **7:51 pm** 4:51 pm
☽ enters ♑ **11:44 pm** 8:44 pm

30 Sunday

2nd ♑

June 2023

S	M	T	W	T	F	S
				1	2	3
4	5	6	7	8	9	10
11	12	13	14	15	16	17
18	19	20	21	22	23	24
25	26	27	28	29	30	

July 2023

S	M	T	W	T	F	S
						1
2	3	4	5	6	7	8
9	10	11	12	13	14	15
16	17	18	19	20	21	22
23	24	25	26	27	28	29
30	31					

August 2023

S	M	T	W	T	F	S
		1	2	3	4	5
6	7	8	9	10	11	12
13	14	15	16	17	18	19
20	21	22	23	24	25	26
27	28	29	30	31		

Eastern time in bold type
Pacific time in medium type

31 Monday

2nd ♑
☽ v/c **10:13 pm** 7:13 pm
☽ enters ♒ **11:58 pm** 8:58 pm

1 Tuesday

2nd ♒
Full Moon **2:32 pm** 11:32 am

Lammas

2 Wednesday

3rd ♒
☽ v/c **5:15 pm** 2:15 pm
☽ enters ♓ **11:05 pm** 8:05 pm

3 Thursday

3rd ♓

Eastern time in bold type
Pacific time in medium type

4 Friday

3rd ♓

☽ v/c	**9:21 pm**	6:21 pm
☽ enters ♈	**11:19 pm**	8:19 pm

5 Saturday

3rd ♈

6 Sunday

3rd ♈

☽ v/c		9:13 pm
☽ enters ♉		11:25 pm

July 2023

S	M	T	W	T	F	S
						1
2	3	4	5	6	7	8
9	10	11	12	13	14	15
16	17	18	19	20	21	22
23	24	25	26	27	28	29
30	31					

August 2023

S	M	T	W	T	F	S
		1	2	3	4	5
6	7	8	9	10	11	12
13	14	15	16	17	18	19
20	21	22	23	24	25	26
27	28	29	30	31		

September 2023

S	M	T	W	T	F	S
					1	2
3	4	5	6	7	8	9
10	11	12	13	14	15	16
17	18	19	20	21	22	23
24	25	26	27	28	29	30

7 Monday

3rd ♈

☽ v/c **12:13 am**

☽ enters ♉ **2:25 am**

8 Tuesday

3rd ♉

4th Quarter **6:28 am** 3:28 am

9 Wednesday

4th ♉

☽ v/c **6:39 am** 3:39 am

☽ enters ♊ **9:05 am** 6:05 am

10 Thursday

4th ♊

Eastern time in bold type

Pacific time in medium type

11 Friday

4th ♊

☽ v/c	**1:27 pm**	10:27 am
☽ enters ♋	**6:52 pm**	3:52 pm

12 Saturday

4th ♋

13 Sunday

4th ♋

July 2023

S	M	T	W	T	F	S
						1
2	3	4	5	6	7	8
9	10	11	12	13	14	15
16	17	18	19	20	21	22
23	24	25	26	27	28	29
30	31					

August 2023

S	M	T	W	T	F	S
		1	2	3	4	5
6	7	8	9	10	11	12
13	14	15	16	17	18	19
20	21	22	23	24	25	26
27	28	29	30	31		

September 2023

S	M	T	W	T	F	S
					1	2
3	4	5	6	7	8	9
10	11	12	13	14	15	16
17	18	19	20	21	22	23
24	25	26	27	28	29	30

14 Monday

4th ♋
☽ v/c **3:46 am** 12:46 am
☽ enters ♌ **6:36 am** 3:36 am

15 Tuesday

4th ♌
⚵ enters ♌ **3:29 pm** 12:29 pm

16 Wednesday

4th ♌
☽ v/c **5:38 am** 2:38 am
New Moon **5:38 am** 2:38 am
☽ enters ♍ **7:14 pm** 4:14 pm

17 Thursday

1st ♍

Eastern time in bold type
Pacific time in medium type

18 Friday

1st ♍

19 Saturday

1st ♍

☽ v/c	**4:51 am**	1:51 am
☽ enters ♎	**7:53 am**	4:53 am

20 Sunday

1st ♎

July 2023

S	M	T	W	T	F	S
						1
2	3	4	5	6	7	8
9	10	11	12	13	14	15
16	17	18	19	20	21	22
23	24	25	26	27	28	29
30	31					

August 2023

S	M	T	W	T	F	S
		1	2	3	4	5
6	7	8	9	10	11	12
13	14	15	16	17	18	19
20	21	22	23	24	25	26
27	28	29	30	31		

September 2023

S	M	T	W	T	F	S
					1	2
3	4	5	6	7	8	9
10	11	12	13	14	15	16
17	18	19	20	21	22	23
24	25	26	27	28	29	30

21 Monday

1st ♎

☽ v/c	**4:31 pm**	1:31 pm
☽ enters ♏	**7:22 pm**	4:22 pm

22 Tuesday

1st ♏

23 Wednesday

1st ♏

☉ enters ♍	**5:01 am**	2:01 am
☿ ℞	**3:59 pm**	12:59 pm
☽ v/c		10:10 pm

Sun enters Virgo • Mercury retrograde until 9/15

24 Thursday

1st ♏

☽ v/c	**1:10 am**	
☽ enters ♐	**4:07 am**	1:07 am
2nd Quarter	**5:57 am**	2:57 am

Eastern time in bold type
Pacific time in medium type

25 Friday

2nd ♐

26 Saturday

2nd ♐

☽ v/c	**7:56 am**	4:56 am
☽ enters ♑	**9:05 am**	6:05 am

27 Sunday

2nd ♑

♂ enters ♎	**9:20 am**	6:20 am

July 2023

S	M	T	W	T	F	S
						1
2	3	4	5	6	7	8
9	10	11	12	13	14	15
16	17	18	19	20	21	22
23	24	25	26	27	28	29
30	31					

August 2023

S	M	T	W	T	F	S
		1	2	3	4	5
6	7	8	9	10	11	12
13	14	15	16	17	18	19
20	21	22	23	24	25	26
27	28	29	30	31		

September 2023

S	M	T	W	T	F	S
					1	2
3	4	5	6	7	8	9
10	11	12	13	14	15	16
17	18	19	20	21	22	23
24	25	26	27	28	29	30

28 Monday

2nd ♑

☽ v/c	**7:49 am**	4:49 am
☽ enters ♒	**10:32 am**	7:32 am
♅ ℞	**10:39 pm**	7:39 pm

29 Tuesday

2nd ♒

☽ v/c	**11:04 pm**	8:04 pm

30 Wednesday

2nd ♒

☽ enters ♓	**9:56 am**	6:56 am
Full Moon	**9:36 pm**	6:36 pm

31 Thursday

3rd ♓

Eastern time in bold type
Pacific time in medium type

1 Friday

3rd ♓
☽ v/c **6:36 am** 3:36 am
☽ enters ♈ **9:25 am** 6:25 am

2 Saturday

3rd ♈

3 Sunday

3rd ♈
☽ v/c **7:57 am** 4:57 am
☽ enters ♉ **11:00 am** 8:00 am
♀ D **9:20 pm** 6:20 pm

August 2023

S	M	T	W	T	F	S
		1	2	3	4	5
6	7	8	9	10	11	12
13	14	15	16	17	18	19
20	21	22	23	24	25	26
27	28	29	30	31		

September 2023

S	M	T	W	T	F	S
					1	2
3	4	5	6	7	8	9
10	11	12	13	14	15	16
17	18	19	20	21	22	23
24	25	26	27	28	29	30

October 2023

S	M	T	W	T	F	S
1	2	3	4	5	6	7
8	9	10	11	12	13	14
15	16	17	18	19	20	21
22	23	24	25	26	27	28
29	30	31				

Eastern time in bold type
Pacific time in medium type

4 Monday

3rd ♉
♃ ℞ **10:10 am** 7:10 am

Labor Day

5 Tuesday

3rd ♉
☽ v/c **12:46 pm** 9:46 am
☽ enters ♊ **4:07 pm** 1:07 pm

6 Wednesday

3rd ♊
4th Quarter **6:21 pm** 3:21 pm

7 Thursday

4th ♊
☽ v/c **6:22 pm** 3:22 pm
☽ enters ♋ 10:00 pm

Eastern time in bold type
Pacific time in medium type

8 Friday

4th ♊
☽ enters ♋ **1:00 am**

9 Saturday

4th ♋

10 Sunday

4th ♋
☽ v/c **8:47 am** 5:47 am
☽ enters ♌ **12:36 pm** 9:36 am

August 2023

S	M	T	W	T	F	S
		1	2	3	4	5
6	7	8	9	10	11	12
13	14	15	16	17	18	19
20	21	22	23	24	25	26
27	28	29	30	31		

September 2023

S	M	T	W	T	F	S
					1	2
3	4	5	6	7	8	9
10	11	12	13	14	15	16
17	18	19	20	21	22	23
24	25	26	27	28	29	30

October 2023

S	M	T	W	T	F	S
1	2	3	4	5	6	7
8	9	10	11	12	13	14
15	16	17	18	19	20	21
22	23	24	25	26	27	28
29	30	31				

Eastern time in bold type
Pacific time in medium type

11 Monday
4th ♌

12 Tuesday
4th ♌

☽ v/c **11:06 am** 8:06 am
☽ enters ♍ 10:18 pm

13 Wednesday
4th ♌

☽ enters ♍ **1:18 am**
⚳ enters ♎ **12:38 pm** 9:38 am
⚵ enters ♋ **7:28 pm** 4:28 pm

14 Thursday
4th ♍

New Moon **9:40 pm** 6:40 pm

Eastern time in bold type
Pacific time in medium type

15 Friday

1st ♍

⚳ enters ♏	**8:50 am**	5:50 am
☽ v/c	**9:49 am**	6:49 am
☽ enters ♎	**1:44 pm**	10:44 am
☿ D	**4:21 pm**	1:21 pm

Rosh Hashanah begins at sundown

16 Saturday

1st ♎

17 Sunday

1st ♎

☽ v/c	**9:06 pm**	6:06 pm
☽ enters ♏		9:58 pm

August 2023

S	M	T	W	T	F	S
		1	2	3	4	5
6	7	8	9	10	11	12
13	14	15	16	17	18	19
20	21	22	23	24	25	26
27	28	29	30	31		

September 2023

S	M	T	W	T	F	S
					1	2
3	4	5	6	7	8	9
10	11	12	13	14	15	16
17	18	19	20	21	22	23
24	25	26	27	28	29	30

October 2023

S	M	T	W	T	F	S
1	2	3	4	5	6	7
8	9	10	11	12	13	14
15	16	17	18	19	20	21
22	23	24	25	26	27	28
29	30	31				

Eastern time in bold type
Pacific time in medium type

18 Monday

1st ♎
☽ enters ♏ **12:58 am**

19 Tuesday

1st ♏

20 Wednesday

1st ♏

☽ v/c	**6:21 am**	3:21 am
☽ enters ♐	**10:06 am**	7:06 am

21 Thursday

1st ♐

UN International Day of Peace

Eastern time in bold type
Pacific time in medium type

22 Friday

1st ♐
☽ v/c	**3:32 pm**	12:32 pm
2nd Quarter	**3:32 pm**	12:32 pm
☽ enters ♑	**4:20 pm**	1:20 pm
☉ enters ♎		11:50 pm

Sun enters Libra • 11:50 pm PDT

23 Saturday

2nd ♑

☉ enters ♎ **2:50 am**

Sun enters Libra • Mabon • Fall Equinox • 2:50 am EDT

24 Sunday

2nd ♑
☽ v/c	**4:05 pm**	1:05 pm
☽ enters ♒	**7:29 pm**	4:29 pm

Yom Kippur begins at sundown

August 2023

S	M	T	W	T	F	S
		1	2	3	4	5
6	7	8	9	10	11	12
13	14	15	16	17	18	19
20	21	22	23	24	25	26
27	28	29	30	31		

September 2023

S	M	T	W	T	F	S
					1	2
3	4	5	6	7	8	9
10	11	12	13	14	15	16
17	18	19	20	21	22	23
24	25	26	27	28	29	30

October 2023

S	M	T	W	T	F	S
1	2	3	4	5	6	7
8	9	10	11	12	13	14
15	16	17	18	19	20	21
22	23	24	25	26	27	28
29	30	31				

25 Monday
2nd ♒

26 Tuesday
2nd ♒

☽ v/c **8:38 am** 5:38 am

☽ enters ♓ **8:18 pm** 5:18 pm

27 Wednesday

2nd ♓

28 Thursday

2nd ♓

☽ v/c **4:58 pm** 1:58 pm

☽ enters ♈ **8:17 pm** 5:17 pm

Eastern time in bold type
Pacific time in medium type

29 Friday

2nd ♈
Full Moon **5:58 am** 2:58 am

Sukkot begins at sundown

30 Saturday

3rd ♈
☽ v/c **5:50 pm** 2:50 pm
☽ enters ♉ **9:18 pm** 6:18 pm

1 Sunday

3rd ♉

September 2023

S	M	T	W	T	F	S
					1	2
3	4	5	6	7	8	9
10	11	12	13	14	15	16
17	18	19	20	21	22	23
24	25	26	27	28	29	30

October 2023

S	M	T	W	T	F	S
1	2	3	4	5	6	7
8	9	10	11	12	13	14
15	16	17	18	19	20	21
22	23	24	25	26	27	28
29	30	31				

November 2023

S	M	T	W	T	F	S
			1	2	3	4
5	6	7	8	9	10	11
12	13	14	15	16	17	18
19	20	21	22	23	24	25
26	27	28	29	30		

Eastern time in bold type
Pacific time in medium type

2 Monday

3rd ♉
☽ v/c **9:20 pm** 6:20 pm
☽ enters ♊ 10:03 pm

3 Tuesday

3rd ♉
☽ enters ♊ **1:03 am**

4 Wednesday

3rd ♊
☿ enters ♎ **8:09 pm** 5:09 pm
☽ v/c 11:34 pm

5 Thursday

3rd ♊
☽ v/c **2:34 am**
☽ enters ♋ **8:32 am** 5:32 am

Eastern time in bold type
Pacific time in medium type

6 Friday

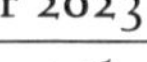

3rd ♋
4th Quarter **9:48 am** 6:48 am

Sukkot ends

7 Saturday

4th ♋
☽ v/c **3:12 pm** 12:12 pm
☽ enters ♌ **7:24 pm** 4:24 pm

8 Sunday

4th ♌
♀ enters ♍ **9:11 pm** 6:11 pm

September 2023

S	M	T	W	T	F	S
					1	2
3	4	5	6	7	8	9
10	11	12	13	14	15	16
17	18	19	20	21	22	23
24	25	26	27	28	29	30

October 2023

S	M	T	W	T	F	S
1	2	3	4	5	6	7
8	9	10	11	12	13	14
15	16	17	18	19	20	21
22	23	24	25	26	27	28
29	30	31				

November 2023

S	M	T	W	T	F	S
			1	2	3	4
5	6	7	8	9	10	11
12	13	14	15	16	17	18
19	20	21	22	23	24	25
26	27	28	29	30		

9 Monday

4th ♌

Indigenous Peoples' Day

10 Tuesday

4th ♌

☽ v/c **5:37 am** 2:37 am
☽ enters ♍ **8:02 am** 5:02 am
♇ D **9:10 pm** 6:10 pm

11 Wednesday

4th ♍

♂ enters ♏ 9:04 pm

12 Thursday

4th ♍

♂ enters ♏ **12:04 am**
☽ v/c **4:10 pm** 1:10 pm
☽ enters ♎ **8:22 pm** 5:22 pm

Eastern time in bold type
Pacific time in medium type

13 Friday
4th ♎

14 Saturday
4th ♎
New Moon **1:55 pm** 10:55 am

Solar Eclipse 21° ♎ 08'

15 Sunday

1st ♎
☽ v/c **3:01 am** 12:01 am
☽ enters ♏ **7:04 am** 4:04 am

September 2023

S	M	T	W	T	F	S
					1	2
3	4	5	6	7	8	9
10	11	12	13	14	15	16
17	18	19	20	21	22	23
24	25	26	27	28	29	30

October 2023

S	M	T	W	T	F	S
1	2	3	4	5	6	7
8	9	10	11	12	13	14
15	16	17	18	19	20	21
22	23	24	25	26	27	28
29	30	31				

November 2023

S	M	T	W	T	F	S
			1	2	3	4
5	6	7	8	9	10	11
12	13	14	15	16	17	18
19	20	21	22	23	24	25
26	27	28	29	30		

16 Monday

1st ♏

17 Tuesday

1st ♏

⚵ enters ♍ **9:27 am** 6:27 am

☽ v/c **11:44 am** 8:44 am

☽ enters ♐ **3:36 pm** 12:36 pm

18 Wednesday

1st ♐

19 Thursday

1st ♐

☽ v/c **3:02 pm** 12:02 pm

☽ enters ♑ **9:55 pm** 6:55 pm

Eastern time in bold type
Pacific time in medium type

20 Friday
1st ♑

21 Saturday

1st ♑
2nd Quarter **11:29 pm** 8:29 pm
☽ v/c 11:00 pm
☽ enters ♒ 11:06 pm
☿ enters ♏ 11:49 pm

22 Sunday
2nd ♑
☽ v/c **2:00 am**
☽ enters ♒ **2:06 am**
☿ enters ♏ **2:49 am**

September 2023

S	M	T	W	T	F	S
					1	2
3	4	5	6	7	8	9
10	11	12	13	14	15	16
17	18	19	20	21	22	23
24	25	26	27	28	29	30

October 2023

S	M	T	W	T	F	S
1	2	3	4	5	6	7
8	9	10	11	12	13	14
15	16	17	18	19	20	21
22	23	24	25	26	27	28
29	30	31				

November 2023

S	M	T	W	T	F	S
			1	2	3	4
5	6	7	8	9	10	11
12	13	14	15	16	17	18
19	20	21	22	23	24	25
26	27	28	29	30		

Eastern time in bold type
Pacific time in medium type

23 Monday

2nd ♒
☉ enters ♏ **12:21 pm** 9:21 am
☽ v/c **3:04 pm** 12:04 pm

Sun enters Scorpio

24 Tuesday

2nd ♒
☽ enters ♓ **4:33 am** 1:33 am

25 Wednesday

2nd ♓
☽ v/c 11:39 pm

26 Thursday

2nd ♓
☽ v/c **2:39 am**
☽ enters ♈ **6:02 am** 3:02 am

Eastern time in bold type
Pacific time in medium type

27 Friday

2nd ♈

28 Saturday

2nd ♈

☽ v/c	**4:20 am**	1:20 am
☽ enters ♉	**7:44 am**	4:44 am
Full Moon	**4:24 pm**	1:24 pm

Lunar Eclipse 5° ♉ 09'

29 Sunday

3rd ♉

September 2023

S	M	T	W	T	F	S
					1	2
3	4	5	6	7	8	9
10	11	12	13	14	15	16
17	18	19	20	21	22	23
24	25	26	27	28	29	30

October 2023

S	M	T	W	T	F	S
1	2	3	4	5	6	7
8	9	10	11	12	13	14
15	16	17	18	19	20	21
22	23	24	25	26	27	28
29	30	31				

November 2023

S	M	T	W	T	F	S
			1	2	3	4
5	6	7	8	9	10	11
12	13	14	15	16	17	18
19	20	21	22	23	24	25
26	27	28	29	30		

Eastern time in bold type
Pacific time in medium type

30 Monday

3rd ♉
☽ v/c **7:36 am** 4:36 am
☽ enters ♊ **11:08 am** 8:08 am

31 Tuesday

3rd ♊

Halloween • Samhain

1 Wednesday

3rd ♊
☽ v/c **8:36 am** 5:36 am
☽ enters ♋ **5:30 pm** 2:30 pm

All Saints' Day

2 Thursday

3rd ♋
⚶ ℞ **9:50 pm** 6:50 pm

Eastern time in bold type
Pacific time in medium type

3 Friday

3rd ♋
☽ v/c **11:28 pm** 8:28 pm

4 Saturday

3rd ♋
♄ D **3:03 am** 12:03 am
☽ enters ♌ **3:21 am** 12:21 am

5 Sunday

3rd ♌
4th Quarter **3:37 am** 1:37 am
☽ v/c 11:25 pm

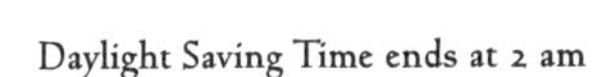
Daylight Saving Time ends at 2 am

October 2023

S	M	T	W	T	F	S
1	2	3	4	5	6	7
8	9	10	11	12	13	14
15	16	17	18	19	20	21
22	23	24	25	26	27	28
29	30	31				

November 2023

S	M	T	W	T	F	S
			1	2	3	4
5	6	7	8	9	10	11
12	13	14	15	16	17	18
19	20	21	22	23	24	25
26	27	28	29	30		

December 2023

S	M	T	W	T	F	S
					1	2
3	4	5	6	7	8	9
10	11	12	13	14	15	16
17	18	19	20	21	22	23
24	25	26	27	28	29	30
31						

6 Monday

4th ♌
☽ v/c **2:25 am**
☽ enters ♍ **2:39 pm** 11:39 am

7 Tuesday

4th ♍

Election Day (general)

8 Wednesday

4th ♍
♀ enters ♎ **4:30 am** 1:30 am
☽ v/c **11:55 pm** 8:55 pm

9 Thursday

4th ♍
☽ enters ♎ **3:08 am** 12:08 am
☿ enters ♐ 10:25 pm

Eastern time in bold type
Pacific time in medium type

10 Friday
4th ♎
☿ enters ♐ **1:25 am**

11 Saturday
4th ♎
☽ v/c **10:05 am** 7:05 am
☽ enters ♏ **1:39 pm** 10:39 am

Veterans Day

12 Sunday

4th ♏

October 2023

S	M	T	W	T	F	S
1	2	3	4	5	6	7
8	9	10	11	12	13	14
15	16	17	18	19	20	21
22	23	24	25	26	27	28
29	30	31				

November 2023

S	M	T	W	T	F	S
			1	2	3	4
5	6	7	8	9	10	11
12	13	14	15	16	17	18
19	20	21	22	23	24	25
26	27	28	29	30		

December 2023

S	M	T	W	T	F	S
					1	2
3	4	5	6	7	8	9
10	11	12	13	14	15	16
17	18	19	20	21	22	23
24	25	26	27	28	29	30
31						

Eastern time in bold type
Pacific time in medium type

13 Monday

4th ♏
New Moon **4:27 am** 1:27 am
☽ v/c **6:03 pm** 3:03 pm
☽ enters ♐ **9:23 pm** 6:23 pm

14 Tuesday

1st ♐

15 Wednesday

1st ♐
☽ v/c **5:57 pm** 2:57 pm
☽ enters ♑ 11:41 pm

16 Thursday

1st ♐
☽ enters ♑ **2:41 am**

Eastern time in bold type
Pacific time in medium type

17 Friday

1st ♑

18 Saturday

1st ♑

☽ v/c **3:27 am** 12:27 am

☽ enters ♒ **6:28 am** 3:28 am

19 Sunday

1st ♒

♀ enters ♏ **4:03 am** 1:03 am

October 2023

S	M	T	W	T	F	S
1	2	3	4	5	6	7
8	9	10	11	12	13	14
15	16	17	18	19	20	21
22	23	24	25	26	27	28
29	30	31				

November 2023

S	M	T	W	T	F	S
			1	2	3	4
5	6	7	8	9	10	11
12	13	14	15	16	17	18
19	20	21	22	23	24	25
26	27	28	29	30		

December 2023

S	M	T	W	T	F	S
					1	2
3	4	5	6	7	8	9
10	11	12	13	14	15	16
17	18	19	20	21	22	23
24	25	26	27	28	29	30
31						

Eastern time in bold type
Pacific time in medium type

20 Monday

1st ♒

☽ v/c	**5:50 am**	2:50 am
2nd Quarter	**5:50 am**	2:50 am
☽ enters ♓	**9:29 am**	6:29 am

21 Tuesday

2nd ♓

22 Wednesday

2nd ♓

☉ enters ♐	**9:03 am**	6:03 am
☽ v/c	**10:10 am**	7:10 am
☽ enters ♈	**12:19 pm**	9:19 am

Sun enters Sagittarius

23 Thursday

2nd ♈

Thanksgiving Day

Eastern time in bold type
Pacific time in medium type

24 Friday

2nd ♈
♂ enters ♐ **5:15 am** 2:15 am
☽ v/c **12:40 pm** 9:40 am
☽ enters ♉ **3:29 pm** 12:29 pm
⚳ enters ♐ 9:14 pm

25 Saturday

2nd ♉
⚳ enters ♐ **12:14 am**

26 Sunday

2nd ♉
☽ v/c **4:52 pm** 1:52 pm
☽ enters ♊ **7:40 pm** 4:40 pm

October 2023

S	M	T	W	T	F	S
1	2	3	4	5	6	7
8	9	10	11	12	13	14
15	16	17	18	19	20	21
22	23	24	25	26	27	28
29	30	31				

November 2023

S	M	T	W	T	F	S
			1	2	3	4
5	6	7	8	9	10	11
12	13	14	15	16	17	18
19	20	21	22	23	24	25
26	27	28	29	30		

December 2023

S	M	T	W	T	F	S
					1	2
3	4	5	6	7	8	9
10	11	12	13	14	15	16
17	18	19	20	21	22	23
24	25	26	27	28	29	30
31						

Eastern time in bold type
Pacific time in medium type

27 Monday

2nd ♊

Full Moon **4:16 am** 1:16 am

28 Tuesday

3rd ♊

☽ v/c **8:03 pm** 5:03 pm

☽ enters ♋ 10:54 pm

29 Wednesday

3rd ♊

☽ enters ♋ **1:54 am**

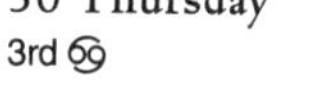

30 Thursday

3rd ♋

Eastern time in bold type
Pacific time in medium type

1 Friday

3rd ♋

☽ v/c	**8:07 am**	5:07 am
☿ enters ♑	**9:31 am**	6:31 am
☽ enters ♌	**11:00 am**	8:00 am

2 Saturday

3rd ♌

3 Sunday

3rd ♌

☽ v/c	**9:11 pm**	6:11 pm
☽ enters ♍	**10:50 pm**	7:50 pm

November 2023

S	M	T	W	T	F	S
			1	2	3	4
5	6	7	8	9	10	11
12	13	14	15	16	17	18
19	20	21	22	23	24	25
26	27	28	29	30		

December 2023

S	M	T	W	T	F	S
					1	2
3	4	5	6	7	8	9
10	11	12	13	14	15	16
17	18	19	20	21	22	23
24	25	26	27	28	29	30
31						

January 2024

S	M	T	W	T	F	S
	1	2	3	4	5	6
7	8	9	10	11	12	13
14	15	16	17	18	19	20
21	22	23	24	25	26	27
28	29	30	31			

4 Monday

3rd ♍
♀ enters ♏ **1:51 pm** 10:51 am
4th Quarter 9:49 pm

5 Tuesday

3rd ♍
4th Quarter **12:49 am**

6 Wednesday

4th ♍
♆ D **8:20 am** 5:20 am
☽ v/c **8:50 am** 5:50 am
☽ enters ♎ **11:35 am** 8:35 am

7 Thursday

4th ♎

Hanukkah begins at sundown

Eastern time in bold type
Pacific time in medium type

8 Friday

4th ♎

☽ v/c	**8:05 pm**	5:05 pm
☽ enters ♏	**10:35 pm**	7:35 pm

9 Saturday

4th ♏

10 Sunday

4th ♏

November 2023

S	M	T	W	T	F	S
			1	2	3	4
5	6	7	8	9	10	11
12	13	14	15	16	17	18
19	20	21	22	23	24	25
26	27	28	29	30		

December 2023

S	M	T	W	T	F	S
					1	2
3	4	5	6	7	8	9
10	11	12	13	14	15	16
17	18	19	20	21	22	23
24	25	26	27	28	29	30
31						

January 2024

S	M	T	W	T	F	S
	1	2	3	4	5	6
7	8	9	10	11	12	13
14	15	16	17	18	19	20
21	22	23	24	25	26	27
28	29	30	31			

11 Monday

4th ♏

☽ v/c	**3:57 am**	12:57 am
☽ enters ♐	**6:11 am**	3:11 am

12 Tuesday

4th ♐

New Moon	**6:32 pm**	3:32 pm
☽ v/c		10:48 pm
☿ ℞		11:09 pm

Mercury retrograde until 1/1/24

13 Wednesday

1st ♐

☽ v/c	**1:48 am**	
☿ ℞	**2:09 am**	
☽ enters ♑	**10:31 am**	7:31 am

Mercury retrograde until 1/1/24

14 Thursday

1st ♑

Eastern time in bold type
Pacific time in medium type

15 Friday

1st ♑
☽ v/c **11:04 am** 8:04 am
☽ enters ♒ **12:56 pm** 9:56 am

Hanukkah ends

16 Saturday

1st ♒

17 Sunday

1st ♒
☽ v/c **7:04 am** 4:04 am
☽ enters ♓ **2:58 pm** 11:58 am

November 2023

S	M	T	W	T	F	S
			1	2	3	4
5	6	7	8	9	10	11
12	13	14	15	16	17	18
19	20	21	22	23	24	25
26	27	28	29	30		

December 2023

S	M	T	W	T	F	S
					1	2
3	4	5	6	7	8	9
10	11	12	13	14	15	16
17	18	19	20	21	22	23
24	25	26	27	28	29	30
31						

January 2024

S	M	T	W	T	F	S
	1	2	3	4	5	6
7	8	9	10	11	12	13
14	15	16	17	18	19	20
21	22	23	24	25	26	27
28	29	30	31			

Eastern time in bold type
Pacific time in medium type

18 Monday

1st ♓

19 Tuesday

1st ♓
2nd Quarter **1:39 pm** 10:39 am
☽ v/c **4:03 pm** 1:03 pm
☽ enters ♈ **5:47 pm** 2:47 pm

20 Wednesday

2nd ♈
⚳ enters ♊ **4:56 am** 1:56 am

21 Thursday

2nd ♈
☽ v/c **9:47 pm** 6:47 pm
☽ enters ♉ **9:50 pm** 6:50 pm
☉ enters ♑ **10:27 pm** 7:27 pm

Sun enters Capricorn • Yule • Winter Solstice • 10:27 pm EST/7:27 pm PST

Eastern time in bold type
Pacific time in medium type

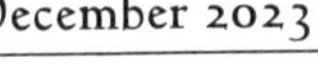

22 Friday

2nd ♉
☿ enters ♐ 10:18 pm

23 Saturday

2nd ♉
☿ enters ♐ **1:18 am**
☽ v/c 10:40 pm

24 Sunday

2nd ♉
☽ v/c **1:40 am**
☽ enters ♊ **3:15 am** 12:15 am

Christmas Eve

November 2023

S	M	T	W	T	F	S
			1	2	3	4
5	6	7	8	9	10	11
12	13	14	15	16	17	18
19	20	21	22	23	24	25
26	27	28	29	30		

December 2023

S	M	T	W	T	F	S
					1	2
3	4	5	6	7	8	9
10	11	12	13	14	15	16
17	18	19	20	21	22	23
24	25	26	27	28	29	30
31						

January 2024

S	M	T	W	T	F	S
	1	2	3	4	5	6
7	8	9	10	11	12	13
14	15	16	17	18	19	20
21	22	23	24	25	26	27
28	29	30	31			

Eastern time in bold type
Pacific time in medium type

25 Monday

2nd ♊
☽ v/c 11:55 pm

Christmas Day

26 Tuesday

2nd ♊
☽ v/c **2:55 am**
☽ enters ♋ **10:15 am** 7:15 am
Full Moon **7:33 pm** 4:33 pm
⚷ D **10:10 pm** 7:10 pm

Kwanzaa begins

27 Wednesday

3rd ♋

28 Thursday

3rd ♋
☽ v/c **5:57 pm** 2:57 pm
☽ enters ♌ **7:23 pm** 4:23 pm

Eastern time in bold type
Pacific time in medium type

29 Friday

3rd ♌
♀ enters ♐ **3:24 pm** 12:24 pm

30 Saturday

3rd ♌
♃ D **9:40 pm** 6:40 pm
☽ v/c 9:18 pm

31 Sunday

3rd ♌
☽ v/c **12:18 am**
☽ enters ♍ **6:53 am** 3:53 am

New Year's Eve

November 2023

S	M	T	W	T	F	S
			1	2	3	4
5	6	7	8	9	10	11
12	13	14	15	16	17	18
19	20	21	22	23	24	25
26	27	28	29	30		

December 2023

S	M	T	W	T	F	S
					1	2
3	4	5	6	7	8	9
10	11	12	13	14	15	16
17	18	19	20	21	22	23
24	25	26	27	28	29	30
31						

January 2024

S	M	T	W	T	F	S
	1	2	3	4	5	6
7	8	9	10	11	12	13
14	15	16	17	18	19	20
21	22	23	24	25	26	27
28	29	30	31			

The Year 2023

January

S	M	T	W	T	F	S
1	2	3	4	5	6	7
8	9	10	11	12	13	14
15	16	17	18	19	20	21
22	23	24	25	26	27	28
29	30	31				

February

S	M	T	W	T	F	S
			1	2	3	4
5	6	7	8	9	10	11
12	13	14	15	16	17	18
19	20	21	22	23	24	25
26	27	28				

March

S	M	T	W	T	F	S
			1	2	3	4
5	6	7	8	9	10	11
12	13	14	15	16	17	18
19	20	21	22	23	24	25
26	27	28	29	30	31	

April

S	M	T	W	T	F	S
						1
2	3	4	5	6	7	8
9	10	11	12	13	14	15
16	17	18	19	20	21	22
23	24	25	26	27	28	29
30						

May

S	M	T	W	T	F	S
	1	2	3	4	5	6
7	8	9	10	11	12	13
14	15	16	17	18	19	20
21	22	23	24	25	26	27
28	29	30	31			

June

S	M	T	W	T	F	S
				1	2	3
4	5	6	7	8	9	10
11	12	13	14	15	16	17
18	19	20	21	22	23	24
25	26	27	28	29	30	

July

S	M	T	W	T	F	S
						1
2	3	4	5	6	7	8
9	10	11	12	13	14	15
16	17	18	19	20	21	22
23	24	25	26	27	28	29
30	31					

August

S	M	T	W	T	F	S
		1	2	3	4	5
6	7	8	9	10	11	12
13	14	15	16	17	18	19
20	21	22	23	24	25	26
27	28	29	30	31		

September

S	M	T	W	T	F	S
					1	2
3	4	5	6	7	8	9
10	11	12	13	14	15	16
17	18	19	20	21	22	23
24	25	26	27	28	29	30

October

S	M	T	W	T	F	S
1	2	3	4	5	6	7
8	9	10	11	12	13	14
15	16	17	18	19	20	21
22	23	24	25	26	27	28
29	30	31				

November

S	M	T	W	T	F	S
			1	2	3	4
5	6	7	8	9	10	11
12	13	14	15	16	17	18
19	20	21	22	23	24	25
26	27	28	29	30		

December

S	M	T	W	T	F	S
					1	2
3	4	5	6	7	8	9
10	11	12	13	14	15	16
17	18	19	20	21	22	23
24	25	26	27	28	29	30
31						

The Year 2024

January

S	M	T	W	T	F	S
	1	2	3	4	5	6
7	8	9	10	11	12	13
14	15	16	17	18	19	20
21	22	23	24	25	26	27
28	29	30	31			

February

S	M	T	W	T	F	S
				1	2	3
4	5	6	7	8	9	10
11	12	13	14	15	16	17
18	19	20	21	22	23	24
25	26	27	28	29		

March

S	M	T	W	T	F	S
					1	2
3	4	5	6	7	8	9
10	11	12	13	14	15	16
17	18	19	20	21	22	23
24	25	26	27	28	29	30
31						

April

S	M	T	W	T	F	S
	1	2	3	4	5	6
7	8	9	10	11	12	13
14	15	16	17	18	19	20
21	22	23	24	25	26	27
28	29	30				

May

S	M	T	W	T	F	S
			1	2	3	4
5	6	7	8	9	10	11
12	13	14	15	16	17	18
19	20	21	22	23	24	25
26	27	28	29	30	31	

June

S	M	T	W	T	F	S
						1
2	3	4	5	6	7	8
9	10	11	12	13	14	15
16	17	18	19	20	21	22
23	24	25	26	27	28	29
30						

July

S	M	T	W	T	F	S
	1	2	3	4	5	6
7	8	9	10	11	12	13
14	15	16	17	18	19	20
21	22	23	24	25	26	27
28	29	30	31			

August

S	M	T	W	T	F	S
				1	2	3
4	5	6	7	8	9	10
11	12	13	14	15	16	17
18	19	20	21	22	23	24
25	26	27	28	29	30	31

September

S	M	T	W	T	F	S
1	2	3	4	5	6	7
8	9	10	11	12	13	14
15	16	17	18	19	20	21
22	23	24	25	26	27	28
29	30					

October

S	M	T	W	T	F	S
		1	2	3	4	5
6	7	8	9	10	11	12
13	14	15	16	17	18	19
20	21	22	23	24	25	26
27	28	29	30	31		

November

S	M	T	W	T	F	S
					1	2
3	4	5	6	7	8	9
10	11	12	13	14	15	16
17	18	19	20	21	22	23
24	25	26	27	28	29	30

December

S	M	T	W	T	F	S
1	2	3	4	5	6	7
8	9	10	11	12	13	14
15	16	17	18	19	20	21
22	23	24	25	26	27	28
29	30	31				

JANUARY 2022

☽ Last Aspect day	ET / hr:mn / PT	asp	☽ Ingress sign	day	ET / hr:mn / PT
1	**3:16 am** 12:16 am	□♆	♑	1	**6:02 pm** 3:02 pm
3	**11:21 am** 8:21 am	☌♇	♒	3	**5:44 pm** 2:44 pm
4	**7:45 pm** 4:45 pm	⚹♂	♓	5	**7:17 pm** 4:17 pm
7	**5:23 pm** 2:23 pm	⚹♇	♈	7	9:26 pm
7	**5:23 pm** 2:23 pm	⚹♇	♈	8	**12:26 am**
9	11:23 pm	□♇	♉	10	**9:47 am** 6:47 am
10	**2:23 am**	□♇	♉	10	**9:47 am** 6:47 am
12	**2:39 pm** 11:39 am	△♇	♊	12	**10:08 pm** 7:08 pm
14	**9:22 pm** 6:22 pm	☍♂	♋	15	**11:11 am** 8:11 am
17	**6:48 pm** 3:48 pm	☍☉	♌	17	**11:03 pm** 8:03 pm
20	**3:15 am** 12:15 am	△♂	♍	20	**9:02 am** 6:02 am
22	**2:46 pm** 11:46 am	□♂	♎	22	**5:03 pm** 2:03 pm
24	**5:10 pm** 2:10 pm	□♇	♏	24	**10:57 pm** 7:57 pm
26	9:28 pm	⚹☿	♐	26	11:34 pm
27	**12:28 am**	⚹☿	♐	27	**2:34 am**
28	**2:00 pm** 11:00 am	□♆	♑	29	**4:09 am** 1:09 am
30	**11:44 pm** 8:44 pm	☌♇	♒	31	**4:43 am** 1:43 am

☽ Phases & Eclipses phase	day	ET / hr:mn / PT
New Moon	2	**1:33 pm** 10:33 am
2nd Quarter	9	**1:11 pm** 10:11 am
Full Moon	17	**6:48 pm** 3:48 pm
4th Quarter	25	**8:41 am** 5:41 am
New Moon	31	9:46 pm
New Moon	2/1	**12:46 am**

Planet Ingress		day	ET / hr:mn / PT
☿	♒	1	11:10 pm
☿	♒	2	**2:10 am**
⚵	♑	10	9:19 pm
⚵	♑	11	**12:19 am**
☉	♒	19	**9:39 pm** 6:39 pm
♂	♑	24	**7:53 am** 4:53 am
☿	♑	25	**10:05 pm** 7:05 pm

Planetary Motion		day	ET / hr:mn / PT
☿	℞	14	**6:41 am** 3:41 am
⚳	D	14	**4:20 pm** 1:20 pm
♅	D	18	**10:27 am** 7:27 am
♀	D	29	**3:46 am** 12:46 am

1 SATURDAY
☽ □ ♆ **3:16 am** 12:16 am
☉ △ ♅ **4:50 am** 1:50 am
☽ ⚺ ♀ **7:02 am** 4:02 am
☽ ⚺ ♇ **11:38 am** 8:38 am
☽ ⚺ ☿ **5:13 pm** 2:13 pm
☽ ⚹ ♃ **7:13 pm** 4:13 pm

2 SUNDAY
☉ ⚺ ♄ **7:12 am** 4:12 am
☽ △ ♅ **11:20 am** 8:20 am
☽ ⚺ ♄ **1:10 pm** 10:10 am
☽ ☌ ☉ **1:33 pm** 10:33 am
☽ ⚺ ♂ **4:56 pm** 1:56 pm
☿ ⚺ ♃ **6:44 pm** 3:44 pm
☽ ⚹ ♆ 11:52 pm

3 MONDAY
☽ ⚹ ♆ **2:52 am**
☽ ☌ ♀ **4:59 am** 1:59 am
☽ ☌ ♇ **11:21 am** 8:21 am
☽ ⚺ ♃ **7:34 pm** 4:34 pm
☽ ☌ ☿ **9:37 pm** 6:37 pm

4 TUESDAY
☽ □ ♅ **11:25 am** 8:25 am
☽ ☌ ♄ **1:44 pm** 10:44 am
☽ ⚺ ☉ **5:23 pm** 2:23 pm
☽ ⚹ ♂ **7:45 pm** 4:45 pm

5 WEDNESDAY
☽ ⚺ ♆ **3:41 am** 12:41 am
☽ ⚺ ♀ **3:59 am** 12:59 am
♀ ⚹ ♆ **11:03 am** 8:03 am
☽ ⚺ ♇ **12:39 pm** 9:39 am
☽ ☌ ♃ **9:57 pm** 6:57 pm

6 THURSDAY
☽ ⚺ ☿ **4:07 am** 1:07 am
☽ ⚹ ♅ **2:04 pm** 11:04 am
☽ ⚺ ♄ **5:01 pm** 2:01 pm
☽ ⚹ ☉ 9:41 pm
☽ □ ♂ 10:55 pm

7 FRIDAY
☽ ⚹ ☉ **12:41 am**
☽ □ ♂ **1:55 am**
☽ ⚹ ♀ **5:41 am** 2:41 am
☽ ☌ ♆ **7:40 am** 4:40 am
☽ ⚹ ♇ **5:23 pm** 2:23 pm

8 SATURDAY
☽ ⚺ ♃ **4:11 am** 1:11 am
☽ ⚹ ☿ **2:37 pm** 11:37 am
♀ ⚺ ♂ **5:48 pm** 2:48 pm
☉ ☌ ♀ **7:48 pm** 4:48 pm
☽ ⚺ ♅ **8:44 pm** 5:44 pm
☽ ⚹ ♄ 9:27 pm

9 SUNDAY
☽ ⚹ ♄ **12:27 am**
☉ ⚺ ♂ **4:32 am** 1:32 am
☽ □ ♀ **11:01 am** 8:01 am

☽ △ ♂ **12:58 pm** 9:58 am
☽ □ ☉ **1:11 pm** 10:11 am
☽ ⚺ ♆ **3:52 pm** 12:52 pm
☽ □ ♇ 11:23 pm

10 MONDAY
☽ □ ♇ **2:23 am**
☽ ⚹ ♃ **2:48 pm** 11:48 am
☉ ⚹ ♆ **10:28 pm** 7:28 pm

11 TUESDAY
☽ □ ☿ **4:38 am** 1:38 am
☽ ☌ ♅ **7:21 am** 4:21 am
☽ □ ♄ **11:53 am** 8:53 am
♂ □ ♆ **4:43 pm** 1:43 pm
☽ △ ♀ **7:34 pm** 4:34 pm

12 WEDNESDAY
☽ ⚹ ♆ **3:38 am** 12:38 am
☽ ⚻ ♂ **4:19 am** 1:19 am
☽ △ ☉ **6:20 am** 3:20 am
☽ △ ♇ **2:39 pm** 11:39 am

13 THURSDAY
☽ □ ♃ **4:24 am** 1:24 am
☽ △ ☿ **7:10 pm** 4:10 pm
☽ ⚺ ♅ **8:12 pm** 5:12 pm
☽ △ ♄ 10:26 pm

14 FRIDAY
☽ △ ♄ **1:26 am**
☽ ⚻ ♀ **5:46 am** 2:46 am
☽ □ ♆ **4:50 pm** 1:50 pm
☽ ☍ ♂ **9:22 pm** 6:22 pm
☽ ⚻ ☉ 10:10 pm

15 SATURDAY
☽ ⚻ ☉ **1:10 am**
☽ ⚻ ♇ **3:54 am** 12:54 am
☽ △ ♃ **6:31 pm** 3:31 pm

16 SUNDAY
☽ ⚻ ☿ **7:12 am** 4:12 am
☽ ⚹ ♅ **8:58 am** 5:58 am
☉ ☌ ♇ **9:51 am** 6:51 am
☽ ⚻ ♄ **2:42 pm** 11:42 am
☽ ☍ ♀ **3:50 pm** 12:50 pm

17 MONDAY
☽ △ ♆ **5:19 am** 2:19 am
☽ ⚻ ♂ **1:24 pm** 10:24 am
♀ ⚺ ♄ **2:44 pm** 11:44 am
☽ ☍ ♇ **4:08 pm** 1:08 pm
☽ ☍ ☉ **6:48 pm** 3:48 pm

18 TUESDAY
☽ ⚻ ♃ **7:15 am** 4:15 am
☽ ☍ ☿ **3:39 pm** 12:39 pm
☽ □ ♅ **8:11 pm** 5:11 pm
☽ ⚻ ♀ 9:47 pm
☽ ☍ ♄ 11:19 pm

19 WEDNESDAY
☽ ⚻ ♀ **12:47 am**
☽ ☍ ♄ **2:19 am**
♂ ⚺ ♇ **1:30 pm** 10:30 am
☽ ⚻ ♆ **4:00 pm** 1:00 pm
☽ ⚻ ♇ 11:30 pm

20 THURSDAY
☽ ⚻ ♇ **2:30 am**
☽ △ ♂ **3:15 am** 12:15 am
☽ ⚻ ☉ **10:02 am** 7:02 am
☽ ☍ ♃ **5:58 pm** 2:58 pm
☽ ⚻ ☿ **8:55 pm** 5:55 pm

21 FRIDAY
☽ △ ♅ **5:28 am** 2:28 am
☽ △ ♀ **8:19 am** 5:19 am
☽ ⚻ ♄ **11:54 am** 8:54 am
☿ ⚺ ♃ **11:00 pm** 8:00 pm
☽ ☍ ♆ 9:43 pm

22 SATURDAY
☽ ☍ ♆ **12:43 am**
☽ △ ♇ **10:53 am** 7:53 am
☽ □ ♂ **2:46 pm** 11:46 am
☽ △ ☉ **10:43 pm** 7:43 pm
☽ △ ☿ **11:47 pm** 8:47 pm
☽ ⚻ ♃ 11:37 pm

23 SUNDAY
☽ ⚻ ♃ **2:37 am**
☉ ☌ ☿ **5:28 am** 2:28 am
☽ ⚻ ♅ **12:45 pm** 9:45 am
☽ □ ♀ **2:22 pm** 11:22 am
☽ △ ♄ **7:26 pm** 4:26 pm

24 MONDAY
☽ ⚻ ♆ **7:23 am** 4:23 am
☽ □ ♇ **5:10 pm** 2:10 pm
☽ ⚹ ♂ **11:48 pm** 8:48 pm
☽ □ ☿ 9:51 pm

25 TUESDAY
☽ □ ☿ **12:51 am**
☿ ⚺ ♂ **7:46 am** 4:46 am
☽ □ ☉ **8:41 am** 5:41 am
☽ △ ♃ **9:01 am** 6:01 am
☉ ⚺ ♃ **2:32 pm** 11:32 am
☽ ☍ ♅ **5:52 pm** 2:52 pm
☽ ⚹ ♀ **6:41 pm** 3:41 pm
☽ □ ♄ 9:42 pm

26 WEDNESDAY
☽ □ ♄ **12:42 am**
☽ △ ♆ **11:47 am** 8:47 am
☽ ⚹ ♇ **9:10 pm** 6:10 pm
☽ ⚹ ☿ 9:28 pm

27 THURSDAY
☽ ⚹ ☿ **12:28 am**
☽ ⚺ ♂ **6:09 am** 3:09 am
☽ □ ♃ **1:02 pm** 10:02 am
☽ ⚹ ☉ **3:47 pm** 12:47 pm
☽ ⚻ ♅ **8:43 pm** 5:43 pm
☽ ⚺ ♀ **9:08 pm** 6:08 pm

28 FRIDAY
☽ ⚹ ♄ **3:39 am** 12:39 am
☽ □ ♆ **2:00 pm** 11:00 am
☽ ⚺ ♇ **11:02 pm** 8:02 pm
☽ ⚺ ☿ **11:03 pm** 8:03 pm
☿ ☌ ♇ **11:16 pm** 8:16 pm

29 SATURDAY
☽ ☌ ♂ **10:10 am** 7:10 am
☽ ⚹ ♃ **3:03 pm** 12:03 pm

☽ ⚺ ☉ **8:34 pm** 5:34 pm
☽ △ ♅ **9:47 pm** 6:47 pm
☽ ☌ ♀ **10:08 pm** 7:08 pm

30 SUNDAY
☽ ⚺ ♄ **4:56 am** 1:56 am
☉ □ ♅ **2:32 pm** 11:32 am
☽ ⚹ ♆ **2:48 pm** 11:48 am
☉ ⚺ ♀ **8:29 pm** 5:29 pm
☽ ☌ ☿ **9:26 pm** 6:26 pm
☽ ☌ ♇ **11:44 pm** 8:44 pm

31 MONDAY
☽ ⚺ ♂ **1:14 pm** 10:14 am
☽ ⚺ ♃ **4:22 pm** 1:22 pm
☽ □ ♅ **10:25 pm** 7:25 pm
☽ ⚺ ♀ **10:58 pm** 7:58 pm
☽ ☌ ☉ 9:46 pm

Eastern time in bold type
Pacific time in medium type

JANUARY 2022

DATE	SID.TIME	SUN	MOON	NODE	MERCURY	VENUS	MARS	JUPITER	SATURN	URANUS	NEPTUNE	PLUTO	CERES	PALLAS	JUNO	VESTA	CHIRON
1 Sa	6 42 30	10♑31 44	15♐29	1♊12℞	28♑11	23♑18℞	13♐06	0♓33	11♒54	10♉57℞	20♓40	25♑56	28♉38℞	16♓28	17♑23	24♐32	8♈30
2 Su	6 46 27	11 32 55	0♑37	1 10	29 35	22 48	13 49	0 45	12 01	10 56	20 41	25 58	28 32	16 43	17 46	25 04	8 31
3 M	6 50 23	12 34 06	15 46	1 05	0♒57	22 16	14 31	0 56	12 07	10 55	20 42	26 00	28 27	16 58	18 10	25 36	8 32
4 T	6 54 20	13 35 17	0♒47	0 59	2 16	21 43	15 14	1 08	12 14	10 55	20 43	26 02	28 22	17 13	18 33	26 08	8 33
5 W	6 58 17	14 36 28	15 31	0 51	3 32	21 09	15 57	1 20	12 20	10 54	20 45	26 04	28 18	17 29	18 56	26 40	8 34
6 Th	7 2 13	15 37 38	29 50	0 44	4 43	20 34	16 40	1 33	12 27	10 53	20 46	26 06	28 14	17 45	19 20	27 13	8 34
7 F	7 6 10	16 38 48	13♓41	0 38	5 50	19 58	17 23	1 45	12 34	10 53	20 47	26 08	28 11	18 01	19 43	27 45	8 35
8 Sa	7 10 6	17 39 58	27 03	0 34	6 52	19 21	18 05	1 57	12 41	10 52	20 48	26 10	28 08	18 17	20 07	28 17	8 36
9 Su	7 14 3	18 41 07	9♈57	0 32D	7 47	18 44	18 48	2 09	12 47	10 52	20 49	26 12	28 05	18 33	20 30	28 49	8 38
10 M	7 17 59	19 42 16	22 27	0 32	8 35	18 08	19 31	2 22	12 54	10 51	20 51	26 14	28 03	18 49	20 54	29 21	8 39
11 T	7 21 56	20 43 24	4♉39	0 32	9 15	17 31	20 14	2 34	13 01	10 51	20 52	26 16	28 01	19 06	21 18	29 53	8 40
12 W	7 25 52	21 44 32	16 38	0 34	9 46	16 55	20 57	2 47	13 08	10 50	20 53	26 18	28 00	19 23	21 41	0♑25	8 41
13 Th	7 29 49	22 45 40	28 28	0 34℞	10 08	16 20	21 40	3 00	13 15	10 50	20 55	26 20	27 59	19 40	22 05	0 57	8 42
14 F	7 33 45	23 46 46	10♊14	0 34	10 19℞	15 46	22 24	3 12	13 22	10 50	20 56	26 22	27 58D	19 57	22 28	1 29	8 44
15 Sa	7 37 42	24 47 53	22 01	0 31	10 19	15 13	23 07	3 25	13 28	10 49	20 58	26 24	27 58	20 14	22 52	2 01	8 45
16 Su	7 41 39	25 48 58	3♋52	0 26	10 07	14 41	23 50	3 38	13 35	10 49	20 59	26 26	27 58	20 32	23 16	2 33	8 47
17 M	7 45 35	26 50 03	15 50	0 18	9 43	14 11	24 33	3 51	13 42	10 49	21 01	26 28	27 59	20 49	23 40	3 04	8 48
18 T	7 49 32	27 51 08	27 57	0 09	9 08	13 43	25 16	4 04	13 49	10 49D	21 02	26 29	28 00	21 07	24 03	3 36	8 50
19 W	7 53 28	28 52 12	10♌12	29♉57	8 22	13 17	26 00	4 17	13 56	10 49	21 04	26 31	28 01	21 25	24 27	4 08	8 51
20 Th	7 57 25	29 53 15	22 39	29 46	7 26	12 53	26 43	4 30	14 03	10 49	21 05	26 33	28 03	21 43	24 51	4 40	8 53
21 F	8 1 21	0♒54 18	5♍16	29 34	6 22	12 31	27 26	4 44	14 11	10 49	21 07	26 35	28 05	22 01	25 15	5 12	8 54
22 Sa	8 5 18	1 55 21	18 04	29 25	5 11	12 12	28 10	4 57	14 18	10 49	21 08	26 37	28 08	22 19	25 38	5 43	8 56
23 Su	8 9 15	2 56 22	1♎04	29 18	3 56	11 55	28 53	5 10	14 25	10 50	21 10	26 39	28 11	22 38	26 02	6 15	8 58
24 M	8 13 11	3 57 24	14 17	29 14	2 40	11 40	29 37	5 24	14 32	10 50	21 12	26 41	28 14	22 56	26 26	6 47	9 00
25 T	8 17 8	4 58 25	27 45	29 12D	1 23	11 28	0♑20	5 37	14 39	10 50	21 13	26 43	28 18	23 15	26 50	7 18	9 02
26 W	8 21 4	5 59 25	11♏30	29 12	0 09	11 19	1 04	5 51	14 46	10 51	21 15	26 45	28 22	23 34	27 14	7 50	9 04
27 Th	8 25 1	7 00 25	25 31	29 12℞	29♑00	11 12	1 47	6 04	14 53	10 51	21 17	26 47	28 27	23 53	27 38	8 21	9 06
28 F	8 28 57	8 01 25	9♐49	29 12	27 57	11 07	2 31	6 18	15 00	10 51	21 19	26 49	28 32	24 12	28 01	8 53	9 08
29 Sa	8 32 54	9 02 24	24 23	29 10	27 01	11 05D	3 15	6 31	15 08	10 52	21 20	26 51	28 37	24 31	28 25	9 24	9 10
30 Su	8 36 50	10 03 23	9♑09	29 05	26 13	11 05	3 58	6 45	15 15	10 52	21 22	26 53	28 43	24 50	28 49	9 55	9 12
31 M	8 40 47	11 04 20	24 00	28 57	25 34	11 08	4 42	6 59	15 22	10 53	21 24	26 55	28 49	25 10	29 13	10 27	9 14

EPHEMERIS CALCULATED FOR 12 MIDNIGHT GREENWICH MEAN TIME. ALL OTHER DATA AND FACING ASPECTARIAN PAGE IN **EASTERN TIME (BOLD)** AND PACIFIC TIME (REGULAR).

FEBRUARY 2022

☽ Last Aspect day	ET / hr:mn / PT		asp	☽ Ingress sign	day	ET / hr:mn / PT	
1	**6:01 am**	3:01 am	☌ ♄	♓	2	**6:00 am**	3:00 am
4	**4:41 am**	1:41 am	⚹ ♇	♈	4	**9:57 am**	6:57 am
6	**12:21 pm**	9:21 am	□ ♇	♉	6	**5:52 pm**	2:52 pm
8	**11:48 pm**	8:48 pm	△ ♇	♊	9	**5:27 am**	2:27 am
11	**3:23 am**	12:23 am	△ ☉	♋	11	**6:27 pm**	3:27 pm
14	**5:27 am**	2:27 am	☍ ☿	♌	14	**6:17 am**	3:17 am
16	**11:56 am**	8:56 am	☍ ☉	♍	16	**3:42 pm**	12:42 pm
18	**6:20 pm**	3:20 pm	△ ♇	♎	18	**10:51 pm**	7:51 pm
20		9:02 pm	□ ♇	♏	21	**4:19 am**	1:19 am
21	**12:02 am**		□ ♇	♏	21	**4:19 am**	1:19 am
23	**4:24 am**	1:24 am	⚹ ♇	♐	23	**8:29 am**	5:29 am
24	**10:24 pm**	7:24 pm	□ ♆	♑	25	**11:27 am**	8:27 am
27	**9:49 am**	6:49 am	☌ ♇	♒	27	**1:36 pm**	10:36 am
28	**9:01 pm**	6:01 pm	☌ ♄	♓	3/1	**3:53 pm**	12:53 pm

☽ Phases & Eclipses phase	day	ET / hr:mn / PT	
New Moon	1/31		9:46 pm
New Moon	1	**12:46 am**	
2nd Quarter	8	**8:50 am**	5:50 am
Full Moon	16	**11:56 am**	8:56 am
4th Quarter	23	**5:32 pm**	2:32 pm

Planet Ingress		day	ET / hr:mn / PT	
⚵	♒	1	**6:04 pm**	3:04 pm
⚳	♊	8	**9:13 pm**	6:13 pm
♀	♈	13		9:53 pm
♀	♈	14	**12:53 am**	
☿	♒	14	**4:54 pm**	1:54 pm
☉	♓	18	**11:43 am**	8:43 am

Planetary Motion		day	ET / hr:mn / PT	
☿	D	3	**11:13 pm**	8:13 pm

1 TUESDAY
☽ ☌ ☉ **12:46 am**
☽ ☌ ♄ **6:01 am** 3:01 am
☽ ⚺ ♆ **3:46 pm** 12:46 pm
☽ ⚺ ☿ **9:05 pm** 6:05 pm
☽ ⚺ ♇ 9:57 pm

2 WEDNESDAY
☽ ⚺ ♇ **12:57 am**
☽ ⚹ ♂ **5:33 pm** 2:33 pm
☽ ☌ ♃ **6:57 pm** 3:57 pm
☽ ⚹ ♅ 9:30 pm
☽ ⚹ ♀ 10:35 pm

3 THURSDAY
☽ ⚹ ♅ **12:30 am**
☽ ⚹ ♀ **1:35 am**
☽ ⚺ ☉ **6:52 am** 3:52 am
☽ ⚺ ♄ **8:54 am** 5:54 am
☽ ☌ ♆ **6:54 pm** 3:54 pm
☽ ⚹ ☿ **11:55 pm** 8:55 pm

4 FRIDAY
☽ ⚹ ♇ **4:41 am** 1:41 am
♂ ⚹ ♃ **8:38 am** 5:38 am
☉ ☌ ♄ **2:05 pm** 11:05 am
☽ ⚺ ♃ 9:48 pm
☽ □ ♂ 10:27 pm

5 SATURDAY
☽ ⚺ ♃ **12:48 am**
☽ □ ♂ **1:27 am**
☽ ⚺ ♅ **5:53 am** 2:53 am
☽ □ ♀ **7:56 am** 4:56 am
☽ ⚹ ♄ **3:22 pm** 12:22 pm
☽ ⚹ ☉ **5:17 pm** 2:17 pm
☽ ⚺ ♆ 10:47 pm

6 SUNDAY
☽ ⚺ ♆ **1:47 am**
☽ □ ☿ **7:42 am** 4:42 am
☽ □ ♇ **12:21 pm** 9:21 am

7 MONDAY
☽ ⚹ ♃ **10:58 am** 7:58 am
☽ △ ♂ **2:12 pm** 11:12 am
☽ ☌ ♅ **3:22 pm** 12:22 pm
☽ △ ♀ **7:00 pm** 4:00 pm
☽ □ ♄ 11:01 pm

8 TUESDAY
☽ □ ♄ **2:01 am**
☽ □ ☉ **8:50 am** 5:50 am
♂ △ ♅ **9:57 am** 6:57 am
☽ ⚹ ♆ **12:40 pm** 9:40 am
☽ △ ☿ **8:48 pm** 5:48 pm
☽ △ ♇ **11:48 pm** 8:48 pm

9 WEDNESDAY
☽ □ ♃ 9:28 pm

10 THURSDAY
☽ □ ♃ **12:28 am**
☽ ⚺ ♅ **3:53 am** 12:53 am
☽ ⚻ ♂ **6:36 am** 3:36 am
☉ ⚺ ♆ **7:29 am** 4:29 am
☽ ⚻ ♀ **9:35 am** 6:35 am
☽ △ ♄ **3:20 pm** 12:20 pm
☽ □ ♆ 10:43 pm

11 FRIDAY
☽ □ ♆ **1:43 am**
☽ △ ☉ **3:23 am** 12:23 am
☿ ☌ ♇ **9:04 am** 6:04 am
☽ ⚻ ♇ **12:56 pm** 9:56 am
☽ ⚻ ☿ **1:11 pm** 10:11 am

12 SATURDAY
☽ △ ♃ **2:35 pm** 11:35 am
☽ ⚹ ♅ **4:49 pm** 1:49 pm
☽ ☍ ♂ **11:21 pm** 8:21 pm
☽ ☍ ♀ 9:45 pm

13 SUNDAY
☽ ☍ ♀ **12:45 am**
☽ ⚻ ♄ **4:33 am** 1:33 am
☽ △ ♆ **2:15 pm** 11:15 am
☽ ⚻ ☉ **9:09 pm** 6:09 pm
☽ ☍ ♇ 10:07 pm

14 MONDAY
☽ ☍ ♇ **1:07 am**
☽ ☍ ☿ **5:27 am** 2:27 am
☽ ⚻ ♃ 11:49 pm

15 TUESDAY
☽ ⚻ ♃ **2:49 am**
☽ □ ♅ **3:56 am** 12:56 am
☽ ⚻ ♂ **1:45 pm** 10:45 am
☽ ⚻ ♀ **2:02 pm** 11:02 am
☽ ☍ ♄ **3:38 pm** 12:38 pm
☉ ⚺ ♇ **10:17 pm** 7:17 pm
☽ ⚻ ♆ 9:31 pm

16 WEDNESDAY
☽ ⚻ ♆ **12:31 am**
♀ ☌ ♂ **9:29 am** 6:29 am
☽ ⚻ ♇ **10:53 am** 7:53 am
☽ ☍ ☉ **11:56 am** 8:56 am
☽ ⚻ ☿ **7:31 pm** 4:31 pm

17 THURSDAY
♂ ⚺ ♄ **3:34 am** 12:34 am
♀ ⚺ ♄ **9:09 am** 6:09 am
☽ ☍ ♃ **12:26 pm** 9:26 am
☽ △ ♅ **12:33 pm** 9:33 am
♃ ⚹ ♅ **7:13 pm** 4:13 pm
☽ ⚻ ♄ 9:11 pm
☽ △ ♀ 9:47 pm
☽ △ ♂ 10:13 pm

18 FRIDAY
☽ ⚻ ♄ **12:11 am**
☽ △ ♀ **12:47 am**
☽ △ ♂ **1:13 am**
☽ ☍ ♆ **8:22 am** 5:22 am
☽ △ ♇ **6:20 pm** 3:20 pm
☽ ⚻ ☉ **11:46 pm** 8:46 pm

19 SATURDAY
☽ △ ☿ **7:18 am** 4:18 am
☽ ⚻ ♅ **7:06 pm** 4:06 pm
☽ ⚻ ♃ **7:53 pm** 4:53 pm

20 SUNDAY
☽ △ ♄ **6:46 am** 3:46 am
☽ □ ♀ **9:33 am** 6:33 am
☽ □ ♂ **10:25 am** 7:25 am
☽ ⚻ ♆ **2:22 pm** 11:22 am
☽ □ ♇ 9:02 pm

21 MONDAY
☽ □ ♇ **12:02 am**
☽ △ ☉ **9:28 am** 6:28 am
☽ □ ☿ **5:28 pm** 2:28 pm
☽ ☍ ♅ 9:10 pm
☽ △ ♃ 10:45 pm

22 TUESDAY
☽ ☍ ♅ **12:10 am**
☽ △ ♃ **1:45 am**
☽ □ ♄ **11:53 am** 8:53 am
☽ ⚹ ♀ **4:55 pm** 1:55 pm
☽ ⚹ ♂ **5:58 pm** 2:58 pm
☽ △ ♆ **7:00 pm** 4:00 pm

23 WEDNESDAY
☽ ⚹ ♇ **4:24 am** 1:24 am
♂ ⚹ ♆ **2:12 pm** 11:12 am
☽ □ ☉ **5:32 pm** 2:32 pm
☽ ⚹ ☿ 11:17 pm

24 THURSDAY
☽ ⚹ ☿ **2:17 am**
☽ ⚻ ♅ **3:59 am** 12:59 am
☽ □ ♃ **6:19 am** 3:19 am
♀ ⚹ ♆ **11:04 am** 8:04 am
☽ ⚹ ♄ **3:45 pm** 12:45 pm
☿ □ ♅ **9:22 pm** 6:22 pm
☽ □ ♆ **10:24 pm** 7:24 pm
☽ ⚺ ♀ **11:00 pm** 8:00 pm
☽ ⚺ ♂ 9:06 pm

25 FRIDAY
☽ ⚺ ♂ **12:06 am**
☽ ⚺ ♇ **7:33 am** 4:33 am
☽ ⚹ ☉ 9:10 pm

26 SATURDAY
☽ ⚹ ☉ **12:10 am**
☽ △ ♅ **6:40 am** 3:40 am
☿ ⚺ ♃ **7:16 am** 4:16 am
☽ ⚹ ♃ **9:43 am** 6:43 am
☽ ⚺ ☿ **9:55 am** 6:55 am
☽ ⚺ ♄ **6:32 pm** 3:32 pm
☽ ⚹ ♆ 9:49 pm

27 SUNDAY
☽ ⚹ ♆ **12:49 am**
☽ ☌ ♀ **4:06 am** 1:06 am
☽ ☌ ♂ **5:06 am** 2:06 am
☽ ☌ ♇ **9:49 am** 6:49 am

28 MONDAY
☽ ⚺ ☉ **5:59 am** 2:59 am
☽ □ ♅ **8:50 am** 5:50 am
☽ ⚺ ♃ **12:37 pm** 9:37 am
☽ ☌ ☿ **5:11 pm** 2:11 pm
☽ ☌ ♄ **9:01 pm** 6:01 pm

Eastern time in bold type
Pacific time in medium type

FEBRUARY 2022

DATE	SID.TIME	SUN	MOON	NODE	MERCURY	VENUS	MARS	JUPITER	SATURN	URANUS	NEPTUNE	PLUTO	CERES	PALLAS	JUNO	VESTA	CHIRON
1 T	8 44 44	12♒05 17	8♒48	28♉47℞	25♑03℞	11♑13	5♑26	7♓13	15♒29	10♉54	21♓26	26♑57	28♉55	25♓29	29♑37	10♑58	9♈16
2 W	8 48 40	13 06 12	23 25	28 35	24 41	11 20	6 10	7 27	15 36	10 55	21 28	26 59	29 02	25 49	0♒01	11 29	9 18
3 Th	8 52 37	14 07 07	7♓42	28 23	24 28	11 30	6 54	7 40	15 43	10 55	21 30	27 01	29 09	26 09	0 25	12 01	9 21
4 F	8 56 33	15 08 00	21 35	28 12	24 23D	11 42	7 37	7 54	15 51	10 56	21 32	27 03	29 17	26 29	0 49	12 32	9 23
5 Sa	9 0 30	16 08 52	5♈01	28 04	24 25	11 56	8 21	8 08	15 58	10 57	21 33	27 05	29 25	26 49	1 13	13 03	9 25
6 Su	9 4 26	17 09 42	18 00	27 58	24 35	12 12	9 05	8 22	16 05	10 58	21 35	27 07	29 33	27 09	1 37	13 34	9 28
7 M	9 8 23	18 10 31	0♉35	27 55	24 51	12 30	9 49	8 36	16 12	10 59	21 37	27 08	29 41	27 30	2 01	14 05	9 30
8 T	9 12 19	19 11 19	12 50	27 54D	25 13	12 50	10 33	8 50	16 19	11 00	21 39	27 10	29 50	27 50	2 24	14 36	9 33
9 W	9 16 16	20 12 05	24 50	27 54℞	25 41	13 12	11 17	9 05	16 27	11 01	21 41	27 12	29 59	28 11	2 48	15 07	9 35
10 Th	9 20 13	21 12 50	6♊41	27 54	26 15	13 35	12 01	9 19	16 34	11 02	21 43	27 14	0♊09	28 31	3 12	15 38	9 38
11 F	9 24 9	22 13 33	18 28	27 52	26 53	14 01	12 45	9 33	16 41	11 03	21 45	27 16	0 18	28 52	3 36	16 09	9 40
12 Sa	9 28 6	23 14 14	0♋16	27 49	27 35	14 28	13 30	9 47	16 48	11 05	21 47	27 18	0 28	29 13	4 00	16 39	9 43
13 Su	9 32 2	24 14 54	12 11	27 42	28 21	14 57	14 14	10 01	16 55	11 06	21 49	27 19	0 39	29 34	4 24	17 10	9 45
14 M	9 35 59	25 15 33	24 15	27 33	29 11	15 27	14 58	10 16	17 02	11 07	21 52	27 21	0 49	29 55	4 48	17 41	9 48
15 T	9 39 55	26 16 10	6♌32	27 21	0♒05	15 59	15 42	10 30	17 10	11 09	21 54	27 23	1 00	0♈16	5 12	18 11	9 51
16 W	9 43 52	27 16 45	19 02	27 08	1 01	16 32	16 26	10 44	17 17	11 10	21 56	27 25	1 12	0 37	5 36	18 42	9 54
17 Th	9 47 48	28 17 19	1♍46	26 54	2 01	17 07	17 11	10 59	17 24	11 11	21 58	27 27	1 23	0 59	6 00	19 13	9 56
18 F	9 51 45	29 17 51	14 43	26 40	3 03	17 43	17 55	11 13	17 31	11 13	22 00	27 28	1 35	1 20	6 24	19 43	9 59
19 Sa	9 55 42	0♓18 22	27 52	26 29	4 07	18 20	18 39	11 27	17 38	11 15	22 02	27 30	1 47	1 42	6 47	20 13	10 02
20 Su	9 59 38	1 18 51	11♎13	26 20	5 14	18 59	19 24	11 42	17 45	11 16	22 04	27 32	2 00	2 03	7 11	20 44	10 05
21 M	10 3 35	2 19 19	24 43	26 14	6 23	19 39	20 08	11 56	17 52	11 18	22 06	27 33	2 12	2 25	7 35	21 14	10 08
22 T	10 7 31	3 19 46	8♏22	26 11	7 34	20 20	20 52	12 10	17 59	11 20	22 09	27 35	2 25	2 47	7 59	21 44	10 11
23 W	10 11 28	4 20 11	22 11	26 10	8 47	21 02	21 37	12 25	18 06	11 21	22 11	27 37	2 38	3 09	8 23	22 14	10 14
24 Th	10 15 24	5 20 35	6♐08	26 10	10 01	21 45	22 21	12 39	18 13	11 23	22 13	27 38	2 52	3 31	8 47	22 44	10 17
25 F	10 19 21	6 20 58	20 15	26 10	11 18	22 29	23 06	12 54	18 20	11 25	22 15	27 40	3 05	3 53	9 10	23 14	10 20
26 Sa	10 23 17	7 21 20	4♑30	26 08	12 35	23 14	23 51	13 08	18 27	11 27	22 17	27 42	3 19	4 15	9 34	23 44	10 23
27 Su	10 27 14	8 21 40	18 51	26 03	13 55	24 00	24 35	13 23	18 34	11 29	22 20	27 43	3 33	4 37	9 58	24 14	10 26
28 M	10 31 11	9 21 58	3♒15	25 55	15 15	24 47	25 20	13 37	18 41	11 31	22 22	27 45	3 48	5 00	10 22	24 44	10 29

EPHEMERIS CALCULATED FOR 12 MIDNIGHT GREENWICH MEAN TIME. ALL OTHER DATA AND FACING ASPECTARIAN PAGE IN **EASTERN TIME (BOLD)** AND PACIFIC TIME (REGULAR).

MARCH 2022

☽ Last Aspect day	ET / hr:mn / PT	asp	☽ Ingress sign	day	ET / hr:mn / PT
2/28	**9:01 pm** 6:01 pm	☌ ♄	♓	1	**3:53 pm** 12:53 pm
3	**4:45 pm** 1:45 pm	⚹ ♂	♈	3	**7:52 pm** 4:52 pm
5	**11:02 pm** 8:02 pm	□ ♇	♉	6	**3:00 am** 12:00 am
8	**9:35 am** 6:35 am	△ ♇	♊	8	**1:40 pm** 10:40 am
10	**11:43 am** 8:43 am	□ ♆	♋	10	11:24 pm
10	**11:43 am** 8:43 am	□ ♆	♋	11	**2:24 am**
13	**11:44 am** 8:44 am	☍ ♇	♌	13	**3:32 pm** 12:32 pm
15	**6:56 am** 3:56 am	☍ ♄	♍	15	9:59 pm
15	**6:56 am** 3:56 am	☍ ♄	♍	16	**12:59 am**
18	**4:11 am** 1:11 am	△ ♇	♎	18	**7:26 am** 4:26 am
20	**8:40 am** 5:40 am	□ ♇	♏	20	**11:45 am** 8:45 am
22	**12:01 pm** 9:01 am	⚹ ♇	♐	22	**2:59 pm** 11:59 am
24	**8:59 am** 5:59 am	□ ☿	♑	24	**5:54 pm** 2:54 pm
26	**7:51 pm** 4:51 pm	⚹ ☿	♒	26	**8:55 pm** 5:55 pm
28	**10:11 am** 7:11 am	☌ ♄	♓	28	9:32 pm
28	**10:11 am** 7:11 am	☌ ♄	♓	29	**12:32 am**
30	11:37 pm	⚹ ♇	♈	31	**5:30 am** 2:30 am
31	**2:37 am**	⚹ ♇	♈	31	**5:30 am** 2:30 am

☽ Phases & Eclipses phase	day	ET / hr:mn / PT
New Moon	2	**12:35 pm** 9:35 am
2nd Quarter	10	**5:45 am** 2:45 am
Full Moon	18	**3:18 am** 12:18 am
4th Quarter	24	10:37 pm
4th Quarter	25	**1:37 am**
New Moon	31	11:24 pm
New Moon	4/1	**2:24 am**

Planet Ingress		day	ET / hr:mn / PT
♂	♒	5	10:23 pm
♂	♒	6	**1:23 am**
♀	♒	5	10:30 pm
♀	♒	6	**1:30 am**
☿	♓	9	**8:32 pm** 5:32 pm
⚵	♒	10	**1:22 pm** 10:22 am
☉	♈	20	**11:33 am** 8:33 am
☿	♈	27	**3:44 am** 12:44 am

Planetary Motion	day	ET / hr:mn / PT

1 TUESDAY

	ET	PT
☽ ⚺ ♆	**3:05 am**	12:05 am
☽ ⚺ ♀	**9:14 am**	6:14 am
☽ ⚺ ♂	**10:02 am**	7:02 am
☽ ⚺ ♇	**12:09 pm**	9:09 am
☉ ⚹ ♅		9:05 pm

2 WEDNESDAY

	ET	PT
☉ ⚹ ♅	**12:05 am**	
☿ ☌ ♄	**11:33 am**	8:33 am
☽ ⚹ ♅	**11:43 am**	8:43 am
☽ ☌ ☉	**12:35 pm**	9:35 am
☽ ☌ ♃	**4:24 pm**	1:24 pm
☽ ⚺ ♄		9:37 pm
☽ ⚺ ☿		11:00 pm

3 THURSDAY

	ET	PT
☽ ⚺ ♄	**12:37 am**	
☽ ⚺ ☿	**2:00 am**	
♂ ☌ ♇	**3:43 am**	12:43 am
☽ ☌ ♆	**6:37 am**	3:37 am
♀ ☌ ♇	**12:56 pm**	9:56 am
☽ ⚹ ♇	**4:03 pm**	1:03 pm
☽ ⚹ ♀	**4:15 pm**	1:15 pm
☽ ⚹ ♂	**4:45 pm**	1:45 pm

4 FRIDAY

	ET	PT
☽ ⚺ ♅	**4:55 pm**	1:55 pm
☽ ⚺ ☉	**10:05 pm**	7:05 pm
☽ ⚺ ♃	**10:45 pm**	7:45 pm
☿ ⚺ ♆	**10:50 pm**	7:50 pm

5 SATURDAY

	ET	PT
☽ ⚹ ♄	**6:56 am**	3:56 am
☉ ☌ ♃	**9:06 am**	6:06 am
☽ ⚺ ♆	**1:01 pm**	10:01 am
☽ ⚹ ☿	**2:49 pm**	11:49 am
☽ □ ♇	**11:02 pm**	8:02 pm
♀ ☌ ♂		11:12 pm

6 SUNDAY

	ET	PT
♀ ☌ ♂	**2:12 am**	
☽ □ ♂	**3:06 am**	12:06 am
☽ □ ♀	**3:07 am**	12:07 am
☽ ☌ ♅		10:38 pm

7 MONDAY

	ET	PT
☽ ☌ ♅	**1:38 am**	
☽ ⚹ ♃	**8:49 am**	5:49 am
☽ ⚹ ☉	**12:03 pm**	9:03 am
☽ □ ♄	**4:56 pm**	1:56 pm
☽ ⚹ ♆	**11:03 pm**	8:03 pm

8 TUESDAY

	ET	PT
☽ □ ☿	**9:04 am**	6:04 am
☽ △ ♇	**9:35 am**	6:35 am
☿ ⚺ ♇	**1:05 pm**	10:05 am
☽ △ ♂	**5:40 pm**	2:40 pm
☽ △ ♀	**6:27 pm**	3:27 pm

9 WEDNESDAY

	ET	PT
☽ ⚺ ♅	**1:35 pm**	10:35 am
☽ □ ♃	**10:07 pm**	7:07 pm

10 THURSDAY

	ET	PT
☽ □ ☉	**5:45 am**	2:45 am
☽ △ ♄	**5:48 am**	2:48 am
☉ ⚺ ♄	**6:17 am**	3:17 am
☽ □ ♆	**11:43 am**	8:43 am
☽ ⚻ ♇	**10:23 pm**	7:23 pm

11 FRIDAY

	ET	PT
☽ △ ☿	**7:00 am**	4:00 am
☽ ⚻ ♂	**10:34 am**	7:34 am
☽ ⚻ ♀	**12:19 pm**	9:19 am
☽ ⚹ ♅		11:37 pm

12 SATURDAY

	ET	PT
☽ ⚹ ♅	**2:37 am**	
☽ △ ♃	**12:07 pm**	9:07 am
☽ ⚻ ♄	**6:59 pm**	3:59 pm
☽ △ ☉	**11:52 pm**	8:52 pm
☽ △ ♆		9:25 pm

13 SUNDAY

	ET	PT
☽ △ ♆	**12:25 am**	
☿ ⚺ ♂	**5:44 am**	1:44 am
☉ ☌ ♆	**7:43 am**	4:43 am
☽ ☍ ♇	**11:44 am**	8:44 am

14 MONDAY

	ET	PT
☽ ☍ ♂	**3:17 am**	12:17 am
☽ ⚻ ☿	**5:05 am**	2:05 am
☽ ☍ ♀	**6:00 am**	3:00 am
☽ □ ♅	**3:02 pm**	12:02 pm
☿ ⚺ ♀	**7:51 pm**	4:51 pm
☽ ⚻ ♃		10:02 pm

15 TUESDAY

	ET	PT
☽ ⚻ ♃	**1:02 am**	
☽ ☍ ♄	**6:56 am**	3:56 am
☽ ⚻ ♆	**11:46 am**	8:46 am
☽ ⚻ ☉	**4:01 pm**	1:01 pm
☽ ⚻ ♇	**9:29 pm**	6:29 pm

16 WEDNESDAY

	ET	PT
☽ ⚻ ♂	**3:35 pm**	12:35 pm
☽ ⚻ ♀	**7:09 pm**	4:09 pm
☽ ☍ ☿	**10:08 pm**	7:08 pm
☽ △ ♅	**11:25 pm**	8:25 pm

17 THURSDAY

	ET	PT
☿ ⚹ ♅	**8:13 am**	5:13 am
☽ ☍ ♃	**9:44 am**	6:44 am
☽ ⚻ ♄	**2:44 pm**	11:44 am
☽ ☍ ♆	**7:02 pm**	4:02 pm

18 FRIDAY

	ET	PT
☽ ☍ ☉	**3:18 am**	12:18 am
☽ △ ♇	**4:11 am**	1:11 am
☉ ⚹ ♇	**3:37 pm**	12:37 pm
☽ △ ♂		9:29 pm

19 SATURDAY

	ET	PT
☽ △ ♂	**12:29 am**	
☽ △ ♀	**4:52 am**	1:52 am
☽ ⚻ ♅	**5:02 am**	2:02 am
♀ □ ♅	**7:16 am**	4:16 am
☽ ⚻ ☿	**11:20 am**	8:20 am
☽ ⚻ ♃	**3:43 pm**	12:43 pm
☽ △ ♄	**7:59 pm**	4:59 pm
☽ ⚻ ♆	**11:53 pm**	8:53 pm

20 SUNDAY

	ET	PT
☽ □ ♇	**8:40 am**	5:40 am
☽ ⚻ ☉	**11:45 am**	8:45 am
☿ ☌ ♃		11:06 pm

21 MONDAY

	ET	PT
☿ ☌ ♃	**2:06 am**	
☽ □ ♂	**7:17 am**	4:17 am
☽ ☍ ♅	**8:58 am**	5:58 am
☽ □ ♀	**12:34 pm**	9:34 am
☽ △ ♃	**8:09 pm**	5:09 pm
☽ △ ☿	**10:26 pm**	7:26 pm
☽ □ ♄	**11:49 pm**	8:49 pm

22 TUESDAY

	ET	PT
☽ △ ♆	**3:26 am**	12:26 am
☿ ⚺ ♄	**9:48 am**	6:48 am
☽ ⚹ ♇	**12:01 pm**	9:01 am
♂ □ ♅	**4:44 pm**	1:44 pm
☽ △ ☉	**6:52 pm**	3:52 pm

23 WEDNESDAY

	ET	PT
☽ ⚻ ♅	**12:10 pm**	9:10 am
☽ ⚹ ♂	**1:12 pm**	10:12 am
☿ ☌ ♆	**1:44 pm**	10:44 am
☽ ⚹ ♀	**7:29 pm**	4:29 pm
☽ □ ♃	**11:59 pm**	8:59 pm

24 THURSDAY

	ET	PT
☽ ⚹ ♄	**3:09 am**	12:09 am
☽ □ ♆	**6:30 am**	3:30 am
☽ □ ☿	**8:59 am**	5:59 am
☽ ⚺ ♇	**3:00 pm**	12:00 pm
☽ □ ☉		10:37 pm

25 FRIDAY

	ET	PT
☽ □ ☉	**1:37 am**	
☽ △ ♅	**3:16 pm**	12:16 pm
☽ ⚺ ♂	**6:59 pm**	3:59 pm
☽ ⚺ ♀		11:22 pm

26 SATURDAY

	ET	PT
☽ ⚺ ♀	**2:22 am**	
☽ ⚹ ♃	**3:48 am**	12:48 am
☽ ⚺ ♄	**6:27 am**	3:27 am
☿ ⚹ ♇	**6:35 am**	3:35 am
☽ ⚹ ♆	**9:37 am**	6:37 am
☽ ☌ ♇	**6:04 pm**	3:04 pm
☽ ⚹ ☿	**7:51 pm**	4:51 pm

27 SUNDAY

	ET	PT
♀ ⚺ ♃	**3:34 am**	12:34 am
☽ ⚹ ☉	**8:35 am**	5:35 am
☽ □ ♅	**6:38 pm**	3:38 pm
☽ ☌ ♂		10:08 pm

28 MONDAY

	ET	PT
☽ ☌ ♂	**1:08 am**	
☽ ⚺ ♃	**8:02 am**	5:02 am
☽ ☌ ♀	**9:48 am**	6:48 am
☽ ☌ ♄	**10:11 am**	7:11 am
☽ ⚺ ♆	**1:10 pm**	10:10 am
♀ ☌ ♄	**3:27 pm**	12:27 pm
☽ ⚺ ♇	**9:40 pm**	6:40 pm

29 TUESDAY

	ET	PT
☽ ⚺ ☿	**7:52 am**	4:52 am
☽ ⚺ ☉	**4:27 pm**	1:27 pm
☽ ⚹ ♅	**10:54 pm**	7:54 pm

30 WEDNESDAY

	ET	PT
♀ ⚺ ♆	**8:15 am**	5:15 am
☽ ⚺ ♂	**8:27 am**	5:27 am
☽ ☌ ♃	**1:24 pm**	10:24 am
☽ ⚺ ♄	**3:04 pm**	12:04 pm
☽ ☌ ♆	**5:55 pm**	2:55 pm
☽ ⚺ ♀	**6:42 pm**	3:42 pm
☽ ⚹ ♇		11:37 pm

31 THURSDAY

	ET	PT
☽ ⚹ ♇	**2:37 am**	
☽ ☌ ☿	**10:35 pm**	7:35 pm
☽ ☌ ☉		11:24 pm

Eastern time in bold type
Pacific time in medium type

MARCH 2022

DATE	SID.TIME	SUN	MOON	NODE	MERCURY	VENUS	MARS	JUPITER	SATURN	URANUS	NEPTUNE	PLUTO	CERES	PALLAS	JUNO	VESTA	CHIRON
1 T	10 35 7	10♓22 15	17♒36	25♉45℞	16♒38	25♑35	26♑04	13♓52	18♒48	11♉33	22♓24	27♑46	4♊02	5♈22	10♒46	25♑14	10♈32
2 W	10 39 4	11 22 31	1♓50	25 33	18 01	26 24	26 49	14 06	18 55	11 35	22 26	27 48	4 17	5 45	11 09	25 43	10 35
3 Th	10 43 0	12 22 44	15 50	25 21	19 26	27 13	27 34	14 21	19 02	11 37	22 29	27 50	4 32	6 07	11 33	26 13	10 38
4 F	10 46 57	13 22 56	29 30	25 10	20 52	28 03	28 19	14 35	19 08	11 39	22 31	27 51	4 48	6 30	11 57	26 42	10 42
5 Sa	10 50 53	14 23 06	12♈50	25 01	22 19	28 54	29 03	14 50	19 15	11 41	22 33	27 53	5 03	6 53	12 20	27 12	10 45
6 Su	10 54 50	15 23 13	25 46	24 55	23 48	29 46	29 48	15 04	19 22	11 43	22 35	27 54	5 19	7 15	12 44	27 41	10 48
7 M	10 58 46	16 23 19	8♉21	24 51	25 18	0♒38	0♒33	15 19	19 29	11 46	22 38	27 55	5 35	7 38	13 07	28 11	10 51
8 T	11 2 43	17 23 23	20 38	24 50D	26 49	1 31	1 18	15 33	19 35	11 48	22 40	27 57	5 51	8 01	13 31	28 40	10 55
9 W	11 6 39	18 23 25	2♊40	24 50	28 21	2 25	2 03	15 48	19 42	11 50	22 42	27 58	6 08	8 24	13 55	29 09	10 58
10 Th	11 10 36	19 23 24	14 32	24 51℞	29 54	3 19	2 47	16 02	19 49	11 53	22 44	28 00	6 24	8 48	14 18	29 38	11 01
11 F	11 14 33	20 23 22	26 21	24 51	1♓28	4 13	3 32	16 17	19 55	11 55	22 47	28 01	6 41	9 11	14 42	0♒07	11 05
12 Sa	11 18 29	21 23 17	8♋12	24 49	3 04	5 09	4 17	16 31	20 02	11 58	22 49	28 02	6 58	9 34	15 05	0 36	11 08
13 Su	11 22 26	22 23 10	20 09	24 45	4 41	6 04	5 02	16 46	20 08	12 00	22 51	28 04	7 15	9 57	15 29	1 04	11 11
14 M	11 26 22	23 23 01	2♌17	24 39	6 19	7 01	5 47	17 00	20 14	12 03	22 54	28 05	7 33	10 21	15 52	1 33	11 15
15 T	11 30 19	24 22 50	14 40	24 30	7 58	7 58	6 32	17 15	20 21	12 05	22 56	28 06	7 50	10 44	16 15	2 02	11 18
16 W	11 34 15	25 22 36	27 20	24 21	9 38	8 55	7 17	17 29	20 27	12 08	22 58	28 07	8 08	11 08	16 39	2 30	11 22
17 Th	11 38 12	26 22 21	10♍19	24 10	11 20	9 53	8 02	17 44	20 34	12 10	23 00	28 09	8 26	11 32	17 02	2 59	11 25
18 F	11 42 8	27 22 03	23 35	24 00	13 02	10 51	8 47	17 58	20 40	12 13	23 03	28 10	8 44	11 55	17 25	3 27	11 28
19 Sa	11 46 5	28 21 43	7♎07	23 51	14 46	11 49	9 32	18 13	20 46	12 16	23 05	28 11	9 02	12 19	17 48	3 55	11 32
20 Su	11 50 2	29 21 22	20 53	23 45	16 31	12 48	10 17	18 27	20 52	12 18	23 07	28 12	9 21	12 43	18 12	4 23	11 35
21 M	11 53 58	0♈20 58	4♏48	23 41	18 18	13 48	11 02	18 41	20 58	12 21	23 09	28 13	9 39	13 07	18 35	4 51	11 39
22 T	11 57 55	1 20 33	18 51	23 39D	20 05	14 48	11 47	18 56	21 04	12 24	23 12	28 14	9 58	13 31	18 58	5 19	11 42
23 W	12 1 51	2 20 06	2♐57	23 39	21 54	15 48	12 33	19 10	21 10	12 27	23 14	28 15	10 17	13 55	19 21	5 47	11 46
24 Th	12 5 48	3 19 37	17 06	23 40	23 45	16 48	13 18	19 24	21 16	12 30	23 16	28 17	10 36	14 19	19 44	6 15	11 49
25 F	12 9 44	4 19 07	1♑14	23 41℞	25 36	17 49	14 03	19 39	21 22	12 33	23 18	28 18	10 56	14 43	20 07	6 43	11 53
26 Sa	12 13 41	5 18 34	15 22	23 41	27 29	18 51	14 48	19 53	21 28	12 35	23 21	28 19	11 15	15 07	20 30	7 10	11 56
27 Su	12 17 37	6 18 01	29 28	23 38	29 23	19 52	15 33	20 07	21 34	12 38	23 23	28 20	11 35	15 32	20 53	7 38	12 00
28 M	12 21 34	7 17 25	13♒29	23 34	1♈18	20 54	16 19	20 21	21 40	12 41	23 25	28 20	11 54	15 56	21 16	8 05	12 03
29 T	12 25 31	8 16 47	27 24	23 28	3 15	21 56	17 04	20 36	21 46	12 44	23 27	28 21	12 14	16 20	21 39	8 32	12 07
30 W	12 29 27	9 16 08	11♓09	23 21	5 13	22 59	17 49	20 50	21 51	12 47	23 30	28 22	12 34	16 45	22 01	8 59	12 10
31 Th	12 33 24	10 15 27	24 42	23 13	7 12	24 02	18 34	21 04	21 57	12 50	23 32	28 23	12 54	17 09	22 24	9 26	12 14

EPHEMERIS CALCULATED FOR 12 MIDNIGHT GREENWICH MEAN TIME. ALL OTHER DATA AND FACING ASPECTARIAN PAGE IN **EASTERN TIME (BOLD)** AND PACIFIC TIME (REGULAR).

APRIL 2022

☽ Last Aspect day	ET / hr:mn / PT	asp	☽ Ingress sign	day	ET / hr:mn / PT
2	**9:51 am** 6:51 am	□♇	♉	2	**12:50 pm** 9:50 am
4	**9:53 pm** 6:53 pm	□♀	♊	4	**11:04 pm** 8:04 pm
6	**11:15 pm** 8:15 pm	△♂	♋	7	**11:30 am** 8:30 am
9	**9:01 pm** 6:01 pm	☍♇	♌	9	9:00 pm
9	**9:01 pm** 6:01 pm	☍♇	♌	10	**12:00 am**
12	**6:16 am** 3:16 am	☍♂	♍	12	**10:07 am** 7:07 am
14	**2:11 pm** 11:11 am	△♇	♎	14	**4:46 pm** 1:46 pm
16	**5:57 pm** 2:57 pm	□♇	♏	16	**8:23 pm** 5:23 pm
18	**7:55 pm** 4:55 pm	⚹♇	♐	18	**10:16 pm** 7:16 pm
20	**4:56 pm** 1:56 pm	□♃	♑	20	**11:52 pm** 8:52 pm
22	**11:53 pm** 8:53 pm	☌♇	♒	22	11:17 pm
22	**11:53 pm** 8:53 pm	☌♇	♒	23	**2:17 am**
24	**8:33 pm** 5:33 pm	□☿	♓	25	**6:15 am** 3:15 am
27	**9:36 am** 6:36 am	⚹♇	♈	27	**12:10 pm** 9:10 am
29	**5:38 pm** 2:38 pm	□♇	♉	29	**8:19 pm** 5:19 pm

☽ Phases & Eclipses phase	day	ET / hr:mn / PT
New Moon	3/31	11:24 pm
New Moon	1	**2:24 am**
2nd Quarter	8	11:48 pm
2nd Quarter	9	**2:48 am**
Full Moon	16	**2:55 pm** 11:55 am
4th Quarter	23	**7:56 am** 4:56 am
New Moon	30	**4:28 pm** 1:28 pm
●	30	10° ♉ 28'

Planet Ingress		day	ET / hr:mn / PT
♀	♓	5	**11:18 am** 8:18 am
☿	♉	10	**10:09 pm** 7:09 pm
♂	♓	14	**11:06 pm** 8:06 pm
☉	♉	19	**10:24 pm** 7:24 pm
⚵	♓	20	**11:51 am** 8:51 am
☿	♊	29	**6:23 pm** 3:23 pm
♀	♉	30	**4:50 am** 1:50 am

Planetary Motion		day	ET / hr:mn / PT
♇	℞	29	**2:38 pm** 11:38 am

1 FRIDAY
☽ ☌ ☉ **2:24 am**
☽ ⚺ ♅ **4:59 am** 1:59 am
☽ ⚹ ♂ **6:07 pm** 3:07 pm
☽ ⚺ ♃ **8:57 pm** 5:57 pm
☽ ⚹ ♄ **10:04 pm** 7:04 pm
☽ ⚺ ♆ 9:49 pm

2 SATURDAY
☽ ⚺ ♆ **12:49 am**
☽ ⚹ ♀ **6:24 am** 3:24 am
☽ □ ♇ **9:51 am** 6:51 am
☉ ⚺ ♅ **2:10 pm** 11:10 am
☿ ⚺ ♅ **4:49 pm** 1:49 pm
☉ ☌ ☿ **7:11 pm** 4:11 pm

3 SUNDAY
☽ ☌ ♅ **1:47 pm** 10:47 am
☽ ⚺ ☉ **3:43 pm** 12:43 pm
☽ ⚺ ☿ **5:50 pm** 2:50 pm
♀ ⚺ ♇ 9:16 pm

4 MONDAY
♀ ⚺ ♇ **12:16 am**
☽ □ ♂ **7:09 am** 4:09 am
☽ ⚹ ♃ **7:29 am** 4:29 am
☽ □ ♄ **7:58 am** 4:58 am
☽ ⚹ ♆ **10:36 am** 7:36 am
♂ ⚺ ♃ **2:47 pm** 11:47 am
☽ △ ♇ **8:00 pm** 5:00 pm
♂ ☌ ♄ **9:51 pm** 6:51 pm
☽ □ ♀ **9:53 pm** 6:53 pm

Eastern time in bold type
Pacific time in medium type

5 TUESDAY
♃ ⚺ ♄ **11:24 pm** 8:24 pm
☽ ⚺ ♅ 10:25 pm

6 WEDNESDAY
☽ ⚺ ♅ **1:25 am**
☽ ⚹ ☉ **8:32 am** 5:32 am
♂ ⚺ ♆ **5:34 pm** 2:34 pm
☽ ⚹ ☿ **5:57 pm** 2:57 pm
☽ △ ♄ **8:26 pm** 5:26 pm
☽ □ ♃ **8:42 pm** 5:42 pm
☽ □ ♆ **10:54 pm** 7:54 pm
☽ △ ♂ **11:15 pm** 8:15 pm

7 THURSDAY
☽ ⚻ ♇ **8:25 am** 5:25 am
☿ ⚹ ♄ **8:37 am** 5:37 am
☿ ⚺ ♃ **11:14 am** 8:14 am
☽ △ ♀ **4:20 pm** 1:20 pm
☿ ⚺ ♆ **10:33 pm** 7:33 pm

8 FRIDAY
☿ ⚹ ♂ **2:19 pm** 11:19 am
☽ ⚹ ♅ **2:28 pm** 11:28 am
☽ □ ☉ 11:48 pm

9 SATURDAY
☽ □ ☉ **2:48 am**
☽ ⚻ ♄ **9:35 am** 6:35 am
☽ △ ♃ **10:36 am** 7:36 am
☽ △ ♆ **11:46 am** 8:46 am
☽ ⚻ ♂ **4:01 pm** 1:01 pm
☽ □ ☿ **7:25 pm** 4:25 pm
☽ ☍ ♇ **9:01 pm** 6:01 pm

10 SUNDAY
☿ □ ♇ **4:45 am** 1:45 am
☽ ⚻ ♀ **10:37 am** 7:37 am
☽ □ ♅ 11:25 pm

11 MONDAY
☽ □ ♅ **2:25 am**
☽ △ ☉ **7:01 pm** 4:01 pm
☽ ☍ ♄ **8:50 pm** 5:50 pm
☽ ⚻ ♃ **10:30 pm** 7:30 pm
☽ ⚻ ♆ **10:42 pm** 7:42 pm

12 TUESDAY
☽ ☍ ♂ **6:16 am** 3:16 am
☽ ⚻ ♇ **7:21 am** 4:21 am
♃ ☌ ♆ **10:42 am** 7:42 am
☽ △ ☿ **4:55 pm** 1:55 pm
☉ ⚹ ♄ **8:14 pm** 5:14 pm
♂ ⚺ ♇ 9:30 pm
☽ ☍ ♀ 10:27 pm

13 WEDNESDAY
♂ ⚺ ♇ **12:30 am**
☽ ☍ ♀ **1:27 am**
☽ △ ♅ **11:15 am** 8:15 am
☉ ⚺ ♆ **7:48 pm** 4:48 pm

14 THURSDAY
☉ ⚺ ♃ **4:14 am** 1:14 am
☽ ⚻ ♄ **4:37 am** 1:37 am
☽ ☍ ♆ **6:11 am** 3:11 am
☽ ☍ ♃ **6:49 am** 3:49 am
☽ ⚻ ☉ **6:58 am** 3:58 am
☽ △ ♇ **2:11 pm** 11:11 am
☽ ⚻ ♂ **4:23 pm** 1:23 pm

15 FRIDAY
☽ ⚻ ☿ **8:12 am** 5:12 am
☽ ⚻ ♀ **11:48 am** 8:48 am
☽ ⚻ ♅ **4:37 pm** 1:37 pm

16 SATURDAY
☽ △ ♄ **9:06 am** 6:06 am
☽ ⚻ ♆ **10:26 am** 7:26 am
☽ ⚻ ♃ **11:45 am** 8:45 am
☽ ☍ ☉ **2:55 pm** 11:55 am
☽ □ ♇ **5:57 pm** 2:57 pm
☽ △ ♂ **10:55 pm** 7:55 pm

17 SUNDAY
☽ ☍ ☿ **6:43 pm** 3:43 pm
☽ △ ♀ **6:51 pm** 3:51 pm
☽ ☍ ♅ **7:28 pm** 4:28 pm
☿ ⚹ ♀ **9:09 pm** 6:09 pm
☿ ☌ ♅ 9:51 pm

18 MONDAY
☿ ☌ ♅ **12:51 am**
♀ ⚹ ♅ **3:15 am** 12:15 am
☉ □ ♇ **11:14 am** 8:14 am
☽ □ ♄ **11:31 am** 8:31 am
☽ △ ♆ **12:40 pm** 9:40 am
☽ △ ♃ **2:37 pm** 11:37 am
☽ ⚹ ♇ **7:55 pm** 4:55 pm
☽ ⚻ ☉ **8:32 pm** 5:32 pm

19 TUESDAY
☽ □ ♂ **3:30 am** 12:30 am
☽ ⚻ ♅ **9:15pm** 6:15pm
☽ □ ♀ 9:33 pm

20 WEDNESDAY
☽ □ ♀ **12:33 am**
☽ ⚻ ☿ **3:02 am** 12:02 am
☽ ⚹ ♄ **1:18 pm** 10:18 am
☽ □ ♆ **2:20 pm** 11:20 am
☽ □ ♃ **4:56 pm** 1:56 pm
☽ ⚺ ♇ **9:31 pm** 6:31 pm
☽ △ ☉ 10:43 pm

21 THURSDAY
☽ △ ☉ **1:43 am**
☽ ⚹ ♂ **7:53 am** 4:53 am
☽ △ ♅ **11:18 pm** 8:18 pm

22 FRIDAY
☽ ⚹ ♀ **6:43 am** 3:43 am
☽ △ ☿ **11:13 am** 8:13 am
☽ ⚺ ♄ **3:43 pm** 12:43 pm
☽ ⚹ ♆ **4:38 pm** 1:38 pm
☽ ⚹ ♃ **7:58 pm** 4:58 pm
☽ ☌ ♇ **11:53 pm** 8:53 pm

23 SATURDAY
☽ □ ☉ **7:56 am** 4:56 am
☽ ⚺ ♂ **1:24 pm** 10:24 am
☽ □ ♅ 11:35 pm

24 SUNDAY
☽ □ ♅ **2:35 am**
☿ □ ♄ **9:50 am** 6:50 am
☽ ⚺ ♀ **2:33 pm** 11:33 am
☿ ⚹ ♆ **6:37 pm** 3:37 pm
☽ ☌ ♄ **7:33 pm** 4:33 pm
☽ ⚺ ♆ **8:22 pm** 5:22 pm
☽ □ ☿ **8:33 pm** 5:33 pm
☽ ⚺ ♃ 9:32 pm

25 MONDAY
☽ ⚺ ♃ **12:32 am**
☽ ⚺ ♇ **3:46 am** 12:46 am
☽ ⚹ ☉ **4:09 pm** 1:09 pm
☽ ☌ ♂ **8:51 pm** 5:51 pm

26 TUESDAY
☽ ⚹ ♅ **7:39 am** 4:39 am
☽ ☌ ♀ 9:50 pm
☿ ⚹ ♃ 10:11 pm
☽ ⚺ ♄ 10:18 pm
☽ ☌ ♆ 11:02 pm

27 WEDNESDAY
☽ ☌ ♀ **12:50 am**
☿ ⚹ ♃ **1:11 am**
☽ ⚺ ♄ **1:18 am**
☽ ☌ ♆ **2:02 am**
♀ ⚺ ♄ **6:43 am** 3:43 am
☽ ☌ ♃ **7:07 am** 4:07 am
☽ ⚹ ☿ **7:35 am** 4:35 am
☽ ⚹ ♇ **9:36 am** 6:36 am
♀ ☌ ♆ **3:12 pm** 12:12 pm
☽ ⚺ ☉ 11:52 pm

28 THURSDAY
☽ ⚺ ☉ **2:52 am**
☽ ⚺ ♂ **6:45 am** 3:45 am
☿ △ ♇ **8:05 am** 5:05 am
☽ ⚺ ♅ **2:52 pm** 11:52 am

29 FRIDAY
☽ ⚹ ♄ **9:16 am** 6:16 am
☽ ⚺ ♆ **9:53 am** 6:53 am
☽ ⚺ ♀ **1:59 pm** 10:59 am
☽ ⚺ ♃ **4:01 pm** 1:01 pm
☽ □ ♇ **5:38 pm** 2:38 pm
☽ ⚺ ☿ **8:28 pm** 5:28 pm

30 SATURDAY
☽ ☌ ☉ **4:28 pm** 1:28 pm
♀ ☌ ♃ **5:14 pm** 2:14 pm
☽ ⚹ ♂ **7:23 pm** 4:23 pm
☽ ☌ ♅ 9:24 pm

APRIL 2022

DATE	SID.TIME	SUN	MOON	NODE	MERCURY	VENUS	MARS	JUPITER	SATURN	URANUS	NEPTUNE	PLUTO	CERES	PALLAS	JUNO	VESTA	CHIRON
1 F	12 37 20	11♈14 43	8♈00	23♉06℞	9♈12	25♒05	19♒20	21♓18	22♒02	12♉53	23♓34	28♑24	13♊15	17♈34	22♒47	9♒53	12♈17
2 Sa	12 41 17	12 13 58	21 02	23 01	11 13	26 08	20 05	21 32	22 08	12 56	23 36	28 25	13 35	17 59	23 09	10 20	12 21
3 Su	12 45 13	13 13 10	3♉46	22 57	13 15	27 11	20 50	21 46	22 13	13 00	23 38	28 26	13 56	18 23	23 32	10 46	12 24
4 M	12 49 10	14 12 21	16 14	22 55D	15 18	28 15	21 35	22 00	22 19	13 03	23 41	28 26	14 16	18 48	23 54	11 13	12 28
5 T	12 53 6	15 11 29	28 27	22 55	17 22	29 19	22 21	22 14	22 24	13 06	23 43	28 27	14 37	19 13	24 17	11 39	12 31
6 W	12 57 3	16 10 35	10♊28	22 56	19 27	0♓23	23 06	22 28	22 29	13 09	23 45	28 28	14 58	19 38	24 39	12 06	12 35
7 Th	13 1 0	17 09 39	22 21	22 58	21 31	1 28	23 51	22 42	22 34	13 12	23 47	28 28	15 19	20 03	25 02	12 32	12 38
8 F	13 4 56	18 08 41	4♋11	23 00	23 36	2 32	24 37	22 56	22 39	13 15	23 49	28 29	15 40	20 28	25 24	12 58	12 42
9 Sa	13 8 53	19 07 40	16 02	23 01℞	25 41	3 37	25 22	23 09	22 44	13 19	23 51	28 30	16 02	20 53	25 46	13 24	12 45
10 Su	13 12 49	20 06 37	28 00	23 00	27 45	4 42	26 07	23 23	22 49	13 22	23 53	28 30	16 23	21 18	26 08	13 49	12 49
11 M	13 16 46	21 05 32	10♌08	22 59	29 49	5 48	26 53	23 37	22 54	13 25	23 55	28 31	16 44	21 43	26 30	14 15	12 52
12 T	13 20 42	22 04 25	22 33	22 56	1♉52	6 53	27 38	23 50	22 59	13 28	23 57	28 31	17 06	22 08	26 52	14 40	12 56
13 W	13 24 39	23 03 15	5♍17	22 52	3 53	7 59	28 23	24 04	23 04	13 32	24 00	28 32	17 28	22 34	27 14	15 06	12 59
14 Th	13 28 35	24 02 03	18 22	22 47	5 53	9 04	29 09	24 18	23 08	13 35	24 02	28 32	17 50	22 59	27 36	15 31	13 03
15 F	13 32 32	25 00 49	1♎50	22 43	7 50	10 10	29 54	24 31	23 13	13 38	24 04	28 33	18 12	23 24	27 58	15 56	13 06
16 Sa	13 36 29	25 59 32	15 39	22 39	9 45	11 16	0♓40	24 45	23 18	13 42	24 06	28 33	18 34	23 50	28 20	16 21	13 10
17 Su	13 40 25	26 58 14	29 47	22 36	11 38	12 23	1 25	24 58	23 22	13 45	24 08	28 34	18 56	24 15	28 41	16 46	13 13
18 M	13 44 22	27 56 54	14♏08	22 35D	13 27	13 29	2 10	25 11	23 26	13 48	24 10	28 34	19 18	24 41	29 03	17 10	13 17
19 T	13 48 18	28 55 32	28 37	22 35	15 13	14 36	2 56	25 25	23 31	13 52	24 12	28 34	19 41	25 06	29 24	17 35	13 20
20 W	13 52 15	29 54 08	13♐10	22 35	16 56	15 43	3 41	25 38	23 35	13 55	24 13	28 35	20 03	25 32	29 46	17 59	13 23
21 Th	13 56 11	0♉52 42	27 40	22 37	18 35	16 49	4 26	25 51	23 39	13 58	24 15	28 35	20 26	25 57	0♓07	18 23	13 27
22 F	14 0 8	1 51 15	12♑04	22 38	20 09	17 57	5 12	26 04	23 43	14 02	24 17	28 35	20 48	26 23	0 29	18 47	13 30
23 Sa	14 4 4	2 49 47	26 18	22 39℞	21 40	19 04	5 57	26 17	23 47	14 05	24 19	28 35	21 11	26 49	0 50	19 11	13 34
24 Su	14 8 1	3 48 16	10♒21	22 39	23 06	20 11	6 42	26 30	23 51	14 09	24 21	28 35	21 34	27 15	1 11	19 35	13 37
25 M	14 11 58	4 46 44	24 10	22 38	24 27	21 19	7 28	26 43	23 55	14 12	24 23	28 36	21 57	27 40	1 32	19 58	13 40
26 T	14 15 54	5 45 11	7♓46	22 36	25 44	22 26	8 13	26 56	23 59	14 16	24 25	28 36	22 20	28 06	1 53	20 22	13 44
27 W	14 19 51	6 43 36	21 08	22 34	26 57	23 34	8 59	27 09	24 02	14 19	24 27	28 36	22 43	28 32	2 14	20 45	13 47
28 Th	14 23 47	7 41 59	4♈16	22 32	28 04	24 42	9 44	27 21	24 06	14 22	24 28	28 36	23 06	28 58	2 34	21 08	13 50
29 F	14 27 44	8 40 20	17 10	22 30	29 06	25 50	10 29	27 34	24 10	14 26	24 30	28 36℞	23 30	29 24	2 55	21 31	13 54
30 Sa	14 31 40	9 38 40	29 50	22 29	0♊04	26 58	11 15	27 47	24 13	14 29	24 32	28 36	23 53	29 50	3 16	21 53	13 57

EPHEMERIS CALCULATED FOR 12 MIDNIGHT GREENWICH MEAN TIME. ALL OTHER DATA AND FACING ASPECTARIAN PAGE IN **EASTERN TIME (BOLD)** AND PACIFIC TIME (REGULAR).

MAY 2022

☽ Last Aspect day	ET / hr:mn / PT	asp	☽ Ingress sign day	ET / hr:mn / PT
2	**6:13 am** 3:13 am	✶♀	♊ 2	**6:47 am** 3:47 am
4	**4:37 pm** 1:37 pm	□♃	♋ 4	**7:05 pm** 4:05 pm
7	**6:26 am** 3:26 am	△♃	♌ 7	**7:50 am** 4:50 am
9	**8:39 am** 5:39 am	☍♄	♍ 9	**6:53 pm** 3:53 pm
11	9:00 pm	△♇	♎ 11	11:34 pm
12	**12:00 am**	△♇	♎ 12	**2:34 am**
14	**4:07 am** 1:07 am	□♇	♏ 14	**6:34 am** 3:34 am
16	**5:28 am** 2:28 am	✶♇	♐ 16	**7:50 am** 4:50 am
17	**11:59 pm** 8:59 pm	✶♄	♑ 18	**8:02 am** 5:02 am
20	**8:00 am** 5:00 am	△☉	♒ 20	**8:53 am** 5:53 am
22	**3:19 am** 12:19 am	☌♄	♓ 22	**11:49 am** 8:49 am
24	**5:33 pm** 2:33 pm	☌♂	♈ 24	**5:39 pm** 2:39 pm
26	**11:20 pm** 8:20 pm	□♇	♉ 26	11:22 pm
26	**11:20 pm** 8:20 pm	□♇	♉ 27	**2:22 am**
29	**10:11 am** 7:11 am	△♇	♊ 29	**1:23 pm** 10:23 am
31	**4:10 pm** 1:10 pm	△♄	♋ 31	10:49 pm
31	**4:10 pm** 1:10 pm	△♄	♋ 6/1	**1:49 am**

☽ Phases & Eclipses phase	day	ET / hr:mn / PT
2nd Quarter	8	**8:21 pm** 5:21 pm
Full Moon	15	9:14 pm
Full Moon	16	**12:14 am**
●	15/16	25° ♏ 18'
4th Quarter	22	**2:43 pm** 11:43 am
New Moon	30	**7:30 am** 4:30 am

Planet Ingress	day	ET / hr:mn / PT
♀ ♈	2	**12:10 pm** 9:10 am
♃ ♈	10	**7:22 pm** 4:22 pm
⚳ ♋	15	**3:11 am** 12:11 am
☉ ♊	20	**9:23 pm** 6:23 pm
☿ ♉	22	**9:15 pm** 6:15 pm
⚶ ♓	24	**5:46 am** 2:46 am
♂ ♈	24	**7:17 pm** 4:17 pm
♀ ♉	28	**10:46 am** 7:46 am

Planetary Motion	day	ET / hr:mn / PT
☿ ℞	10	**7:47 am** 4:47 am

1 SUNDAY
☽ ☌ ♅ **12:24 am**
♀ ✶ ♇ **6:37 am** 3:37 am
☽ □ ♄ **7:33 pm** 4:33 pm
☽ ✶ ♆ **8:04 pm** 5:04 pm

2 MONDAY
☽ ✶ ♃ **3:19 am** 12:19 am
☽ △ ♇ **4:00 am** 1:00 am
☽ ✶ ♀ **6:13 am** 3:13 am
☽ ☌ ☿ **11:05 am** 8:05 am

3 TUESDAY
☽ ⚺ ☉ **8:54 am** 5:54 am
☽ □ ♂ **10:41 am** 7:41 am
☽ ⚺ ♅ **12:10 pm** 9:10 am
♃ ✶ ♇ **6:33 pm** 3:33 pm

4 WEDNESDAY
☽ △ ♄ **7:51 am** 4:51 am
☽ □ ♆ **8:16 am** 5:16 am
♂ ✶ ♅ **11:47 am** 8:47 am
☽ ⚻ ♇ **4:14 pm** 1:14 pm
☽ □ ♃ **4:37 pm** 1:37 pm
☽ □ ♀ 9:57 pm
☽ ⚺ ☿ 11:33 pm

5 THURSDAY
☽ □ ♀ **12:57 am**
☽ ⚺ ☿ **2:33 am**
☉ ☌ ♅ **3:22 am** 12:22 am
☽ ✶ ♅ 10:13 pm
☿ ✶ ♀ 11:01 pm

6 FRIDAY
☽ ✶ ♅ **1:13 am**
☿ ✶ ♀ **2:01 am**
☽ ✶ ☉ **3:03 am** 12:03 am
☽ △ ♂ **3:34 am** 12:34 am
☽ ⚻ ♄ **8:55 pm** 5:55 pm
☽ △ ♆ **9:13 pm** 6:13 pm

7 SATURDAY
☽ ☍ ♇ **4:59 am** 1:59 am
☉ ✶ ♂ **5:48 am** 2:48 am
☽ △ ♃ **6:26 am** 3:26 am
☽ ✶ ☿ **4:59 pm** 1:59 pm
☽ △ ♀ **8:02 pm** 5:02 pm

8 SUNDAY
☽ □ ♅ **1:41 pm** 10:41 am
☽ ⚻ ♂ **7:38 pm** 4:38 pm
☽ □ ☉ **8:21 pm** 5:21 pm

9 MONDAY
☽ ☍ ♄ **8:39 am** 5:39 am
☽ ⚻ ♆ **8:50 am** 5:50 am
☽ ⚻ ♇ **4:09 pm** 1:09 pm
☽ ⚻ ♃ **6:30 pm** 3:30 pm

10 TUESDAY
☽ □ ☿ **4:10 am** 1:10 am
☽ ⚻ ♀ **12:19 pm** 9:19 am
☽ △ ♅ **11:27 pm** 8:27 pm

11 WEDNESDAY
☽ ☍ ♂ **8:17 am** 5:17 am
☽ △ ☉ **10:02 am** 7:02 am
☽ ⚻ ♄ **5:10 pm** 2:10 pm
☽ ☍ ♆ **5:17 pm** 2:17 pm
☽ △ ♇ 9:00 pm

12 THURSDAY
☽ △ ♇ **12:00 am**
☽ ☍ ♃ **3:02 am** 12:02 am
☽ △ ☿ **10:54 am** 7:54 am
☽ ☍ ♀ **11:49 pm** 8:49 pm

13 FRIDAY
☽ ⚻ ♅ **5:27 am** 2:27 am
☽ ⚻ ♂ **4:28 pm** 1:28 pm
☽ ⚻ ☉ **7:00 pm** 4:00 pm
☽ △ ♄ **9:54 pm** 6:54 pm
☽ ⚻ ♆ **9:57 pm** 6:57 pm

14 SATURDAY
☽ □ ♇ **4:07 am** 1:07 am
☽ ⚻ ♃ **7:42 am** 4:42 am
☽ ⚻ ☿ **1:31 pm** 10:31 am

15 SUNDAY
☽ ⚻ ♀ **6:55 am** 3:55 am
☽ ☍ ♅ **8:04 am** 5:04 am
☉ □ ♄ **2:49 pm** 11:49 am
☉ ✶ ♆ **3:15 pm** 12:15 pm
☽ △ ♂ **9:02 pm** 6:02 pm
♀ ⚺ ♅ **10:14 pm** 7:14 pm
☽ □ ♄ **11:38 pm** 8:38 pm
☽ △ ♆ **11:40 pm** 8:40 pm
☽ ☍ ☉ 9:14 pm

16 MONDAY
☽ ☍ ☉ **12:14 am**
☽ ✶ ♇ **5:28 am** 2:28 am
☽ △ ♃ **9:34 am** 6:34 am
☽ ☍ ☿ **1:19 pm** 10:19 am

17 TUESDAY
☽ ⚻ ♅ **8:46 am** 5:46 am
☽ △ ♀ **11:31 am** 8:31 am
♄ ⚺ ♆ **11:39 am** 8:39 am
☽ □ ♂ **11:51 pm** 8:51 pm
☽ □ ♆ **11:59 pm** 8:59 pm
☽ ✶ ♄ **11:59 pm** 8:59 pm
♂ ☌ ♆ 11:33 pm
♂ ⚺ ♄ 11:43 pm

18 WEDNESDAY
♂ ☌ ♆ **2:33 am**
♂ ⚺ ♄ **2:43 am**
☽ ⚻ ☉ **3:48 am** 12:48 am
☽ ⚺ ♇ **5:39 am** 2:39 am
☽ □ ♃ **10:21 am** 7:21 am
☽ ⚻ ☿ **12:00 pm** 9:00 am

19 THURSDAY
☉ △ ♇ **8:11 am** 5:11 am
☽ △ ♅ **9:16 am** 6:16 am
☽ □ ♀ **4:02 pm** 1:02 pm
☿ ✶ ♃ **9:33 pm** 6:33 pm
☽ ✶ ♆ 9:41 pm
☽ ⚺ ♄ 9:43 pm

20 FRIDAY
☽ ✶ ♆ **12:41 am**
☽ ⚺ ♄ **12:43 am**
☽ ✶ ♂ **3:07 am** 12:07 am
☽ ☌ ♇ **6:24 am** 3:24 am
☽ △ ☉ **8:00 am** 5:00 am
☽ △ ☿ **11:11 am** 8:11 am
☽ ✶ ♃ **11:54 am** 8:54 am

21 SATURDAY
☽ □ ♅ **11:16 am** 8:16 am
☉ ☌ ☿ **3:18 pm** 12:18 pm
☽ ✶ ♀ **10:40 pm** 7:40 pm

22 SUNDAY
☽ ⚺ ♆ **3:17 am** 12:17 am
☽ ☌ ♄ **3:19 am** 12:19 am
☽ ⚺ ♂ **8:39 am** 5:39 am
☽ ⚺ ♇ **9:11 am** 6:11 am
☽ □ ☿ **12:12 pm** 9:12 am
☽ □ ☉ **2:43 pm** 11:43 am
☽ ⚺ ♃ **3:40 pm** 12:40 pm
♂ ✶ ♇ **6:15 pm** 3:15 pm

23 MONDAY
☉ ✶ ♃ **7:05 am** 4:05 am
☽ ✶ ♅ **3:54 pm** 12:54 pm
☿ ✶ ♂ **11:27 pm** 8:27 pm

24 TUESDAY
♀ ⚺ ♆ **6:30 am** 3:30 am
♀ ✶ ♄ **7:06 am** 4:06 am
☽ ☌ ♆ **8:41 am** 5:41 am
☽ ⚺ ♄ **8:45 am** 5:45 am
☽ ⚺ ♀ **8:54 am** 5:54 am
☽ ✶ ♇ **2:49 pm** 11:49 am
☽ ✶ ☿ **3:50 pm** 12:50 pm
☽ ☌ ♂ **5:33 pm** 2:33 pm
☽ ☌ ♃ **10:27 pm** 7:27 pm
☽ ✶ ☉ 10:03 pm

25 WEDNESDAY
☽ ✶ ☉ **1:03 am**
☿ △ ♇ **5:49 pm** 2:49 pm
☽ ⚺ ♅ **11:33 pm** 8:33 pm

26 THURSDAY
☽ ⚺ ♆ **5:03 pm** 2:03 pm
☽ ✶ ♄ **5:06 pm** 2:06 pm
☿ ⚺ ♀ **5:07 pm** 2:07 pm
☽ ⚺ ☿ **10:16 pm** 7:16 pm
☽ ☌ ♀ **11:00 pm** 8:00 pm
☽ □ ♇ **11:20 pm** 8:20 pm
♀ □ ♇ 11:29 pm

27 FRIDAY
♀ □ ♇ **2:29 am**
☽ ⚺ ♂ **5:54 am** 2:54 am
☽ ⚺ ♃ **8:12 am** 5:12 am
☽ ⚺ ☉ **2:56 pm** 11:56 am

28 SATURDAY
☽ ☌ ♅ **9:50 am** 6:50 am

29 SUNDAY
☽ ✶ ♆ **3:49 am** 12:49 am
☽ □ ♄ **3:51 am** 12:51 am
♂ ☌ ♃ **6:31 am** 3:31 am
☽ ☌ ☿ **7:15 am** 4:15 am
☽ △ ♇ **10:11 am** 7:11 am
☽ ⚺ ♀ **4:15 pm** 1:15 pm
☽ ✶ ♃ **8:12 pm** 5:12 pm
☽ ✶ ♂ **8:55 pm** 5:55 pm

30 MONDAY
☽ ☌ ☉ **7:30 am** 4:30 am
☽ ⚺ ♅ **10:00 pm** 7:00 pm

31 TUESDAY
♀ ⚺ ♃ **2:34 pm** 11:34 am
☽ □ ♆ **4:10 pm** 1:10 pm
☽ △ ♄ **4:10 pm** 1:10 pm
♄ ⚺ ♆ **6:03 pm** 3:03 pm
☽ ⚺ ☿ **6:19 pm** 3:19 pm
☽ ⚻ ♇ **10:30 pm** 7:30 pm

Eastern time in bold type
Pacific time in medium type

MAY 2022

DATE	SID.TIME	SUN	MOON	NODE	MERCURY	VENUS	MARS	JUPITER	SATURN	URANUS	NEPTUNE	PLUTO	CERES	PALLAS	JUNO	VESTA	CHIRON
1 Su	14 35 37	10♉36 58	12♉18	22♉28D	0♊56	28♓06	12♓00	27♓59	24♒16	14♉33	24♓34	28♑36℞	24♊16	0♉17	3♓36	22♒16	14♈00
2 M	14 39 33	11 35 14	24 33	22 28	1 43	29 14	12 45	28 12	24 20	14 36	24 35	28 36	24 40	0 43	3 57	22 38	14 03
3 T	14 43 30	12 33 29	6♊38	22 28	2 25	0♈22	13 30	28 24	24 23	14 40	24 37	28 36	25 04	1 09	4 17	23 00	14 06
4 W	14 47 27	13 31 42	18 36	22 29	3 02	1 31	14 16	28 36	24 26	14 43	24 39	28 36	25 27	1 35	4 37	23 22	14 10
5 Th	14 51 23	14 29 52	0♋27	22 30	3 33	2 39	15 01	28 49	24 29	14 47	24 40	28 36	25 51	2 01	4 57	23 43	14 13
6 F	14 55 20	15 28 01	12 16	22 30	3 59	3 48	15 46	29 01	24 32	14 50	24 42	28 35	26 15	2 28	5 17	24 05	14 16
7 Sa	14 59 16	16 26 09	24 08	22 31	4 20	4 57	16 31	29 13	24 35	14 54	24 43	28 35	26 39	2 54	5 37	24 26	14 19
8 Su	15 3 13	17 24 14	6♌05	22 31	4 36	6 05	17 17	29 25	24 37	14 57	24 45	28 35	27 03	3 21	5 57	24 47	14 22
9 M	15 7 9	18 22 17	18 12	22 32℞	4 46	7 14	18 02	29 37	24 40	15 01	24 47	28 35	27 27	3 47	6 16	25 08	14 25
10 T	15 11 6	19 20 18	0♍35	22 32	4 51℞	8 23	18 47	29 49	24 42	15 04	24 48	28 34	27 51	4 14	6 36	25 29	14 28
11 W	15 15 2	20 18 17	13 17	22 31	4 51	9 32	19 32	0♈00	24 45	15 07	24 50	28 34	28 15	4 40	6 55	25 49	14 31
12 Th	15 18 59	21 16 15	26 21	22 31	4 46	10 41	20 17	0 12	24 47	15 11	24 51	28 34	28 40	5 07	7 14	26 09	14 34
13 F	15 22 56	22 14 11	9♎50	22 31D	4 36	11 51	21 02	0 24	24 49	15 14	24 52	28 33	29 04	5 33	7 33	26 29	14 37
14 Sa	15 26 52	23 12 04	23 45	22 31	4 22	13 00	21 47	0 35	24 52	15 18	24 54	28 33	29 28	6 00	7 52	26 49	14 40
15 Su	15 30 49	24 09 57	8♏03	22 31℞	4 04	14 09	22 32	0 46	24 54	15 21	24 55	28 33	29 53	6 27	8 11	27 08	14 43
16 M	15 34 45	25 07 47	22 41	22 31	3 42	15 19	23 17	0 58	24 56	15 25	24 57	28 32	0♋17	6 53	8 30	27 28	14 46
17 T	15 38 42	26 05 37	7♐33	22 31	3 16	16 28	24 02	1 09	24 58	15 28	24 58	28 32	0 42	7 20	8 49	27 47	14 49
18 W	15 42 38	27 03 25	22 30	22 31	2 48	17 38	24 47	1 20	24 59	15 31	24 59	28 31	1 06	7 47	9 07	28 06	14 51
19 Th	15 46 35	28 01 12	7♑26	22 30	2 17	18 47	25 32	1 31	25 01	15 35	25 01	28 31	1 31	8 14	9 25	28 24	14 54
20 F	15 50 31	28 58 57	22 11	22 30	1 45	19 57	26 17	1 42	25 03	15 38	25 02	28 30	1 56	8 41	9 44	28 42	14 57
21 Sa	15 54 28	29 56 41	6♒41	22 29	1 11	21 07	27 02	1 53	25 04	15 42	25 03	28 30	2 21	9 08	10 02	29 00	15 00
22 Su	15 58 25	0♊54 25	20 51	22 29D	0 36	22 16	27 47	2 03	25 06	15 45	25 04	28 29	2 45	9 35	10 20	29 18	15 02
23 M	16 2 21	1 52 07	4♓40	22 29	0 02	23 26	28 32	2 14	25 07	15 48	25 05	28 28	3 10	10 02	10 37	29 36	15 05
24 T	16 6 18	2 49 48	18 08	22 29	29♉28	24 36	29 17	2 24	25 08	15 52	25 06	28 28	3 35	10 29	10 55	29 53	15 08
25 W	16 10 14	3 47 28	1♈16	22 30	28 55	25 46	0♈01	2 35	25 09	15 55	25 08	28 27	4 00	10 56	11 13	0♓10	15 10
26 Th	16 14 11	4 45 07	14 07	22 31	28 24	26 56	0 46	2 45	25 10	15 58	25 09	28 26	4 25	11 23	11 30	0 27	15 13
27 F	16 18 7	5 42 45	26 42	22 32	27 55	28 07	1 31	2 55	25 11	16 02	25 10	28 26	4 51	11 50	11 47	0 43	15 15
28 Sa	16 22 4	6 40 22	9♉04	22 33	27 28	29 17	2 15	3 05	25 12	16 05	25 11	28 25	5 16	12 18	12 04	0 59	15 18
29 Su	16 26 0	7 37 58	21 16	22 33℞	27 05	0♉27	3 00	3 15	25 13	16 08	25 12	28 24	5 41	12 45	12 21	1 15	15 20
30 M	16 29 57	8 35 33	3♊19	22 33	26 45	1 37	3 45	3 25	25 13	16 12	25 13	28 23	6 06	13 12	12 37	1 31	15 23
31 T	16 33 54	9 33 07	15 16	22 32	26 29	2 48	4 29	3 35	25 14	16 15	25 14	28 23	6 32	13 39	12 54	1 46	15 25

EPHEMERIS CALCULATED FOR 12 MIDNIGHT GREENWICH MEAN TIME. ALL OTHER DATA AND FACING ASPECTARIAN PAGE IN **EASTERN TIME (BOLD)** AND PACIFIC TIME (REGULAR).

JUNE 2022

☽ Last Aspect day	ET / hr:mn / PT	asp	☽ Ingress sign	day	ET / hr:mn / PT
3	**11:15 am** 8:15 am	☍♇	♌	3	**2:38 pm** 11:38 am
5	**7:12 pm** 4:12 pm	□☿	♍	5	11:22 pm
5	**7:12 pm** 4:12 pm	□☿	♍	6	**2:22 am**
8	**8:09 am** 5:09 am	△♇	♎	8	**11:23 am** 8:23 am
10	**1:36 pm** 10:36 am	□♇	♏	10	**4:41 pm** 1:41 pm
12	**5:40 pm** 2:40 pm	☍☿	♐	12	**6:31 pm** 3:31 pm
14	**10:58 am** 7:58 am	□♆	♑	14	**6:14 pm** 3:14 pm
16	**2:41 pm** 11:41 am	☌♇	♒	16	**5:44 pm** 2:44 pm
18	**2:50 pm** 11:50 am	△☉	♓	18	**7:01 pm** 4:01 pm
20	**11:11 pm** 8:11 pm	□☉	♈	20	**11:37 pm** 8:37 pm
23	**4:02 am** 1:02 am	□♇	♉	23	**7:58 am** 4:58 am
25	**3:02 pm** 12:02 pm	△♇	♊	25	**7:13 pm** 4:13 pm
27	**10:38 pm** 7:38 pm	□♆	♋	28	**7:53 am** 4:53 am
30	**4:14 pm** 1:14 pm	☍♇	♌	30	**8:40 pm** 5:40 pm

☽ Phases & Eclipses phase	day	ET / hr:mn / PT
2nd Quarter	7	**10:48 am** 7:48 am
Full Moon	14	**7:52 am** 4:52 am
4th Quarter	20	**11:11 pm** 8:11 pm
New Moon	28	**10:52 pm** 7:52 pm

Planet Ingress		day	ET / hr:mn / PT
☿	♊	13	**11:27 am** 8:27 am
☉	♋	21	**5:14 am** 2:14 am
♀	♊	22	**8:34 pm** 5:34 pm

Planetary Motion		day	ET / hr:mn / PT
☿	D	3	**4:00 am** 1:00 am
♄	℞	4	**5:47 pm** 2:47 pm
♆	℞	28	**3:55 am** 12:55 am

1 WEDNESDAY
☽□♃ **9:35 am** 6:35 am
☽⚹♀ **11:24 am** 8:24 am
☽□♂ **1:31 pm** 10:31 am
☽⚺☉ 10:33 pm

2 THURSDAY
☽⚺☉ **1:33 am**
☽⚹♅ **11:05 am** 8:05 am

3 FRIDAY
☽⚻♄ **5:02 am** 2:02 am
☽△♆ **5:05 am** 2:05 am
☽⚹☿ **6:44 am** 3:44 am
☽☍♇ **11:15 am** 8:15 am
♀⚺♂ **5:18 pm** 2:18 pm
☽△♃ **11:09 pm** 8:09 pm

4 SATURDAY
☽△♂ **6:15 am** 3:15 am
☽□♀ **6:47 am** 3:47 am
☽⚹☉ **7:23 pm** 4:23 pm
☽□♅ **11:47 pm** 8:47 pm

5 SUNDAY
☽☍♄ **5:03 pm** 2:03 pm
☽⚻♆ **5:10 pm** 2:10 pm
☽□☿ **7:12 pm** 4:12 pm
☽⚻♇ **11:01 pm** 8:01 pm

6 MONDAY
☽⚻♃ **11:19 am** 8:19 am
☽⚻♂ **9:09 pm** 6:09 pm
☽△♀ 9:05 pm

7 TUESDAY
☽△♀ **12:05 am**
☉⚺♅ **5:36 am** 2:36 am
☽△♅ **10:26 am** 7:26 am
☽□☉ **10:48 am** 7:48 am
☽⚻♄ 11:34 pm
☽☍♆ 11:44 pm

8 WEDNESDAY
☽⚻♄ **2:34 am**
☽☍♆ **2:44 am**
☽△☿ **5:56 am** 2:56 am
☽△♇ **8:09 am** 5:09 am
☽☍♃ **8:26 pm** 5:26 pm

9 THURSDAY
☽☍♂ **8:16 am** 5:16 am
☽⚻♀ **1:08 pm** 10:08 am
☽⚻♅ **5:39 pm** 2:39 pm
☽△☉ **9:57 pm** 6:57 pm

10 FRIDAY
☽△♄ **8:27 am** 5:27 am
☽⚻♆ **8:41 am** 5:41 am
☽⚻☿ **1:27 pm** 10:27 am
☽□♇ **1:36 pm** 10:36 am
☿△♇ **5:21 pm** 2:21 pm
☽⚻♃ 10:38 pm

11 SATURDAY
☽⚻♃ **1:38 am**
☽⚻♂ **2:55 pm** 11:55 am
♀☌♅ **6:58 pm** 3:58 pm
☽☍♅ **9:05 pm** 6:05 pm
☽☍♀ **9:16 pm** 6:16 pm

12 SUNDAY
☽⚻☉ **4:29 am** 1:29 am
☽□♄ **10:45 am** 7:45 am
☽△♆ **11:01 am** 8:01 am
☽⚹♇ **3:34 pm** 12:34 pm
☽☍☿ **5:40 pm** 2:40 pm

13 MONDAY
☽△♃ **3:26 am** 12:26 am
☽△♂ **6:05 pm** 3:05 pm
☽⚻♅ **9:40 pm** 6:40 pm
☽⚻♀ 10:47 pm

14 TUESDAY
☽⚻♀ **1:47 am**
☽☍☉ **7:52 am** 4:52 am
☽⚹♄ **10:38 am** 7:38 am
☽□♆ **10:58 am** 7:58 am
☽⚺♇ **3:18 pm** 12:18 pm
☽⚻☿ **7:55 pm** 4:55 pm

15 WEDNESDAY
☽□♃ **3:21 am** 12:21 am
☽□♂ **7:50 pm** 4:50 pm
☽△♅ **9:10 pm** 6:10 pm

16 THURSDAY
☉△♄ **3:13 am** 12:13 am
☽△♀ **5:09 am** 2:09 am
☉□♆ **9:41 am** 6:41 am
☽⚺♄ **9:58 am** 6:58 am
☽⚹♆ **10:23 am** 7:23 am
☽⚻☉ **10:26 am** 7:26 am
☽☌♇ **2:41 pm** 11:41 am
☽△☿ **10:30 pm** 7:30 pm
♂⚺♅ 10:37 pm

17 FRIDAY
♂⚺♅ **1:37 am**
☽⚹♃ **3:28 am** 12:28 am
☽□♅ **9:37 pm** 6:37 pm
☽⚹♂ **10:35 pm** 7:35 pm

18 SATURDAY
☽□♀ **10:10 am** 7:10 am
☽☌♄ **10:47 am** 7:47 am
☽⚺♆ **11:19 am** 8:19 am
☽△☉ **2:50 pm** 11:50 am
☽⚺♇ **3:45 pm** 12:45 pm
♀□♄ **5:32 pm** 2:32 pm
♀⚹♆ 9:06 pm

19 SUNDAY
♀⚹♆ **12:06 am**
☽□☿ **4:01 am** 1:01 am
☉⚻♇ **4:10 am** 1:10 am
☽⚺♃ **5:45 am** 2:45 am
☽⚹♅ 9:50 pm

20 MONDAY
☽⚹♅ **12:50 am**
☿⚹♃ **3:44 am** 12:44 am
☽⚺♂ **4:35 am** 1:35 am
☽⚺♄ **2:41 pm** 11:41 am
☽☌♆ **3:21 pm** 12:21 pm
☽⚹♀ **7:11 pm** 4:11 pm
☽⚹♇ **8:01 pm** 5:01 pm
☽□☉ **11:11 pm** 8:11 pm

21 TUESDAY
♀△♇ **4:23 am** 1:23 am
☽☌♃ **11:37 am** 8:37 am
☽⚹☿ **2:34 pm** 11:34 am

22 WEDNESDAY
☽⚺♅ **7:50 am** 4:50 am
☽☌♂ **2:58 pm** 11:58 am
☽⚹♄ **10:19 pm** 7:19 pm
☽⚺♆ **11:10 pm** 8:10 pm

23 THURSDAY
☽□♇ **4:02 am** 1:02 am
☽⚺♀ **9:10 am** 6:10 am
☽⚹☉ **12:12 pm** 9:12 am
☽⚺♃ **9:13 pm** 6:13 pm

24 FRIDAY
☽⚺☿ **6:48 am** 3:48 am
☽☌♅ **6:15 pm** 3:15 pm

25 SATURDAY
☽⚺♂ **5:14 am** 2:14 am
☽□♄ **9:02 am** 6:02 am
☽⚹♆ **10:05 am** 7:05 am
☽△♇ **3:02 pm** 12:02 pm

26 SUNDAY
☽☌♀ **3:03 am** 12:03 am
☽⚺☉ **4:47 am** 1:47 am
☽⚹♃ **9:27 am** 6:27 am

27 MONDAY
☽☌☿ **3:22 am** 12:22 am
☽⚺♅ **6:44 am** 3:44 am
♂⚹♄ **6:29 pm** 3:29 pm
☽△♄ **9:23 pm** 6:23 pm
☽⚹♂ **9:35 pm** 6:35 pm
☽□♆ **10:38 pm** 7:38 pm

28 TUESDAY
☽⚻♇ **3:33 am** 12:33 am
☿⚺♅ **5:02 am** 2:02 am
♂⚺♆ **3:08 pm** 12:08 pm
☉□♃ **8:59 pm** 5:59 pm
☽⚺♀ **10:37 pm** 7:37 pm
☽□♃ **10:44 pm** 7:44 pm
☽☌☉ **10:52 pm** 7:52 pm
♀⚹♃ **11:52 pm** 8:52 pm

29 WEDNESDAY
☉⚺♀ **10:09 am** 7:09 am
☽⚹♅ **7:48 pm** 4:48 pm
☽⚺☿ 11:00 pm

30 THURSDAY
☽⚺☿ **2:00 am**
☽⚻♄ **10:01 am** 7:01 am
☽△♆ **11:28 am** 8:28 am
☽□♂ **2:17 pm** 11:17 am
☽☍♇ **4:14 pm** 1:14 pm

Eastern time in bold type
Pacific time in medium type

JUNE 2022

DATE	SID.TIME	SUN	MOON	NODE	MERCURY	VENUS	MARS	JUPITER	SATURN	URANUS	NEPTUNE	PLUTO	CERES	PALLAS	JUNO	VESTA	CHIRON
1 W	16 37 50	10♊30 40	27♊08	22♉30℞	26♉17℞	3♉58	5♈14	3♈44	25♒14	16♉18	25♓14	28♑22℞	6♋57	14♉07	13♓10	2♓01	15♈27
2 Th	16 41 47	11 28 12	8♋58	22 27	26 09	5 09	5 58	3 54	25 15	16 21	25 15	28 21	7 22	14 34	13 26	2 16	15 30
3 F	16 45 43	12 25 43	20 47	22 24	26 05D	6 19	6 42	4 03	25 15	16 25	25 16	28 20	7 48	15 02	13 42	2 30	15 32
4 Sa	16 49 40	13 23 12	2♌40	22 20	26 06	7 30	7 27	4 12	25 15℞	16 28	25 17	28 19	8 13	15 29	13 58	2 44	15 34
5 Su	16 53 36	14 20 40	14 38	22 18	26 11	8 40	8 11	4 21	25 15	16 31	25 18	28 18	8 39	15 57	14 13	2 58	15 36
6 M	16 57 33	15 18 07	26 45	22 15	26 21	9 51	8 55	4 30	25 15	16 34	25 18	28 17	9 04	16 24	14 29	3 11	15 38
7 T	17 1 29	16 15 33	9♍06	22 14D	26 35	11 01	9 39	4 39	25 15	16 37	25 19	28 16	9 30	16 52	14 44	3 24	15 40
8 W	17 5 26	17 12 58	21 44	22 14	26 54	12 12	10 23	4 48	25 15	16 40	25 20	28 15	9 56	17 19	14 59	3 37	15 42
9 Th	17 9 23	18 10 21	4♎43	22 15	27 17	13 23	11 07	4 57	25 14	16 43	25 20	28 14	10 21	17 47	15 14	3 49	15 44
10 F	17 13 19	19 07 43	18 06	22 16	27 44	14 34	11 51	5 05	25 14	16 47	25 21	28 13	10 47	18 15	15 28	4 01	15 46
11 Sa	17 17 16	20 05 04	1♏56	22 18	28 16	15 45	12 35	5 13	25 13	16 50	25 22	28 12	11 13	18 42	15 42	4 12	15 48
12 Su	17 21 12	21 02 25	16 13	22 19℞	28 52	16 56	13 19	5 21	25 13	16 53	25 22	28 11	11 39	19 10	15 56	4 24	15 50
13 M	17 25 9	21 59 44	0♐55	22 19	29 32	18 06	14 03	5 29	25 12	16 56	25 23	28 10	12 05	19 38	16 10	4 35	15 52
14 T	17 29 5	22 57 03	15 55	22 17	0♊16	19 17	14 47	5 37	25 11	16 59	25 23	28 09	12 30	20 06	16 24	4 45	15 54
15 W	17 33 2	23 54 21	1♑07	22 14	1 04	20 28	15 31	5 45	25 10	17 01	25 24	28 08	12 56	20 33	16 37	4 55	15 55
16 Th	17 36 59	24 51 38	16 20	22 10	1 56	21 40	16 14	5 53	25 09	17 04	25 24	28 07	13 22	21 01	16 51	5 05	15 57
17 F	17 40 55	25 48 55	1♒25	22 05	2 52	22 51	16 58	6 00	25 08	17 07	25 24	28 06	13 48	21 29	17 04	5 14	15 59
18 Sa	17 44 52	26 46 12	16 12	22 01	3 52	24 02	17 41	6 08	25 07	17 10	25 25	28 05	14 14	21 57	17 16	5 24	16 00
19 Su	17 48 48	27 43 28	0♓35	21 57	4 55	25 13	18 25	6 15	25 06	17 13	25 25	28 03	14 40	22 25	17 29	5 32	16 02
20 M	17 52 45	28 40 43	14 31	21 55	6 02	26 24	19 08	6 22	25 04	17 16	25 25	28 02	15 06	22 53	17 41	5 40	16 04
21 T	17 56 41	29 37 59	28 00	21 54D	7 12	27 36	19 51	6 29	25 03	17 19	25 26	28 01	15 33	23 21	17 53	5 48	16 05
22 W	18 0 38	0♋35 14	11♈04	21 54	8 26	28 47	20 35	6 35	25 01	17 21	25 26	28 00	15 59	23 49	18 05	5 56	16 06
23 Th	18 4 34	1 32 29	23 47	21 56	9 44	29 58	21 18	6 42	24 59	17 24	25 26	27 58	16 25	24 17	18 16	6 03	16 08
24 F	18 8 31	2 29 44	6♉11	21 57	11 05	1♊10	22 01	6 48	24 58	17 27	25 26	27 57	16 51	24 45	18 27	6 09	16 09
25 Sa	18 12 28	3 26 59	18 22	21 58℞	12 29	2 21	22 44	6 55	24 56	17 29	25 26	27 56	17 17	25 13	18 38	6 15	16 10
26 Su	18 16 24	4 24 14	0♊23	21 58	13 56	3 33	23 27	7 01	24 54	17 32	25 26	27 55	17 44	25 42	18 49	6 21	16 12
27 M	18 20 21	5 21 29	12 18	21 56	15 27	4 44	24 10	7 07	24 52	17 35	25 27	27 53	18 10	26 10	18 59	6 26	16 13
28 T	18 24 17	6 18 43	24 09	21 52	17 02	5 56	24 53	7 12	24 50	17 37	25 27℞	27 52	18 36	26 38	19 09	6 31	16 14
29 W	18 28 14	7 15 58	5♋58	21 45	18 39	7 07	25 35	7 18	24 47	17 40	25 27	27 51	19 03	27 06	19 19	6 35	16 15
30 Th	18 32 10	8 13 12	17 48	21 38	20 20	8 19	26 18	7 24	24 45	17 42	25 27	27 49	19 29	27 34	19 28	6 39	16 16

EPHEMERIS CALCULATED FOR 12 MIDNIGHT GREENWICH MEAN TIME. ALL OTHER DATA AND FACING ASPECTARIAN PAGE IN **EASTERN TIME (BOLD)** AND PACIFIC TIME (REGULAR).

JULY 2022

☽ Last Aspect day	ET / hr:mn / PT		asp	☽ Ingress sign	day	ET / hr:mn / PT	
3	**5:59 am**	2:59 am	△♂	♍	3	**8:31 am**	5:31 am
5	**2:04 pm**	11:04 am	△♇	♎	5	**6:25 pm**	3:25 pm
7	**9:04 pm**	6:04 pm	□♇	♏	7		10:15 pm
7	**9:04 pm**	6:04 pm	□♇	♏	8	**1:15 am**	
9		9:34 pm	⚹♇	♐	10	**4:34 am**	1:34 am
10	**12:34 am**		⚹♇	♐	10	**4:34 am**	1:34 am
11	**9:42 pm**	6:42 pm	□♆	♑	12	**5:01 am**	2:01 am
13		9:17 pm	☌♇	♒	14	**4:13 am**	1:13 am
14	**12:17 am**		☌♇	♒	14	**4:13 am**	1:13 am
15		9:36 pm	△♀	♓	16	**4:18 am**	1:18 am
16	**12:36 am**		△♀	♓	16	**4:18 am**	1:18 am

☽ Last Aspect day	ET / hr:mn / PT		asp	☽ Ingress sign	day	ET / hr:mn / PT	
17		11:43 pm	⚹♇	♈	18	**7:17 am**	4:17 am
18	**2:43 am**		⚹♇	♈	18	**7:17 am**	4:17 am
20	**10:19 am**	7:19 am	□☉	♉	20	**2:23 pm**	11:23 am
22	**7:45 pm**	4:45 pm	△♇	♊	22		10:11 pm
22	**7:45 pm**	4:45 pm	△♇	♊	23	**1:11 am**	
25	**4:14 am**	1:14 am	□♆	♋	25	**1:54 pm**	10:54 am
27	**8:54 pm**	5:54 pm	☍♇	♌	27		11:36 pm
27	**8:54 pm**	5:54 pm	☍♇	♌	28	**2:36 am**	
29		9:29 pm	☍♄	♍	30	**2:11 pm**	11:11 am
30	**12:29 am**		☍♄	♍	30	**2:11 pm**	11:11 am

☽ Phases & Eclipses phase	day	ET / hr:mn / PT	
2nd Quarter	6	**10:14 pm**	7:14 pm
Full Moon	13	**2:38 pm**	11:38 am
4th Quarter	20	**10:19 am**	7:19 am
New Moon	28	**1:55 pm**	10:55 am

Planet Ingress		day	ET / hr:mn / PT	
♀	♊	4	**11:16 pm**	8:16 pm
♂	♉	4		11:04 pm
♂	♉	5	**2:04 am**	
☿	♋	4		11:25 pm
☿	♋	5	**2:25 am**	
♀	♋	17	**9:32 pm**	6:32 pm
☿	♌	19	**8:35 am**	5:35 am
☉	♌	22	**4:07 pm**	1:07 pm
⚳	♌	23	**1:29 pm**	10:29 am

Planetary Motion		day	ET / hr:mn / PT	
⚶	℞	7	**5:30 pm**	2:30 pm
⚷	℞	19	**11:21 am**	8:21 am
⚵	℞	24		11:48 pm
⚵	℞	25	**2:48 am**	
♃	℞	28	**4:37 pm**	1:37 pm

1 FRIDAY
☽△♃ **11:49 am** 8:49 am
☽⊻☉ **4:46 pm** 1:46 pm
☽⚹♀ **5:59 pm** 2:59 pm
♂□♇ **10:14 pm** 7:14 pm

2 SATURDAY
☿△♄ **6:39 am** 3:39 am
☽□♅ **8:22 am** 5:22 am
☿□♆ **4:53 pm** 1:53 pm
☽☍♄ **9:55 pm** 6:55 pm
☽⊼♆ **11:31 pm** 8:31 pm
☽⚹☿ 9:43 pm

3 SUNDAY
☽⚹☿ **12:43 am**
☽⊼♇ **4:05 am** 1:05 am
☽△♂ **5:59 am** 2:59 am
☿⊼♇ **10:13 pm** 7:13 pm
☽⊼♃ **11:41 pm** 8:41 pm

4 MONDAY
☽⚹☉ **9:03 am** 6:03 am
☽□♀ **11:38 am** 8:38 am
☽△♅ **7:23 pm** 4:23 pm
☿⚹♂ 11:37 pm

5 TUESDAY
☿⚹♂ **2:37 am**
☽⊼♄ **8:02 am** 5:02 am
☽☍♆ **9:46 am** 6:46 am
☽△♇ **2:04 pm** 11:04 am

☽⊼♂ **7:22 pm** 4:22 pm
☽□☿ **9:20 pm** 6:20 pm

6 WEDNESDAY
☽☍♃ **9:13 am** 6:13 am
☽□☉ **10:14 pm** 7:14 pm
☽△♀ 10:54 pm

7 THURSDAY
☽△♀ **1:54 am**
☽⊼♅ **3:43 am** 12:43 am
☽△♄ **3:18 pm** 12:18 pm
☽⊼♆ **5:06 pm** 2:06 pm
☽□♇ **9:04 pm** 6:04 pm
♀⊻♅ **10:27 pm** 7:27 pm

8 FRIDAY
☽☍♂ **5:06 am** 2:06 am
☽△☿ **1:31 pm** 10:31 am
☽⊼♃ **3:23 pm** 12:23 pm
☿□♃ 11:14 pm

9 SATURDAY
☿□♃ **2:14 am**
☽△☉ **7:10 am** 4:10 am
☽☍♅ **8:34 am** 5:34 am
☽⊼♀ **11:38 am** 8:38 am
☽□♄ **7:04 pm** 4:04 pm
☽△♆ **8:56 pm** 5:56 pm
☽⚹♇ 9:34 pm

10 SUNDAY
☽⚹♇ **12:34 am**
☉⚹♅ **4:39 am** 1:39 am
☽⊼♂ **10:44 am** 7:44 am
☽△♃ **6:02 pm** 3:02 pm
☽⊼☿ 9:29 pm

11 MONDAY
☽⊼☿ **12:29 am**
☽⊼♅ **10:07 am** 7:07 am
☽⊼☉ **12:03 pm** 9:03 am
☽☍♀ **5:12 pm** 2:12 pm
☽⚹♄ **7:48 pm** 4:48 pm
☽□♆ **9:42 pm** 6:42 pm
☽⊻♇ 10:07 pm

12 TUESDAY
☽⊻♇ **1:07 am**
☽△♂ **1:12 pm** 10:12 am
☽□♃ **6:07 pm** 3:07 pm
♀△♄ 9:28 pm

13 WEDNESDAY
♀△♄ **12:28 am**
☽☍☿ **7:59 am** 4:59 am
☽△♅ **9:41 am** 6:41 am
☽☍☉ **2:38 pm** 11:38 am
☽⊻♄ **6:55 pm** 3:55 pm
☿⚹♅ **8:17 pm** 5:17 pm
☽⊼♀ **8:34 pm** 5:34 pm
☽⚹♆ **8:57 pm** 5:57 pm
☽☌♇ 9:17 pm
♀□♆ 10:24 pm

14 THURSDAY
☽☌♇ **12:17 am**
♀□♆ **1:24 am**
☽□♂ **2:39 pm** 11:39 am
☽⚹♃ **5:30 pm** 2:30 pm

15 FRIDAY
☽□♅ **9:16 am** 6:16 am
☽⊼☿ **3:25 pm** 12:25 pm
☽⊼☉ **5:30 pm** 2:30 pm
☽☌♄ **6:27 pm** 3:27 pm
♀⊼♇ **6:51 pm** 3:51 pm
☽⊻♆ **8:43 pm** 5:43 pm
☽⊻♇ 9:08 pm
☽△♀ 9:36 pm

16 SATURDAY
☽⊻♇ **12:08 am**
☽△♀ **12:36 am**
☉⊼♄ **7:34 am** 4:34 am
☿⊼♄ **11:55 am** 8:55 am
☉☌☿ **3:38 pm** 12:38 pm
☽⚹♂ **5:37 pm** 2:37 pm
☽⊻♃ **6:21 pm** 3:21 pm

17 SUNDAY
☿△♆ **3:52 am** 12:52 am
♂⊻♃ **9:58 am** 6:58 am
☽⚹♅ **11:01 am** 8:01 am
☉△♆ **6:55 pm** 3:55 pm
☽⊻♄ **8:31 pm** 5:31 pm
☽☌♆ **11:07 pm** 8:07 pm

☽△☉ **11:26 pm** 8:26 pm
☽△☿ 11:40 pm
☽⚹♇ 11:43 pm

18 MONDAY
☽△☿ **2:40 am**
☽⚹♇ **2:43 am**
☿☍♇ **3:01 am** 12:01 am
☽□♀ **8:15 am** 5:15 am
☽☌♃ **10:35 pm** 7:35 pm
☽⊻♂ 9:27 pm

19 TUESDAY
☽⊻♂ **12:27 am**
☽⊻♅ **4:35 pm** 1:35 pm
☉☍♇ **9:39 pm** 6:39 pm
☽⚹♄ 11:28 pm

20 WEDNESDAY
☽⚹♄ **2:28 am**
☽⊻♆ **5:30 am** 2:30 am
☽□♇ **9:20 am** 6:20 am
☽□☉ **10:19 am** 7:19 am
☽□☿ **8:19 pm** 5:19 pm
☽⚹♀ **9:17 pm** 6:17 pm

21 THURSDAY
☽⊻♃ **6:58 am** 3:58 am
☿⊻♀ **9:02 am** 6:02 am
☽☌♂ **12:06 pm** 9:06 am
☽☌♅ 11:14 pm

22 FRIDAY
☽☌♅ **2:14 am**
☽□♄ **12:18 pm** 9:18 am

☽⚹♆ **3:45 pm** 12:45 pm
☽△♇ **7:45 pm** 4:45 pm
☽⚹☉ 10:58 pm

23 SATURDAY
☽⚹☉ **1:58 am**
☿△♃ **1:52 pm** 10:52 am
☽⊻♀ **3:06 pm** 12:06 pm
☽⚹♃ **6:38 pm** 3:38 pm
☽⚹☿ **7:36 pm** 4:36 pm

24 SUNDAY
☽⊻♂ **3:26 am** 12:26 am
☽⊻♅ **2:36 pm** 11:36 am
☽△♄ 9:27 pm
♀□♃ 11:13 pm

25 MONDAY
☽△♄ **12:27 am**
♀□♃ **2:13 am**
☽□♆ **4:14 am** 1:14 am
☽⊼♇ **8:15 am** 5:15 am
☽⊻☉ **8:02 pm** 5:02 pm

26 TUESDAY
☽□♃ **7:35 am** 4:35 am
☽☌♀ **10:54 am** 7:54 am
☿□♂ **3:13 pm** 12:13 pm
☽⚹♂ **7:57 pm** 4:57 pm
☽⊻☿ **8:33 pm** 5:33 pm

27 WEDNESDAY
☽⚹♅ **3:36 am** 12:36 am
☽⊼♄ **12:56 pm** 9:56 am

☽△♆ **4:58 pm** 1:58 pm
☽☍♇ **8:54 pm** 5:54 pm

28 THURSDAY
☽☌☉ **1:55 pm** 10:55 am
☿□♅ **5:16 pm** 2:16 pm
☽△♃ **8:03 pm** 5:03 pm

29 FRIDAY
☽⊻♀ **6:04 am** 3:04 am
☽□♂ **11:38 am** 8:38 am
☽□♅ **3:48 pm** 12:48 pm
☽☌☿ **7:49 pm** 4:49 pm
☽☍♄ 9:29 pm

30 SATURDAY
☽☍♄ **12:29 am**
☽⊼♆ **4:42 am** 1:42 am
☽⊼♇ **8:30 am** 5:30 am
☿☍♄ 11:05 pm

31 SUNDAY
☿☍♄ **2:05 am**
☽⊻☉ **6:12 am** 3:12 am
☽⊼♃ **7:11 am** 4:11 am
☉△♃ **6:36 pm** 3:36 pm
☽⚹♀ **11:19 pm** 8:19 pm
☽△♂ 10:35 pm
☽△♅ 11:30 pm

Eastern time in bold type
Pacific time in medium type

JULY 2022

DATE	SID.TIME	SUN	MOON	NODE	MERCURY	VENUS	MARS	JUPITER	SATURN	URANUS	NEPTUNE	PLUTO	CERES	PALLAS	JUNO	VESTA	CHIRON
1 F	18 36 7	9♋10 26	29♋40	21♉29R	22♊04	9♊31	27♈00	7♈29	24♒43R	17♉45	25♓26R	27♑48R	19♋55	28♉03	19♓37	6♓43	16♈17
2 Sa	18 40 3	10 07 39	11♌37	21 20	23 51	10 43	27 43	7 34	24 40	17 47	25 26	27 47	20 22	28 31	19 46	6 46	16 18
3 Su	18 44 0	11 04 53	23 40	21 12	25 41	11 54	28 25	7 39	24 38	17 49	25 26	27 45	20 48	28 59	19 54	6 48	16 19
4 M	18 47 57	12 02 06	5♍51	21 05	27 33	13 06	29 07	7 44	24 35	17 52	25 26	27 44	21 15	29 28	20 03	6 50	16 20
5 T	18 51 53	12 59 19	18 14	21 00	29 29	14 18	29 49	7 48	24 32	17 54	25 26	27 43	21 41	29 56	20 10	6 52	16 20
6 W	18 55 50	13 56 31	0♎51	20 57	1♋27	15 30	0♉31	7 53	24 30	17 56	25 26	27 41	22 08	0♊25	20 18	6 53	16 21
7 Th	18 59 46	14 53 44	13 46	20 56D	3 27	16 42	1 13	7 57	24 27	17 59	25 25	27 40	22 34	0 53	20 25	6 54R	16 22
8 F	19 3 43	15 50 56	27 03	20 56	5 29	17 54	1 55	8 01	24 24	18 01	25 25	27 39	23 01	1 21	20 32	6 54	16 22
9 Sa	19 7 39	16 48 07	10♏44	20 57R	7 33	19 06	2 37	8 05	24 21	18 03	25 25	27 37	23 27	1 50	20 38	6 54	16 23
10 Su	19 11 36	17 45 19	24 51	20 57	9 39	20 18	3 18	8 08	24 18	18 05	25 24	27 36	23 54	2 18	20 44	6 53	16 24
11 M	19 15 32	18 42 31	9♐24	20 56	11 46	21 30	4 00	8 12	24 15	18 07	25 24	27 34	24 20	2 47	20 50	6 52	16 24
12 T	19 19 29	19 39 43	24 19	20 53	13 54	22 42	4 41	8 15	24 11	18 09	25 24	27 33	24 47	3 15	20 56	6 50	16 24
13 W	19 23 26	20 36 54	9♑30	20 47	16 03	23 54	5 23	8 18	24 08	18 11	25 23	27 31	25 14	3 44	21 01	6 48	16 25
14 Th	19 27 22	21 34 06	24 47	20 39	18 12	25 06	6 04	8 21	24 05	18 13	25 23	27 30	25 40	4 12	21 05	6 45	16 25
15 F	19 31 19	22 31 19	9♒58	20 30	20 21	26 18	6 45	8 24	24 01	18 15	25 22	27 29	26 07	4 41	21 10	6 42	16 25
16 Sa	19 35 15	23 28 31	24 55	20 21	22 30	27 31	7 26	8 27	23 58	18 17	25 22	27 27	26 33	5 10	21 14	6 38	16 26
17 Su	19 39 12	24 25 44	9♓28	20 13	24 39	28 43	8 07	8 29	23 54	18 19	25 21	27 26	27 00	5 38	21 17	6 34	16 26
18 M	19 43 8	25 22 58	23 33	20 07	26 47	29 55	8 48	8 31	23 51	18 21	25 20	27 24	27 27	6 07	21 20	6 30	16 26
19 T	19 47 5	26 20 12	7♈08	20 04	28 54	1♋08	9 28	8 33	23 47	18 23	25 20	27 23	27 54	6 36	21 23	6 25	16 26R
20 W	19 51 1	27 17 27	20 15	20 02D	1♌00	2 20	10 09	8 35	23 43	18 24	25 19	27 21	28 20	7 04	21 26	6 19	16 26
21 Th	19 54 58	28 14 43	2♉56	20 02	3 05	3 33	10 49	8 37	23 39	18 26	25 18	27 20	28 47	7 33	21 28	6 13	16 26
22 F	19 58 55	29 11 59	15 18	20 02R	5 08	4 45	11 29	8 38	23 36	18 28	25 18	27 19	29 14	8 02	21 29	6 07	16 26
23 Sa	20 2 51	0♌09 16	27 25	20 02	7 10	5 58	12 09	8 40	23 32	18 29	25 17	27 17	29 40	8 30	21 30	6 00	16 26
24 Su	20 6 48	1 06 35	9♊21	20 01	9 11	7 10	12 49	8 41	23 28	18 31	25 16	27 16	0♌07	8 59	21 31	5 52	16 26
25 M	20 10 44	2 03 53	21 12	19 57	11 10	8 23	13 29	8 42	23 24	18 32	25 15	27 14	0 34	9 28	21 31R	5 44	16 25
26 T	20 14 41	3 01 13	3♋00	19 50	13 08	9 36	14 09	8 42	23 20	18 34	25 14	27 13	1 01	9 56	21 31	5 36	16 25
27 W	20 18 37	3 58 34	14 50	19 41	15 04	10 48	14 49	8 43	23 16	18 35	25 14	27 11	1 28	10 25	21 31	5 28	16 25
28 Th	20 22 34	4 55 55	26 43	19 29	16 58	12 01	15 28	8 43R	23 12	18 36	25 13	27 10	1 54	10 54	21 30	5 18	16 24
29 F	20 26 30	5 53 17	8♌41	19 16	18 50	13 14	16 07	8 43	23 07	18 38	25 12	27 09	2 21	11 23	21 29	5 09	16 24
30 Sa	20 30 27	6 50 40	20 46	19 03	20 41	14 27	16 46	8 43	23 03	18 39	25 11	27 07	2 48	11 51	21 27	4 59	16 23
31 Su	20 34 24	7 48 03	2♍58	18 50	22 30	15 40	17 25	8 43	22 59	18 40	25 10	27 06	3 15	12 20	21 24	4 49	16 23

EPHEMERIS CALCULATED FOR 12 MIDNIGHT GREENWICH MEAN TIME. ALL OTHER DATA AND FACING ASPECTARIAN PAGE IN **EASTERN TIME (BOLD)** AND PACIFIC TIME (REGULAR).

☽ Last Aspect day	ET / hr:mn / PT	asp	☽ Ingress sign	day	ET / hr:mn / PT
1	**6:29 pm** 3:29 pm	△♇	♎	1	9:06 pm
1	**6:29 pm** 3:29 pm	△♇	♎	2	**12:06 am**
3	11:20 pm	□♇	♏	4	**7:47 am** 4:47 am
4	**2:20 am**	□♇	♏	4	**7:47 am** 4:47 am
6	**7:24 am** 4:24 am	⚹♇	♐	6	**12:39 pm** 9:39 am
8	**6:30 am** 3:30 am	□♆	♑	8	**2:39 pm** 11:39 am
10	**12:39 pm** 9:39 am	☍♀	♒	10	**2:45 pm** 11:45 am
12	**7:07 am** 4:07 am	□♂	♓	12	**2:44 pm** 11:44 am
14	**11:11 am** 8:11 am	⚹♇	♈	14	**4:43 pm** 1:43 pm
16	**4:18 pm** 1:18 pm	□♇	♉	16	**10:22 pm** 7:22 pm

☽ Last Aspect day	ET / hr:mn / PT	asp	☽ Ingress sign	day	ET / hr:mn / PT
19	**7:06 am** 4:06 am	☌♂	♊	19	**8:06 am** 5:06 am
21	**6:06 pm** 3:06 pm	⚹☉	♋	21	**8:29 pm** 5:29 pm
24	**5:40 am** 2:40 am	⚹☿	♌	24	**9:09 am** 6:09 am
25	11:55 pm	☍♄	♍	26	**8:25 pm** 5:25 pm
26	**2:55 am**	☍♄	♍	26	**8:25 pm** 5:25 pm
28	**11:08 pm** 8:08 pm	△♇	♎	29	**5:45 am** 2:45 am
31	**6:43 am** 3:43 am	□♇	♏	31	**1:11 pm** 10:11 am

☽ Phases & Eclipses phase	day	ET / hr:mn / PT
2nd Quarter	5	**7:07 am** 4:07 am
Full Moon	11	**9:36 pm** 6:36 pm
4th Quarter	18	9:36 pm
4th Quarter	19	**12:36 am**
New Moon	27	**4:17 am** 1:17 am

Planet Ingress		day	ET / hr:mn / PT
☿	♍	3	11:58 pm
☿	♍	4	**2:58 am**
♀	♌	11	**2:30 pm** 11:30 am
♂	♊	20	**3:56 am** 12:56 am
⚶	♒	21	**6:33 am** 3:33 am
☉	♍	22	**11:16 pm** 8:16 pm
☿	♎	25	**9:03 pm** 6:03 pm

Planetary Motion		day	ET / hr:mn / PT
♅	℞	24	**9:54 am** 6:54 am

1 MONDAY
☽ △ ♂ **1:35 am**
☽ △ ♅ **2:30 am**
☿ ⚻ ♆ **7:23 am** 4:23 am
☽ ⚻ ♄ **10:30 am** 7:30 am
☽ ☍ ♆ **2:50 pm** 11:50 am
☽ ⚺ ☿ **4:03 pm** 1:03 pm
☽ △ ♇ **6:29 pm** 3:29 pm
♂ ☌ ♅ **7:53 pm** 4:53 pm

2 TUESDAY
♀ ⚹ ♅ **8:25 am** 5:25 am
☿ ⚻ ♇ **9:24 am** 6:24 am
☽ ☍ ♃ **4:27 pm** 1:27 pm
☽ ⚹ ☉ **8:12 pm** 5:12 pm
♀ ⚹ ♂ **10:00 pm** 7:00 pm

3 WEDNESDAY
☽ ⚻ ♅ **11:11 am** 8:11 am
☽ ⚻ ♂ **1:10 pm** 10:10 am
☽ □ ♀ **1:54 pm** 10:54 am
☽ △ ♄ **6:28 pm** 3:28 pm
☽ ⚻ ♆ **10:51 pm** 7:51 pm
☽ □ ♇ 11:20 pm

4 THURSDAY
☽ □ ♇ **2:20 am**
☽ ⚹ ☿ **8:29 am** 5:29 am
☽ ⚻ ♃ **11:18 pm** 8:18 pm

5 FRIDAY
☽ □ ☉ **7:07 am** 4:07 am
♀ ⚻ ♄ **12:23 pm** 9:23 am
☽ ☍ ♅ **5:13 pm** 2:13 pm
☽ ☍ ♂ **9:38 pm** 6:38 pm
☽ □ ♄ **11:46 pm** 8:46 pm
☽ △ ♀ 9:56 pm

6 SATURDAY
☽ △ ♀ **12:56 am**
☽ △ ♆ **4:08 am** 1:08 am
☽ ⚹ ♇ **7:24 am** 4:24 am
☽ □ ☿ **8:18 pm** 5:18 pm

7 SUNDAY
☽ △ ♃ **3:12 am** 12:12 am
♀ △ ♆ **12:43 pm** 9:43 am
☽ △ ☉ **2:21 pm** 11:21 am
♂ □ ♄ **3:57 pm** 12:57 pm
☽ ⚻ ♅ **8:17 pm** 5:17 pm
☽ ⚹ ♄ 11:11 pm
☽ ⚻ ♂ 11:42 pm

8 MONDAY
☽ ⚹ ♄ **2:11 am**
☽ ⚻ ♂ **2:42 am**
☽ □ ♆ **6:30 am** 3:30 am
☽ ⚻ ♀ **8:08 am** 5:08 am
☽ ⚺ ♇ **9:35 am** 6:35 am
♀ ☍ ♇ 10:18 pm

9 TUESDAY
♀ ☍ ♇ **1:18 am**
☽ △ ☿ **3:51 am** 12:51 am
☽ □ ♃ **4:24 am** 1:24 am
☿ ⚻ ♃ **9:06 am** 6:06 am
☽ ⚻ ☉ **6:33 pm** 3:33 pm
☽ △ ♅ **8:58 pm** 5:58 pm
☽ ⚺ ♄ 11:23 pm

10 WEDNESDAY
☽ ⚺ ♄ **2:23 am**
☽ △ ♂ **5:12 am** 2:12 am
☽ ⚹ ♆ **6:45 am** 3:45 am
☽ ☌ ♇ **9:45 am** 6:45 am
☽ ☍ ♀ **12:39 pm** 9:39 am

11 THURSDAY
☽ ⚹ ♃ **4:08 am** 1:08 am
☉ □ ♅ **8:53 am** 5:53 am
☽ ⚻ ☿ **9:05 am** 6:05 am
♂ ⚹ ♆ **5:44 pm** 2:44 pm
☽ □ ♅ **8:47 pm** 5:47 pm
☽ ☍ ☉ **9:36 pm** 6:36 pm
☽ ☌ ♄ 10:58 pm

12 FRIDAY
☽ ☌ ♄ **1:58 am**
☽ ⚺ ♆ **6:33 am** 3:33 am
☽ □ ♂ **7:07 am** 4:07 am
☽ ⚺ ♇ **9:35 am** 6:35 am
☽ ⚻ ♀ **4:55 pm** 1:55 pm

13 SATURDAY
☽ ⚺ ♃ **4:19 am** 1:19 am
☽ ☍ ☿ **3:02 pm** 12:02 pm
☽ ⚹ ♅ **9:49 pm** 6:49 pm
☽ ⚻ ☉ 11:10 pm
☽ ⚺ ♄ 11:58 pm

14 SUNDAY
☽ ⚻ ☉ **2:10 am**
☽ ⚺ ♄ **2:58 am**
☽ ☌ ♆ **7:58 am** 4:58 am
☽ ⚹ ♂ **10:53 am** 7:53 am
☽ ⚹ ♇ **11:11 am** 8:11 am
☉ ☍ ♄ **1:11 pm** 10:11 am
♂ △ ♇ **5:28 pm** 2:28 pm
☽ △ ♀ **11:53 pm** 8:53 pm

15 MONDAY
☽ ☌ ♃ **6:59 am** 3:59 am
☽ ⚻ ☿ 9:41 pm
☽ ⚺ ♅ 11:01 pm

16 TUESDAY
☽ ⚻ ☿ **12:41 am**
☽ ⚺ ♅ **2:01 am**
☽ ⚹ ♄ **7:14 am** 4:14 am
☽ △ ☉ **10:48 am** 7:48 am
☽ ⚺ ♆ **12:50 pm** 9:50 am
☿ △ ♅ **1:46 pm** 10:46 am
☽ □ ♇ **4:18 pm** 1:18 pm
☽ ⚺ ♂ **6:39 pm** 3:39 pm

17 WEDNESDAY
☽ □ ♀ **11:54 am** 8:54 am
☽ ⚺ ♃ **1:32 pm** 10:32 am
☉ ⚻ ♆ **1:57 pm** 10:57 am

18 THURSDAY
♀ △ ♃ **4:03 am** 1:03 am
☽ ☌ ♅ **10:20 am** 7:20 am
☿ ⚻ ♄ **3:06 pm** 12:06 pm
☽ □ ♄ **3:34 pm** 12:34 pm
☽ △ ☿ **3:37 pm** 12:37 pm
☽ ⚹ ♆ **9:49 pm** 6:49 pm
☽ □ ☉ 9:36 pm
☽ △ ♇ 10:32 pm

19 FRIDAY
☽ □ ☉ **12:36 am**
☽ △ ♇ **1:32 am**
☽ ☌ ♂ **7:06 am** 4:06 am
☉ ⚻ ♇ **12:10 pm** 9:10 am
☽ ⚹ ♃ **11:52 pm** 8:52 pm

20 SATURDAY
☽ ⚹ ♀ **5:09 am** 2:09 am
☽ ⚺ ♅ **10:01 pm** 7:01 pm

21 SUNDAY
☽ △ ♄ **3:04 am** 12:04 am
☿ ☍ ♆ **3:40 am** 12:40 am
☽ □ ♆ **9:47 am** 6:47 am
☽ □ ☿ **10:29 am** 7:29 am
☽ ⚻ ♇ **1:38 pm** 10:38 am
☽ ⚹ ☉ **6:06 pm** 3:06 pm
☽ ⚺ ♂ **10:35 pm** 7:35 pm

22 MONDAY
☽ □ ♃ **12:10 pm** 9:10 am
☿ △ ♇ **5:59 pm** 2:59 pm
☽ ⚺ ♀ 9:55 pm

23 TUESDAY
☽ ⚺ ♀ **12:55 am**
☽ ⚹ ♅ **10:51 am** 7:51 am
☽ ⚻ ♄ **3:30 pm** 12:30 pm
☽ △ ♆ **10:26 pm** 7:26 pm
☽ ☍ ♇ 11:17 pm

24 WEDNESDAY
☽ ☍ ♇ **2:17 am**
☽ ⚹ ☿ **5:40 am** 2:40 am
☽ ⚺ ☉ **12:07 pm** 9:07 am
☽ ⚹ ♂ **2:16 pm** 11:16 am
☽ △ ♃ 9:10 pm

25 THURSDAY
☽ △ ♃ **12:10 am**
☽ ☌ ♀ **7:50 pm** 4:50 pm
☽ □ ♅ **10:45 pm** 7:45 pm
☽ ☍ ♄ 11:55 pm

26 FRIDAY
☽ ☍ ♄ **2:55 am**
☽ ⚻ ♆ **9:53 am** 6:53 am
☽ ⚻ ♇ **1:39 pm** 10:39 am
☽ ⚺ ☿ **10:28 pm** 7:28 pm
♀ □ ♅ 9:34 pm
☉ □ ♂ 10:27 pm

27 SATURDAY
♀ □ ♅ **12:34 am**
☉ □ ♂ **1:27 am**
☽ □ ♂ **4:11 am** 1:11 am
☽ ☌ ☉ **4:17 am** 1:17 am
☽ ⚻ ♃ **10:33 am** 7:33 am

28 SUNDAY
☽ △ ♅ **8:47 am** 5:47 am
☽ ⚺ ♀ **12:17 pm** 9:17 am
☽ ⚻ ♄ **12:30 pm** 9:30 am
♀ ☍ ♄ **2:27 pm** 11:27 am
☽ ☍ ♆ **7:27 pm** 4:27 pm
☽ △ ♇ **11:08 pm** 8:08 pm

29 MONDAY
☽ ☌ ☿ **12:10 pm** 9:10 am
☽ △ ♂ **3:50 pm** 12:50 pm
☽ ⚺ ☉ **6:00 pm** 3:00 pm
☽ ☍ ♃ **7:00 pm** 4:00 pm

30 TUESDAY
☉ ⚻ ♃ **6:09 am** 3:09 am
☽ ⚻ ♅ **4:54 pm** 1:54 pm
☽ △ ♄ **8:13 pm** 5:13 pm
☽ ⚹ ♀ 11:07 pm

31 WEDNESDAY
☽ ⚹ ♀ **2:07 am**
☽ ⚻ ♆ **3:08 am** 12:08 am
☽ □ ♇ **6:43 am** 3:43 am
♀ ⚻ ♆ **12:37 pm** 9:37 am
☽ ⚺ ☿ **10:54 pm** 7:54 pm
☽ ⚻ ♂ 10:16 pm
☽ ⚻ ♃ 10:35 pm

Eastern time in bold type
Pacific time in medium type

AUGUST 2022

DATE	SID.TIME	SUN	MOON	NODE	MERCURY	VENUS	MARS	JUPITER	SATURN	URANUS	NEPTUNE	PLUTO	CERES	PALLAS	JUNO	VESTA	CHIRON
1 M	20 38 20	8♌45 27	15♍20	18♉40℞	24♌18	16♋52	18♉04	8♈42℞	22♒55℞	18♉41	25♓09℞	27♑04℞	3♌42	12♊49	21♓22℞	4♓38℞	16♈22℞
2 T	20 42 17	9 42 52	27 51	18 31	26 04	18 05	18 43	8 41	22 50	18 43	25 08	27 03	4 09	13 18	21 19	4 27	16 21
3 W	20 46 13	10 40 18	10♎34	18 26	27 48	19 18	19 21	8 40	22 46	18 44	25 07	27 02	4 35	13 46	21 15	4 15	16 21
4 Th	20 50 10	11 37 44	23 32	18 23	29 31	20 31	20 00	8 39	22 42	18 45	25 06	27 00	5 02	14 15	21 11	4 04	16 20
5 F	20 54 6	12 35 10	6♏47	18 22	1♍11	21 44	20 38	8 38	22 37	18 46	25 05	26 59	5 29	14 44	21 07	3 51	16 19
6 Sa	20 58 3	13 32 38	20 22	18 22	2 51	22 58	21 16	8 36	22 33	18 47	25 04	26 57	5 56	15 13	21 02	3 39	16 18
7 Su	21 1 59	14 30 06	4♐19	18 22	4 28	24 11	21 54	8 35	22 29	18 48	25 02	26 56	6 23	15 41	20 57	3 26	16 17
8 M	21 5 56	15 27 35	18 38	18 20	6 04	25 24	22 31	8 33	22 24	18 48	25 01	26 55	6 50	16 10	20 51	3 13	16 16
9 T	21 9 53	16 25 05	3♑18	18 15	7 39	26 37	23 09	8 31	22 20	18 49	25 00	26 53	7 17	16 39	20 45	3 00	16 15
10 W	21 13 49	17 22 35	18 14	18 08	9 12	27 50	23 46	8 29	22 15	18 50	24 59	26 52	7 43	17 08	20 38	2 46	16 14
11 Th	21 17 46	18 20 07	3♒18	17 59	10 43	29 03	24 23	8 26	22 11	18 51	24 58	26 51	8 10	17 36	20 31	2 33	16 13
12 F	21 21 42	19 17 39	18 22	17 48	12 12	0♌17	25 00	8 23	22 06	18 51	24 56	26 50	8 37	18 05	20 24	2 19	16 12
13 Sa	21 25 39	20 15 13	3♓14	17 37	13 40	1 30	25 37	8 21	22 02	18 52	24 55	26 48	9 04	18 34	20 16	2 05	16 11
14 Su	21 29 35	21 12 47	17 47	17 27	15 06	2 44	26 13	8 17	21 57	18 52	24 54	26 47	9 31	19 02	20 08	1 50	16 10
15 M	21 33 32	22 10 23	1♈54	17 19	16 31	3 57	26 50	8 14	21 53	18 53	24 52	26 46	9 58	19 31	19 59	1 36	16 08
16 T	21 37 28	23 08 01	15 33	17 14	17 54	5 10	27 26	8 11	21 48	18 53	24 51	26 44	10 24	20 00	19 50	1 21	16 07
17 W	21 41 25	24 05 40	28 43	17 11	19 15	6 24	28 02	8 07	21 44	18 54	24 50	26 43	10 51	20 28	19 41	1 06	16 06
18 Th	21 45 22	25 03 20	11♉28	17 10D	20 34	7 37	28 37	8 03	21 39	18 54	24 48	26 42	11 18	20 57	19 31	0 52	16 04
19 F	21 49 18	26 01 02	23 52	17 10℞	21 51	8 51	29 13	7 59	21 35	18 54	24 47	26 41	11 45	21 26	19 21	0 37	16 03
20 Sa	21 53 15	26 58 46	5♊59	17 10	23 07	10 05	29 48	7 55	21 30	18 55	24 46	26 40	12 12	21 54	19 11	0 22	16 01
21 Su	21 57 11	27 56 32	17 55	17 08	24 21	11 18	0♊23	7 51	21 26	18 55	24 44	26 38	12 38	22 23	19 00	0 07	16 00
22 M	22 1 8	28 54 19	29 46	17 05	25 32	12 32	0 58	7 46	21 21	18 55	24 43	26 37	13 05	22 51	18 49	29♒52	15 58
23 T	22 5 4	29 52 07	11♋35	16 58	26 42	13 46	1 33	7 42	21 17	18 55	24 41	26 36	13 32	23 20	18 37	29 37	15 56
24 W	22 9 1	0♍49 58	23 27	16 50	27 49	15 00	2 07	7 37	21 13	18 55℞	24 40	26 35	13 59	23 48	18 25	29 22	15 55
25 Th	22 12 57	1 47 50	5♌25	16 38	28 55	16 13	2 42	7 32	21 08	18 55	24 38	26 34	14 26	24 17	18 13	29 07	15 53
26 F	22 16 54	2 45 43	17 32	16 26	29 57	17 27	3 16	7 27	21 04	18 55	24 37	26 33	14 52	24 45	18 00	28 52	15 51
27 Sa	22 20 51	3 43 38	29 47	16 13	0♎58	18 41	3 49	7 21	20 59	18 55	24 35	26 32	15 19	25 13	17 48	28 37	15 49
28 Su	22 24 47	4 41 35	12♍13	16 01	1 55	19 55	4 23	7 16	20 55	18 55	24 34	26 31	15 46	25 42	17 35	28 22	15 47
29 M	22 28 44	5 39 33	24 50	15 50	2 50	21 09	4 56	7 10	20 51	18 55	24 32	26 29	16 13	26 10	17 21	28 08	15 46
30 T	22 32 40	6 37 32	7♎37	15 42	3 42	22 23	5 29	7 05	20 47	18 55	24 31	26 28	16 39	26 38	17 08	27 53	15 44
31 W	22 36 37	7 35 33	20 35	15 37	4 31	23 37	6 01	6 59	20 42	18 54	24 29	26 27	17 06	27 06	16 54	27 39	15 42

EPHEMERIS CALCULATED FOR 12 MIDNIGHT GREENWICH MEAN TIME. ALL OTHER DATA AND FACING ASPECTARIAN PAGE IN **EASTERN TIME (BOLD)** AND PACIFIC TIME (REGULAR).

SEPTEMBER 2022

☽ Last Aspect day	ET / hr:mn / PT	asp	☽ Ingress sign	day	ET / hr:mn / PT
2	**1:22 pm** 10:22 am	□ ♀	♐	2	**6:39 pm** 3:39 pm
4	**9:51 pm** 6:51 pm	△ ♀	♑	4	**10:03 pm** 7:03 pm
6	**5:43 pm** 2:43 pm	☌ ♇	♒	6	**11:41 pm** 8:41 pm
8	**8:34 am** 5:34 am	☌ ♄	♓	8	9:42 pm
8	**8:34 am** 5:34 am	☌ ♄	♓	9	**12:42 am**
10	**8:29 pm** 5:29 pm	⚹ ♇	♈	10	11:47 pm
10	**8:29 pm** 5:29 pm	⚹ ♇	♈	11	**2:47 am**
12	9:53 pm	□ ♇	♉	13	**7:39 am** 4:39 am
13	**12:53 am**	□ ♇	♉	13	**7:39 am** 4:39 am
15	**8:59 am** 5:59 am	△ ♇	♊	15	**4:16 pm** 1:16 pm
17	**5:52 pm** 2:52 pm	□ ☉	♋	18	**3:59 am** 12:59 am
20	**11:57 am** 8:57 am	⚹ ☉	♌	20	**4:38 pm** 1:38 pm
22	**7:07 am** 4:07 am	☍ ♄	♍	23	**3:53 am** 12:53 am
25	**8:49 am** 5:49 am	☌ ☿	♎	25	**12:43 pm** 9:43 am
27	**12:21 pm** 9:21 am	□ ♇	♏	27	**7:15 pm** 4:15 pm
29	**5:20 pm** 2:20 pm	⚹ ♇	♐	29	9:03 pm
29	**5:20 pm** 2:20 pm	⚹ ♇	♐	30	**12:03 am**

☽ Phases & Eclipses phase	day	ET / hr:mn / PT
2nd Quarter	3	**2:08 pm** 11:08 am
Full Moon	10	**5:59 am** 2:59 am
4th Quarter	17	**5:52 pm** 2:52 pm
New Moon	25	**5:55 pm** 2:55 pm

Planet Ingress	day	ET / hr:mn / PT
♀ ♍	4	9:05 pm
♀ ♍	5	**12:05 am**
⚴ ♋	5	10:04 pm
⚴ ♋	6	**1:04 am**
☉ ♎	22	**9:04 pm** 6:04 pm
☿ ♍	23	**8:04 am** 5:04 am
♀ ♎	29	**3:49 am** 12:49 am
⚳ ♍	29	**4:59 am** 1:59 am

Planetary Motion	day	ET / hr:mn / PT
☿ ℞	9	**11:38 pm** 8:38 pm

1 THURSDAY
☽ ⚻ ♂ **1:16 am**
☽ ⚻ ♃ **1:35 am**
☽ ⚹ ☉ **5:20 am** 2:20 am
♂ ⚹ ♃ **7:52 am** 4:52 am
☽ ☍ ♅ **11:06 pm** 8:06 pm
☽ □ ♄ 11:02 pm
♀ ⚻ ♇ 11:33 pm

2 FRIDAY
☽ □ ♄ **2:02 am**
♀ ⚻ ♇ **2:33 am**
☽ △ ♆ **8:52 am** 5:52 am
☽ ⚹ ♇ **12:23 pm** 9:23 am
☽ □ ♀ **1:22 pm** 10:22 am
☿ ☍ ♃ **9:49 pm** 6:49 pm

3 SATURDAY
☽ △ ♃ **6:10 am** 3:10 am
☽ ⚹ ☿ **6:37 am** 3:37 am
☽ ☍ ♂ **8:23 am** 5:23 am
☽ □ ☉ **2:08 pm** 11:08 am

4 SUNDAY
☽ ⚻ ♅ **3:13 am** 12:13 am
☽ ⚹ ♄ **5:50 am** 2:50 am
☽ □ ♆ **12:32 pm** 9:32 am
☽ ⚺ ♇ **3:57 pm** 12:57 pm
☽ △ ♀ **9:51 pm** 6:51 pm

5 MONDAY
☽ □ ♃ **8:44 am** 5:44 am
☽ □ ☿ **11:21 am** 8:21 am
☽ ⚻ ♂ **1:09 pm** 10:09 am
☽ △ ☉ **8:25 pm** 5:25 pm

6 TUESDAY
☽ △ ♅ **5:23 am** 2:23 am
☽ ⚺ ♄ **7:43 am** 4:43 am
☽ ⚹ ♆ **2:21 pm** 11:21 am
☽ ☌ ♇ **5:43 pm** 2:43 pm

7 WEDNESDAY
☽ ⚻ ♀ **4:04 am** 1:04 am
☽ ⚹ ♃ **9:45 am** 6:45 am
☽ △ ☿ **1:48 pm** 10:48 am
☽ △ ♂ **4:13 pm** 1:13 pm
☽ ⚻ ☉ 10:04 pm

8 THURSDAY
☽ ⚻ ☉ **1:04 am**
☽ □ ♅ **6:26 am** 3:26 am
☽ ☌ ♄ **8:34 am** 5:34 am
☽ ⚺ ♆ **3:17 pm** 12:17 pm
☽ ⚺ ♇ **6:41 pm** 3:41 pm

9 FRIDAY
☽ ☍ ♀ **9:39 am** 6:39 am
☽ ⚺ ♃ **10:26 am** 7:26 am
☽ ⚻ ☿ **3:24 pm** 12:24 pm
♀ ⚻ ♃ **6:06 pm** 3:06 pm
☽ □ ♂ **7:08 pm** 4:08 pm

10 SATURDAY
☽ ☍ ☉ **5:59 am** 2:59 am
☽ ⚹ ♅ **7:51 am** 4:51 am
☽ ⚺ ♄ **9:52 am** 6:52 am
☽ ☌ ♆ **4:56 pm** 1:56 pm
☽ ⚹ ♇ **8:29 pm** 5:29 pm

11 SUNDAY
☉ △ ♅ **9:09 am** 6:09 am
☽ ☌ ♃ **12:31 pm** 9:31 am
☽ ⚻ ♀ **5:05 pm** 2:05 pm
☽ ☍ ☿ **5:52 pm** 2:52 pm
☽ ⚹ ♂ **11:56 pm** 8:56 pm
☿ ⚺ ♀ 9:49 pm

12 MONDAY
☿ ⚺ ♀ **12:49 am**
☽ ⚺ ♅ **11:27 am** 8:27 am
☉ ⚻ ♄ **12:09 pm** 9:09 am
☽ ⚹ ♄ **1:25 pm** 10:25 am
☽ ⚻ ☉ **1:31 pm** 10:31 am
☽ ⚺ ♆ **9:02 pm** 6:02 pm
☽ □ ♇ 9:53 pm

13 TUESDAY
☽ □ ♇ **12:53 am**
☽ ⚺ ♃ **5:33 pm** 2:33 pm
☽ ⚻ ☿ **10:32 pm** 7:32 pm

14 WEDNESDAY
☽ △ ♀ **4:41 am** 1:41 am
☽ ⚺ ♂ **8:23 am** 5:23 am
☽ ☌ ♅ **6:34 pm** 3:34 pm
☽ □ ♄ **8:30 pm** 5:30 pm
☽ △ ☉ 10:31 pm

15 THURSDAY
☽ △ ☉ **1:31 am**
☽ ⚹ ♆ **4:47 am** 1:47 am
☽ △ ♇ **8:59 am** 5:59 am
☽ ⚹ ♃ 11:14 pm

16 FRIDAY
☽ ⚹ ♃ **2:14 am**
☽ △ ☿ **5:36 am** 2:36 am
♀ □ ♂ **2:49 pm** 11:49 am
☉ ☍ ♆ **6:21 pm** 3:21 pm
☽ ☌ ♂ **8:52 pm** 5:52 pm
☽ □ ♀ **9:18 pm** 6:18 pm

17 SATURDAY
☽ ⚺ ♅ **5:13 am** 2:13 am
☽ △ ♄ **7:04 am** 4:04 am
☽ □ ♆ **3:54 pm** 12:54 pm
☽ □ ☉ **5:52 pm** 2:52 pm
☽ ⚻ ♇ **8:21 pm** 5:21 pm

18 SUNDAY
☽ □ ♃ **1:38 pm** 10:38 am
☽ □ ☿ **1:56 pm** 10:56 am
☿ ☍ ♃ **6:34 pm** 3:34 pm
☉ △ ♇ **11:58 pm** 8:58 pm

19 MONDAY
☽ ⚺ ♂ **11:41 am** 8:41 am
☽ ⚹ ♀ **4:53 pm** 1:53 pm
☽ ⚹ ♅ **5:43 pm** 2:43 pm
☽ ⚻ ♄ **7:25 pm** 4:25 pm
♀ △ ♅ 9:44 pm

20 TUESDAY
♀ △ ♅ **12:44 am**
☽ △ ♆ **4:25 am** 1:25 am
☽ ☍ ♇ **8:58 am** 5:58 am
☽ ⚹ ☉ **11:57 am** 8:57 am
♀ ⚻ ♄ **4:12 pm** 1:12 pm
☽ ⚹ ☿ **9:52 pm** 6:52 pm
☽ △ ♃ 10:32 pm

21 WEDNESDAY
☽ △ ♃ **1:32 am**
☽ ⚹ ♂ 11:00 pm

22 THURSDAY
☽ ⚹ ♂ **2:00 am**
☽ □ ♅ **5:36 am** 2:36 am
☽ ☍ ♄ **7:07 am** 4:07 am
☽ ⚺ ♀ **11:42 am** 8:42 am
☽ ⚻ ♆ **3:57 pm** 12:57 pm
☽ ⚻ ♇ **8:28 pm** 5:28 pm
☉ ☌ ☿ 11:50 pm

23 FRIDAY
☉ ☌ ☿ **2:50 am**
☽ ⚺ ☿ **4:13 am** 1:13 am
☽ ⚺ ☉ **4:28 am** 1:28 am
☽ ⚻ ♃ **11:50 am** 8:50 am

24 SATURDAY
♀ ☍ ♆ **4:51 am** 1:51 am
☽ □ ♂ **1:51 pm** 10:51 am
☽ △ ♅ **3:17 pm** 12:17 pm
☽ ⚻ ♄ **4:38 pm** 1:38 pm
☽ ☍ ♆ 10:10 pm

25 SUNDAY
☽ ☍ ♆ **1:10 am**
☽ ☌ ♀ **3:24 am** 12:24 am
☽ △ ♇ **5:35 am** 2:35 am
☽ ☌ ☿ **8:49 am** 5:49 am
☽ ☌ ☉ **5:55 pm** 2:55 pm
☽ ☍ ♃ **7:45 pm** 4:45 pm
♀ △ ♇ 10:46 pm

26 MONDAY
♀ △ ♇ **1:46 am**
♂ ⚺ ♅ **10:14 am** 7:14 am
☿ ☌ ♀ **1:59 pm** 10:59 am
☉ ☍ ♃ **3:33 pm** 12:33 pm
☽ ⚻ ♅ **10:31 pm** 7:31 pm
☽ △ ♂ **10:54 pm** 7:54 pm
☽ △ ♄ **11:44 pm** 8:44 pm

27 TUESDAY
☽ ⚻ ♆ **8:01 am** 5:01 am
☿ △ ♇ **8:56 am** 5:56 am
☽ ⚺ ☿ **12:10 pm** 9:10 am
☽ □ ♇ **12:21 pm** 9:21 am
☽ ⚺ ♀ **3:54 pm** 12:54 pm
☽ ⚻ ♃ 10:29 pm
♂ △ ♄ 10:49 pm

28 WEDNESDAY
☽ ⚻ ♃ **1:29 am**
♂ △ ♄ **1:49 am**
☽ ⚺ ☉ **4:31 am** 1:31 am

29 THURSDAY
☽ ☍ ♅ **3:49 am** 12:49 am
☽ □ ♄ **4:57 am** 1:57 am
☽ ⚻ ♂ **5:46 am** 2:46 am
☽ △ ♆ **1:03 pm** 10:03 am
☽ ⚹ ☿ **2:58 pm** 11:58 am
☽ ⚹ ♇ **5:20 pm** 2:20 pm
☽ ⚹ ♀ 11:04 pm

30 FRIDAY
☽ ⚹ ♀ **2:04 am**
☽ △ ♃ **5:38 am** 2:38 am
☽ ⚹ ☉ **1:05 pm** 10:05 am

Eastern time in bold type
Pacific time in medium type

SEPTEMBER 2022

DATE	SID.TIME	SUN	MOON	NODE	MERCURY	VENUS	MARS	JUPITER	SATURN	URANUS	NEPTUNE	PLUTO	CERES	PALLAS	JUNO	VESTA	CHIRON
1 Th	22 40 33	8♍33 35	3♏46	15♉35D	5♎17	24♌51	6♊34	6♈53℞	20♒38℞	18♉54℞	24♓28℞	26♑26℞	17♌33	27♊34	16♓40℞	27♒25℞	15♈40℞
2 F	22 44 30	9 31 39	17 09	15 34	5 59	26 05	7 06	6 46	20 34	18 53	24 26	26 25	17 59	28 02	16 26	27 11	15 38
3 Sa	22 48 26	10 29 44	0♐46	15 35℞	6 37	27 19	7 37	6 40	20 30	18 53	24 24	26 25	18 26	28 30	16 12	26 58	15 36
4 Su	22 52 23	11 27 51	14 39	15 35	7 11	28 33	8 09	6 33	20 26	18 53	24 23	26 24	18 53	28 58	15 57	26 44	15 33
5 M	22 56 20	12 25 59	28 47	15 34	7 41	29 47	8 40	6 27	20 22	18 52	24 21	26 23	19 19	29 26	15 43	26 31	15 31
6 T	23 0 16	13 24 08	13♑10	15 31	8 06	1♍02	9 11	6 20	20 18	18 51	24 20	26 22	19 46	29 54	15 28	26 18	15 29
7 W	23 4 13	14 22 19	27 45	15 25	8 27	2 16	9 42	6 13	20 14	18 51	24 18	26 21	20 12	0♋22	15 13	26 06	15 27
8 Th	23 8 9	15 20 32	12♒26	15 17	8 42	3 30	10 12	6 06	20 10	18 50	24 16	26 20	20 39	0 50	14 59	25 54	15 25
9 F	23 12 6	16 18 45	27 08	15 09	8 51	4 44	10 42	5 59	20 06	18 49	24 15	26 19	21 06	1 17	14 44	25 42	15 22
10 Sa	23 16 2	17 17 01	11♓42	14 59	8 55℞	5 59	11 11	5 52	20 03	18 49	24 13	26 19	21 32	1 45	14 29	25 30	15 20
11 Su	23 19 59	18 15 18	26 01	14 51	8 53	7 13	11 41	5 45	19 59	18 48	24 11	26 18	21 59	2 12	14 14	25 19	15 18
12 M	23 23 55	19 13 37	9♈59	14 45	8 45	8 27	12 10	5 38	19 55	18 47	24 10	26 17	22 25	2 40	13 59	25 08	15 15
13 T	23 27 52	20 11 58	23 34	14 40	8 30	9 42	12 38	5 30	19 52	18 46	24 08	26 16	22 51	3 07	13 44	24 58	15 13
14 W	23 31 49	21 10 21	6♉43	14 38D	8 08	10 56	13 07	5 23	19 48	18 45	24 07	26 16	23 18	3 34	13 30	24 48	15 11
15 Th	23 35 45	22 08 46	19 29	14 38	7 39	12 11	13 35	5 15	19 45	18 44	24 05	26 15	23 44	4 01	13 15	24 38	15 08
16 F	23 39 42	23 07 13	1♊55	14 39	7 04	13 25	14 02	5 07	19 41	18 43	24 03	26 14	24 11	4 28	13 00	24 29	15 06
17 Sa	23 43 38	24 05 42	14 04	14 40℞	6 22	14 40	14 29	5 00	19 38	18 42	24 02	26 14	24 37	4 55	12 46	24 20	15 03
18 Su	23 47 35	25 04 14	26 03	14 41	5 34	15 54	14 56	4 52	19 35	18 41	24 00	26 13	25 03	5 22	12 32	24 12	15 01
19 M	23 51 31	26 02 48	7♋55	14 40	4 41	17 09	15 22	4 44	19 32	18 39	23 58	26 13	25 29	5 49	12 17	24 04	14 58
20 T	23 55 28	27 01 24	19 46	14 37	3 43	18 23	15 48	4 36	19 29	18 38	23 57	26 12	25 56	6 16	12 03	23 56	14 56
21 W	23 59 24	28 00 02	1♌41	14 32	2 42	19 38	16 14	4 28	19 26	18 37	23 55	26 12	26 22	6 42	11 50	23 49	14 53
22 Th	0 3 21	28 58 42	13 43	14 26	1 38	20 52	16 39	4 20	19 23	18 36	23 53	26 11	26 48	7 09	11 36	23 43	14 51
23 F	0 7 18	29 57 24	25 56	14 18	0 33	22 07	17 04	4 12	19 20	18 34	23 52	26 11	27 14	7 35	11 23	23 36	14 48
24 Sa	0 11 14	0♎56 09	8♍22	14 10	29♍28	23 22	17 28	4 04	19 17	18 33	23 50	26 10	27 40	8 01	11 10	23 31	14 45
25 Su	0 15 11	1 54 55	21 02	14 02	28 26	24 37	17 52	3 56	19 14	18 31	23 48	26 10	28 06	8 27	10 57	23 25	14 43
26 M	0 19 7	2 53 43	3♎57	13 56	27 28	25 51	18 15	3 48	19 12	18 30	23 47	26 09	28 32	8 53	10 44	23 21	14 40
27 T	0 23 4	3 52 34	17 05	13 51	26 35	27 06	18 38	3 40	19 09	18 28	23 45	26 09	28 58	9 19	10 32	23 16	14 37
28 W	0 27 0	4 51 26	0♏25	13 49D	25 48	28 21	19 01	3 32	19 07	18 27	23 43	26 09	29 24	9 44	10 20	23 12	14 35
29 Th	0 30 57	5 50 20	13 58	13 48	25 10	29 36	19 23	3 24	19 04	18 25	23 42	26 08	29 50	10 10	10 08	23 09	14 32
30 F	0 34 53	6 49 17	27 40	13 48	24 41	0♎50	19 44	3 16	19 02	18 24	23 40	26 08	0♍16	10 35	9 57	23 06	14 29

EPHEMERIS CALCULATED FOR 12 MIDNIGHT GREENWICH MEAN TIME. ALL OTHER DATA AND FACING ASPECTARIAN PAGE IN **EASTERN TIME (BOLD)** AND PACIFIC TIME (REGULAR).

OCTOBER 2022

☽ Last Aspect day	ET / hr:mn / PT		asp	☽ Ingress sign	day	ET / hr:mn / PT	
1	**5:46 pm**	2:46 pm	□ ☿	♑	2	**3:38 am**	12:38 am
3	**11:49 pm**	8:49 pm	☌ ♇	♒	4	**6:20 am**	3:20 am
5	**6:46 pm**	3:46 pm	△ ♂	♓	6	**8:47 am**	5:47 am
8	**7:10 am**	4:10 am	☍ ☿	♈	8	**11:57 am**	8:57 am
10	**10:02 am**	7:02 am	□ ♇	♉	10	**5:04 pm**	2:04 pm
12	**5:42 pm**	2:42 pm	△ ♇	♊	12		10:08 pm
12	**5:42 pm**	2:42 pm	△ ♇	♊	13	**1:08 am**	
14		9:11 pm	☌ ♂	♋	15	**12:11 pm**	9:11 am
15	**12:11 am**		☌ ♂	♋	15	**12:11 pm**	9:11 am
17	**4:56 pm**	1:56 pm	☍ ♇	♌	17		9:45 pm
17	**4:56 pm**	1:56 pm	☍ ♇	♌	18	**12:45 am**	
20	**6:35 am**	3:35 am	⚹ ☉	♍	20	**12:25 pm**	9:25 am
22	**2:17 pm**	11:17 am	△ ♇	♎	22	**9:24 pm**	6:24 pm
24	**8:36 pm**	5:36 pm	□ ♇	♏	25	**3:18 am**	12:18 am
26		9:27 pm	⚹ ♇	♐	27	**6:55 am**	3:55 am
27	**12:27 am**		⚹ ♇	♐	27	**6:55 am**	3:55 am
29	**9:10 am**	6:10 am	□ ♃	♑	29	**9:21 am**	6:21 am
31	**11:14 am**	8:14 am	⚹ ♃	♒	31	**11:43 am**	8:43 am

☽ Phases & Eclipses phase	day	ET / hr:mn / PT	
2nd Quarter	2	**8:14 pm**	5:14 pm
Full Moon	9	**4:55 pm**	1:55 pm
4th Quarter	17	**1:15 pm**	10:15 am
New Moon	25	**6:49 am**	3:49 am
●	25	2° ♏ 00'	
2nd Quarter	31		11:37 pm
2nd Quarter	11/1	**2:37 am**	

Planet Ingress		day	ET / hr:mn / PT	
☿	♎	10	**7:51 pm**	4:51 pm
♀	♏	23	**3:52 am**	12:52 am
☉	♏	23	**6:36 am**	3:36 am
♃	♓	27		10:10 pm
♃	♓	28	**1:10 am**	
☿	♏	29	**3:22 pm**	12:22 pm

Planetary Motion		day	ET / hr:mn / PT	
☿	D	2	**5:07 am**	2:07 am
⚶	D	5	**2:10 pm**	11:10 am
♇	D	8	**5:56 pm**	2:56 pm
♄	D	22		9:07 pm
♄	D	23	**12:07 am**	
⚵	D	23	**9:05 am**	6:05 pm
♂	℞	30	**9:26 am**	6:26 am

1 SATURDAY
☽ ⚻ ♅ **7:43 am** 4:43 am
☽ ⚹ ♄ **8:48 am** 5:48 am
☽ ☍ ♂ **11:03 am** 8:03 am
♀ ☍ ♃ **2:12 pm** 11:12 am
☽ □ ♆ **4:45 pm** 1:45 pm
☽ □ ☿ **5:46 pm** 2:46 pm
☽ ⚺ ♇ **9:02 pm** 6:02 pm

2 SUNDAY
☽ □ ♃ **8:37 am** 5:37 am
☽ □ ♀ **10:35 am** 7:35 am
☽ □ ☉ **8:14 pm** 5:14 pm

3 MONDAY
☽ △ ♅ **10:37 am** 7:37 am
☽ ⚺ ♄ **11:39 am** 8:39 am
☽ ⚻ ♂ **3:12 pm** 12:12 pm
☽ ⚹ ♆ **7:31 pm** 4:31 pm
☽ △ ☿ **8:59 pm** 5:59 pm
☽ ☌ ♇ **11:49 pm** 8:49 pm

4 TUESDAY
☽ ⚹ ♃ **10:48 am** 7:48 am
☽ △ ♀ **6:04 pm** 3:04 pm
☽ △ ☉ 11:31 pm

5 WEDNESDAY
☽ △ ☉ **2:31 am**
☽ □ ♅ **12:58 pm** 9:58 am
☽ ☌ ♄ **2:00 pm** 11:00 am
☽ △ ♂ **6:46 pm** 3:46 pm
☽ ⚺ ♆ **9:51 pm** 6:51 pm
☽ ⚻ ☿ 10:06 pm
☽ ⚺ ♇ 11:14 pm

6 THURSDAY
☽ ⚻ ☿ **1:06 am**
☽ ⚺ ♇ **2:14 am**
☽ ⚺ ♃ **12:49 pm** 9:49 am
☿ △ ♇ **11:56 pm** 8:56 pm
☽ ⚻ ♀ 10:28 pm

7 FRIDAY
☽ ⚻ ♀ **1:28 am**
☽ ⚻ ☉ **8:54 am** 5:54 am
☽ ⚹ ♅ **3:35 pm** 12:35 pm
☽ ⚺ ♄ **4:39 pm** 1:39 pm
☽ □ ♂ **10:40 pm** 7:40 pm
☽ ☌ ♆ 9:40 pm

8 SATURDAY
☽ ☌ ♆ **12:40 am**
☽ ⚹ ♇ **5:14 am** 2:14 am
☽ ☍ ☿ **7:10 am** 4:10 am
☽ ☌ ♃ **3:37 pm** 12:37 pm

9 SUNDAY
☽ ☍ ♀ **10:20 am** 7:20 am
☽ ☍ ☉ **4:55 pm** 1:55 pm
☽ ⚺ ♅ **7:39 pm** 4:39 pm
☽ ⚹ ♄ **8:48 pm** 5:48 pm

10 MONDAY
☽ ⚹ ♂ **4:14 am** 1:14 am
☽ ⚺ ♆ **5:09 am** 2:09 am
☽ □ ♇ **10:02 am** 7:02 am
☽ ⚻ ☿ **4:47 pm** 1:47 pm
☽ ⚺ ♃ **8:25 pm** 5:25 pm

11 TUESDAY
☉ ⚻ ♅ **5:13 am** 2:13 am
☉ △ ♄ **9:07 pm** 6:07 pm
☽ ⚻ ♀ **10:29 pm** 7:29 pm
♂ □ ♆ 10:46 pm
☽ ☌ ♅ 11:20 pm

12 WEDNESDAY
♂ □ ♆ **1:46 am**
☽ ☌ ♅ **2:20 am**
☿ ☍ ♃ **3:24 am** 12:24 am
☽ □ ♄ **3:37 am** 12:37 am
☽ ⚻ ☉ **4:10 am** 1:10 am
☽ ⚹ ♆ **12:25 pm** 9:25 am
☽ ⚺ ♂ **12:38 pm** 9:38 am
☽ △ ♇ **5:42 pm** 2:42 pm

13 THURSDAY
☽ ⚹ ♃ **4:08 am** 1:08 am
☽ △ ☿ **7:29 am** 4:29 am
♀ ⚻ ♅ **12:57 pm** 9:57 am
♀ △ ♄ 11:21 pm

14 FRIDAY
♀ △ ♄ **2:21 am**
☽ ⚺ ♅ **12:07 pm** 9:07 am
☽ △ ♄ **1:33 pm** 10:33 am
☽ △ ♀ **2:51 pm** 11:51 am
☽ △ ☉ **7:23 pm** 4:23 pm
☽ □ ♆ **10:46 pm** 7:46 pm
☽ ☌ ♂ 9:11 pm

15 SATURDAY
☽ ☌ ♂ **12:11 am**
☽ ⚻ ♇ **4:26 am** 1:26 am
☽ □ ♃ **2:44 pm** 11:44 am

16 SUNDAY
☽ □ ☿ **3:19 am** 12:19 am
☉ ⚻ ♆ **11:39 am** 8:39 am
☽ ⚹ ♅ 9:09 pm
☽ ⚻ ♄ 10:44 pm

17 MONDAY
☽ ⚹ ♅ **12:09 am**
☽ ⚻ ♄ **1:44 am**
☽ □ ♀ **10:14 am** 7:14 am
☽ △ ♆ **11:04 am** 8:04 am
☽ □ ☉ **1:15 pm** 10:15 am
☽ ⚺ ♂ **1:35 pm** 10:35 am
☽ ☍ ♇ **4:56 pm** 1:56 pm
♀ ⚻ ♆ **6:00 pm** 3:00 pm
☉ △ ♂ **6:05 pm** 3:05 pm
☽ △ ♃ 11:44 pm

18 TUESDAY
☽ △ ♃ **2:44 am**
♀ △ ♂ **10:20 pm** 7:20 pm
☽ ⚹ ☿ 10:16 pm

19 WEDNESDAY
☽ ⚹ ☿ **1:16 am**
☉ □ ♇ **9:33 am** 6:33 am
☽ □ ♅ **12:17 pm** 9:17 am
☽ ☍ ♄ **1:59 pm** 10:59 am
☽ ⚻ ♆ **11:02 pm** 8:02 pm
♀ □ ♇ 11:03 pm
☽ ⚹ ♂ 11:23 pm

20 THURSDAY
♀ □ ♇ **2:03 am**
☽ ⚹ ♂ **2:23 am**
☽ ⚻ ♇ **4:53 am** 1:53 am
☽ ⚹ ♀ **5:13 am** 2:13 am
☽ ⚹ ☉ **6:35 am** 3:35 am
☽ ⚻ ♃ **1:50 pm** 10:50 am

21 FRIDAY
☽ ⚺ ☿ **8:54 pm** 5:54 pm
☽ △ ♅ **10:19 pm** 7:19 pm
☽ ⚻ ♄ 9:06 pm

22 SATURDAY
☽ ⚻ ♄ **12:06 am**
☿ ⚻ ♅ **7:24 am** 4:24 am
☽ ☍ ♆ **8:37 am** 5:37 am
☽ □ ♂ **12:27 pm** 9:27 am
☽ △ ♇ **2:17 pm** 11:17 am
☉ ☌ ♀ **5:17 pm** 2:17 pm
☽ ⚺ ☉ **8:38 pm** 5:38 pm
☽ ⚺ ♀ **8:43 pm** 5:43 pm
☿ △ ♄ **9:00 pm** 6:00 pm
☽ ☍ ♃ **10:17 pm** 7:17 pm

23 SUNDAY
♀ ⚻ ♃ **11:58 am** 8:58 am
☉ ⚻ ♃ **4:21 pm** 1:21 pm

24 MONDAY
☽ ⚻ ♅ **5:18 am** 2:18 am
☽ △ ♄ **7:08 am** 4:08 am
☽ ☌ ☿ **12:01 pm** 9:01 am
☽ ⚻ ♆ **3:07 pm** 12:07 pm
☽ △ ♂ **7:12 pm** 4:12 pm
☽ □ ♇ **8:36 pm** 5:36 pm

25 TUESDAY
☽ ⚻ ♃ **3:46 am** 12:46 am
☽ ☌ ☉ **6:49 am** 3:49 am
☽ ☌ ♀ **8:04 am** 5:04 am
☿ ⚻ ♆ **12:30 pm** 9:30 am

26 WEDNESDAY
☽ ☍ ♅ **9:34 am** 6:34 am
☽ □ ♄ **11:30 am** 8:30 am
☽ △ ♆ **7:04 pm** 4:04 pm
☽ ⚺ ☿ **11:17 pm** 8:17 pm
☽ ⚻ ♂ **11:19 pm** 8:19 pm
☿ △ ♂ **11:37 pm** 8:37 pm
☽ ⚹ ♇ 9:27 pm

27 THURSDAY
☽ ⚹ ♇ **12:27 am**
☽ △ ♃ **7:01 am** 4:01 am
☿ □ ♇ **9:09 am** 6:09 am
☽ ⚺ ☉ **2:11 pm** 11:11 am
☽ ⚺ ♀ **4:30 pm** 1:30 pm

28 FRIDAY
☽ ⚻ ♅ **12:13 pm** 9:13 am
☽ ⚹ ♄ **2:17 pm** 11:17 am
☽ □ ♆ **9:37 pm** 6:37 pm
☽ ☍ ♂ 10:59 pm

29 SATURDAY
☽ ☍ ♂ **1:59 am**
☽ ⚺ ♇ **3:01 am** 12:01 am
☽ ⚹ ☿ **8:34 am** 5:34 am
☽ □ ♃ **9:10 am** 6:10 am
☿ ⚻ ♃ **1:32 pm** 10:32 am
☽ ⚹ ☉ **8:20 pm** 5:20 pm
☽ ⚹ ♀ **11:41 pm** 8:41 pm

30 SUNDAY
☽ △ ♅ **2:21 pm** 11:21 am
☽ ⚺ ♄ **4:36 pm** 1:36 pm
☽ ⚹ ♆ **11:51 pm** 8:51 pm

31 MONDAY
☽ ⚻ ♂ **4:19 am** 1:19 am
☽ ☌ ♇ **5:23 am** 2:23 am
☽ ⚹ ♃ **11:14 am** 8:14 am
☽ □ ☿ **5:37 pm** 2:37 pm
☽ □ ☉ 11:37 pm

Eastern time in bold type
Pacific time in medium type

OCTOBER 2022

DATE	SID.TIME	SUN	MOON	NODE	MERCURY	VENUS	MARS	JUPITER	SATURN	URANUS	NEPTUNE	PLUTO	CERES	PALLAS	JUNO	VESTA	CHIRON
1 Sa	0 38 50	7♎48 15	11♐32	13♉50	24♍22℞	2♎05	20♊05	3♈08℞	19♒00℞	18♉22℞	23♓39℞	26♑08℞	0♍42	11♋00	9♓46℞	23♒03℞	14♈27℞
2 Su	0 42 47	8 47 14	25 32	13 51	24 13D	3 20	20 25	3 00	18 58	18 20	23 37	26 08	1 08	11 25	9 36	23 02	14 24
3 M	0 46 43	9 46 16	9♑39	13 52℞	24 14	4 35	20 45	2 52	18 56	18 18	23 35	26 07	1 34	11 50	9 26	23 00	14 21
4 T	0 50 40	10 45 19	23 51	13 51	24 26	5 50	21 04	2 44	18 54	18 17	23 34	26 07	1 59	12 15	9 16	22 59	14 19
5 W	0 54 36	11 44 24	8♒08	13 49	24 47	7 05	21 23	2 36	18 52	18 15	23 32	26 07	2 25	12 39	9 07	22 58D	14 16
6 Th	0 58 33	12 43 31	22 25	13 45	25 19	8 20	21 41	2 29	18 50	18 13	23 31	26 07	2 50	13 03	8 58	22 58	14 13
7 F	1 2 29	13 42 39	6♓38	13 41	26 00	9 35	21 59	2 21	18 48	18 11	23 29	26 07	3 16	13 27	8 50	22 59	14 11
8 Sa	1 6 26	14 41 49	20 44	13 37	26 49	10 50	22 16	2 13	18 47	18 09	23 28	26 07D	3 41	13 51	8 42	22 59	14 08
9 Su	1 10 22	15 41 01	4♈38	13 33	27 46	12 04	22 32	2 06	18 45	18 07	23 26	26 07	4 07	14 15	8 35	23 01	14 05
10 M	1 14 19	16 40 15	18 17	13 29	28 50	13 19	22 48	1 58	18 44	18 05	23 25	26 07	4 32	14 38	8 28	23 02	14 02
11 T	1 18 15	17 39 31	1♉37	13 28D	0♎00	14 34	23 03	1 51	18 43	18 03	23 23	26 07	4 57	15 02	8 21	23 04	14 00
12 W	1 22 12	18 38 49	14 38	13 27	1 17	15 49	23 18	1 43	18 42	18 01	23 22	26 07	5 23	15 25	8 15	23 07	13 57
13 Th	1 26 9	19 38 10	27 19	13 28	2 37	17 04	23 32	1 36	18 41	17 59	23 20	26 07	5 48	15 47	8 10	23 10	13 54
14 F	1 30 5	20 37 32	9♊44	13 29	4 03	18 19	23 45	1 29	18 40	17 57	23 19	26 07	6 13	16 10	8 05	23 14	13 52
15 Sa	1 34 2	21 36 57	21 54	13 31	5 31	19 35	23 58	1 22	18 39	17 55	23 18	26 08	6 38	16 32	8 00	23 17	13 49
16 Su	1 37 58	22 36 24	3♋54	13 32	7 03	20 50	24 10	1 15	18 38	17 53	23 16	26 08	7 03	16 54	7 56	23 22	13 46
17 M	1 41 55	23 35 54	15 47	13 33℞	8 37	22 05	24 21	1 08	18 37	17 50	23 15	26 08	7 28	17 16	7 52	23 27	13 44
18 T	1 45 51	24 35 26	27 39	13 33	10 13	23 20	24 31	1 01	18 37	17 48	23 13	26 08	7 53	17 38	7 49	23 32	13 41
19 W	1 49 48	25 35 00	9♌35	13 33	11 51	24 35	24 41	0 55	18 36	17 46	23 12	26 08	8 18	17 59	7 47	23 37	13 38
20 Th	1 53 45	26 34 36	21 38	13 31	13 30	25 50	24 50	0 48	18 36	17 44	23 11	26 09	8 43	18 20	7 45	23 43	13 36
21 F	1 57 41	27 34 14	3♍54	13 29	15 09	27 05	24 59	0 42	18 36	17 41	23 09	26 09	9 07	18 41	7 43	23 50	13 33
22 Sa	2 1 38	28 33 55	16 25	13 27	16 50	28 20	25 06	0 35	18 35	17 39	23 08	26 09	9 32	19 01	7 42	23 57	13 30
23 Su	2 5 34	29 33 38	29 15	13 25	18 31	29 35	25 13	0 29	18 35D	17 37	23 07	26 10	9 56	19 21	7 42D	24 04	13 28
24 M	2 9 31	0♏33 23	12♎23	13 23	20 12	0♏51	25 19	0 23	18 35	17 34	23 06	26 10	10 21	19 41	7 42	24 11	13 25
25 T	2 13 27	1 33 10	25 51	13 22	21 54	2 06	25 24	0 18	18 35	17 32	23 04	26 11	10 45	20 00	7 42	24 19	13 23
26 W	2 17 24	2 32 59	9♏35	13 22D	23 35	3 21	25 28	0 12	18 36	17 30	23 03	26 11	11 10	20 19	7 43	24 28	13 20
27 Th	2 21 20	3 32 50	23 35	13 22	25 17	4 36	25 31	0 06	18 36	17 27	23 02	26 12	11 34	20 38	7 45	24 36	13 18
28 F	2 25 17	4 32 43	7♐45	13 22	26 58	5 51	25 34	0 01	18 37	17 25	23 01	26 12	11 58	20 56	7 47	24 46	13 15
29 Sa	2 29 13	5 32 37	22 02	13 23	28 39	7 06	25 36	29♓56	18 37	17 23	23 00	26 13	12 22	21 14	7 49	24 55	13 13
30 Su	2 33 10	6 32 34	6♑21	13 24	0♏19	8 22	25 37℞	29 51	18 38	17 20	22 59	26 14	12 46	21 32	7 52	25 05	13 10
31 M	2 37 7	7 32 32	20 40	13 24	2 00	9 37	25 37	29 46	18 38	17 18	22 58	26 14	13 10	21 49	7 56	25 15	13 08

EPHEMERIS CALCULATED FOR 12 MIDNIGHT GREENWICH MEAN TIME. ALL OTHER DATA AND FACING ASPECTARIAN PAGE IN **EASTERN TIME (BOLD)** AND PACIFIC TIME (REGULAR).

NOVEMBER 2022

☽ Last Aspect day	ET / hr:mn / PT	asp	☽ Ingress sign day	ET / hr:mn / PT
2	**7:08 am** 4:08 am	△♂	♓ 2	**2:46 pm** 11:46 am
4	**6:05 pm** 3:05 pm	☌♃	♈ 4	**7:07 pm** 4:07 pm
6	**5:30 pm** 2:30 pm	□♇	♉ 6	9:15 pm
6	**5:30 pm** 2:30 pm	□♇	♉ 7	**12:15 am**
9	**7:00 am** 4:00 am	⚹♃	♊ 9	**8:37 am** 5:37 am
11	**5:28 pm** 2:28 pm	□♃	♋ 11	**7:22 pm** 4:22 pm
14	**5:41 am** 2:41 am	△♃	♌ 14	**7:48 am** 4:48 am
16	**6:55 pm** 3:55 pm	□☿	♍ 16	**8:04 pm** 5:04 pm
19	**3:47 am** 12:47 am	☍♃	♎ 19	**5:58 am** 2:58 am
21	**6:14 am** 3:14 am	□♇	♏ 21	**12:16 pm** 9:16 am
23	**1:16 pm** 10:16 am	△♃	♐ 23	**3:16 pm** 12:16 pm
25	**2:22 pm** 11:22 am	□♃	♑ 25	**4:18 pm** 1:18 pm
27	**3:11 pm** 12:11 pm	⚹♃	♒ 27	**5:07 pm** 2:07 pm
28	10:53 pm	☌♄	♓ 29	**7:15 pm** 4:15 pm
29	**1:53 am**	☌♄	♓ 29	**7:15 pm** 4:15 pm

☽ Phases & Eclipses phase	day	ET / hr:mn / PT
2nd Quarter	10/31	11:37 pm
2nd Quarter	1	**2:37 am**
Full Moon	8	**6:02 am** 3:02 am
●	8	16° ♉ 01'
4th Quarter	16	**8:27 am** 5:27 am
New Moon	23	**5:57 pm** 2:57 pm
2nd Quarter	30	**9:37 am** 6:37 am

Planet Ingress	day	ET / hr:mn / PT
♀ ♐	15	10:09 pm
♀ ♐	16	**1:09 am**
☿ ♐	17	**3:42 am** 12:42 am
⚶ ♓	20	**4:25 pm** 1:25 pm
☉ ♐	22	**3:20 am** 12:20 am

Planetary Motion	day	ET / hr:mn / PT
♃ D	23	**6:02 pm** 3:02 pm
♀ R	30	**3:33 am** 12:33 am

1 TUESDAY
☽□☉ **2:37 am**
☽□♀ **7:05 am** 4:05 am
☽□♅ **4:54 pm** 1:54 pm
☽☌♄ **7:22 pm** 4:22 pm
☽⚺♆ 11:38 pm

2 WEDNESDAY
☽⚺♆ **2:38 am**
☽△♂ **7:08 am** 4:08 am
☽⚺♇ **8:21 am** 5:21 am
☽⚺♃ **2:01 pm** 11:01 am

3 THURSDAY
☽△☿ **3:43 am** 12:43 am
☽△☉ **10:01 am** 7:01 am
☽△♀ **3:43 pm** 12:43 pm
☽⚹♅ **8:28 pm** 5:28 pm
☽⚺♄ **11:14 pm** 8:14 pm

4 FRIDAY
☽☌♆ **6:34 am** 3:34 am
☽□♂ **11:02 am** 8:02 am
☽⚹♇ **12:34 pm** 9:34 am
☽☌♃ **6:05 pm** 3:05 pm

5 SATURDAY
☽⚻☿ **3:49 pm** 12:49 pm
♀☍♅ **6:22 pm** 3:22 pm
☽⚻☉ **7:15 pm** 4:15 pm
☽⚺♅ 10:37 pm
☽⚻♀ 11:23 pm

6 SUNDAY
☽⚺♅ **1:37 am**
☽⚻♀ **1:23 am**
☽⚹♄ **3:44 am** 1:44 am
☽⚺♆ **11:10 am** 8:10 am
☽⚹♂ **3:30 pm** 12:30 pm
☽□♇ **5:30 pm** 2:30 pm
☽⚺♃ **10:56 pm** 7:56 pm
♀□♄ 11:34 pm

7 MONDAY
♀□♄ **2:34 am**

8 TUESDAY
☽☍☿ **5:44 am** 2:44 am
☽☍☉ **6:02 am** 3:02 am
☽☌♅ **7:47 am** 4:47 am
☽□♄ **11:20 am** 8:20 am
☉☌☿ **11:42 am** 8:42 am
☽☍♀ **2:51 pm** 11:51 am
☽⚹♆ **6:54 pm** 3:54 pm
☿☍♅ **9:40 pm** 6:40 pm
☽⚺♂ **10:57 pm** 7:57 pm
☽△♇ 10:38 pm

9 WEDNESDAY
☽△♇ **1:38 am**
☉☍♅ **3:26 am** 12:26 am
☽⚹♃ **7:00 am** 4:00 am
☿□♄ 11:52 pm

10 THURSDAY
☿□♄ **2:52 am**
♀△♆ **7:22 am** 4:22 am
☽⚺♅ **5:20 pm** 2:20 pm
☽⚻☉ **8:52 pm** 5:52 pm
☽△♄ **9:22 pm** 6:22 pm
☽⚻☿ 9:06 pm

11 FRIDAY
☽⚻☿ **12:06 am**
☉□♄ **3:04 am** 12:04 am
☽□♆ **5:03 am** 2:03 am
☽⚻♀ **7:34 am** 4:34 am
☽☌♂ **8:34 am** 5:34 am
☽⚻♇ **12:12 pm** 9:12 am
♀⚻♂ **4:07 pm** 1:07 pm
☽□♃ **5:28 pm** 2:28 pm

12 SATURDAY
☿△♆ **1:36 pm** 10:36 am

13 SUNDAY
♀⚹♇ **4:41 am** 1:41 am
☽⚹♅ **4:59 am** 1:59 am
☽⚻♄ **9:30 am** 6:30 am
☿⚻♂ **10:47 am** 7:47 am
☽△☉ **2:22 pm** 11:22 am
☽△♆ **5:08 pm** 2:08 pm
☽⚺♂ **7:50 pm** 4:50 pm
☽△☿ **9:25 pm** 6:25 pm
☽☍♇ 9:35 pm
☽△♀ 11:54 pm

14 MONDAY
☽☍♇ **12:35 am**
☽△♀ **2:54 am**
☽△♃ **5:41 am** 2:41 am
☿⚹♇ **9:27 pm** 6:27 pm
☉△♆ **10:43 pm** 7:43 pm

15 TUESDAY
♀△♃ **4:36 am** 1:36 am
☽□♅ **5:23 pm** 2:23 pm
☉⚻♂ **8:07 pm** 5:07 pm
☽☍♄ **10:17 pm** 7:17 pm

16 WEDNESDAY
☽⚻♆ **5:36 am** 2:36 am
☽⚹♂ **7:12 am** 4:12 am
☽□☉ **8:27 am** 5:27 am
☿△♃ **10:43 am** 7:43 am
☽⚻♇ **1:04 pm** 10:04 am
☽⚻♃ **5:51 pm** 2:51 pm
☽□☿ **6:55 pm** 3:55 pm
☽□♀ **10:14 pm** 7:14 pm

18 FRIDAY
☽△♅ **4:23 am** 1:23 am
☽⚻♄ **9:28 am** 6:28 am
☽☍♆ **4:12 pm** 1:12 pm
☽□♂ **4:35 pm** 1:35 pm
☉⚹♇ **4:38 pm** 1:38 pm
☽△♇ **11:26 pm** 8:26 pm
☽⚹☉ 9:00 pm

19 SATURDAY
☽⚹☉ **12:00 am**
☽☍♃ **3:47 am** 12:47 am

♂□♆ **10:43 am** 7:43 am
☽⚹☿ **12:54 pm** 9:54 am
☽⚹♀ **2:15 pm** 11:15 am

20 SUNDAY
☽⚻♅ **12:11 pm** 9:11 am
☽△♄ **5:18 pm** 2:18 pm
☽△♂ **10:37 pm** 7:37 pm
☉△♃ **11:07 pm** 8:07 pm
☽⚻♆ **11:22 pm** 8:22 pm

21 MONDAY
☽□♇ **6:14 am** 3:14 am
☽⚻♃ **10:10 am** 7:10 am
☽⚺☉ **11:04 am** 8:04 am
☿☌♀ **5:55 pm** 2:55 pm
☽⚺♀ 10:21 pm
☽⚺☿ 10:32 pm

22 TUESDAY
☽⚺♀ **1:21 am**
☽⚺☿ **1:32 am**
☽☍♅ **4:24 pm** 1:24 pm
☽□♄ **9:33 pm** 6:33 pm
☽⚻♂ 10:16 pm

23 WEDNESDAY
☽⚻♂ **1:16 am**
☽△♆ **3:03 am** 12:03 am
☽⚹♇ **9:38 am** 6:38 am
☽△♃ **1:16 pm** 10:16 am
☽☌☉ **5:57 pm** 2:57 pm

24 THURSDAY
☽☌♀ **8:26 am** 5:26 am
☽☌☿ **9:49 am** 6:49 am
☽⚻♅ **6:00 pm** 3:00 pm

☽⚹♄ **11:16 pm** 8:16 pm
☽☍♂ 10:36 pm

25 FRIDAY
☽☍♂ **1:36 am**
☽□♆ **4:24 am** 1:24 am
☽⚺♇ **10:53 am** 7:53 am
☽□♃ **2:22 pm** 11:22 am
☽⚺☉ **10:32 pm** 7:32 pm

26 SATURDAY
☽⚺♀ **1:43 pm** 10:43 am
☽⚺☿ **4:14 pm** 1:14 pm
☽△♅ **6:35 pm** 3:35 pm
☽⚺♄ 9:09 pm
☽⚻♂ 10:11 pm

27 SUNDAY
☽⚺♄ **12:09 am**
☽⚻♂ **1:11 am**
☽⚹♆ **5:06 am** 2:06 am
☽☌♇ **11:43 am** 8:43 am
☿⚻♅ **2:16 pm** 11:16 am
☽⚹♃ **3:11 pm** 12:11 pm

28 MONDAY
☽⚹☉ **3:06 am** 12:06 am
♂△♄ **12:56 pm** 9:56 am
☽⚹♀ **7:40 pm** 4:40 pm
☽□♅ **7:48 pm** 4:48 pm

♀⚻♅ **9:19 pm** 6:19 pm
☽⚹☿ **11:26 pm** 8:26 pm
☽△♂ 10:31 pm
☽☌♄ 10:53 pm

29 TUESDAY
☽△♂ **1:31 am**
☽☌♄ **1:53 am**
☽⚺♆ **6:47 am** 3:47 am
☽⚺♇ **1:44 pm** 10:44 am
☿☍♂ **3:30 pm** 12:30 pm
☽⚺♃ **5:19 pm** 2:19 pm
☿⚹♄ **11:18 pm** 8:18 pm

30 WEDNESDAY
☽□☉ **9:37 am** 6:37 am
☽⚹♅ **10:58 pm** 7:58 pm
♀☍♂ 9:28 pm

Eastern time in bold type
Pacific time in medium type

NOVEMBER 2022

DATE	SID.TIME	SUN	MOON	NODE	MERCURY	VENUS	MARS	JUPITER	SATURN	URANUS	NEPTUNE	PLUTO	CERES	PALLAS	JUNO	VESTA	CHIRON
1 T	2 41 3	8♏32 32	4♒54	13♉24℞	3♏40	10♏52	25♊36℞	29♓42℞	18♒39	17♉15℞	22♓57℞	26♑15	13♍34	22♋06	8♓00	25♒26	13♈05℞
2 W	2 45 0	9 32 33	19 02	13 24	5 19	12 07	25 34	29 37	18 40	17 13	22 56	26 15	13 57	22 22	8 04	25 37	13 03
3 Th	2 48 56	10 32 36	3♓02	13 24	6 58	13 23	25 32	29 33	18 41	17 10	22 55	26 16	14 21	22 38	8 09	25 48	13 01
4 F	2 52 53	11 32 40	16 52	13 24	8 37	14 38	25 28	29 29	18 43	17 08	22 54	26 17	14 44	22 54	8 15	25 59	12 58
5 Sa	2 56 49	12 32 45	0♈30	13 24D	10 15	15 53	25 24	29 25	18 44	17 05	22 53	26 18	15 08	23 09	8 21	26 11	12 56
6 Su	3 0 46	13 32 53	13 56	13 24	11 53	17 08	25 19	29 21	18 45	17 03	22 52	26 19	15 31	23 24	8 27	26 24	12 54
7 M	3 4 42	14 33 02	27 09	13 24	13 31	18 23	25 13	29 18	18 47	17 00	22 51	26 19	15 54	23 38	8 34	26 36	12 52
8 T	3 8 39	15 33 13	10♉07	13 24℞	15 08	19 39	25 06	29 14	18 48	16 58	22 50	26 20	16 17	23 52	8 41	26 49	12 49
9 W	3 12 36	16 33 25	22 52	13 24	16 44	20 54	24 58	29 11	18 50	16 55	22 49	26 21	16 40	24 05	8 49	27 02	12 47
10 Th	3 16 32	17 33 39	5♊23	13 24	18 21	22 09	24 49	29 08	18 52	16 53	22 48	26 22	17 03	24 18	8 58	27 16	12 45
11 F	3 20 29	18 33 56	17 42	13 23	19 57	23 24	24 40	29 05	18 54	16 51	22 48	26 23	17 26	24 30	9 06	27 29	12 43
12 Sa	3 24 25	19 34 14	29 49	13 22	21 32	24 40	24 29	29 03	18 56	16 48	22 47	26 24	17 48	24 42	9 16	27 43	12 41
13 Su	3 28 22	20 34 34	11♋47	13 21	23 08	25 55	24 18	29 00	18 58	16 46	22 46	26 25	18 11	24 53	9 25	27 58	12 39
14 M	3 32 18	21 34 56	23 41	13 20	24 43	27 10	24 06	28 58	19 00	16 43	22 45	26 26	18 33	25 04	9 35	28 12	12 37
15 T	3 36 15	22 35 19	5♌32	13 19	26 17	28 25	23 53	28 56	19 02	16 41	22 45	26 27	18 56	25 14	9 46	28 27	12 35
16 W	3 40 12	23 35 45	17 26	13 19D	27 52	29 41	23 39	28 55	19 04	16 38	22 44	26 28	19 18	25 24	9 57	28 42	12 33
17 Th	3 44 8	24 36 12	29 28	13 19	29 26	0♐56	23 25	28 53	19 07	16 36	22 44	26 29	19 40	25 33	10 08	28 58	12 31
18 F	3 48 5	25 36 41	11♍41	13 19	1♐00	2 11	23 09	28 52	19 09	16 33	22 43	26 30	20 02	25 41	10 20	29 13	12 29
19 Sa	3 52 1	26 37 12	24 11	13 20	2 34	3 27	22 53	28 50	19 12	16 31	22 43	26 31	20 24	25 49	10 32	29 29	12 28
20 Su	3 55 58	27 37 45	7♎01	13 22	4 07	4 42	22 36	28 50	19 15	16 28	22 42	26 33	20 45	25 56	10 45	29 45	12 26
21 M	3 59 54	28 38 20	20 14	13 23	5 40	5 57	22 19	28 49	19 18	16 26	22 42	26 34	21 07	26 03	10 58	0♓02	12 24
22 T	4 3 51	29 38 56	3♏52	13 24℞	7 13	7 12	22 01	28 48	19 21	16 24	22 41	26 35	21 28	26 09	11 11	0 18	12 23
23 W	4 7 47	0♐39 34	17 53	13 24	8 46	8 28	21 42	28 48D	19 24	16 21	22 41	26 36	21 49	26 14	11 25	0 35	12 21
24 Th	4 11 44	1 40 13	2♐16	13 23	10 19	9 43	21 22	28 48	19 27	16 19	22 40	26 37	22 10	26 19	11 39	0 52	12 19
25 F	4 15 40	2 40 54	16 53	13 21	11 51	10 58	21 02	28 48	19 30	16 16	22 40	26 39	22 31	26 23	11 54	1 10	12 18
26 Sa	4 19 37	3 41 36	1♑40	13 19	13 24	12 14	20 42	28 48	19 33	16 14	22 40	26 40	22 52	26 26	12 09	1 27	12 16
27 Su	4 23 34	4 42 20	16 27	13 16	14 56	13 29	20 21	28 49	19 37	16 12	22 40	26 41	23 13	26 29	12 24	1 45	12 15
28 M	4 27 30	5 43 04	1♒09	13 13	16 28	14 44	19 59	28 50	19 40	16 09	22 39	26 43	23 33	26 31	12 40	2 03	12 14
29 T	4 31 27	6 43 50	15 38	13 11	18 00	16 00	19 37	28 51	19 44	16 07	22 39	26 44	23 53	26 32	12 56	2 22	12 12
30 W	4 35 23	7 44 36	29 51	13 09D	19 32	17 15	19 15	28 52	19 47	16 05	22 39	26 46	24 14	26 33℞	13 12	2 40	12 11

EPHEMERIS CALCULATED FOR 12 MIDNIGHT GREENWICH MEAN TIME. ALL OTHER DATA AND FACING ASPECTARIAN PAGE IN **EASTERN TIME (BOLD)** AND PACIFIC TIME (REGULAR).

DECEMBER 2022

☽ Last Aspect day	ET / hr:mn / PT	asp	☽ Ingress sign	day	ET / hr:mn / PT
1	**9:44 pm** 6:44 pm	☌ ♃	♈	1	**11:41 pm** 8:41 pm
3	9:46 pm	□ ♇	♉	4	**6:38 am** 3:38 am
4	**12:46 am**	□ ♇	♉	4	**6:38 am** 3:38 am
6	**2:02 pm** 11:02 am	⚹ ♃	♊	6	**3:49 pm** 12:49 pm
8	10:13 pm	□ ♃	♋	8	11:49 pm
9	**1:13 am**	□ ♃	♋	9	**2:49 am**
11	**1:49 pm** 10:49 am	△ ♃	♌	11	**3:09 pm** 12:09 pm
13	**10:52 am** 7:52 am	△ ☉	♍	14	**3:45 am** 12:45 am
16	**2:13 pm** 11:13 am	☍ ♃	♎	16	**2:49 pm** 11:49 am
18	**5:35 pm** 2:35 pm	□ ♇	♏	18	**10:31 pm** 7:31 pm
20	**9:45 pm** 6:45 pm	⚹ ♇	♐	20	11:12 pm

☽ Last Aspect day	ET / hr:mn / PT	asp	☽ Ingress sign	day	ET / hr:mn / PT
20	**9:45 pm** 6:45 pm	⚹ ♇	♐	21	**2:12 am**
22	**3:16 pm** 12:16 pm	□ ♆	♑	22	11:49 pm
22	**3:16 pm** 12:16 pm	□ ♆	♑	23	**2:49 am**
24	**10:11 pm** 7:11 pm	☌ ♇	♒	24	11:14 pm
24	**10:11 pm** 7:11 pm	☌ ♇	♒	25	**2:14 am**
26	**1:19 pm** 10:19 am	☌ ♄	♓	26	11:34 pm
26	**1:19 pm** 10:19 am	☌ ♄	♓	27	**2:34 am**
28	10:21 pm	⚹ ♇	♈	29	**5:36 am** 2:36 am
29	**1:21 am**	⚹ ♇	♈	29	**5:36 am** 2:36 am
31	**7:44 am** 4:44 am	□ ♇	♉	31	**12:08 pm** 9:08 am

☽ Phases & Eclipses phase	day	ET / hr:mn / PT
Full Moon	7	**11:08 pm** 8:08 pm
4th Quarter	16	**3:56 am** 12:56 am
New Moon	23	**5:17 am** 2:17 am
2nd Quarter	29	**8:21 pm** 5:21 pm

Planet Ingress		day	ET / hr:mn / PT
☿	♑	6	**5:08 pm** 2:08 pm
♀	♑	9	**10:54 pm** 7:54 pm
⚳	♎	18	**6:34 pm** 3:34 pm
♃	♈	20	**9:32 am** 6:32 am
☉	♑	21	**4:48 pm** 1:48 pm

Planetary Motion		day	ET / hr:mn / PT
♆	D	3	**7:15 pm** 4:15 pm
⚷	D	23	**4:31 am** 1:31 am
☿	℞	29	**4:32 am** 1:32 am

1 THURSDAY
♀ ☍ ♂ **12:28 am**
☽ □ ♂ **3:42 am** 12:42 am
☽ □ ♀ **4:08 am** 1:08 am
☽ ⚺ ♄ **5:43 am** 2:43 am
☽ □ ☿ **9:23 am** 6:23 am
☽ ☌ ♆ **10:36 am** 7:36 am
☽ ⚹ ♇ **5:59 pm** 2:59 pm
☿ □ ♆ **8:08 pm** 5:08 pm
☽ ☌ ♃ **9:44 pm** 6:44 pm
♀ ⚹ ♄ **10:09 pm** 7:09 pm

2 FRIDAY
☽ △ ☉ **7:10 pm** 4:10 pm

3 SATURDAY
☽ ⚺ ♅ **4:36 am** 1:36 am
☽ ⚹ ♂ **8:11 am** 5:11 am
☽ ⚹ ♄ **12:06 pm** 9:06 am
☽ △ ♀ **3:57 pm** 12:57 pm
☽ ⚺ ♆ **4:56 pm** 1:56 pm
☽ △ ☿ **10:53 pm** 7:53 pm
☽ □ ♇ 9:46 pm
♀ □ ♆ 11:12 pm

4 SUNDAY
☽ □ ♇ **12:46 am**
♀ □ ♆ **2:12 am**
☽ ⚺ ♃ **4:44 am** 1:44 am
☿ ⚺ ♇ **3:11 pm** 12:11 pm

5 MONDAY
☽ ⚻ ☉ **7:50 am** 4:50 am
☽ ☌ ♅ **12:38 pm** 9:38 am
☽ ⚺ ♂ **2:50 pm** 11:50 am
☽ □ ♄ **8:54 pm** 5:54 pm
☽ ⚹ ♆ 10:37 pm
☿ □ ♃ 11:05 pm

6 TUESDAY
☽ ⚹ ♆ **1:37 am**
☿ □ ♃ **2:05 am**
☽ ⚻ ♀ **6:55 am** 3:55 am
☽ △ ♇ **9:51 am** 6:51 am
☽ ⚹ ♃ **2:02 pm** 11:02 am
☽ ⚻ ☿ **3:38 pm** 12:38 pm

7 WEDNESDAY
♀ ⚺ ♇ **12:33 pm** 9:33 am
☉ ⚻ ♅ **5:35 pm** 2:35 pm
☽ ⚺ ♅ **10:40 pm** 7:40 pm
☽ ☍ ☉ **11:08 pm** 8:08 pm
☽ ☌ ♂ **11:19 pm** 8:19 pm
☉ ☍ ♂ 9:42 pm

8 THURSDAY
☉ ☍ ♂ **12:42 am**
☽ △ ♄ **7:41 am** 4:41 am
☽ □ ♆ **12:13 pm** 9:13 am
☽ ⚻ ♇ **8:49 pm** 5:49 pm
♂ ⚺ ♅ **10:05 pm** 7:05 pm
☽ ☍ ♀ 9:29 pm
☽ □ ♃ 10:13 pm

9 FRIDAY
☽ ☍ ♀ **12:29 am**
☽ □ ♃ **1:13 am**
♀ □ ♃ **7:55 am** 4:55 am
☽ ☍ ☿ **10:55 am** 7:55 am

10 SATURDAY
☽ ⚺ ♂ **9:16 am** 6:16 am
☽ ⚹ ♅ **10:17 am** 7:17 am
☽ ⚻ ☉ **4:30 pm** 1:30 pm
☽ ⚻ ♄ **8:03 pm** 5:03 pm
☽ △ ♆ 9:18 pm

11 SUNDAY
☽ △ ♆ **12:18 am**
☽ ☍ ♇ **9:11 am** 6:11 am
☽ △ ♃ **1:49 pm** 10:49 am
☽ ⚻ ♀ **7:54 pm** 4:54 pm

12 MONDAY
☽ ⚻ ☿ **7:47 am** 4:47 am
☉ ⚹ ♄ **1:12 pm** 10:12 am
☽ ⚹ ♂ **8:04 pm** 5:04 pm
☽ □ ♅ **10:47 pm** 7:47 pm

13 TUESDAY
☽ ☍ ♄ **9:09 am** 6:09 am
☽ △ ☉ **10:52 am** 7:52 am
☽ ⚻ ♆ **1:01 pm** 10:01 am
☽ ⚻ ♇ **9:59 pm** 6:59 pm
☽ ⚻ ♃ 11:46 pm

14 WEDNESDAY
☽ ⚻ ♃ **2:46 am**
☉ □ ♆ **12:10 pm** 9:10 am
☽ △ ♀ **3:32 pm** 12:32 pm

15 THURSDAY
☽ △ ☿ **4:02 am** 1:02 am
☽ □ ♂ **6:29 am** 3:29 am
☽ △ ♅ **10:41 am** 7:41 am
☽ ⚻ ♄ **9:18 pm** 6:18 pm
☿ ⚻ ♂ **10:12 pm** 7:12 pm
☽ ☍ ♆ 9:41 pm

16 FRIDAY
☽ ☍ ♆ **12:41 am**
☽ □ ☉ **3:56 am** 12:56 am
☽ △ ♇ **9:25 am** 6:25 am
☽ ☍ ♃ **2:13 pm** 11:13 am

17 SATURDAY
☽ □ ♀ **8:28 am** 5:28 am
☽ △ ♂ **2:44 pm** 11:44 am
☿ △ ♅ **4:37 pm** 1:37 pm
☽ ⚻ ♅ **8:03 pm** 5:03 pm
☽ □ ☿ **8:26 pm** 5:26 pm

18 SUNDAY
☽ △ ♄ **6:31 am** 3:31 am
☽ ⚻ ♆ **9:20 am** 6:20 am
☽ ⚹ ☉ **5:03 pm** 2:03 pm
☽ □ ♇ **5:35 pm** 2:35 pm
☽ ⚻ ♃ **10:17 pm** 7:17 pm
☉ ⚺ ♇ 9:26 pm

19 MONDAY
☉ ⚺ ♇ **12:26 am**
♀ ⚻ ♂ **12:37 pm** 9:37 am
☽ ⚻ ♂ **7:30 pm** 4:30 pm
☽ ⚹ ♀ **8:22 pm** 5:22 pm
☽ ☍ ♅ 10:33 pm

20 TUESDAY
☽ ☍ ♅ **1:33 am**
☽ ⚹ ☿ **6:58 am** 3:58 am
☽ □ ♄ **11:41 am** 8:41 am
☽ △ ♆ **2:01 pm** 11:01 am
☽ ⚹ ♇ **9:45 pm** 6:45 pm
☽ ⚺ ☉ 10:06 pm
☽ △ ♃ 11:19 pm

21 WEDNESDAY
☽ ⚺ ☉ **1:06 am**
☽ △ ♃ **2:19 am**
☉ □ ♃ **7:50 pm** 4:50 pm
☽ ☍ ♂ **8:48 pm** 5:48 pm

22 THURSDAY
☽ ⚺ ♀ **3:15 am** 12:15 am
☽ ⚻ ♅ **3:23 am** 12:23 am
♀ △ ♅ **4:48 am** 1:48 am
☽ ⚺ ☿ **12:15 pm** 9:15 am
☽ ⚹ ♄ **1:19 pm** 10:19 am
☽ □ ♆ **3:16 pm** 12:16 pm
☽ ⚺ ♇ **10:40 pm** 7:40 pm

23 FRIDAY
☽ □ ♃ **3:13 am** 12:13 am
☽ ☌ ☉ **5:17 am** 2:17 am
☿ ⚺ ♄ **8:08 am** 5:08 am
☽ ⚻ ♂ **7:51 pm** 4:51 pm

24 SATURDAY
☽ △ ♅ **3:02 am** 12:02 am
☽ ☌ ♀ **7:16 am** 4:16 am
☽ ⚺ ♄ **1:09 pm** 10:09 am
☽ ☌ ☿ **2:32 pm** 11:32 am
☽ ⚹ ♆ **2:48 pm** 11:48 am
☿ ⚹ ♆ **8:17 pm** 5:17 pm
☽ ☌ ♇ **10:11 pm** 7:11 pm
☽ ⚹ ♃ 11:56 pm

25 SUNDAY
☽ ⚹ ♃ **2:56 am**
☽ ⚺ ☉ **8:07 am** 5:07 am
☽ △ ♂ **6:34 pm** 3:34 pm
☽ □ ♅ 11:35 pm

26 MONDAY
☽ □ ♅ **2:35 am**
☽ ⚺ ♀ **11:24 am** 8:24 am
☽ ☌ ♄ **1:19 pm** 10:19 am
☽ ⚺ ♆ **2:46 pm** 11:46 am
☽ ⚺ ☿ **4:24 pm** 1:24 pm
☽ ⚺ ♇ **10:28 pm** 7:28 pm

27 TUESDAY
☽ ⚺ ♃ **3:39 am** 12:39 am
♀ ⚺ ♄ **11:53 am** 8:53 am
☽ ⚹ ☉ **12:23 pm** 9:23 am
☽ □ ♂ **6:54 pm** 3:54 pm

28 WEDNESDAY
♀ ⚹ ♆ **3:32 am** 12:32 am
☽ ⚹ ♅ **4:02 am** 1:02 am
☽ ⚺ ♄ **3:51 pm** 12:51 pm
☽ ☌ ♆ **5:05 pm** 2:05 pm
☽ ⚹ ♀ **6:25 pm** 3:25 pm
☽ ⚹ ☿ **7:43 pm** 4:43 pm
☽ ⚹ ♇ 10:21 pm

29 THURSDAY
☽ ⚹ ♇ **1:21 am**
☽ ☌ ♃ **7:11 am** 4:11 am
☿ ☌ ♀ **8:58 am** 5:58 am
☽ □ ☉ **8:21 pm** 5:21 pm
☽ ⚹ ♂ **10:17 pm** 7:17 pm

30 FRIDAY
☽ ⚺ ♅ **8:45 am** 5:45 am
☉ ⚻ ♂ **6:21 pm** 3:21 pm
☽ ⚹ ♄ **9:52 pm** 6:52 pm
☽ ⚺ ♆ **10:51 pm** 7:51 pm
☽ □ ☿ 10:00 pm

31 SATURDAY
☽ □ ☿ **1:00 am**
☽ □ ♀ **5:59 am** 2:59 am
☽ □ ♇ **7:44 am** 4:44 am
☽ ⚺ ♃ **2:20 pm** 11:20 am
♀ ☌ ♇ 9:25 pm

Eastern time in bold type
Pacific time in medium type

DECEMBER 2022

DATE	SID.TIME	SUN	MOON	NODE	MERCURY	VENUS	MARS	JUPITER	SATURN	URANUS	NEPTUNE	PLUTO	CERES	PALLAS	JUNO	VESTA	CHIRON
1 Th	4 39 20	8♐45 24	13♓46	13♉09	21♐03	18♐30	18♊53℞	28♓53	19♒51	16♉03℞	22♓39℞	26♑47	24♍34	26♋33℞	13♓29	2♓59	12♈10℞
2 F	4 43 16	9 46 12	27 23	13 10	22 34	19 46	18 30	28 55	19 55	16 00	22 39	26 48	24 53	26 32	13 46	3 18	12 09
3 Sa	4 47 13	10 47 01	10♈42	13 12	24 06	21 01	18 07	28 56	19 59	15 58	22 39	26 50	25 13	26 30	14 03	3 37	12 08
4 Su	4 51 10	11 47 51	23 45	13 13	25 36	22 16	17 44	28 58	20 03	15 56	22 39D	26 51	25 32	26 28	14 21	3 56	12 06
5 M	4 55 6	12 48 41	6♉35	13 15℞	27 07	23 31	17 21	29 01	20 07	15 54	22 39	26 53	25 52	26 25	14 39	4 16	12 05
6 T	4 59 3	13 49 33	19 12	13 15	28 37	24 47	16 58	29 03	20 11	15 52	22 39	26 54	26 11	26 22	14 57	4 35	12 04
7 W	5 2 59	14 50 26	1♊39	13 13	0♑07	26 02	16 34	29 06	20 15	15 50	22 39	26 56	26 30	26 17	15 16	4 55	12 04
8 Th	5 6 56	15 51 20	13 56	13 10	1 36	27 17	16 11	29 08	20 20	15 48	22 39	26 57	26 48	26 12	15 35	5 15	12 03
9 F	5 10 52	16 52 15	26 04	13 05	3 05	28 32	15 48	29 11	20 24	15 46	22 39	26 59	27 07	26 06	15 55	5 35	12 02
10 Sa	5 14 49	17 53 10	8♋06	12 59	4 33	29 48	15 25	29 14	20 29	15 44	22 39	27 01	27 25	25 59	16 14	5 56	12 01
11 Su	5 18 45	18 54 07	20 02	12 52	6 01	1♑03	15 03	29 18	20 33	15 42	22 40	27 02	27 43	25 52	16 34	6 16	12 00
12 M	5 22 42	19 55 05	1♌54	12 45	7 27	2 18	14 40	29 21	20 38	15 40	22 40	27 04	28 01	25 44	16 54	6 37	12 00
13 T	5 26 39	20 56 04	13 45	12 38	8 53	3 34	14 18	29 25	20 42	15 38	22 40	27 05	28 19	25 35	17 15	6 58	11 59
14 W	5 30 35	21 57 03	25 39	12 33	10 17	4 49	13 57	29 29	20 47	15 36	22 40	27 07	28 36	25 26	17 36	7 19	11 59
15 Th	5 34 32	22 58 04	7♍38	12 30	11 40	6 04	13 35	29 33	20 52	15 34	22 41	27 09	28 54	25 15	17 57	7 40	11 58
16 F	5 38 28	23 59 06	19 47	12 29D	13 01	7 19	13 14	29 38	20 57	15 32	22 41	27 11	29 11	25 04	18 18	8 01	11 58
17 Sa	5 42 25	25 00 09	2♎11	12 29	14 20	8 35	12 54	29 42	21 02	15 30	22 42	27 12	29 27	24 53	18 40	8 23	11 57
18 Su	5 46 21	26 01 12	14 55	12 30	15 36	9 50	12 34	29 47	21 07	15 29	22 42	27 14	29 44	24 41	19 02	8 44	11 57
19 M	5 50 18	27 02 17	28 03	12 31	16 50	11 05	12 14	29 52	21 12	15 27	22 43	27 16	0♎00	24 28	19 24	9 06	11 57
20 T	5 54 14	28 03 22	11♏38	12 32℞	18 01	12 20	11 55	29 57	21 18	15 25	22 43	27 17	0 16	24 14	19 46	9 28	11 56
21 W	5 58 11	29 04 29	25 41	12 31	19 08	13 36	11 37	0♈02	21 23	15 24	22 44	27 19	0 32	24 00	20 09	9 50	11 56
22 Th	6 2 8	0♑05 36	10♐12	12 28	20 10	14 51	11 20	0 08	21 28	15 22	22 44	27 21	0 48	23 45	20 32	10 12	11 56
23 F	6 6 4	1 06 44	25 05	12 23	21 08	16 06	11 03	0 13	21 34	15 21	22 45	27 23	1 03	23 30	20 55	10 35	11 56D
24 Sa	6 10 1	2 07 52	10♑13	12 16	21 59	17 21	10 46	0 19	21 39	15 19	22 46	27 25	1 18	23 14	21 18	10 57	11 56
25 Su	6 13 57	3 09 01	25 26	12 08	22 44	18 37	10 31	0 25	21 45	15 18	22 46	27 26	1 33	22 57	21 42	11 20	11 56
26 M	6 17 54	4 10 09	10♒32	12 00	23 22	19 52	10 16	0 31	21 50	15 16	22 47	27 28	1 48	22 40	22 06	11 42	11 56
27 T	6 21 50	5 11 18	25 24	11 53	23 51	21 07	10 02	0 37	21 56	15 15	22 48	27 30	2 02	22 23	22 30	12 05	11 56
28 W	6 25 47	6 12 27	9♓52	11 48	24 11	22 22	9 49	0 44	22 02	15 14	22 49	27 32	2 16	22 05	22 54	12 28	11 57
29 Th	6 29 44	7 13 36	23 56	11 45	24 21℞	23 37	9 36	0 51	22 07	15 12	22 50	27 34	2 30	21 46	23 19	12 51	11 57
30 F	6 33 40	8 14 45	7♈33	11 44D	24 19	24 53	9 25	0 57	22 13	15 11	22 50	27 36	2 43	21 28	23 44	13 14	11 57
31 Sa	6 37 37	9 15 54	20 46	11 44	24 07	26 08	9 14	1 04	22 19	15 10	22 51	27 38	2 56	21 09	24 09	13 38	11 58

EPHEMERIS CALCULATED FOR 12 MIDNIGHT GREENWICH MEAN TIME. ALL OTHER DATA AND FACING ASPECTARIAN PAGE IN **EASTERN TIME (BOLD)** AND PACIFIC TIME (REGULAR).

JANUARY 2023

☽ Last Aspect				☽ Ingress			
day	ET / hr:mn / PT		asp	sign	day	ET / hr:mn / PT	
2	**5:16 pm**	2:16 pm	△♇	♊	2	**9:44 pm**	6:44 pm
4	**7:08 pm**	4:08 pm	□♆	♋	5	**9:15 am**	6:15 am
7	**5:23 pm**	2:23 pm	☍♇	♌	7	**9:40 pm**	6:40 pm
9	**8:52 pm**	5:52 pm	☍♄	♍	10	**10:15 am**	7:15 am
12	**6:06 pm**	3:06 pm	△♇	♎	12	**9:56 pm**	6:56 pm
15	**3:40 am**	12:40 am	□♇	♏	15	**7:08 am**	4:08 am
17	**9:27 am**	6:27 am	⚹♇	♐	17	**12:33 pm**	9:33 am
19	**5:09 am**	2:09 am	⚹♄	♑	19	**2:11 pm**	11:11 am
21	**10:52 am**	7:52 am	☌♇	♒	21	**1:29 pm**	10:29 am
23	**5:19 am**	2:19 am	☌♀	♓	23	**12:36 pm**	9:36 am
25	**11:12 am**	8:12 am	⚹♇	♈	25	**1:48 pm**	10:48 am
27	**4:01 pm**	1:01 pm	□♇	♉	27	**6:42 pm**	3:42 pm
29		9:52 pm	△♇	♊	30	**3:35 am**	12:35 am
30	**12:52 am**		△♇	♊	30	**3:35 am**	12:35 am

☽ Phases & Eclipses			
phase	day	ET / hr:mn / PT	
Full Moon	6	**6:08 pm**	3:08 pm
4th Quarter	14	**9:10 pm**	6:10 pm
New Moon	21	**3:53 pm**	12:53 pm
2nd Quarter	28	**10:19 am**	7:19 am

Planet Ingress				
		day	ET / hr:mn / PT	
♀	♒	2	**9:09 pm**	6:09 pm
⚵	♈	12		10:30 pm
⚵	♈	13	**1:30 am**	
☉	♒	20	**3:30 am**	12:30 am
♀	♓	26	**9:33 pm**	6:33 pm

Planetary Motion				
		day	ET / hr:mn / PT	
♂	D	12	**3:56 pm**	12:56 pm
☿	D	18	**8:12 am**	5:12 am
♅	D	22	**5:59 pm**	2:59 pm

1 SUNDAY
♀ ☌ ♇ **12:25 am**
☽ ⚺ ♂ **5:09 am** 2:09 am
☽ △ ☉ **8:42 am** 5:42 am
☽ ☌ ♅ **4:52 pm** 1:52 pm
☿ ⚹ ♆ 10:44 pm

2 MONDAY
☿ ⚹ ♆ **1:44 am**
☽ □ ♄ **7:15 am** 4:15 am
☽ △ ☿ **7:30 am** 4:30 am
☽ ⚹ ♆ **7:53 am** 4:53 am
☿ ⚺ ♄ **10:59 am** 7:59 am
☽ △ ♇ **5:16 pm** 2:16 pm
☽ △ ♀ **9:48 pm** 6:48 pm
☽ ⚹ ♃ 9:37 pm

3 TUESDAY
☽ ⚹ ♃ **12:37 am**
☽ ☌ ♂ **2:47 pm** 11:47 am
☽ ⚻ ☉ 9:30 pm

4 WEDNESDAY
☽ ⚻ ☉ **12:30 am**
☽ ⚺ ♅ **3:30 am** 12:30 am
♀ ⚹ ♃ **4:08 am** 1:08 am
☽ ⚻ ☿ **2:10 pm** 11:10 am
☽ △ ♄ **6:54 pm** 3:54 pm
☽ □ ♆ **7:08 pm** 4:08 pm

5 THURSDAY
☽ ⚻ ♇ **4:50 am** 1:50 am
☉ △ ♅ **11:43 am** 8:43 am

☽ □ ♃ **12:50 pm** 9:50 am
☽ ⚻ ♀ **4:16 pm** 1:16 pm
☽ ⚺ ♂ 11:08 pm
♄ ⚺ ♆ 11:56 pm

6 FRIDAY
☽ ⚺ ♂ **2:08 am**
♄ ⚺ ♆ **2:56 am**
☽ ⚹ ♅ **3:30 pm** 12:30 pm
☽ ☍ ☉ **6:08 pm** 3:08 pm
☽ ☍ ☿ **8:36 pm** 5:36 pm

7 SATURDAY
☽ △ ♆ **7:30 am** 4:30 am
☽ ⚻ ♄ **7:42 am** 4:42 am
☉ ☌ ☿ **7:57 am** 4:57 am
☽ ☍ ♇ **5:23 pm** 2:23 pm
☽ △ ♃ 11:00 pm

8 SUNDAY
☽ △ ♃ **2:00 am**
☽ ☍ ♀ **11:52 am** 8:52 am
☽ ⚹ ♂ **2:19 pm** 11:19 am
☿ △ ♅ **6:23 pm** 3:23 pm

9 MONDAY
☽ ⚻ ☿ **3:05 am** 12:05 am
☽ □ ♅ **4:02 am** 1:02 am
♀ △ ♂ **10:22 am** 7:22 am
☽ ⚻ ☉ **12:26 pm** 9:26 am
☽ ⚻ ♆ **8:13 pm** 5:13 pm
☽ ☍ ♄ **8:52 pm** 5:52 pm

10 TUESDAY
☽ ⚻ ♇ **6:09 am** 3:09 am
☽ ⚻ ♃ **3:17 pm** 12:17 pm
☽ □ ♂ 11:36 pm

11 WEDNESDAY
☽ □ ♂ **2:36 am**
☽ ⚻ ♀ **7:25 am** 4:25 am
☽ △ ☿ **9:58 am** 6:58 am
☽ △ ♅ **4:17 pm** 1:17 pm
☿ ⚺ ♀ **10:02 pm** 7:02 pm

12 THURSDAY
☽ △ ☉ **6:08 am** 3:08 am
☽ ☍ ♆ **8:21 am** 5:21 am
☽ ⚻ ♄ **9:25 am** 6:25 am
☽ △ ♇ **6:06 pm** 3:06 pm

13 FRIDAY
☽ ☍ ♃ **3:34 am** 12:34 am
☉ ⚹ ♆ **9:11 am** 6:11 am
☽ △ ♂ **1:46 pm** 10:46 am
☽ □ ☿ **4:55 pm** 1:55 pm
☽ △ ♀ 9:58 pm
☉ ⚺ ♄ 10:47 pm
☽ ⚻ ♅ 11:54 pm

14 SATURDAY
☽ △ ♀ **12:58 am**
☉ ⚺ ♄ **1:47 am**
☽ ⚻ ♅ **2:54 am**
☽ ⚻ ♆ **6:22 pm** 3:22 pm
☽ △ ♄ **7:47 pm** 4:47 pm

♀ □ ♅ **8:22 pm** 5:22 pm
☽ □ ☉ **9:10 pm** 6:10 pm

15 SUNDAY
☽ □ ♇ **3:40 am** 12:40 am
☽ ⚻ ♃ **1:07 pm** 10:07 am
☽ ⚻ ♂ **10:08 pm** 7:08 pm
☽ ⚹ ☿ **10:47 pm** 7:47 pm

16 MONDAY
☽ ☍ ♅ **10:17 am** 7:17 am
☽ □ ♀ **2:09 pm** 11:09 am
☽ △ ♆ 9:48 pm
☿ ⚻ ♂ 10:42 pm
☽ □ ♄ 11:27 pm

17 TUESDAY
☽ △ ♆ **12:48 am**
☿ ⚻ ♂ **1:42 am**
☽ □ ♄ **2:27 am**
☽ ⚹ ☉ **7:36 am** 4:36 am
☽ ⚹ ♇ **9:27 am** 6:27 am
☽ △ ♃ **6:41 pm** 3:41 pm
☽ ⚺ ☿ 11:21 pm
☽ ☍ ♂ 11:39 pm

18 WEDNESDAY
☽ ⚺ ☿ **2:21 am**
☽ ☍ ♂ **2:39 am**
☉ ☌ ♇ **9:44 am** 6:44 am
☽ ⚻ ♅ **1:42 pm** 10:42 am
☽ ⚹ ♀ **10:05 pm** 7:05 pm

19 THURSDAY
☽ □ ♆ **3:17 am** 12:17 am
☽ ⚹ ♄ **5:09 am** 2:09 am
☽ ⚺ ♇ **11:24 am** 8:24 am
☽ ⚺ ☉ **1:13 pm** 10:13 am
☽ □ ♃ **8:29 pm** 5:29 pm

20 FRIDAY
☽ ☌ ☿ **3:30 am** 12:30 am
☽ ⚻ ♂ **3:42 am** 12:42 am
☽ △ ♅ **1:55 pm** 10:55 am
☿ ⚻ ♂ **8:06 pm** 5:06 pm
☽ ⚺ ♀ 11:10 pm

21 SATURDAY
☽ ⚺ ♀ **2:10 am**
☽ ⚹ ♆ **3:01 am** 12:01 am
☽ ⚺ ♄ **5:04 am** 2:04 am
☽ ☌ ♇ **10:52 am** 7:52 am
♀ ⚺ ♆ **12:43 pm** 9:43 am
☽ ☌ ☉ **3:53 pm** 12:53 pm
☽ ⚹ ♃ **8:09 pm** 5:09 pm

22 SUNDAY
☽ △ ♂ **3:02 am** 12:02 am
☽ ⚺ ☿ **3:36 am** 12:36 am
☽ □ ♅ **12:49 pm** 9:49 am
♀ ☌ ♄ **5:13 pm** 2:13 pm
☽ ⚺ ♆ 11:03 pm

23 MONDAY
☽ ⚺ ♆ **2:03 am**
☽ ☌ ♄ **4:25 am** 1:25 am
☽ ☌ ♀ **5:19 am** 2:19 am

☽ ⚺ ♇ **10:02 am** 7:02 am
☽ ⚺ ☉ **6:30 pm** 3:30 pm
☽ ⚺ ♃ **7:59 pm** 4:59 pm
☽ □ ♂ 11:56 pm

24 TUESDAY
☽ □ ♂ **2:56 am**
☽ ⚹ ☿ **4:59 am** 1:59 am
☽ ⚹ ♅ **12:43 pm** 9:43 am
☉ ⚹ ♃ **8:30 pm** 5:30 pm
☽ ☌ ♆ 11:42 pm

25 WEDNESDAY
☽ ☌ ♆ **2:42 am**
☽ ⚺ ♄ **5:30 am** 2:30 am
☽ ⚺ ♀ **10:45 am** 7:45 am
☽ ⚹ ♇ **11:12 am** 8:12 am
♀ ⚺ ♇ **3:59 pm** 12:59 pm
☽ ☌ ♃ **10:18 pm** 7:18 pm
☽ ⚹ ☉ **11:59 pm** 8:59 pm

26 THURSDAY
☽ ⚹ ♂ **5:40 am** 2:40 am
☽ □ ☿ **10:08 am** 7:08 am
☽ ⚺ ♅ **3:38 pm** 12:38 pm

27 FRIDAY
☽ ⚺ ♆ **6:50 am** 3:50 am
☽ ⚹ ♄ **10:13 am** 7:13 am
☽ □ ♇ **4:01 pm** 1:01 pm
☽ ⚹ ♀ **8:56 pm** 5:56 pm

28 SATURDAY
☽ ⚺ ♃ **4:39 am** 1:39 am
☽ □ ☉ **10:19 am** 7:19 am

☽ ⚺ ♂ **12:34 pm** 9:34 am
☽ △ ☿ **8:44 pm** 5:44 pm
☽ ☌ ♅ **10:37 pm** 7:37 pm

29 SUNDAY
☽ ⚹ ♆ **3:02 pm** 12:02 pm
☽ □ ♄ **7:03 pm** 4:03 pm
☉ △ ♂ **8:45 pm** 5:45 pm
☿ △ ♅ **9:16 pm** 6:16 pm
☽ △ ♇ 9:52 pm

30 MONDAY
☽ △ ♇ **12:52 am**
☽ □ ♀ **12:24 pm** 9:24 am
☽ ⚹ ♃ **3:01 pm** 12:01 pm
☽ ☌ ♂ **11:27 pm** 8:27 pm
☽ △ ☉ 10:24 pm

31 TUESDAY
☽ △ ☉ **1:24 am**
☽ ⚺ ♅ **9:06 am** 6:06 am
☽ ⚻ ☿ **12:27 pm** 9:27 am
♀ ⚺ ♃ **6:14 pm** 3:14 pm
☽ □ ♆ 11:21 pm

Eastern time in bold type
Pacific time in medium type

JANUARY 2023

DATE	SID.TIME	SUN	MOON	NODE	MERCURY	VENUS	MARS	JUPITER	SATURN	URANUS	NEPTUNE	PLUTO	CERES	PALLAS	JUNO	VESTA	CHIRON
1 Su	6 41 33	10♑17 02	3♉39	11♉45℞	23♑42℞	27♑23	9♊04℞	1♈12	22♒25	15♉09℞	22♓52	27♑39	3♎09	20♋49℞	24♓34	14♓01	11♈58
2 M	6 45 30	11 18 11	16 14	11 45	23 06	28 38	8 55	1 19	22 31	15 08	22 53	27 41	3 22	20 30	25 00	14 25	11 59
3 T	6 49 26	12 19 19	28 36	11 44	22 18	29 53	8 46	1 26	22 37	15 07	22 54	27 43	3 34	20 10	25 25	14 48	11 59
4 W	6 53 23	13 20 27	10♊48	11 39	21 20	1♒08	8 39	1 34	22 43	15 06	22 55	27 45	3 46	19 50	25 51	15 12	12 00
5 Th	6 57 19	14 21 35	22 53	11 33	20 13	2 23	8 32	1 42	22 49	15 05	22 56	27 47	3 58	19 30	26 17	15 36	12 00
6 F	7 1 16	15 22 43	4♋52	11 23	18 59	3 39	8 26	1 50	22 56	15 04	22 57	27 49	4 09	19 10	26 43	16 00	12 01
7 Sa	7 5 13	16 23 51	16 47	11 11	17 40	4 54	8 21	1 58	23 02	15 03	22 59	27 51	4 20	18 50	27 10	16 24	12 02
8 Su	7 9 9	17 24 59	28 41	10 58	16 20	6 09	8 17	2 06	23 08	15 02	23 00	27 53	4 31	18 29	27 37	16 48	12 03
9 M	7 13 6	18 26 06	10♌33	10 44	15 00	7 24	8 14	2 14	23 15	15 02	23 01	27 55	4 41	18 09	28 03	17 12	12 04
10 T	7 17 2	19 27 14	22 26	10 32	13 42	8 39	8 11	2 23	23 21	15 01	23 02	27 57	4 51	17 49	28 30	17 37	12 05
11 W	7 20 59	20 28 21	4♍21	10 21	12 31	9 54	8 09	2 32	23 28	15 00	23 03	27 59	5 01	17 29	28 58	18 01	12 06
12 Th	7 24 55	21 29 29	16 21	10 13	11 26	11 09	8 08D	2 40	23 34	15 00	23 05	28 01	5 10	17 09	29 25	18 26	12 07
13 F	7 28 52	22 30 36	28 30	10 08	10 30	12 24	8 08	2 49	23 41	14 59	23 06	28 03	5 19	16 49	29 53	18 50	12 08
14 Sa	7 32 48	23 31 43	10♎51	10 05	9 42	13 39	8 08	2 58	23 47	14 59	23 07	28 05	5 28	16 29	0♈20	19 15	12 09
15 Su	7 36 45	24 32 50	23 29	10 04D	9 05	14 54	8 09	3 08	23 54	14 58	23 09	28 07	5 36	16 10	0 48	19 40	12 10
16 M	7 40 42	25 33 57	6♏28	10 05℞	8 37	16 09	8 11	3 17	24 00	14 58	23 10	28 09	5 44	15 51	1 16	20 05	12 11
17 T	7 44 38	26 35 04	19 53	10 04	8 19	17 24	8 14	3 26	24 07	14 57	23 11	28 11	5 52	15 32	1 44	20 29	12 13
18 W	7 48 35	27 36 10	3♐47	10 02	8 09D	18 39	8 18	3 36	24 14	14 57	23 13	28 12	5 59	15 13	2 13	20 54	12 14
19 Th	7 52 31	28 37 17	18 10	9 58	8 09	19 54	8 22	3 46	24 21	14 57	23 14	28 14	6 06	14 55	2 41	21 20	12 15
20 F	7 56 28	29 38 23	3♑00	9 51	8 17	21 08	8 27	3 56	24 27	14 57	23 16	28 16	6 12	14 38	3 10	21 45	12 17
21 Sa	8 0 24	0♒39 29	18 11	9 41	8 32	22 23	8 32	4 06	24 34	14 57	23 17	28 18	6 18	14 20	3 39	22 10	12 18
22 Su	8 4 21	1 40 34	3♒32	9 30	8 54	23 38	8 39	4 16	24 41	14 56D	23 19	28 20	6 23	14 04	4 08	22 35	12 20
23 M	8 8 17	2 41 38	18 53	9 18	9 22	24 53	8 46	4 26	24 48	14 56	23 21	28 22	6 29	13 47	4 37	23 01	12 22
24 T	8 12 14	3 42 42	4♓00	9 07	9 56	26 08	8 53	4 36	24 55	14 56	23 22	28 24	6 33	13 32	5 06	23 26	12 23
25 W	8 16 11	4 43 44	18 46	8 59	10 35	27 23	9 02	4 47	25 02	14 57	23 24	28 26	6 38	13 16	5 36	23 52	12 25
26 Th	8 20 7	5 44 46	3♈03	8 53	11 19	28 37	9 10	4 57	25 09	14 57	23 25	28 28	6 42	13 02	6 05	24 17	12 27
27 F	8 24 4	6 45 46	16 51	8 51	12 07	29 52	9 20	5 08	25 16	14 57	23 27	28 30	6 45	12 48	6 35	24 43	12 28
28 Sa	8 28 0	7 46 46	0♉10	8 50	12 58	1♓07	9 30	5 19	25 23	14 57	23 29	28 32	6 48	12 34	7 05	25 08	12 30
29 Su	8 31 57	8 47 44	13 03	8 50	13 54	2 21	9 41	5 30	25 30	14 57	23 31	28 34	6 51	12 22	7 35	25 34	12 32
30 M	8 35 53	9 48 41	25 35	8 49	14 52	3 36	9 52	5 41	25 37	14 58	23 32	28 36	6 53	12 09	8 05	26 00	12 34
31 T	8 39 50	10 49 37	7♊51	8 47	15 53	4 51	10 04	5 52	25 44	14 58	23 34	28 38	6 55	11 58	8 36	26 26	12 36

EPHEMERIS CALCULATED FOR 12 MIDNIGHT GREENWICH MEAN TIME. ALL OTHER DATA AND FACING ASPECTARIAN PAGE IN **EASTERN TIME (BOLD)** AND PACIFIC TIME (REGULAR).

FEBRUARY 2023

☽ Last Aspect day	ET / hr:mn / PT		asp	☽ Ingress sign	day	ET / hr:mn / PT	
1	6:58 am	3:58 am	△ ♄	♋	1	3:11 pm	12:11 pm
3		10:19 pm	☍ ♇	♌	4	3:48 am	12:48 am
4	1:19 am		☍ ♇	♌	4	3:48 am	12:48 am
6	9:15 am	6:15 am	☍ ♄	♍	6	4:14 pm	1:14 pm
8		10:40 pm	△ ♇	♎	9	3:47 am	12:47 am
9	1:40 am		△ ♇	♎	9	3:47 am	12:47 am
11	11:41 am	8:41 am	□ ♇	♏	11	1:34 pm	10:34 am
13	6:52 pm	3:52 pm	⚹ ♇	♐	13	8:31 pm	5:31 pm
15	8:06 pm	5:06 pm	⚹ ♄	♑	15		9:00 pm
15	8:06 pm	5:06 pm	⚹ ♄	♑	16	12:00 am	
17	11:18 pm	8:18 pm	☌ ♇	♒	17		9:35 pm
17	11:18 pm	8:18 pm	☌ ♇	♒	18	12:35 am	
19	9:00 pm	6:00 pm	☌ ♄	♓	19	11:56 pm	8:56 pm
21	11:06 pm	8:06 pm	⚹ ♇	♈	21		9:14 pm
21	11:06 pm	8:06 pm	⚹ ♇	♈	22	12:14 am	
23		11:22 pm	□ ♇	♉	24	3:29 am	12:29 am
24	2:22 am		□ ♇	♉	24	3:29 am	12:29 am
26	9:42 am	6:42 am	△ ♇	♊	26	10:48 am	7:48 am
28	8:07 pm	5:07 pm	△ ♄	♋	28	9:40 pm	6:40 pm

☽ Phases & Eclipses phase	day	ET / hr:mn / PT	
Full Moon	5	1:29 pm	10:29 am
4th Quarter	13	11:01 am	8:01 am
New Moon	19		11:06 pm
New Moon	20	2:06 am	
2nd Quarter	27	3:06 am	12:06 am

Planet Ingress		day	ET / hr:mn / PT	
⚵	♈	7	11:47 pm	8:47 pm
☿	♒	11	6:22 am	3:22 am
☉	♓	18	5:34 pm	2:34 pm
♀	♈	19		11:56 pm
♀	♈	20	2:56 am	

Planetary Motion		day	ET / hr:mn / PT	
⚳	R	3	2:13 pm	11:13 am
♀	D	16	9:26 am	6:26 am

1 WEDNESDAY
☽ □ ♆ **2:21 am**
☽ △ ♄ **6:58 am** 3:58 am
☽ ⚻ ♇ **12:33 pm** 9:33 am

2 THURSDAY
☽ □ ♃ **3:55 am** 12:55 am
☽ △ ♀ **7:15 am** 4:15 am
☽ ⚺ ♂ **12:42 pm** 9:42 am
☽ ⚻ ☉ **7:12 pm** 4:12 pm
☽ ⚹ ♅ **9:27 pm** 6:27 pm

3 FRIDAY
☽ ☍ ☿ **7:09 am** 3:09 am
☽ △ ♆ **3:02 pm** 12:02 pm
☽ ⚻ ♄ **8:09 pm** 5:09 pm
☉ □ ♅ **9:50 pm** 6:50 pm
☽ ☍ ♇ 10:19 pm

4 SATURDAY
☽ ☍ ♇ **1:19 am**
☽ △ ♃ **5:34 pm** 2:34 pm
♀ □ ♂ **10:29 pm** 7:29 pm
☽ ⚹ ♂ 11:35 pm
☽ ⚻ ♀ 11:58 pm

5 SUNDAY
☽ ⚹ ♂ **2:35 am**
☽ ⚻ ♀ **2:58 am**
☽ □ ♅ **10:08 am** 7:08 am
☽ ☍ ☉ **1:29 pm** 10:29 am
☽ ⚻ ☿ 11:37 pm

6 MONDAY
☽ ⚻ ☿ **2:37 am**
☽ ⚻ ♆ **3:44 am** 12:44 am
☽ ☍ ♄ **9:15 am** 6:15 am
☿ ⚹ ♆ **1:26 pm** 10:26 am
☽ ⚻ ♇ **1:56 pm** 10:56 am

7 TUESDAY
☽ ⚻ ♃ **6:51 am** 3:51 am
☽ □ ♂ **4:05 pm** 1:05 pm
☽ ☍ ♀ **10:01 pm** 7:01 pm
☽ △ ♅ **10:16 pm** 7:16 pm
♀ ⚹ ♅ 9:29 pm

8 WEDNESDAY
♀ ⚹ ♅ **12:29 am**
☽ ⚻ ☉ **6:58 am** 3:58 am
☽ ☍ ♆ **3:40 pm** 12:40 pm
☽ △ ☿ **9:30 pm** 6:30 pm
☽ ⚻ ♄ **9:32 pm** 6:32 pm
☿ ⚺ ♄ **9:49 pm** 6:49 pm
☽ △ ♇ 10:40 pm

9 THURSDAY
☽ △ ♇ **1:40 am**
☽ ☍ ♃ **7:02 pm** 4:02 pm

10 FRIDAY
☽ △ ♂ **4:25 am** 1:25 am
☽ ⚻ ♅ **9:08 am** 6:08 am
☿ ☌ ♇ **12:16 pm** 9:16 am
☽ ⚻ ♀ **3:18 pm** 12:18 pm
☽ △ ☉ **10:39 pm** 7:39 pm
☽ ⚻ ♆ 11:04 pm

11 SATURDAY
☽ ⚻ ♆ **2:04 am**
☽ △ ♄ **8:07 am** 5:07 am
☽ □ ♇ **11:41 am** 8:41 am
☽ □ ☿ **2:27 pm** 11:27 am

12 SUNDAY
☽ ⚻ ♃ **5:07 am** 2:07 am
☽ ⚻ ♂ **2:28 pm** 11:28 am
☽ ☍ ♅ **5:43 pm** 2:43 pm
☉ ⚺ ♆ **6:37 pm** 3:37 pm

13 MONDAY
☽ △ ♀ **5:16 am** 2:16 am
☽ △ ♆ **9:49 am** 6:49 am
☽ □ ☉ **11:01 am** 8:01 am
☽ □ ♄ **3:53 pm** 12:53 pm
☽ ⚹ ♇ **6:52 pm** 3:52 pm

14 TUESDAY
☽ ⚹ ☿ **3:39 am** 12:39 am
☽ △ ♃ **11:56 am** 8:56 am
☽ ☍ ♂ **9:06 pm** 6:06 pm
☽ ⚻ ♅ **10:59 pm** 7:59 pm

15 WEDNESDAY
♀ ☌ ♆ **7:25 am** 4:25 am
☽ □ ♆ **2:06 pm** 11:06 am
☽ □ ♀ **2:43 pm** 11:43 am
☽ ⚹ ☉ **7:03 pm** 4:03 pm
☽ ⚹ ♄ **8:06 pm** 5:06 pm
☽ ⚺ ♇ **10:33 pm** 7:33 pm

16 THURSDAY
☉ ☌ ♄ **11:48 am** 8:48 am
☽ ⚺ ☿ **12:17 pm** 9:17 am
☽ □ ♃ **3:11 pm** 12:11 pm
☽ ⚻ ♂ 9:12 pm
☽ △ ♅ 9:55 pm

17 FRIDAY
☽ ⚻ ♂ **12:12 am**
☽ △ ♅ **12:55 am**
☽ ⚹ ♆ **3:16 pm** 12:16 pm
☽ ⚹ ♀ **8:06 pm** 5:06 pm
☿ ⚹ ♃ **9:13 pm** 6:13 pm
☽ ⚺ ♄ **9:15 pm** 6:15 pm
☉ ⚺ ♇ **10:23 pm** 7:23 pm
☽ ☌ ♇ **11:18 pm** 8:18 pm
☽ ⚺ ☉ **11:22 pm** 8:22 pm

18 SATURDAY
♂ ⚺ ♅ **9:51 am** 6:51 am
♀ ⚺ ♄ **11:32 am** 8:32 am
☽ ⚹ ♃ **3:51 pm** 12:51 pm
☽ ☌ ☿ **5:35 pm** 2:35 pm
☽ □ ♅ 9:42 pm
☽ △ ♂ 10:01 pm

19 SUNDAY
☽ □ ♅ **12:42 am**
☽ △ ♂ **1:01 am**
♀ ⚹ ♇ **12:05 pm** 9:05 am
☽ ⚺ ♆ **2:48 pm** 11:48 am
☽ ☌ ♄ **9:00 pm** 6:00 pm
☽ ⚺ ♇ **10:45 pm** 7:45 pm
☽ ⚺ ♀ **11:40 pm** 8:40 pm
☽ ☌ ☉ 11:06 pm

20 MONDAY
☽ ☌ ☉ **2:06 am**
☽ ⚺ ♃ **3:57 pm** 12:57 pm
☽ ⚺ ☿ **10:24 pm** 7:24 pm
☽ ⚹ ♅ 9:20 pm
☽ □ ♂ 10:44 pm

21 TUESDAY
☽ ⚹ ♅ **12:20 am**
☽ □ ♂ **1:44 am**
☽ ☌ ♆ **2:52 pm** 11:52 am
☿ □ ♅ **5:22 pm** 2:22 pm
☽ ⚺ ♄ **9:35 pm** 6:35 pm
☽ ⚹ ♇ **11:06 pm** 8:06 pm

22 WEDNESDAY
☽ ☌ ♀ **4:26 am** 1:26 am
☽ ⚺ ☉ **6:07 am** 3:07 am
☿ △ ♂ **3:14 pm** 12:14 pm
☽ ☌ ♃ **5:48 pm** 2:48 pm
☽ ⚺ ♅ 11:01 pm

23 THURSDAY
☽ ⚺ ♅ **2:01 am**
☽ ⚹ ♂ **4:44 am** 1:44 am
☽ ⚹ ☿ **6:03 am** 3:03 am
☽ ⚺ ♆ **5:34 pm** 2:34 pm
☽ ⚹ ♄ 10:06 pm
☽ □ ♇ 11:22 pm

24 FRIDAY
☽ ⚹ ♄ **1:06 am**
☽ □ ♇ **2:22 am**
☽ ⚺ ♀ **1:12 pm** 10:12 am
☽ ⚹ ☉ **2:02 pm** 11:02 am
☽ ⚺ ♃ **11:19 pm** 8:19 pm

25 SATURDAY
☽ ☌ ♅ **7:25 am** 4:25 am
☽ ⚺ ♂ **11:51 am** 8:51 am
☽ □ ☿ **7:16 pm** 4:16 pm
☽ ⚹ ♆ 9:15 pm

26 SUNDAY
☽ ⚹ ♆ **12:15 am**
☽ □ ♄ **8:45 am** 5:45 am
☽ △ ♇ **9:42 am** 6:42 am
☉ ⚺ ♀ **11:11 am** 8:11 am

27 MONDAY
☽ □ ☉ **3:06 am** 12:06 am
☽ ⚹ ♀ **3:24 am** 12:24 am
☽ ⚹ ♃ **9:08 am** 6:08 am
☿ ⚺ ♆ **11:03 am** 8:03 am
☽ ⚺ ♅ **4:51 pm** 1:51 pm
☽ ☌ ♂ **11:21 pm** 8:21 pm

28 TUESDAY
☽ □ ♆ **10:46 am** 7:46 am
☽ △ ☿ **2:27 pm** 11:27 am
☽ △ ♄ **8:07 pm** 5:07 pm
☽ ⚻ ♇ **8:40 pm** 5:40 pm

Eastern time in bold type
Pacific time in medium type

FEBRUARY 2023

DATE	SID.TIME	SUN	MOON	NODE	MERCURY	VENUS	MARS	JUPITER	SATURN	URANUS	NEPTUNE	PLUTO	CERES	PALLAS	JUNO	VESTA	CHIRON
1 W	8 43 46	11 ♒ 50 31	19 ♊ 56	8 ♉ 42 ℞	16 ♑ 57	6 ♓ 05	10 ♊ 17	6 ♈ 03	25 ♒ 51	14 ♉ 59	23 ♓ 36	28 ♑ 40	6 ♎ 57	11 ♋ 47 ℞	9 ♈ 06	26 ♓ 52	12 ♈ 38
2 Th	8 47 43	12 51 25	1 ♋ 54	8 35	18 03	7 20	10 30	6 15	25 58	14 59	23 38	28 42	6 58	11 37	9 37	27 18	12 40
3 F	8 51 40	13 52 17	13 47	8 24	19 12	8 34	10 43	6 26	26 05	15 00	23 40	28 44	6 58 ℞	11 28	10 07	27 44	12 42
4 Sa	8 55 36	14 53 08	25 39	8 11	20 22	9 49	10 57	6 38	26 13	15 00	23 41	28 46	6 58	11 19	10 38	28 10	12 45
5 Su	8 59 33	15 53 58	7 ♌ 31	7 56	21 35	11 03	11 12	6 49	26 20	15 01	23 43	28 48	6 58	11 11	11 09	28 36	12 47
6 M	9 3 29	16 54 46	19 25	7 41	22 49	12 18	11 27	7 01	26 27	15 02	23 45	28 49	6 57	11 03	11 40	29 02	12 49
7 T	9 7 26	17 55 34	1 ♍ 23	7 27	24 04	13 32	11 43	7 13	26 34	15 02	23 47	28 51	6 56	10 56	12 11	29 28	12 51
8 W	9 11 22	18 56 20	13 25	7 15	25 21	14 46	11 59	7 25	26 41	15 03	23 49	28 53	6 54	10 50	12 42	29 55	12 54
9 Th	9 15 19	19 57 05	25 32	7 06	26 40	16 01	12 15	7 37	26 48	15 04	23 51	28 55	6 52	10 45	13 14	0 ♈ 21	12 56
10 F	9 19 15	20 57 49	7 ♎ 48	7 00	28 00	17 15	12 32	7 49	26 56	15 05	23 53	28 57	6 50	10 40	13 45	0 47	12 58
11 Sa	9 23 12	21 58 32	20 13	6 56	29 21	18 29	12 49	8 01	27 03	15 06	23 55	28 59	6 47	10 36	14 17	1 14	13 01
12 Su	9 27 9	22 59 14	2 ♏ 53	6 55 D	0 ♒ 43	19 43	13 07	8 13	27 10	15 07	23 57	29 01	6 44	10 33	14 48	1 40	13 03
13 M	9 31 5	23 59 54	15 50	6 55 ℞	2 07	20 58	13 25	8 25	27 17	15 08	23 59	29 02	6 40	10 30	15 20	2 07	13 06
14 T	9 35 2	25 00 34	29 09	6 55	3 32	22 12	13 44	8 38	27 25	15 09	24 01	29 04	6 36	10 28	15 52	2 33	13 08
15 W	9 38 58	26 01 13	12 ♐ 51	6 54	4 57	23 26	14 03	8 50	27 32	15 10	24 03	29 06	6 31	10 27	16 24	3 00	13 11
16 Th	9 42 55	27 01 51	27 00	6 51	6 24	24 40	14 22	9 03	27 39	15 12	24 05	29 08	6 26	10 26 D	16 56	3 26	13 14
17 F	9 46 51	28 02 27	11 ♑ 34	6 45	7 52	25 54	14 42	9 15	27 46	15 13	24 07	29 10	6 20	10 26	17 28	3 53	13 16
18 Sa	9 50 48	29 03 02	26 30	6 37	9 21	27 08	15 02	9 28	27 54	15 14	24 09	29 11	6 14	10 26	18 00	4 20	13 19
19 Su	9 54 45	0 ♓ 03 36	11 ♒ 39	6 27	10 51	28 22	15 23	9 41	28 01	15 16	24 11	29 13	6 08	10 28	18 33	4 46	13 22
20 M	9 58 41	1 04 09	26 53	6 16	12 22	29 36	15 44	9 54	28 08	15 17	24 14	29 15	6 01	10 29	19 05	5 13	13 24
21 T	10 2 38	2 04 39	11 ♓ 59	6 07	13 53	0 ♈ 49	16 05	10 07	28 16	15 18	24 16	29 17	5 54	10 32	19 38	5 40	13 27
22 W	10 6 34	3 05 09	26 49	5 59	15 26	2 03	16 27	10 20	28 23	15 20	24 18	29 18	5 46	10 35	20 10	6 07	13 30
23 Th	10 10 31	4 05 36	11 ♈ 14	5 54	17 00	3 17	16 49	10 33	28 30	15 21	24 20	29 20	5 38	10 39	20 43	6 34	13 33
24 F	10 14 27	5 06 01	25 11	5 52 D	18 35	4 31	17 11	10 46	28 37	15 23	24 22	29 22	5 30	10 43	21 16	7 01	13 36
25 Sa	10 18 24	6 06 25	8 ♉ 39	5 51	20 10	5 44	17 33	10 59	28 44	15 25	24 24	29 23	5 21	10 48	21 49	7 27	13 39
26 Su	10 22 20	7 06 47	21 39	5 52	21 47	6 58	17 56	11 12	28 52	15 26	24 27	29 25	5 12	10 53	22 22	7 54	13 42
27 M	10 26 17	8 07 07	4 ♊ 17	5 53 ℞	23 24	8 11	18 19	11 25	28 59	15 28	24 29	29 26	5 02	10 59	22 55	8 21	13 45
28 T	10 30 13	9 07 25	16 35	5 52	25 03	9 25	18 43	11 39	29 06	15 30	24 31	29 28	4 53	11 06	23 28	8 48	13 48

EPHEMERIS CALCULATED FOR 12 MIDNIGHT GREENWICH MEAN TIME. ALL OTHER DATA AND FACING ASPECTARIAN PAGE IN **EASTERN TIME (BOLD)** AND PACIFIC TIME (REGULAR).

☽ Last Aspect day	ET / hr:mn / PT	asp	☽ Ingress sign	day	ET / hr:mn / PT
3	**9:22 am** 6:22 am	☍♇	♌	3	**10:16 am** 7:16 am
5	**10:18 pm** 7:18 pm	☍♄	♍	5	**10:38 pm** 7:38 pm
8	**9:07 am** 6:07 am	△♇	♎	8	**9:44 am** 6:44 am
10	**6:37 pm** 3:37 pm	□♇	♏	10	**7:06 pm** 4:06 pm
12	11:58 pm	⚹♇	♐	13	**3:21 am** 12:21 am
13	**2:58 am**	⚹♇	♐	13	**3:21 am** 12:21 am
15	**4:50 am** 1:50 am	△♀	♑	15	**8:06 am** 5:06 am
17	**10:14 am** 7:14 am	☌♇	♒	17	**10:25 am** 7:25 am
19	**6:33 am** 3:33 am	△♂	♓	19	**11:12 am** 8:12 am
21	**11:58 am** 8:58 am	⚹♇	♈	21	**12:01 pm** 9:01 am
23	**1:13 pm** 10:13 am	⚹♂	♉	23	**2:42 pm** 11:42 am
25	**12:19 pm** 9:19 am	⚹♆	♊	25	**8:42 pm** 5:42 pm
27	**9:39 pm** 6:39 pm	□♆	♋	28	**6:22 am** 3:22 am
30	**9:45 am** 6:45 am	△♆	♌	30	**6:31 pm** 3:31 pm

☽ Phases & Eclipses phase	day	ET / hr:mn / PT
Full Moon	7	**7:40 am** 4:40 am
4th Quarter	14	**10:08 pm** 7:08 pm
New Moon	21	**1:23 pm** 10:23 am
2nd Quarter	28	**10:32 pm** 7:32 pm

Planet Ingress		day	ET / hr:mn / PT
☿	♓	2	**5:52 pm** 2:52 pm
♄	♓	7	**8:35 am** 5:35 am
⚵	♉	11	**11:15 am** 8:15 am
♀	♉	16	**6:34 pm** 3:34 pm
☿	♈	18	9:24 pm
☿	♈	19	**12:24 am**
☉	♈	20	**5:24 pm** 2:24 pm
⚳	♍	22	**11:38 pm** 8:38 pm
♇	♒	23	**8:13 am** 5:13 am
♂	♋	25	**7:45 am** 4:45 am

Planetary Motion	day	ET / hr:mn / PT

1 WEDNESDAY
☽△☉ **8:10 pm** 5:10 pm
☽□♀ **9:50 pm** 6:50 pm
☽□♃ **10:04 pm** 7:04 pm
♀☌♃ 9:36 pm

2 THURSDAY
♀☌♃ **12:36 am**
☽⚹♅ **5:03 am** 2:03 am
☿☌♄ **9:34 am** 6:34 am
☿⚺♇ **11:21 am** 8:21 am
☽⚺♂ **1:39 pm** 10:39 am
☽△♆ **11:23 pm** 8:23 pm
☉⚺♃ 9:40 pm

3 FRIDAY
☉⚺♃ **12:40 am**
☽⚻♄ **9:19 am** 6:19 am
☽☍♇ **9:22 am** 6:22 am
☽⚻☿ **1:01 pm** 10:01 am
♄⚺♇ **5:26 pm** 2:26 pm

4 SATURDAY
☽△♃ **11:56 am** 8:56 am
☽⚻☉ **2:27 pm** 11:27 am
☽△♀ **5:28 pm** 2:28 pm
☽□♅ **5:54 pm** 2:54 pm
♀⚺♅ **9:46 pm** 6:46 pm

5 SUNDAY
☽⚹♂ **4:26 am** 1:26 am
☽⚻♆ **12:06 pm** 9:06 am
☽⚻♇ **9:54 pm** 6:54 pm
☽☍♄ **10:18 pm** 7:18 pm

6 MONDAY
☉⚹♅ **8:42 am** 5:42 am
☽☍☿ **11:32 am** 8:32 am
☽⚻♃ 10:00 pm

7 TUESDAY
☽⚻♃ **1:00 am**
☽△♅ **5:51 am** 2:51 am
☽☍☉ **7:40 am** 4:40 am
☽⚻♀ **11:53 am** 8:53 am
☽□♂ **6:06 pm** 3:06 pm
☽☍♆ **11:39 pm** 8:39 pm

8 WEDNESDAY
☽△♇ **9:07 am** 6:07 am
☽⚻♄ **9:58 am** 6:58 am

9 THURSDAY
☽⚻☿ **8:10 am** 5:10 am
☽☍♃ **12:27 pm** 9:27 am
☽⚻♅ **4:15 pm** 1:15 pm
☽⚻☉ **10:52 pm** 7:52 pm

10 FRIDAY
☽☍♀ **4:07 am** 1:07 am
☽△♂ **6:00 am** 3:00 am
☽⚻♆ **9:30 am** 6:30 am
☿⚺♃ **5:04 pm** 2:04 pm
☽□♇ **6:37 pm** 3:37 pm
☽△♄ **7:51 pm** 4:51 pm

11 SATURDAY
♀⚹♂ **10:05 am** 7:05 am
☿⚹♅ **4:04 pm** 1:04 pm
☽⚻♃ **9:55 pm** 6:55 pm
☽☍♅ 9:43 pm
☽△☿ 11:07 pm

12 SUNDAY
☽☍♅ **12:43 am**
☽△☿ **3:07 am**
☽△☉ **12:32 pm** 9:32 am
♀⚺♆ **3:09 pm** 12:09 pm
☽⚻♂ **4:43 pm** 1:43 pm
☽△♆ **6:18 pm** 3:18 pm
☽⚻♀ **6:37 pm** 3:37 pm
☽⚹♇ 11:58 pm

13 MONDAY
☽⚹♇ **2:58 am**
☽□♄ **4:34 am** 1:34 am

14 TUESDAY
☽△♃ **5:57 am** 2:57 am
☽⚻♅ **7:49 am** 4:49 am
☽□☿ **5:38 pm** 2:38 pm
♂□♆ **7:39 pm** 4:39 pm
☽□☉ **10:08 pm** 7:08 pm
☽□♆ **11:38 pm** 8:38 pm
☽☍♂ **11:45 pm** 8:45 pm

15 WEDNESDAY
☽△♀ **4:50 am** 1:50 am
☽⚺♇ **7:49 am** 4:49 am
☽⚹♄ **9:41 am** 6:41 am
☉☌♆ **7:39 pm** 4:39 pm

16 THURSDAY
☽□♃ **10:17 am** 7:17 am
☽△♅ **11:22 am** 8:22 am
☿☌♆ **1:13 pm** 10:13 am
☉□♂ **2:10 pm** 11:10 am
♀□♇ **3:59 pm** 12:59 pm
☿□♂ 9:49 pm
☽⚹♆ 11:26 pm

17 FRIDAY
☿□♂ **12:49 am**
☽⚹♆ **2:26 am**
☽⚻♂ **4:04 am** 1:04 am
☽⚹☿ **4:28 am** 1:28 am
☽⚹☉ **4:37 am** 1:37 am
☉☌☿ **6:45 am** 3:45 am
☽☌♇ **10:14 am** 7:14 am
☽□♀ **11:50 am** 8:50 am
☽⚺♄ **12:20 pm** 9:20 am
♀⚹♄ **6:25 pm** 3:25 pm

18 SATURDAY
☽⚹♃ **12:27 pm** 9:27 am
☽□♅ **12:50 pm** 9:50 am
☿⚹♇ **11:24 pm** 8:24 pm

19 SUNDAY
☽⚺♆ **3:30 am** 12:30 am
☽△♂ **6:33 am** 3:33 am
☽⚺☉ **9:02 am** 6:02 am
☽⚺♇ **11:05 am** 8:05 am
☽⚺☿ **12:52 pm** 9:52 am
☽☌♄ **1:28 pm** 10:28 am
☽⚹♀ **4:54 pm** 1:54 pm
☿⚺♄ **5:30 pm** 2:30 pm
♃⚺♅ **6:06 pm** 3:06 pm

20 MONDAY
☽⚹♅ **1:34 pm** 10:34 am
☽⚺♃ **1:49 pm** 10:49 am
☉⚹♇ **4:12 pm** 1:12 pm

21 TUESDAY
☽☌♆ **4:20 am** 1:20 am
☽□♂ **8:55 am** 5:55 am
☽⚹♇ **11:58 am** 8:58 am
☽☌☉ **1:23 pm** 10:23 am
☽⚺♄ **2:43 pm** 11:43 am
☽☌☿ **9:34 pm** 6:34 pm
☽⚺♀ **10:17 pm** 7:17 pm

22 WEDNESDAY
☿⚺♀ **9:14 am** 6:14 am
☉⚺♄ **11:00 am** 8:00 am
☽⚺♅ **3:19 pm** 12:19 pm
☽☌♃ **4:17 pm** 1:17 pm

23 THURSDAY
☽⚺♆ **6:44 am** 3:44 am
☽⚹♂ **1:13 pm** 10:13 am
☽□♇ **2:42 pm** 11:42 am
☽⚹♄ **5:57 pm** 2:57 pm
☽⚺☉ **8:05 pm** 5:05 pm

24 FRIDAY
☽☌♀ **6:31 am** 3:31 am
☽⚺☿ **9:45 am** 6:45 am
☽☌♅ **7:52 pm** 4:52 pm
☽⚺♃ **9:40 pm** 6:40 pm

25 SATURDAY
♂⚻♇ **9:34 am** 6:34 am
☽⚹♆ **12:19 pm** 9:19 am
☽△♇ **8:46 pm** 5:46 pm
☽⚺♂ **9:12 pm** 6:12 pm
☽□♄ 9:38 pm

26 SUNDAY
☽□♄ **12:38 am**
☽⚹☉ **7:03 am** 4:03 am
☽⚺♀ **7:25 pm** 4:25 pm

27 MONDAY
☽⚹☿ **3:39 am** 12:39 am
☽⚺♅ **4:08 am** 1:08 am
☿⚺♅ **6:45 am** 3:45 am
☽⚹♃ **6:57 am** 3:57 am
☽□♆ **9:39 pm** 6:39 pm
☿☌♃ 11:50 pm

28 TUESDAY
☿☌♃ **2:50 am**
☽⚻♇ **6:32 am** 3:32 am
☽☌♂ **9:19 am** 6:19 am
☽△♄ **11:04 am** 8:04 am
☽□☉ **10:32 pm** 7:32 pm

29 WEDNESDAY
☽⚹♀ **12:50 pm** 9:50 am
☽⚹♅ **3:40 pm** 12:40 pm
☽□♃ **7:35 pm** 4:35 pm
☽□☿ 11:30 pm

30 THURSDAY
☽□☿ **2:30 am**
☽△♆ **9:45 am** 6:45 am
♂△♄ **3:03 pm** 12:03 pm
♀☌♅ **6:26 pm** 3:26 pm
☽☍♇ **6:46 pm** 3:46 pm
☽⚻♄ **11:51 pm** 8:51 pm
☽⚺♂ 9:10 pm

31 FRIDAY
☽⚺♂ **12:10 am**
☽△☉ **4:29 pm** 1:29 pm
☿⚺♆ 10:39 pm

Eastern time in bold type
Pacific time in medium type

MARCH 2023

DATE	SID.TIME	SUN	MOON	NODE	MERCURY	VENUS	MARS	JUPITER	SATURN	URANUS	NEPTUNE	PLUTO	CERES	PALLAS	JUNO	VESTA	CHIRON
1 W	10 34 10	10♓07 41	28♊40	5♉50Rx	26♒43	10♈38	19♊07	11♈52	29♒13	15♉32	24♓33	29♑30	4♎42Rx	11♋13	24♈01	9♈15	13♈51
2 Th	10 38 7	11 07 55	10♋36	5 46	28 23	11 52	19 31	12 06	29 20	15 34	24 35	29 31	4 32	11 20	24 34	9 42	13 54
3 F	10 42 3	12 08 06	22 28	5 39	0♓05	13 05	19 55	12 19	29 28	15 36	24 38	29 33	4 21	11 29	25 08	10 09	13 57
4 Sa	10 46 0	13 08 16	4♌19	5 31	1 48	14 18	20 19	12 33	29 35	15 38	24 40	29 34	4 10	11 37	25 41	10 36	14 00
5 Su	10 49 56	14 08 24	16 12	5 21	3 31	15 31	20 44	12 46	29 42	15 40	24 42	29 36	3 59	11 46	26 15	11 03	14 03
6 M	10 53 53	15 08 30	28 11	5 11	5 16	16 44	21 09	13 00	29 49	15 42	24 44	29 37	3 47	11 56	26 48	11 31	14 06
7 T	10 57 49	16 08 34	10♍15	5 01	7 02	17 58	21 35	13 14	29 56	15 44	24 47	29 39	3 35	12 06	27 22	11 58	14 10
8 W	11 1 46	17 08 36	22 27	4 53	8 49	19 10	22 00	13 27	0♓03	15 46	24 49	29 40	3 23	12 17	27 56	12 25	14 13
9 Th	11 5 42	18 08 36	4♎47	4 47	10 37	20 23	22 26	13 41	0 10	15 48	24 51	29 42	3 11	12 28	28 29	12 52	14 16
10 F	11 9 39	19 08 35	17 17	4 43	12 26	21 36	22 52	13 55	0 17	15 50	24 53	29 43	2 58	12 39	29 03	13 19	14 19
11 Sa	11 13 36	20 08 32	29 57	4 42D	14 17	22 49	23 18	14 09	0 24	15 52	24 56	29 45	2 45	12 51	29 37	13 46	14 23
12 Su	11 17 32	21 08 27	12♏50	4 42	16 08	24 02	23 45	14 23	0 31	15 55	24 58	29 46	2 32	13 03	0♉11	14 13	14 26
13 M	11 21 29	22 08 20	25 56	4 43	18 01	25 14	24 11	14 37	0 38	15 57	25 00	29 47	2 19	13 16	0 45	14 41	14 29
14 T	11 25 25	23 08 12	9♐19	4 44	19 54	26 27	24 38	14 51	0 45	15 59	25 02	29 49	2 06	13 29	1 19	15 08	14 32
15 W	11 29 22	24 08 02	22 59	4 45Rx	21 49	27 39	25 05	15 05	0 52	16 02	25 05	29 50	1 52	13 42	1 53	15 35	14 36
16 Th	11 33 18	25 07 50	6♑59	4 44	23 45	28 52	25 32	15 19	0 59	16 04	25 07	29 51	1 39	13 56	2 27	16 02	14 39
17 F	11 37 15	26 07 37	21 17	4 42	25 42	0♉04	26 00	15 33	1 06	16 07	25 09	29 52	1 25	14 10	3 02	16 29	14 43
18 Sa	11 41 11	27 07 22	5♒51	4 38	27 40	1 17	26 27	15 47	1 12	16 09	25 12	29 54	1 11	14 25	3 36	16 57	14 46
19 Su	11 45 8	28 07 06	20 36	4 33	29 38	2 29	26 55	16 01	1 19	16 12	25 14	29 55	0 58	14 40	4 10	17 24	14 49
20 M	11 49 5	29 06 47	5♓27	4 28	1♈38	3 41	27 23	16 15	1 26	16 14	25 16	29 56	0 44	14 55	4 45	17 51	14 53
21 T	11 53 1	0♈06 27	20 14	4 23	3 38	4 53	27 51	16 30	1 33	16 17	25 18	29 57	0 30	15 11	5 19	18 19	14 56
22 W	11 56 58	1 06 04	4♈49	4 18	5 38	6 05	28 20	16 44	1 39	16 20	25 21	29 58	0 16	15 27	5 53	18 46	15 00
23 Th	12 0 54	2 05 40	19 07	4 16	7 39	7 17	28 48	16 58	1 46	16 22	25 23	29 59	0 02	15 43	6 28	19 13	15 03
24 F	12 4 51	3 05 13	3♉02	4 15D	9 40	8 29	29 17	17 12	1 52	16 25	25 25	0♒01	29♍48	16 00	7 03	19 40	15 07
25 Sa	12 8 47	4 04 45	16 32	4 16	11 41	9 41	29 46	17 27	1 59	16 28	25 27	0 02	29 34	16 17	7 37	20 08	15 10
26 Su	12 12 44	5 04 14	29 38	4 17	13 41	10 52	0♋15	17 41	2 05	16 31	25 30	0 03	29 21	16 34	8 12	20 35	15 13
27 M	12 16 40	6 03 41	12♊20	4 19	15 41	12 04	0 44	17 55	2 12	16 33	25 32	0 04	29 07	16 52	8 46	21 02	15 17
28 T	12 20 37	7 03 06	24 44	4 20	17 40	13 15	1 13	18 10	2 18	16 36	25 34	0 05	28 54	17 09	9 21	21 30	15 20
29 W	12 24 34	8 02 28	6♋52	4 21Rx	19 38	14 27	1 43	18 24	2 25	16 39	25 36	0 06	28 40	17 27	9 56	21 57	15 24
30 Th	12 28 30	9 01 48	18 51	4 20	21 33	15 38	2 12	18 38	2 31	16 42	25 39	0 07	28 27	17 46	10 31	22 24	15 27
31 F	12 32 27	10 01 06	0♌44	4 19	23 27	16 49	2 42	18 53	2 37	16 45	25 41	0 07	28 14	18 04	11 06	22 52	15 31

EPHEMERIS CALCULATED FOR 12 MIDNIGHT GREENWICH MEAN TIME. ALL OTHER DATA AND FACING ASPECTARIAN PAGE IN **EASTERN TIME (BOLD)** AND PACIFIC TIME (REGULAR).

APRIL 2023

☽ Last Aspect day	ET / hr:mn / PT	asp	☽ Ingress sign	day	ET / hr:mn / PT
1	11:03 pm	△☿	♍	2	**6:57 am** 3:57 am
2	**2:03 am**	△☿	♍	2	**6:57 am** 3:57 am
4	**9:50 am** 6:50 am	☍♆	♎	4	**5:51 pm** 2:51 pm
6	**8:43 am** 5:43 am	☍♃	♏	6	11:29 pm
6	**8:43 am** 5:43 am	☍♃	♏	7	**2:29 am**
9	**5:09 am** 2:09 am	☍♀	♐	9	**8:57 am** 5:57 am
11	**6:48 am** 3:48 am	□♆	♑	11	**1:33 pm** 10:33 am
13	**10:14 am** 7:14 am	✶♆	♒	13	**4:42 pm** 1:42 pm
15	**11:16 am** 8:16 am	✶☉	♓	15	**6:57 pm** 3:57 pm
17	**2:57 pm** 11:57 am	☌♆	♈	17	**9:09 pm** 6:09 pm

☽ Last Aspect day	ET / hr:mn / PT	asp	☽ Ingress sign	day	ET / hr:mn / PT
19	9:13 pm	☌☉	♉	19	9:30 pm
20	**12:13 am**	☌☉	♉	20	**12:30 am**
21	**11:41 pm** 8:41 pm	✶♆	♊	22	**6:11 am** 3:11 am
24	**8:15 am** 5:15 am	□♆	♋	24	**2:58 pm** 11:58 am
26	**7:41 pm** 4:41 pm	△♆	♌	26	11:30 pm
26	**7:41 pm** 4:41 pm	△♆	♌	27	**2:30 am**
29	**6:53 am** 3:53 am	△♃	♍	29	**2:59 pm** 11:59 am

☽ Phases & Eclipses phase	day	ET / hr:mn / PT
Full Moon	5	9:34 pm
Full Moon	6	**12:34 am**
4th Quarter	13	**5:11 am** 2:11 am
New Moon	19	9:13 pm
New Moon	20	**12:13 am**
●	20	29° ♈ 50'
2nd Quarter	27	**5:20 pm** 2:20 pm

Planet Ingress		day	ET / hr:mn / PT
☿	♉	3	**12:22 pm** 9:22 am
♀	♊	10	9:47 pm
♀	♊	11	**12:47 am**
⚳	♉	15	**1:01 pm** 10:01 am
☉	♉	20	**4:14 am** 1:14 am

Planetary Motion		day	ET / hr:mn / PT
☿	℞	21	**4:35 am** 1:35 am

1 SATURDAY
☿ ⚺ ♆ **1:39 am**
☽ □ ♅ **4:30 am** 1:30 am
☽ □ ♀ **8:06 am** 5:06 am
☽ △ ♃ **9:25 am** 6:25 am
☽ ⚻ ♆ **10:28 pm** 7:28 pm
♀ ⚺ ♃ 9:18 pm
☽ △ ☿ 11:03 pm

2 SUNDAY
♀ ⚺ ♃ **12:18 am**
☽ △ ☿ **2:03 am**
☽ ⚻ ♇ **7:16 am** 4:16 am
☽ ☍ ♄ **12:44 pm** 9:44 am
☽ ✶ ♂ **3:08 pm** 12:08 pm

3 MONDAY
☽ ⚻ ☉ **9:49 am** 6:49 am
☿ □ ♇ **2:55 pm** 11:55 am
☽ △ ♅ **4:28 pm** 1:28 pm
☽ ⚻ ♃ **10:12 pm** 7:12 pm
☽ △ ♀ 11:04 pm

4 TUESDAY
☽ △ ♀ **2:04 am**
☽ ☍ ♆ **9:50 am** 6:50 am
☽ △ ♇ **6:13 pm** 3:13 pm
☽ ⚻ ☿ **10:16 pm** 7:16 pm
☽ ⚻ ♄ **11:54 pm** 8:54 pm

5 WEDNESDAY
☽ □ ♂ **4:12 am** 1:12 am
☿ ✶ ♄ **12:21 pm** 9:21 am
☽ ☍ ☉ 9:34 pm
☽ ⚻ ♅ 11:21 pm

6 THURSDAY
☽ ☍ ☉ **12:34 am**
☽ ⚻ ♅ **2:21 am**
☽ ☍ ♃ **8:43 am** 5:43 am
☽ ⚻ ♀ **5:06 pm** 2:06 pm
☽ ⚻ ♆ **6:57 pm** 3:57 pm
☉ ⚺ ♅ 9:42 pm
☽ □ ♇ 11:54 pm

7 FRIDAY
☉ ⚺ ♅ **12:42 am**
☽ □ ♇ **2:54 am**
☽ △ ♄ **8:44 am** 5:44 am
☽ ☍ ☿ **1:53 pm** 10:53 am
♀ ✶ ♆ **1:58 pm** 10:58 am
☽ △ ♂ **2:42 pm** 11:42 am
☿ ✶ ♂ 11:29 pm

8 SATURDAY
☿ ✶ ♂ **2:29 am**
☽ ☍ ♅ **9:56 am** 6:56 am
☽ ⚻ ☉ **12:27 pm** 9:27 am
☽ ⚻ ♃ **4:51 pm** 1:51 pm
☽ △ ♆ 10:50 pm

9 SUNDAY
☽ △ ♆ **1:50 am**
☽ ☍ ♀ **5:09 am** 2:09 am
☽ ✶ ♇ **9:23 am** 6:23 am
☽ □ ♄ **3:21 pm** 12:21 pm
☽ ⚻ ♂ **10:51 pm** 7:51 pm
☽ ⚻ ☿ 10:23 pm

10 MONDAY
☽ ⚻ ☿ **1:23 am**
☽ ⚻ ♅ **3:29 pm** 12:29 pm
☽ △ ☉ **9:48 pm** 6:48 pm
☽ △ ♃ **10:55 pm** 7:55 pm

11 TUESDAY
♀ △ ♇ **6:14 am** 3:14 am
☽ □ ♆ **6:48 am** 3:48 am
☽ ⚺ ♇ **2:01 pm** 11:01 am
☽ ⚻ ♀ **2:43 pm** 11:43 am
☉ ☌ ♃ **6:07 pm** 3:07 pm
☽ ✶ ♄ **8:08 pm** 5:08 pm

12 WEDNESDAY
☽ ☍ ♂ **5:03 am** 2:03 am
☽ △ ☿ **9:35 am** 6:35 am
☽ △ ♅ **7:24 pm** 4:24 pm

13 THURSDAY
☽ □ ♃ **3:20 am** 12:20 am
☽ □ ☉ **5:11 am** 2:11 am
☽ ✶ ♆ **10:14 am** 7:14 am
☽ ☌ ♇ **5:11 pm** 2:11 pm
☽ △ ♀ **10:23 pm** 7:23 pm
☽ ⚺ ♄ **11:28 pm** 8:28 pm

14 FRIDAY
☽ ⚻ ♂ **9:47 am** 6:47 am
♀ □ ♄ **12:38 pm** 9:38 am
☽ □ ☿ **3:16 pm** 12:16 pm
☽ □ ♅ **10:08 pm** 7:08 pm

15 SATURDAY
☽ ✶ ♃ **6:36 am** 3:36 am
☽ ✶ ☉ **11:16 am** 8:16 am
☽ ⚺ ♆ **12:41 pm** 9:41 am
☽ ⚺ ♇ **7:27 pm** 4:27 pm
☽ ☌ ♄ 10:58 pm

16 SUNDAY
☽ ☌ ♄ **1:58 am**
☽ □ ♀ **4:58 am** 1:58 am
☉ ⚺ ♆ **8:43 am** 5:43 am
☽ △ ♂ **1:49 pm** 10:49 am
☽ ✶ ☿ **7:24 pm** 4:24 pm
☽ ✶ ♅ 9:25 pm

17 MONDAY
☽ ✶ ♅ **12:25 am**
☽ ⚺ ♃ **9:35 am** 6:35 am
☽ ☌ ♆ **2:57 pm** 11:57 am
☽ ⚺ ☉ **5:06 pm** 2:06 pm
☽ ✶ ♇ **9:42 pm** 6:42 pm

18 TUESDAY
☽ ⚺ ♄ **4:34 am** 1:34 am
☽ ✶ ♀ **11:47 am** 8:47 am
☽ □ ♂ **6:16 pm** 3:16 pm
☽ ⚺ ☿ **11:15 pm** 8:15 pm

19 WEDNESDAY
☽ ⚺ ♅ **3:20 am** 12:20 am
☽ ☌ ♃ **1:27 pm** 10:27 am
☽ ⚺ ♆ **6:12 pm** 3:12 pm
☽ ☌ ☉ 9:13 pmc
☽ □ ♇ 10:04 pm

20 THURSDAY
☽ ☌ ☉ **12:13 am**
☽ □ ♇ **1:04 am**
☽ ✶ ♄ **8:30 am** 5:30 am
☉ □ ♇ **12:27 pm** 9:27 am
☽ ⚺ ♀ **8:29 pm** 5:29 pm
☽ ✶ ♂ 9:37 pm

21 FRIDAY
☽ ✶ ♂ **12:37 am**
☽ ☌ ☿ **4:05 am** 1:05 am
☽ ☌ ♅ **8:09 am** 5:09 am
☽ ⚺ ♃ **7:32 pm** 4:32 pm
☽ ✶ ♆ **11:41 pm** 8:41 pm

22 SATURDAY
☽ △ ♇ **6:49 am** 3:49 am
☽ ⚺ ☉ **10:14 am** 7:14 am
☽ □ ♄ **3:00 pm** 12:00 pm

23 SUNDAY
☽ ☌ ♀ **8:43 am** 5:43 am
☽ ⚺ ♂ **10:06 am** 7:06 am
☽ ⚺ ☿ **10:54 am** 7:54 am
☽ ⚺ ♅ **3:55 pm** 12:55 pm
☿ ✶ ♂ **11:19 pm** 8:19 pm

24 MONDAY
☽ ✶ ♃ **4:49 am** 1:49 am
☿ ⚺ ♀ **5:04 am** 2:04 am
☽ □ ♆ **8:15 am** 5:15 am
♀ ⚺ ♂ **12:50 pm** 9:50 am
☽ ⚻ ♇ **3:40 pm** 12:40 pm
☽ ✶ ☉ 9:11 pm
☽ △ ♄ 9:40 pm

25 TUESDAY
☽ ✶ ☉ **12:11 am**
☽ △ ♄ **12:40 am**
☉ ✶ ♄ **6:48 am** 3:48 am
☽ ✶ ☿ **7:47 pm** 4:47 pm
☽ ☌ ♂ **11:08 pm** 8:08 pm
☽ ⚺ ♀ 10:00 pm
☽ ✶ ♅ 11:45 pm

26 WEDNESDAY
☽ ⚺ ♀ **1:00 am**
☽ ✶ ♅ **2:45 am**
☽ □ ♃ **5:09 pm** 2:09 pm
☽ △ ♆ **7:41 pm** 4:41 pm
♀ ⚺ ♅ **8:35 pm** 5:35 pm

27 THURSDAY
☽ ☍ ♇ **3:13 am** 12:13 am
☽ ⚻ ♄ **12:54 pm** 9:54 am
☽ □ ☉ **5:20 pm** 2:20 pm

28 FRIDAY
☽ □ ☿ **5:44 am** 2:44 am
☽ ⚺ ♂ **2:22 pm** 11:22 am
☽ □ ♅ **3:26 pm** 12:26 pm
☽ ✶ ♀ **7:42 pm** 4:42 pm

29 SATURDAY
☽ △ ♃ **6:53 am** 3:53 am
☽ ⚻ ♆ **8:20 am** 5:20 am
☽ ⚻ ♇ **3:43 pm** 12:43 pm
♂ ✶ ♅ **4:05 pm** 1:05 pm
☽ ☍ ♄ 10:41 pm

30 SUNDAY
☽ ☍ ♄ **1:41 am**
☽ △ ☉ **10:59 am** 7:59 am
☽ △ ☿ **3:05 pm** 12:05 pm

Eastern time in bold type
Pacific time in medium type

April 2023

DATE	SID.TIME	SUN	MOON	NODE	MERCURY	VENUS	MARS	JUPITER	SATURN	URANUS	NEPTUNE	PLUTO	CERES	PALLAS	JUNO	VESTA	CHIRON
1 Sa	12 36 23	11♈00 21	12♌36	4♉16℞	25♈18	18♉01	3♋12	19♈07	2♓44	16♉48	25♓43	0♒08	28♍01℞	18♋23	11♉41	23♈19	15♈35
2 Su	12 40 20	11 59 34	24 31	4 13	27 06	19 12	3 42	19 22	2 50	16 51	25 45	0 09	27 48	18 42	12 15	23 46	15 38
3 M	12 44 16	12 58 45	6♍33	4 09	28 51	20 22	4 12	19 36	2 56	16 54	25 48	0 10	27 36	19 02	12 50	24 13	15 42
4 T	12 48 13	13 57 54	18 45	4 06	0♉32	21 33	4 42	19 51	3 02	16 57	25 50	0 11	27 24	19 21	13 25	24 41	15 45
5 W	12 52 9	14 57 00	1♎07	4 03	2 09	22 44	5 13	20 05	3 08	17 00	25 52	0 12	27 12	19 41	14 00	25 08	15 49
6 Th	12 56 6	15 56 05	13 42	4 01	3 41	23 55	5 43	20 20	3 14	17 03	25 54	0 12	27 00	20 01	14 35	25 35	15 52
7 F	13 0 2	16 55 07	26 30	4 00D	5 09	25 05	6 14	20 34	3 20	17 06	25 56	0 13	26 48	20 21	15 10	26 03	15 56
8 Sa	13 3 59	17 54 07	9♏32	4 00	6 32	26 16	6 45	20 48	3 26	17 09	25 58	0 14	26 37	20 42	15 45	26 30	15 59
9 Su	13 7 56	18 53 06	22 46	4 01	7 49	27 26	7 16	21 03	3 32	17 12	26 01	0 14	26 26	21 02	16 21	26 57	16 03
10 M	13 11 52	19 52 02	6♐14	4 02	9 01	28 36	7 47	21 17	3 37	17 15	26 03	0 15	26 16	21 23	16 56	27 24	16 06
11 T	13 15 49	20 50 57	19 53	4 03	10 08	29 46	8 18	21 32	3 43	17 19	26 05	0 16	26 05	21 44	17 31	27 52	16 10
12 W	13 19 45	21 49 51	3♑44	4 04	11 08	0♊56	8 49	21 46	3 49	17 22	26 07	0 16	25 55	22 06	18 06	28 19	16 13
13 Th	13 23 42	22 48 42	17 46	4 04℞	12 03	2 06	9 20	22 01	3 54	17 25	26 09	0 17	25 45	22 27	18 41	28 46	16 17
14 F	13 27 38	23 47 32	1♒57	4 04	12 51	3 16	9 52	22 15	4 00	17 28	26 11	0 17	25 36	22 49	19 16	29 13	16 20
15 Sa	13 31 35	24 46 20	16 16	4 04	13 34	4 25	10 23	22 30	4 05	17 32	26 13	0 18	25 27	23 10	19 52	29 41	16 24
16 Su	13 35 32	25 45 07	0♓38	4 03	14 10	5 35	10 55	22 44	4 11	17 35	26 15	0 18	25 18	23 32	20 27	0♉08	16 27
17 M	13 39 28	26 43 51	15 00	4 02	14 40	6 44	11 26	22 59	4 16	17 38	26 17	0 19	25 10	23 54	21 02	0 35	16 31
18 T	13 43 25	27 42 34	29 19	4 01	15 03	7 53	11 58	23 13	4 22	17 41	26 19	0 19	25 02	24 17	21 38	1 02	16 34
19 W	13 47 21	28 41 15	13♈29	4 01	15 21	9 02	12 30	23 28	4 27	17 45	26 21	0 20	24 55	24 39	22 13	1 30	16 38
20 Th	13 51 18	29 39 54	27 25	4 00D	15 32	10 11	13 02	23 42	4 32	17 48	26 23	0 20	24 48	25 02	22 48	1 57	16 41
21 F	13 55 14	0♉38 31	11♉05	4 00	15 37℞	11 20	13 34	23 57	4 37	17 51	26 25	0 20	24 41	25 24	23 24	2 24	16 45
22 Sa	13 59 11	1 37 07	24 26	4 01	15 36	12 29	14 06	24 11	4 42	17 55	26 27	0 20	24 34	25 47	23 59	2 51	16 48
23 Su	14 3 7	2 35 40	7♊27	4 01	15 30	13 37	14 39	24 25	4 47	17 58	26 29	0 21	24 29	26 10	24 34	3 18	16 52
24 M	14 7 4	3 34 12	20 10	4 01℞	15 18	14 46	15 11	24 40	4 52	18 02	26 31	0 21	24 23	26 33	25 10	3 45	16 55
25 T	14 11 0	4 32 41	2♋35	4 01	15 00	15 54	15 43	24 54	4 57	18 05	26 33	0 21	24 18	26 57	25 45	4 12	16 58
26 W	14 14 57	5 31 08	14 46	4 01	14 39	17 02	16 16	25 08	5 02	18 08	26 35	0 21	24 13	27 20	26 20	4 40	17 02
27 Th	14 18 54	6 29 33	26 46	4 01D	14 13	18 10	16 49	25 23	5 06	18 12	26 37	0 22	24 09	27 43	26 56	5 07	17 05
28 F	14 22 50	7 27 56	8♌41	4 01	13 43	19 18	17 21	25 37	5 11	18 15	26 38	0 22	24 05	28 07	27 31	5 34	17 09
29 Sa	14 26 47	8 26 17	20 34	4 01	13 10	20 26	17 54	25 51	5 15	18 19	26 40	0 22	24 02	28 31	28 07	6 01	17 12
30 Su	14 30 43	9 24 36	2♍30	4 01	12 35	21 33	18 27	26 06	5 20	18 22	26 42	0 22	23 58	28 55	28 42	6 28	17 15

EPHEMERIS CALCULATED FOR 12 MIDNIGHT GREENWICH MEAN TIME. ALL OTHER DATA AND FACING ASPECTARIAN PAGE IN **EASTERN TIME (BOLD)** AND PACIFIC TIME (REGULAR).

MAY 2023

☽ Last Aspect day	ET / hr:mn / PT	asp	☽ Ingress sign	day	ET / hr:mn / PT
1	**7:53 pm** 4:53 pm	☍♆	♎	1	11:09 pm
1	**7:53 pm** 4:53 pm	☍♆	♎	2	**2:09 am**
4	**5:17 am** 2:17 am	☍♃	♏	4	**10:32 am** 7:32 am
6	**10:38 am** 7:38 am	△♆	♐	6	**4:04 pm** 1:04 pm
8	**4:28 pm** 1:28 pm	△♃	♑	8	**7:33 pm** 4:33 pm
10	**7:52 pm** 4:52 pm	□♃	♒	10	**10:05 pm** 7:05 pm
12	**11:15 pm** 8:15 pm	✶♃	♓	12	9:39 pm
12	**11:15 pm** 8:15 pm	✶♃	♓	13	**12:39 am**
14	**10:56 pm** 7:56 pm	☌♆	♈	15	**3:56 am** 12:56 am
17	**5:10 am** 2:10 am	□♂	♉	17	**8:28 am** 5:28 am

☽ Last Aspect day	ET / hr:mn / PT	asp	☽ Ingress sign	day	ET / hr:mn / PT
19	**1:51 pm** 10:51 am	✶♂	♊	19	**2:48 pm** 11:48 am
21	**6:12 pm** 3:12 pm	□♆	♋	21	**11:28 pm** 8:28 pm
24	**5:12 am** 2:12 am	△♆	♌	24	**10:35 am** 7:35 am
25	11:38 pm	□♅	♍	26	**11:05 pm** 8:05 pm
26	**2:38 am**	□♅	♍	26	**11:05 pm** 8:05 pm
29	**5:46 am** 2:46 am	☍♆	♎	29	**10:51 am** 7:51 am
31	**10:53 am** 7:53 am	□♀	♏	31	**7:45 pm** 4:45 pm

☽ Phases & Eclipses phase	day	ET / hr:mn / PT
Full Moon	5	**1:34 pm** 10:34 am
●	5	14° ♏ 58'
4th Quarter	12	**10:28 am** 7:28 am
New Moon	19	**11:53 am** 8:53 am
2nd Quarter	27	**11:22 am** 8:22 am

Planet Ingress		day	ET / hr:mn / PT
⚵	♊	1	9:50 pm
⚵	♊	2	**12:50 am**
♀	♌	2	**1:03 pm** 10:03 am
♀	♋	7	**10:25 am** 7:25 am
♃	♉	16	**1:20 pm** 10:20 am
♂	♌	20	**11:31 am** 8:31 am
☉	♊	21	**3:09 am** 12:09 am

Planetary Motion		day	ET / hr:mn / PT
♇	℞	1	**1:09 pm** 10:09 am
⚳	D	6	**3:24 pm** 12:24 pm
☿	D	14	**11:17 pm** 8:17 pm

1 MONDAY
- ☽△♅ **3:38 am** 12:38 am
- ☽✶♂ **5:08 am** 2:08 am
- ☽□♀ **1:31 pm** 10:31 am
- ☉☌☿ **7:28 pm** 4:28 pm
- ☽⚻♃ **7:30 pm** 4:30 pm
- ☽☍♆ **7:53 pm** 4:53 pm
- ☽△♇ 11:51 pm

2 TUESDAY
- ☽△♇ **2:51 am**
- ☽⚻♄ **12:46 pm** 9:46 am
- ♃⚺♆ **6:03 pm** 3:03 pm
- ☽⚻☿ **10:26 pm** 7:26 pm
- ☽⚻☉ 11:09 pm

3 WEDNESDAY
- ☽⚻☉ **2:09 am**
- ☽⚻♅ **1:26 pm** 10:26 am
- ☽□♂ **5:10 pm** 2:10 pm

4 THURSDAY
- ☽△♀ **3:54 am** 12:54 am
- ☽⚻♆ **4:43 am** 1:43 am
- ☽☍♃ **5:17 am** 2:17 am
- ☽□♇ **11:12 am** 8:12 am
- ♀□♆ **1:40 pm** 10:40 am
- ☽△♄ **8:53 pm** 5:53 pm
- ♀✶♃ 9:03 pm

5 FRIDAY
- ♀✶♃ **12:03 am**
- ☽☍☿ **3:15 am** 12:15 am
- ☽☍☉ **1:34 pm** 10:34 am
- ☽☍♅ **8:13 pm** 5:13 pm
- ☽△♂ 10:51 pm

6 SATURDAY
- ☽△♂ **1:51 am**
- ☽△♆ **10:38 am** 7:38 am
- ☽⚻♃ **11:59 am** 8:59 am
- ☽⚻♀ **2:28 pm** 11:28 am
- ☽✶♇ **4:41 pm** 1:41 pm
- ☽□♄ 11:12 pm

7 SUNDAY
- ☽□♄ **2:12 am**
- ☽⚻☿ **5:58 am** 2:58 am
- ♀⚻♇ **6:10 pm** 3:10 pm
- ☽⚻☉ **9:50 pm** 6:50 pm
- ☽⚻♅ 9:34 pm

8 MONDAY
- ☽⚻♅ **12:34 am**
- ☽⚻♂ **7:55 am** 4:55 am
- ☽□♆ **2:22 pm** 11:22 am
- ☽△♃ **4:28 pm** 1:28 pm
- ☽⚺♇ **8:09 pm** 5:09 pm
- ☽☍♀ **10:20 pm** 7:20 pm

9 TUESDAY
- ☽✶♄ **5:39 am** 2:39 am
- ☽△☿ **7:28 am** 4:28 am
- ☉☌♅ **3:56 pm** 12:56 pm

10 WEDNESDAY
- ☽△♅ **3:32 am** 12:32 am
- ☽△☉ **4:20 am** 1:20 am
- ☽☍♂ **12:38 pm** 9:38 am
- ☽✶♆ **5:03 pm** 2:03 pm
- ☽□♃ **7:52 pm** 4:52 pm
- ☽☌♇ **10:40 pm** 7:40 pm

11 THURSDAY
- ☽⚻♀ **5:01 am** 2:01 am
- ☽⚺♄ **8:20 am** 5:20 am
- ☽□☿ **8:45 am** 5:45 am

12 FRIDAY
- ☿✶♄ **4:42 am** 1:42 am
- ☽□♅ **6:12 am** 3:12 am
- ☽□☉ **10:28 am** 7:28 am
- ☽⚻♂ **5:13 pm** 2:13 pm
- ☽⚺♆ **7:40 pm** 4:40 pm
- ☿✶♀ **10:44 pm** 7:44 pm
- ☽✶♃ **11:15 pm** 8:15 pm
- ☽⚺♇ 10:13 pm
- ♀△♄ 11:57 pm

13 SATURDAY
- ☽⚺♇ **1:13 am**
- ♀△♄ **2:57 am**
- ☽✶☿ **10:44 am** 7:44 am
- ☽☌♄ **11:12 am** 8:12 am
- ☽△♀ **11:51 am** 8:51 am

14 SUNDAY
- ☽✶♅ **9:22 am** 6:22 am
- ☽✶☉ **5:17 pm** 2:17 pm
- ☽△♂ **10:30 pm** 7:30 pm
- ☽☌♆ **10:56 pm** 7:56 pm

15 MONDAY
- ☽⚺♃ **3:22 am** 12:22 am
- ☽✶♇ **4:29 am** 1:29 am
- ♂△♆ **9:44 am** 6:44 am
- ☽⚺☿ **2:05 pm** 11:05 am
- ☽⚺♄ **2:54 pm** 11:54 am
- ☽□♀ **7:42 pm** 4:42 pm

16 TUESDAY
- ☽⚺♅ **1:37 pm** 10:37 am
- ☽⚺☉ 10:30 pm

17 WEDNESDAY
- ☽⚺☉ **1:30 am**
- ☽⚺♆ **3:25 am** 12:25 am
- ☽□♂ **5:10 am** 2:10 am
- ☽☌♃ **8:47 am** 5:47 am
- ☽□♇ **9:00 am** 6:00 am
- ☽☌☿ **7:27 pm** 4:27 pm
- ☽✶♄ **7:57 pm** 4:57 pm
- ♃□♇ **9:11 pm** 6:11 pm

18 THURSDAY
- ☉✶♆ **5:00 am** 2:00 am
- ☽✶♀ **5:18 am** 2:18 am
- ☽☌♅ **7:28 pm** 4:28 pm
- ☿✶♄ 11:40 pm

19 FRIDAY
- ☿✶♄ **2:40 am**
- ☽✶♆ **9:39 am** 6:39 am
- ☽☌☉ **11:53 am** 8:53 am
- ☽✶♂ **1:51 pm** 10:51 am
- ☽△♇ **3:20 pm** 12:20 pm
- ☽⚺♃ **4:06 pm** 1:06 pm
- ☽□♄ 11:58 pm

20 SATURDAY
- ☽□♄ **2:58 am**
- ☽⚺☿ **3:33 am** 12:33 am
- ☽⚺♀ **5:28 pm** 2:28 pm
- ♂☍♇ **11:12 pm** 8:12 pm

21 SUNDAY
- ☽⚺♅ **3:32 am** 12:32 am
- ☉△♇ **9:58 am** 6:58 am
- ☽□♆ **6:12 pm** 3:12 pm
- ☽⚻♇ 9:00 pm
- ☽⚺☉ 10:11 pm
- ☽⚺♂ 10:12 pm
- ☽✶♃ 10:54 pm
- ☉✶♂ 10:57 pm

22 MONDAY
- ☽⚻♇ **12:00 am**
- ☽⚺☉ **1:11 am**
- ☽⚺♂ **1:12 am**
- ☽✶♃ **1:54 am**
- ☉✶♂ **1:57 am**
- ☽△♄ **12:24 pm** 9:24 am
- ☉⚺♃ **12:55 pm** 9:55 am
- ☽✶☿ **3:07 pm** 12:07 pm
- ♂□♃ 10:13 pm

23 TUESDAY
- ♂□♃ **1:13 am**
- ☽☌♀ **8:45 am** 5:45 am
- ☽✶♅ **2:07 pm** 11:07 am

24 WEDNESDAY
- ☽△♆ **5:12 am** 2:12 am
- ☽☍♇ **11:04 am** 8:04 am
- ☽□♃ **2:13 pm** 11:13 am
- ☽☌♂ **3:21 pm** 12:21 pm
- ☽✶☉ **5:31 pm** 2:31 pm
- ☽⚻♄ 9:09 pm

25 THURSDAY
- ☽⚻♄ **12:09 am**
- ☽□☿ **6:11 am** 3:11 am
- ☽⚺♀ 11:33 pm
- ☽□♅ 11:38 pm

26 FRIDAY
- ☽⚺♀ **2:33 am**
- ☽□♅ **2:38 am**
- ♀✶♅ **3:37 am** 12:37 am
- ☽⚻♆ **5:45 pm** 2:45 pm
- ☽⚻♇ **11:31 pm** 8:31 pm

27 SATURDAY
- ☽△♃ **3:53 am** 12:53 am
- ☽⚺♂ **6:57 am** 3:57 am
- ☽□☉ **11:22 am** 8:22 am
- ☽☍♄ **12:53 pm** 9:53 am
- ☽△☿ **11:07 pm** 8:07 pm

28 SUNDAY
- ☉□♄ **6:46 am** 3:46 am
- ☽△♅ **3:12 pm** 12:12 pm
- ☽✶♀ **8:19 pm** 5:19 pm

29 MONDAY
- ☽☍♆ **5:46 am** 2:46 am
- ☽△♇ **11:13 am** 8:13 am
- ☽⚻♃ **4:33 pm** 1:33 pm
- ☽✶♂ **9:21 pm** 6:21 pm
- ☽⚻♄ 9:18 pm

30 TUESDAY
- ☽⚻♄ **12:18 am**
- ☽△☉ **3:39 am** 12:39 am
- ☽⚻☿ **2:50 pm** 11:50 am
- ☽⚻♅ 10:29 pm

31 WEDNESDAY
- ☽⚻♅ **1:29 am**
- ☽□♀ **10:53 am** 7:53 am
- ☽⚻♆ **3:02 pm** 12:02 pm
- ☽□♇ **8:02 pm** 5:02 pm
- ☽☍♃ 11:04 pm

Eastern time in bold type
Pacific time in medium type

MAY 2023

DATE	SID.TIME	SUN	MOON	NODE	MERCURY	VENUS	MARS	JUPITER	SATURN	URANUS	NEPTUNE	PLUTO	CERES	PALLAS	JUNO	VESTA	CHIRON
1 M	14 34 40	10♉22 52	14♍34	4♉02	11♉57℞	22♊40	19♋00	26♈20	5♓24	18♉26	26♓44	0♒22℞	23♍56℞	29♋19	29♉17	6♉55	17♈19
2 T	14 38 36	11 21 07	26 49	4 02	11 19	23 48	19 33	26 34	5 29	18 29	26 46	0 22	23 54	29 43	29 53	7 22	17 22
3 W	14 42 33	12 19 19	9♎19	4 03	10 40	24 55	20 06	26 48	5 33	18 32	26 47	0 22	23 52	0♌07	0♊28	7 49	17 25
4 Th	14 46 29	13 17 30	22 06	4 04℞	10 02	26 01	20 39	27 02	5 37	18 36	26 49	0 22	23 51	0 31	1 04	8 16	17 28
5 F	14 50 26	14 15 39	5♏12	4 04	9 24	27 08	21 12	27 17	5 41	18 39	26 51	0 22	23 50	0 56	1 39	8 43	17 32
6 Sa	14 54 23	15 13 46	18 35	4 03	8 48	28 14	21 45	27 31	5 45	18 43	26 52	0 22	23 49D	1 20	2 15	9 09	17 35
7 Su	14 58 19	16 11 52	2♐16	4 03	8 14	29 20	22 19	27 45	5 49	18 46	26 54	0 21	23 49	1 45	2 50	9 36	17 38
8 M	15 2 16	17 09 56	16 10	4 01	7 43	0♋26	22 52	27 59	5 53	18 50	26 56	0 21	23 49	2 09	3 25	10 03	17 41
9 T	15 6 12	18 07 59	0♑16	3 59	7 15	1 32	23 26	28 13	5 57	18 53	26 57	0 21	23 50	2 34	4 01	10 30	17 44
10 W	15 10 9	19 06 00	14 29	3 58	6 50	2 38	23 59	28 27	6 00	18 57	26 59	0 21	23 51	2 59	4 36	10 57	17 48
11 Th	15 14 5	20 04 00	28 45	3 56	6 30	3 43	24 33	28 41	6 04	19 00	27 00	0 21	23 52	3 24	5 12	11 24	17 51
12 F	15 18 2	21 01 58	13♒02	3 55D	6 13	4 48	25 06	28 55	6 07	19 04	27 02	0 20	23 54	3 49	5 47	11 50	17 54
13 Sa	15 21 59	21 59 55	27 15	3 55	6 01	5 53	25 40	29 09	6 11	19 07	27 03	0 20	23 57	4 14	6 22	12 17	17 57
14 Su	15 25 55	22 57 51	11♓23	3 56	5 54	6 58	26 14	29 23	6 14	19 11	27 05	0 20	23 59	4 39	6 58	12 44	18 00
15 M	15 29 52	23 55 46	25 24	3 57	5 51D	8 02	26 48	29 36	6 17	19 14	27 06	0 19	24 02	5 04	7 33	13 10	18 03
16 T	15 33 48	24 53 39	9♈16	3 59	5 53	9 06	27 22	29 50	6 21	19 18	27 08	0 19	24 06	5 30	8 08	13 37	18 06
17 W	15 37 45	25 51 31	22 58	4 00℞	5 59	10 10	27 56	0♉04	6 24	19 21	27 09	0 19	24 10	5 55	8 44	14 04	18 09
18 Th	15 41 41	26 49 22	6♉28	4 00	6 10	11 14	28 30	0 17	6 27	19 25	27 11	0 18	24 14	6 21	9 19	14 30	18 12
19 F	15 45 38	27 47 12	19 45	3 59	6 25	12 17	29 04	0 31	6 30	19 28	27 12	0 18	24 19	6 46	9 54	14 57	18 15
20 Sa	15 49 34	28 45 00	2♊49	3 57	6 45	13 21	29 38	0 45	6 32	19 31	27 13	0 17	24 24	7 12	10 30	15 24	18 17
21 Su	15 53 31	29 42 47	15 38	3 54	7 09	14 24	0♌12	0 58	6 35	19 35	27 14	0 17	24 29	7 37	11 05	15 50	18 20
22 M	15 57 28	0♊40 33	28 12	3 50	7 38	15 26	0 46	1 12	6 38	19 38	27 16	0 16	24 35	8 03	11 40	16 17	18 23
23 T	16 1 24	1 38 17	10♋33	3 45	8 10	16 28	1 21	1 25	6 40	19 42	27 17	0 16	24 41	8 29	12 16	16 43	18 26
24 W	16 5 21	2 35 59	22 42	3 41	8 47	17 31	1 55	1 39	6 43	19 45	27 18	0 15	24 47	8 55	12 51	17 10	18 29
25 Th	16 9 17	3 33 40	4♌42	3 37	9 27	18 32	2 29	1 52	6 45	19 49	27 19	0 14	24 54	9 21	13 26	17 36	18 31
26 F	16 13 14	4 31 20	16 36	3 34	10 11	19 34	3 04	2 05	6 47	19 52	27 21	0 14	25 01	9 47	14 01	18 02	18 34
27 Sa	16 17 10	5 28 57	28 28	3 33D	10 59	20 35	3 38	2 18	6 49	19 55	27 22	0 13	25 09	10 13	14 37	18 29	18 37
28 Su	16 21 7	6 26 34	10♍24	3 32	11 50	21 35	4 13	2 32	6 52	19 59	27 23	0 12	25 16	10 39	15 12	18 55	18 39
29 M	16 25 3	7 24 09	22 27	3 33	12 45	22 36	4 48	2 45	6 53	20 02	27 24	0 12	25 25	11 05	15 47	19 21	18 42
30 T	16 29 0	8 21 42	4♎42	3 35	13 43	23 36	5 22	2 58	6 55	20 05	27 25	0 11	25 33	11 31	16 22	19 47	18 44
31 W	16 32 57	9 19 15	17 15	3 36	14 45	24 35	5 57	3 11	6 57	20 09	27 26	0 10	25 42	11 57	16 57	20 14	18 47

EPHEMERIS CALCULATED FOR 12 MIDNIGHT GREENWICH MEAN TIME. ALL OTHER DATA AND FACING ASPECTARIAN PAGE IN **EASTERN TIME (BOLD)** AND PACIFIC TIME (REGULAR).

JUNE 2023

☽ Last Aspect day	ET / hr:mn / PT	asp	☽ Ingress sign	day	ET / hr:mn / PT
2	**8:51 pm** 5:51 pm	△♀	♐	2	10:03 pm
2	**8:51 pm** 5:51 pm	△♀	♐	3	**1:03 am**
4	**11:24 pm** 8:24 pm	□♆	♑	5	**3:31 am** 12:31 am
6	9:40 pm	⚹♆	♒	7	**4:42 am** 1:42 am
7	**12:40 am**	⚹♆	♒	7	**4:42 am** 1:42 am
8	9:24 pm	□☿	♓	9	**6:14 am** 3:14 am
9	**12:24 am**	□☿	♓	9	**6:14 am** 3:14 am
11	**9:20 am** 6:20 am	⚹♇	♈	11	**9:20 am** 6:20 am
13	**2:27 pm** 11:27 am	□♇	♉	13	**2:31 pm** 11:31 am
15	**9:36 pm** 6:36 pm	△♇	♊	15	**9:46 pm** 6:46 pm
17	11:24 pm	□♆	♋	18	**6:58 am** 3:58 am
18	**2:24 am**	□♆	♋	18	**6:58 am** 3:58 am
20	**5:43 pm** 2:43 pm	☍♇	♌	20	**6:04 pm** 3:04 pm
22	**1:01 pm** 10:01 am	□♅	♍	23	**6:35 am** 3:35 am
25	**6:24 pm** 3:24 pm	△♇	♎	25	**6:57 pm** 3:57 pm
28	**4:19 am** 1:19 am	□♇	♏	28	**4:55 am** 1:55 am
30	**10:20 am** 7:20 am	⚹♇	♐	30	**10:59 am** 7:59 am

☽ Phases & Eclipses phase	day	ET / hr:mn / PT
Full Moon	3	**11:42 pm** 8:42 pm
4th Quarter	10	**3:31 pm** 12:31 pm
New Moon	17	9:37 pm
New Moon	18	**12:37 am**
2nd Quarter	26	**3:50 am** 12:50 am

Planet Ingress		day	ET / hr:mn / PT
♀	♌	5	**9:46 am** 6:46 am
♇	♑	11	**5:47 am** 2:47 am
☿	♊	11	**6:27 am** 3:27 am
⚳	♎	21	**7:30 am** 4:30 am
☉	♋	21	**10:58 am** 7:58 am
⚵	♋	22	**7:40 am** 4:40 am
⚶	♊	22	**3:17 pm** 12:17 pm
☿	♋	26	**8:24 pm** 5:24 pm

Planetary Motion		day	ET / hr:mn / PT
♄	℞	17	**1:27 pm** 10:27 am
♆	℞	30	**5:07 pm** 2:07 pm

1 THURSDAY
☽☍♃ **2:04 am**
☽□♂ **8:11 am** 5:11 am
☽△♄ **8:30 am** 5:30 am
♂⊼♄ **3:31 pm** 12:31 pm
☽⊼☉ **3:50 pm** 12:50 pm
☽☍☿ 11:53 pm

2 FRIDAY
☽☍☿ **2:53 am**
☽☍♅ **8:10 am** 5:10 am
♀△♆ **6:42 pm** 3:42 pm
☽△♆ **8:42 pm** 5:42 pm
☽△♀ **8:51 pm** 5:51 pm
☽⚹♇ 10:16 pm

3 SATURDAY
☽⚹♇ **1:16 am**
☽⊼♃ **7:48 am** 4:48 am
☽□♄ **1:07 pm** 10:07 am
☽△♂ **2:59 pm** 11:59 am
☽☍☉ **11:42 pm** 8:42 pm

4 SUNDAY
☽⊼☿ **11:12 am** 8:12 am
☽⊼♅ **11:35 am** 8:35 am
☿☌♅ **3:49 pm** 12:49 pm
☽□♆ **11:24 pm** 8:24 pm

5 MONDAY
☽⊼♀ **3:05 am** 12:05 am
☽⊻♇ **3:40 am** 12:40 am
☽△♃ **10:44 am** 7:44 am
♀☍♇ **12:05 pm** 9:05 am
☽⚹♄ **3:12 pm** 12:12 pm
☽⊼♂ **7:00 pm** 4:00 pm

6 TUESDAY
☽⊼☉ **4:51 am** 1:51 am
☽△♅ **1:10 pm** 10:10 am
☽△☿ **5:34 pm** 2:34 pm
☽⚹♆ 9:40 pm

7 WEDNESDAY
☽⚹♆ **12:40 am**
☽☌♇ **4:48 am** 1:48 am
☽☍♀ **7:39 am** 4:39 am
☽□♃ **12:35 pm** 9:35 am
☽⊻♄ **4:23 pm** 1:23 pm
☽☍♂ **10:11 pm** 7:11 pm

8 THURSDAY
☽△☉ **9:29 am** 6:29 am
☽□♅ **2:37 pm** 11:37 am
☽□☿ 9:24 pm
☽⊻♆ 11:10 pm

9 FRIDAY
☽□☿ **12:24 am**
☽⊻♆ **2:10 am**
☽⊻♇ **6:17 am** 3:17 am
☽⊼♀ **12:41 pm** 9:41 am
☽⚹♃ **3:02 pm** 12:02 pm
☿⚹♆ **5:14 pm** 2:14 pm
☽☌♄ **6:16 pm** 3:16 pm
☽⊼♂ 11:20 pm

10 SATURDAY
☽⊼♂ **2:20 am**
☽□☉ **3:31 pm** 12:31 pm
☽⚹♅ **5:21 pm** 2:21 pm

11 SUNDAY
☽☌♆ **5:09 am** 2:09 am
☿△♇ **6:26 am** 3:26 am
☽⚹♇ **9:20 am** 6:20 am
☽⚹☿ **9:43 am** 6:43 am
♀□♃ **11:40 am** 8:40 am
☽⊻♃ **7:16 pm** 4:16 pm
☉⊻♅ **7:37 pm** 4:37 pm
☽△♀ **7:40 pm** 4:40 pm
☽⊻♄ **9:53 pm** 6:53 pm

12 MONDAY
☽△♂ **8:35 am** 5:35 am
☽⊻♅ **10:04 pm** 7:04 pm
☽⚹☉ **11:59 pm** 8:59 pm

13 TUESDAY
♀⊼♄ **5:59 am** 2:59 am
☽⊻♆ **10:12 am** 7:12 am
☽□♇ **2:27 pm** 11:27 am
☽⊻☿ **10:35 pm** 7:35 pm
☽☌♃ 10:40 pm

14 WEDNESDAY
☽☌♃ **1:40 am**
☽⚹♄ **3:36 am** 12:36 am
☽□♀ **5:08 am** 2:08 am
☽□♂ **5:15 pm** 2:15 pm
☿⊻♃ 9:24 pm

15 THURSDAY
☿⊻♃ **12:24 am**
☽☌♅ **4:55 am** 1:55 am
☽⊻☉ **11:04 am** 8:04 am
☿□♄ **12:09 pm** 9:09 am
☽⚹♆ **5:19 pm** 2:19 pm
☽△♇ **9:36 pm** 6:36 pm

16 FRIDAY
☽⊻♃ **10:12 am** 7:12 am
☽□♄ **11:20 am** 8:20 am
☽☌☿ **3:12 pm** 12:12 pm
☽⚹♀ **4:57 pm** 1:57 pm

17 SATURDAY
☽⚹♂ **4:14 am** 1:14 am
☿⚹♀ **11:29 am** 8:29 am
☽⊻♅ **1:45 pm** 10:45 am
☽☌☉ 9:37 pm
☽□♆ 11:24 pm

18 SUNDAY
☽☌☉ **12:37 am**
☽□♆ **2:24 am**
☽⊼♇ **6:43 pm** 3:43 pm
☽⚹♃ **8:45 pm** 5:45 pm
☽△♄ **9:00 pm** 6:00 pm
☉□♆ **11:54 pm** 8:54 pm

19 MONDAY
☽⊻♀ **7:02 am** 4:02 am
☽⊻☿ **11:41 am** 8:41 am
♃⚹♄ **11:53 am** 8:53 am
☽⊻♂ **5:28 pm** 2:28 pm
☽⚹♅ 9:33 pm

20 TUESDAY
☽⚹♅ **12:33 am**
☽△♆ **1:24 pm** 10:24 am
☽⊻☉ **4:37 pm** 1:37 pm
☽☍♇ **5:43 pm** 2:43 pm

21 WEDNESDAY
☉⊼♇ **6:20 am** 3:20 am
☽⊼♄ **8:30 am** 5:30 am
☽□♃ **9:15 am** 6:15 am
☿⚹♂ **11:23 am** 8:23 am
☽☌♀ **11:08 pm** 8:08 pm

22 THURSDAY
☽☌♂ **8:41 am** 5:41 am
☽⚹☿ **11:51 am** 8:51 am
☽□♅ **1:01 pm** 10:01 am
☿⊻♅ **6:37 pm** 3:37 pm
☽⊼♆ 10:52 pm

23 FRIDAY
☽⊼♆ **1:52 am**
☽⊼♇ **6:08 am** 3:08 am
☽⚹☉ **10:24 am** 7:24 am
☽☍♄ **9:07 pm** 6:07 pm
☽△♃ **10:53 pm** 7:53 pm

24 SATURDAY
☽⊻♀ **3:59 pm** 12:59 pm
☽⊻♂ 9:33 pm
☽△♅ 10:53 pm

25 SUNDAY
☽⊻♂ **12:33 am**
☽△♅ **1:53 am**
☽□☿ **1:25 pm** 10:25 am
☽☍♆ **2:20 pm** 11:20 am
☽△♇ **6:24 pm** 3:24 pm
☿□♆ **6:36 pm** 3:36 pm

26 MONDAY
☽□☉ **3:50 am** 12:50 am
♂□♅ **5:23 am** 2:23 am
☽⊼♄ **9:04 am** 6:04 am
☽⊼♃ **11:44 am** 8:44 am
☿⊼♇ **5:07 pm** 2:07 pm

27 TUESDAY
☽⚹♀ **6:56 am** 3:56 am
☽⊼♅ **12:58 pm** 9:58 am
☽⚹♂ **2:26 pm** 11:26 am
☽⊼♆ 9:35 pm

28 WEDNESDAY
☽⊼♆ **12:35 am**
☽□♇ **4:19 am** 1:19 am
☽△☿ **11:32 am** 8:32 am
☽△☉ **5:49 pm** 2:49 pm
☽△♄ **6:07 pm** 3:07 pm
☽☍♃ **9:29 pm** 6:29 pm
☉△♄ **9:43 pm** 6:43 pm

29 THURSDAY
☽□♀ **5:32 pm** 2:32 pm
☽☍♅ **8:22 pm** 5:22 pm
☽□♂ 9:05 pm
☿△♄ 11:24 pm

30 FRIDAY
☽□♂ **12:05 am**
☿△♄ **2:24 am**
☽△♆ **6:58 am** 3:58 am
☽⚹♇ **10:20 am** 7:20 am
☽□♄ **11:08 pm** 8:08 pm
☉☌☿ 10:06 pm
☽⊼☉ 11:48 pm
☽⊼☿ 11:58 pm

Eastern time in bold type
Pacific time in medium type

JUNE 2023

DATE	SID.TIME	SUN	MOON	NODE	MERCURY	VENUS	MARS	JUPITER	SATURN	URANUS	NEPTUNE	PLUTO	CERES	PALLAS	JUNO	VESTA	CHIRON
1 Th	16 36 53	10♊16 45	0♏08	3♉37℞	15♉49	25♋35	6♌32	3♉24	6♓59	20♉12	27♓27	0♒09℞	25♍51	12♌23	17♊32	20♉40	18♈49
2 F	16 40 50	11 14 15	13 24	3 37	16 57	26 33	7 07	3 37	7 00	20 15	27 28	0 09	26 00	12 50	18 07	21 06	18 52
3 Sa	16 44 46	12 11 44	27 04	3 35	18 08	27 32	7 41	3 49	7 02	20 19	27 29	0 08	26 10	13 16	18 42	21 32	18 54
4 Su	16 48 43	13 09 11	11♐07	3 31	19 21	28 30	8 16	4 02	7 03	20 22	27 30	0 07	26 20	13 42	19 18	21 58	18 57
5 M	16 52 39	14 06 38	25 27	3 26	20 38	29 27	8 51	4 15	7 05	20 25	27 30	0 06	26 30	14 09	19 53	22 24	18 59
6 T	16 56 36	15 04 03	10♑01	3 20	21 58	0♌24	9 26	4 28	7 06	20 28	27 31	0 05	26 41	14 35	20 27	22 50	19 01
7 W	17 0 32	16 01 28	24 41	3 14	23 20	1 21	10 01	4 40	7 07	20 32	27 32	0 04	26 52	15 02	21 02	23 16	19 04
8 Th	17 4 29	16 58 52	9♒20	3 08	24 46	2 17	10 36	4 53	7 08	20 35	27 33	0 03	27 03	15 28	21 37	23 42	19 06
9 F	17 8 26	17 56 16	23 52	3 04	26 14	3 13	11 12	5 05	7 09	20 38	27 33	0 02	27 15	15 55	22 12	24 08	19 08
10 Sa	17 12 22	18 53 38	8♓12	3 02D	27 45	4 08	11 47	5 17	7 10	20 41	27 34	0 01	27 26	16 22	22 47	24 33	19 10
11 Su	17 16 19	19 51 01	22 17	3 01	29 18	5 02	12 22	5 30	7 10	20 44	27 35	0 00	27 39	16 48	23 22	24 59	19 12
12 M	17 20 15	20 48 22	6♈07	3 02	0♊55	5 56	12 57	5 42	7 11	20 47	27 35	29♑59	27 51	17 15	23 57	25 25	19 14
13 T	17 24 12	21 45 44	19 41	3 03	2 34	6 50	13 33	5 54	7 12	20 51	27 36	29 58	28 03	17 42	24 32	25 51	19 16
14 W	17 28 8	22 43 05	3♉02	3 04℞	4 16	7 43	14 08	6 06	7 12	20 54	27 37	29 57	28 16	18 08	25 06	26 16	19 18
15 Th	17 32 5	23 40 25	16 09	3 03	6 01	8 35	14 43	6 18	7 12	20 57	27 37	29 56	28 29	18 35	25 41	26 42	19 20
16 F	17 36 1	24 37 45	29 04	3 00	7 48	9 26	15 19	6 30	7 12	21 00	27 38	29 55	28 43	19 02	26 16	27 07	19 22
17 Sa	17 39 58	25 35 05	11♊47	2 55	9 38	10 17	15 54	6 41	7 13℞	21 03	27 38	29 54	28 56	19 29	26 50	27 33	19 24
18 Su	17 43 55	26 32 24	24 20	2 47	11 30	11 08	16 30	6 53	7 13	21 06	27 39	29 53	29 10	19 56	27 25	27 58	19 26
19 M	17 47 51	27 29 42	6♋42	2 38	13 25	11 57	17 05	7 05	7 13	21 09	27 39	29 52	29 24	20 22	28 00	28 24	19 27
20 T	17 51 48	28 27 00	18 54	2 28	15 22	12 46	17 41	7 16	7 12	21 12	27 39	29 51	29 38	20 49	28 34	28 49	19 29
21 W	17 55 44	29 24 17	0♌58	2 18	17 22	13 34	18 17	7 28	7 12	21 15	27 40	29 49	29 53	21 16	29 09	29 14	19 31
22 Th	17 59 41	0♋21 34	12 55	2 08	19 24	14 22	18 53	7 39	7 12	21 18	27 40	29 48	0♎08	21 43	29 43	29 40	19 32
23 F	18 3 37	1 18 50	24 47	2 01	21 27	15 08	19 28	7 50	7 11	21 20	27 40	29 47	0 23	22 10	0♋18	0♊05	19 34
24 Sa	18 7 34	2 16 05	6♍37	1 55	23 33	15 54	20 04	8 02	7 11	21 23	27 40	29 46	0 38	22 37	0 52	0 30	19 35
25 Su	18 11 30	3 13 20	18 31	1 52	25 40	16 39	20 40	8 13	7 10	21 26	27 41	29 45	0 53	23 04	1 26	0 55	19 37
26 M	18 15 27	4 10 34	0♎32	1 51D	27 48	17 22	21 16	8 24	7 09	21 29	27 41	29 43	1 09	23 31	2 01	1 20	19 38
27 T	18 19 24	5 07 47	12 45	1 51	29 58	18 05	21 52	8 34	7 08	21 32	27 41	29 42	1 25	23 58	2 35	1 45	19 40
28 W	18 23 20	6 05 00	25 15	1 51℞	2♋08	18 47	22 28	8 45	7 07	21 34	27 41	29 41	1 41	24 26	3 09	2 10	19 41
29 Th	18 27 17	7 02 13	8♏08	1 51	4 19	19 28	23 04	8 56	7 06	21 37	27 41	29 40	1 57	24 53	3 44	2 35	19 42
30 F	18 31 13	7 59 25	21 27	1 50	6 30	20 08	23 40	9 06	7 05	21 40	27 41℞	29 38	2 14	25 20	4 18	3 00	19 43

EPHEMERIS CALCULATED FOR 12 MIDNIGHT GREENWICH MEAN TIME. ALL OTHER DATA AND FACING ASPECTARIAN PAGE IN **EASTERN TIME (BOLD)** AND PACIFIC TIME (REGULAR).

JULY 2023

☽ Last Aspect day	ET / hr:mn / PT		asp	☽ Ingress sign	day	ET / hr:mn / PT	
2	**9:33 am**	6:33 am	☐ ♆	♑	2	**1:20 pm**	10:20 am
4	**12:45 pm**	9:45 am	☌ ♇	♒	4	**1:30 pm**	10:30 am
6	**9:42 am**	6:42 am	☍ ♂	♓	6	**1:33 pm**	10:33 am
8	**2:22 pm**	11:22 am	⚹ ♇	♈	8	**3:19 pm**	12:19 pm
10	**7:11 pm**	4:11 pm	☐ ☿	♉	10	**7:55 pm**	4:55 pm
12		11:11 pm	△ ♇	♊	13	**3:26 am**	12:26 am
13	**2:11 am**		△ ♇	♊	13	**3:26 am**	12:26 am
15	**8:35 am**	5:35 am	☐ ♆	♋	15	**1:13 pm**	10:13 am
17	**11:06 pm**	8:06 pm	☍ ♇	♌	18		9:39 pm
17	**11:06 pm**	8:06 pm	☍ ♇	♌	18	**12:39 am**	

☽ Last Aspect day	ET / hr:mn / PT		asp	☽ Ingress sign	day	ET / hr:mn / PT	
20	**10:08 am**	7:08 am	☌ ♀	♍	20	**1:13 pm**	10:13 am
22		9:06 pm	△ ♇	♎	22		10:54 pm
23	**12:06 am**		△ ♇	♎	23	**1:54 am**	
25	**11:05 am**	8:05 am	☐ ♇	♏	25	**12:55 pm**	9:55 am
27	**6:36 pm**	3:36 pm	⚹ ♇	♐	27	**8:24 pm**	5:24 pm
29	**7:51 pm**	4:51 pm	△ ♀	♑	29	**11:44 pm**	8:44 pm
31	**10:13 pm**	7:13 pm	☌ ♇	♒	31	**11:58 pm**	8:58 pm

☽ Phases & Eclipses phase	day	ET / hr:mn / PT	
Full Moon	3	**7:39 am**	4:39 am
4th Quarter	9	**9:48 pm**	6:48 pm
New Moon	17	**2:32 pm**	11:32 am
2nd Quarter	25	**6:07 pm**	3:07 pm

Planet Ingress	day	ET / hr:mn / PT	
♀ ♍	9		11:55 pm
♀ ♍	10	**2:55 am**	
♂ ♍	10	**7:40 am**	4:40 am
☿ ♌	10		9:11 pm
☿ ♌	11	**12:11 am**	
☉ ♌	22	**9:50 pm**	6:50 pm
☿ ♍	28	**5:31 pm**	2:31 pm

Planetary Motion	day	ET / hr:mn / PT	
♀ ℞	22	**9:33 pm**	6:33 pm
⚷ ℞	23	**8:42 am**	5:42 am

1 SATURDAY
☉ ☌ ☿ **1:06 am**
☽ ⚻ ☉ **2:48 am**
☽ ⚻ ☿ **2:58 am**
☽ ⚻ ♃ **3:00 am** 12:00 am
☿ ⚹ ♃ **3:10 am** 12:10 am
☉ ⚹ ♃ **6:26 am** 3:26 am
☽ △ ♀ **11:21 pm** 8:21 pm
☽ ⚻ ♅ **11:48 pm** 8:48 pm

2 SUNDAY
☽ △ ♂ **5:19 am** 2:19 am
☽ ☐ ♆ **9:33 am** 6:33 am
♀ ☐ ♅ **10:34 am** 7:34 am
☽ ⚺ ♇ **12:39 pm** 9:39 am
☽ ⚹ ♄ 9:43 pm

3 MONDAY
☽ ⚹ ♄ **12:43 am**
☽ △ ♃ **5:02 am** 2:02 am
☽ ☍ ☉ **7:39 am** 4:39 am
☽ ☍ ☿ **12:50 pm** 9:50 am
☽ △ ♅ 9:30 pm
☽ ⚻ ♀ 10:55 pm

4 TUESDAY
☽ △ ♅ **12:30 am**
☽ ⚻ ♀ **1:55 am**
☽ ⚻ ♂ **7:43 am** 4:43 am
☽ ⚹ ♆ **9:49 am** 6:49 am
☽ ☌ ♇ **12:45 pm** 9:45 am
☽ ⚺ ♄ 9:35 pm

5 WEDNESDAY
☽ ⚺ ♄ **12:35 am**
☽ ☐ ♃ **5:28 am** 2:28 am
☽ ⚻ ☉ **10:46 am** 7:46 am
☽ ⚻ ☿ **8:36 pm** 5:36 pm
☽ ☐ ♅ 9:30 pm

6 THURSDAY
☽ ☐ ♅ **12:30 am**
☽ ☍ ♀ **3:38 am** 12:38 am
☽ ☍ ♂ **9:42 am** 6:42 am
☽ ⚺ ♆ **9:47 am** 6:47 am
♂ ⚻ ♆ **11:48 am** 8:48 am
☽ ⚺ ♇ **12:43 pm** 9:43 am
☽ ☌ ♄ 9:47 pm
☿ ⚹ ♅ 9:55 pm

7 FRIDAY
☽ ☌ ♄ **12:47 am**
☿ ⚹ ♅ **12:55 am**
☽ ⚹ ♃ **6:28 am** 3:28 am
☽ △ ☉ **2:48 pm** 11:48 am
☽ ⚹ ♅ 10:48 pm

8 SATURDAY
☽ ⚹ ♅ **1:48 am**
☽ △ ☿ **5:56 am** 2:56 am
☽ ⚻ ♀ **6:42 am** 3:42 am
☽ ☌ ♆ **11:22 am** 8:22 am
☿ ⚺ ♀ **12:45 pm** 9:45 am
☽ ⚻ ♂ **1:30 pm** 10:30 am
☽ ⚹ ♇ **2:22 pm** 11:22 am

Eastern time in bold type
Pacific time in medium type

9 SUNDAY
☽ ⚺ ♄ **3:02 am** 12:02 am
♂ ⚻ ♇ **8:54 am** 5:54 am
☽ ⚺ ♃ **9:44 am** 6:44 am
☿ △ ♆ **7:57 pm** 4:57 pm
☽ ☐ ☉ **9:48 pm** 6:48 pm

10 MONDAY
☽ ⚺ ♅ **5:45 am** 2:45 am
☽ △ ♀ **12:34 pm** 9:34 am
☽ ⚺ ♆ **3:43 pm** 12:43 pm
☿ ☍ ♇ **4:48 pm** 1:48 pm
☽ ☐ ♇ **6:50 pm** 3:50 pm
☽ ☐ ☿ **7:11 pm** 4:11 pm
☽ △ ♂ **8:31 pm** 5:31 pm

11 TUESDAY
☿ ⚺ ♂ **7:36 am** 4:36 am
☽ ⚹ ♄ **8:11 am** 5:11 am
☽ ☌ ♃ **4:04 pm** 1:04 pm

12 WEDNESDAY
☽ ⚹ ☉ **8:30 am** 5:30 am
☽ ☌ ♅ **12:42 pm** 9:42 am
☽ ☐ ♀ **9:24 pm** 6:24 pm
☽ ⚹ ♆ **10:59 pm** 7:59 pm
☽ △ ♇ 11:11 pm

13 THURSDAY
☽ △ ♇ **2:11 am**
☽ ☐ ♂ **6:51 am** 3:51 am
☽ ⚹ ☿ **12:40 pm** 9:40 am
☽ ☐ ♄ **4:06 pm** 1:06 pm
☽ ⚺ ♃ 10:11 pm

14 FRIDAY
☽ ⚺ ♃ **1:11 am**
☿ ⚻ ♄ **11:17 am** 8:17 am
☉ ⚹ ♅ **7:02 pm** 4:02 pm
☽ ⚺ ♅ **10:08 pm** 7:08 pm
☽ ⚺ ☉ **10:23 pm** 7:23 pm

15 SATURDAY
☽ ⚹ ♀ **8:27 am** 5:27 am
☽ ☐ ♆ **8:35 am** 5:35 am
☽ ⚻ ♇ **11:49 am** 8:49 am
♀ ⚻ ♆ **2:42 pm** 11:42 am
☽ ⚹ ♂ **7:48 pm** 4:48 pm
☽ △ ♄ 11:06 pm

16 SUNDAY
☽ △ ♄ **2:06 am**
☽ ⚺ ☿ **9:08 am** 6:08 am
☽ ⚹ ♃ **12:23 pm** 9:23 am

17 MONDAY
☿ ☐ ♃ **8:49 am** 5:49 am
☽ ⚹ ♅ **9:21 am** 6:21 am
☽ ☌ ☉ **2:32 pm** 11:32 am
☽ △ ♆ **7:52 pm** 4:52 pm
☽ ⚺ ♀ **8:55 pm** 5:55 pm
☽ ☍ ♇ **11:06 pm** 8:06 pm

18 TUESDAY
☽ ⚺ ♂ **10:37 am** 7:37 am
☽ ⚻ ♄ **1:36 pm** 10:36 am
☽ ☐ ♃ 10:02 pm

19 WEDNESDAY
☽ ☐ ♃ **1:02 am**
☽ ☌ ☿ **7:23 am** 4:23 am
☽ ☐ ♅ **9:51 pm** 6:51 pm

20 THURSDAY
☽ ⚺ ☉ **8:14 am** 5:14 am
☽ ⚻ ♆ **8:19 am** 5:19 am
☉ △ ♆ **9:07 am** 6:07 am
☽ ☌ ♀ **10:08 am** 7:08 am
☽ ⚻ ♇ **11:31 am** 8:31 am
♂ ☍ ♄ **4:39 pm** 1:39 pm
☽ ☍ ♄ 11:03 pm
☽ ☌ ♂ 11:36 pm

21 FRIDAY
☽ ☍ ♄ **2:03 am**
☽ ☌ ♂ **2:36 am**
☉ ⚺ ♀ **9:39 am** 6:39 am
☽ △ ♃ **2:30 pm** 11:30 am
☉ ☍ ♇ **11:53 pm** 8:53 pm

22 SATURDAY
☽ ⚺ ☿ **6:07 am** 3:07 am
☽ △ ♅ **10:48 am** 7:48 am
☽ ☍ ♆ **9:00 pm** 6:00 pm
☽ ⚺ ♀ **11:06 pm** 8:06 pm
☽ △ ♇ 9:06 pm
☽ ⚹ ☉ 11:15 pm

23 SUNDAY
☽ △ ♇ **12:06 am**
☽ ⚹ ☉ **2:15 am**
☽ ⚻ ♄ **2:18 pm** 11:18 am

☿ ☐ ♅ **5:39 pm** 2:39 pm
☽ ⚺ ♂ **6:22 pm** 3:22 pm

24 MONDAY
☽ ⚻ ♃ 3:24 am 12:24 am
☽ ⚻ ♅ **10:35 pm** 7:35 pm
☽ ⚹ ☿ 11:39 pm

25 TUESDAY
☽ ⚹ ☿ **2:39 am**
☽ ⚻ ♆ **8:10 am** 5:10 am
☽ ⚹ ♀ **10:00 am** 7:00 am
☽ ☐ ♇ **11:05 am** 8:05 am
☽ ☐ ☉ **6:07 pm** 3:07 pm
☽ △ ♄ 9:27 pm

26 WEDNESDAY
☽ △ ♄ **12:27 am**
☽ ⚹ ♂ **7:31 am** 4:31 am
☽ ☍ ♃ **1:38 pm** 10:38 am
☿ ⚻ ♆ 9:00 pm

27 THURSDAY
☿ ⚻ ♆ **12:00 am**
☽ ☍ ♅ **7:10 am** 4:10 am
☿ ☌ ♀ **11:16 am** 8:16 am
☽ △ ♆ **3:56 pm** 12:56 pm
☽ ☐ ♀ **5:06 pm** 2:06 pm
☽ ☐ ☿ **5:53 pm** 2:53 pm
☽ ⚹ ♇ **6:36 pm** 3:36 pm
☿ ⚻ ♇ 9:24 pm

28 FRIDAY
☿ ⚻ ♇ **12:24 am**
☽ △ ☉ **5:22 am** 2:22 am

☽ ☐ ♄ **6:52 am** 3:52 am
☽ ☐ ♂ **4:09 pm** 1:09 pm
☽ ⚻ ♃ **7:44 pm** 4:44 pm
☉ ⚻ ♄ 10:38 pm

29 SATURDAY
☉ ⚻ ♄ **1:38 am**
☽ ⚻ ♅ **11:35 am** 8:35 am
☽ ☐ ♆ **7:32 pm** 4:32 pm
☽ △ ♀ **7:51 pm** 4:51 pm
☽ ⚺ ♇ **9:59 pm** 6:59 pm
☽ △ ☿ 11:55 pm

30 SUNDAY
☽ △ ☿ **2:55 am**
☽ ⚹ ♄ **9:15 am** 6:15 am
☽ ⚻ ☉ **11:35 am** 8:35 am
♀ ⚻ ♆ **12:25 pm** 9:25 am
☽ △ ♂ **8:18 pm** 5:18 pm
☽ △ ♃ **9:51 pm** 6:51 pm

31 MONDAY
☽ △ ♅ **12:29 pm** 9:29 am
☽ ⚻ ♀ **7:17 pm** 4:17 pm
☽ ⚹ ♆ **7:55 pm** 4:55 pm
☽ ☌ ♇ **10:13 pm** 7:13 pm

JULY 2023

DATE	SID.TIME	SUN	MOON	NODE	MERCURY	VENUS	MARS	JUPITER	SATURN	URANUS	NEPTUNE	PLUTO	CERES	PALLAS	JUNO	VESTA	CHIRON
1 Sa	18 35 10	8♋56 36	5♐14	1♉46℞	8♋41	20♌47	24♌16	9♉17	7♓04℞	21♉42	27♓41℞	29♑37℞	2♎30	25♌47	4♋52	3♊25	19♈45
2 Su	18 39 6	9 53 48	19 28	1 40	10 52	21 24	24 52	9 27	7 03	21 45	27 41	29 36	2 47	26 14	5 26	3 49	19 46
3 M	18 43 3	10 50 59	4♑06	1 31	13 02	22 00	25 28	9 38	7 01	21 47	27 41	29 34	3 04	26 41	6 00	4 14	19 47
4 T	18 47 0	11 48 10	19 01	1 22	15 11	22 36	26 04	9 48	7 00	21 50	27 41	29 33	3 21	27 09	6 34	4 39	19 48
5 W	18 50 56	12 45 21	4♒05	1 12	17 19	23 09	26 41	9 58	6 58	21 52	27 41	29 32	3 39	27 36	7 08	5 03	19 49
6 Th	18 54 53	13 42 32	19 07	1 03	19 26	23 42	27 17	10 08	6 56	21 55	27 41	29 30	3 56	28 03	7 42	5 28	19 50
7 F	18 58 49	14 39 43	3♓58	0 56	21 32	24 13	27 53	10 17	6 55	21 57	27 41	29 29	4 14	28 30	8 16	5 52	19 51
8 Sa	19 2 46	15 36 55	18 32	0 51	23 36	24 42	28 29	10 27	6 53	22 00	27 40	29 28	4 32	28 58	8 49	6 16	19 51
9 Su	19 6 42	16 34 06	2♈45	0 49	25 39	25 11	29 06	10 37	6 51	22 02	27 40	29 26	4 50	29 25	9 23	6 41	19 52
10 M	19 10 39	17 31 18	16 34	0 48D	27 40	25 37	29 42	10 46	6 49	22 04	27 40	29 25	5 08	29 52	9 57	7 05	19 53
11 T	19 14 35	18 28 31	0♉03	0 48℞	29 39	26 02	0♍19	10 56	6 46	22 07	27 40	29 23	5 26	0♍19	10 31	7 29	19 54
12 W	19 18 32	19 25 44	13 11	0 48	1♌37	26 25	0 55	11 05	6 44	22 09	27 39	29 22	5 45	0 47	11 04	7 53	19 54
13 Th	19 22 29	20 22 58	26 04	0 46	3 33	26 47	1 32	11 14	6 42	22 11	27 39	29 21	6 04	1 14	11 38	8 17	19 55
14 F	19 26 25	21 20 12	8♊42	0 41	5 26	27 07	2 08	11 23	6 39	22 13	27 38	29 19	6 22	1 41	12 11	8 41	19 55
15 Sa	19 30 22	22 17 26	21 10	0 34	7 18	27 25	2 45	11 32	6 37	22 15	27 38	29 18	6 41	2 09	12 45	9 05	19 56
16 Su	19 34 18	23 14 41	3♋27	0 24	9 08	27 41	3 22	11 40	6 34	22 17	27 38	29 16	7 01	2 36	13 18	9 28	19 56
17 M	19 38 15	24 11 57	15 37	0 11	10 57	27 55	3 58	11 49	6 32	22 19	27 37	29 15	7 20	3 04	13 52	9 52	19 57
18 T	19 42 11	25 09 13	27 40	29♈58	12 43	28 07	4 35	11 58	6 29	22 21	27 37	29 14	7 39	3 31	14 25	10 16	19 57
19 W	19 46 8	26 06 29	9♌38	29 44	14 27	28 18	5 12	12 06	6 26	22 23	27 36	29 12	7 59	3 58	14 58	10 39	19 57
20 Th	19 50 4	27 03 45	21 31	29 31	16 10	28 26	5 49	12 14	6 23	22 25	27 35	29 11	8 19	4 26	15 32	11 03	19 57
21 F	19 54 1	28 01 02	3♍21	29 20	17 51	28 31	6 26	12 22	6 20	22 27	27 35	29 09	8 39	4 53	16 05	11 26	19 58
22 Sa	19 57 58	28 58 19	15 11	29 12	19 29	28 35	7 03	12 30	6 17	22 29	27 34	29 08	8 59	5 21	16 38	11 50	19 58
23 Su	20 1 54	29 55 36	27 04	29 07	21 06	28 36℞	7 40	12 38	6 14	22 31	27 33	29 06	9 19	5 48	17 11	12 13	19 58℞
24 M	20 5 51	0♌52 54	9♎04	29 04	22 42	28 35	8 17	12 45	6 11	22 33	27 33	29 05	9 39	6 16	17 44	12 36	19 58
25 T	20 9 47	1 50 12	21 15	29 03	24 15	28 32	8 54	12 53	6 08	22 34	27 32	29 04	9 59	6 43	18 17	12 59	19 58
26 W	20 13 44	2 47 31	3♏42	29 03	25 46	28 26	9 31	13 00	6 04	22 36	27 31	29 02	10 20	7 11	18 50	13 22	19 58
27 Th	20 17 40	3 44 49	16 32	29 02	27 16	28 18	10 08	13 07	6 01	22 37	27 30	29 01	10 40	7 38	19 23	13 45	19 57
28 F	20 21 37	4 42 09	29 47	29 01	28 43	28 07	10 45	13 14	5 57	22 39	27 30	28 59	11 01	8 06	19 55	14 08	19 57
29 Sa	20 25 33	5 39 28	13♐31	28 57	0♍09	27 54	11 22	13 21	5 54	22 41	27 29	28 58	11 22	8 33	20 28	14 30	19 57
30 Su	20 29 30	6 36 49	27 44	28 51	1 32	27 39	12 00	13 28	5 50	22 42	27 28	28 56	11 43	9 01	21 01	14 53	19 57
31 M	20 33 27	7 34 10	12♑26	28 42	2 54	27 21	12 37	13 35	5 46	22 44	27 27	28 55	12 04	9 28	21 33	15 15	19 56

EPHEMERIS CALCULATED FOR 12 MIDNIGHT GREENWICH MEAN TIME. ALL OTHER DATA AND FACING ASPECTARIAN PAGE IN **EASTERN TIME (BOLD)** AND PACIFIC TIME (REGULAR).

AUGUST 2023

☽ Last Aspect day	ET / hr:mn / PT		asp	☽ Ingress sign	day	ET / hr:mn / PT	
2	**5:15 pm**	2:15 pm	☍♀	♓	2	**11:05 pm**	8:05 pm
4	**9:21 pm**	6:21 pm	⚹♇	♈	4	**11:19 pm**	8:19 pm
6		9:13 pm	□♇	♉	6		11:25 pm
7	**12:13 am**		□♇	♉	7	**2:25 am**	
9	**6:39 am**	3:39 am	△♇	♊	9	**9:05 am**	6:05 am
11	**1:27 pm**	10:27 am	□♆	♋	11	**6:52 pm**	3:52 pm
14	**3:46 am**	12:46 am	☍♇	♌	14	**6:36 am**	3:36 am
16	**5:38 am**	2:38 am	☌☉	♍	16	**7:14 pm**	4:14 pm
19	**4:51 am**	1:51 am	△♇	♎	19	**7:53 am**	4:53 am
21	**4:31 pm**	1:31 pm	⚹☉	♏	21	**7:22 pm**	4:22 pm
23		10:10 pm	⚹♇	♐	24	**4:07 am**	1:07 am
24	**1:10 am**		⚹♇	♐	24	**4:07 am**	1:07 am
26	**7:56 am**	4:56 am	□♂	♑	27	**9:05 am**	6:05 am
28	**7:49 am**	4:49 am	☌♇	♒	28	**10:32 am**	7:32 am
29	**11:04 pm**	8:04 pm	□♅	♓	30	**9:56 am**	6:56 am

☽ Phases & Eclipses phase	day	ET / hr:mn / PT	
Full Moon	1	**2:32 pm**	11:32 am
4th Quarter	8	**6:28 am**	3:28 am
New Moon	16	**5:38 am**	2:38 am
2nd Quarter	24	**5:57 am**	2:57 am
Full Moon	30	**9:36 pm**	6:36 pm

Planet Ingress	day	ET / hr:mn / PT	
✷ ♌	15	**3:29 pm**	12:29 pm
☉ ♍	23	**5:01 am**	2:01 am
♂ ♎	27	**9:20 am**	6:20 am

Planetary Motion	day	ET / hr:mn / PT	
☿ ℞	23	**3:59 pm**	12:59 pm
♅ ℞	28	**10:39 pm**	7:39 pm

1 TUESDAY
☽⚻☿ **7:37 am** 4:37 am
☽⚺♄ **8:54 am** 5:54 am
☽☍☉ **2:32 pm** 11:32 am
♂△♃ **4:45 pm** 1:45 pm
☽□♃ **9:38 pm** 6:38 pm
☽⚻♂ **9:48 pm** 6:48 pm
☿☍♄ **10:18 pm** 7:18 pm

2 WEDNESDAY
☽□♅ **11:44 am** 8:44 am
☽☍♀ **5:15 pm** 2:15 pm
☽⚺♆ **7:00 pm** 4:00 pm
☽⚺♇ **9:16 pm** 6:16 pm

3 THURSDAY
☽☌♄ **7:53 am** 4:53 am
☽☍☿ **11:03 am** 8:03 am
☽⚻☉ **4:59 pm** 1:59 pm
☽⚹♃ **9:20 pm** 6:20 pm
☽☍♂ **11:15 pm** 8:15 pm

4 FRIDAY
☽⚹♅ **11:35 am** 8:35 am
☽⚻♀ **3:49 pm** 12:49 pm
☽☌♆ **7:00 pm** 4:00 pm
☽⚹♇ **9:21 pm** 6:21 pm

5 SATURDAY
☽⚺♄ **8:18 am** 5:18 am
☽⚻☿ **4:14 pm** 1:14 pm
☽△☉ **9:40 pm** 6:40 pm
☽⚺♃ **11:03 pm** 8:03 pm

Eastern time in bold type
Pacific time in medium type

6 SUNDAY
☽⚻♂ **3:03 am** 12:03 am
☽⚺♅ **1:57 pm** 10:57 am
☽△♀ **4:35 pm** 1:35 pm
☉□♃ **8:03 pm** 5:03 pm
☽⚺♆ **9:43 pm** 6:43 pm
☽□♇ 9:13 pm

7 MONDAY
☽□♇ **12:13 am**
☽⚹♄ **11:46 am** 8:46 am
☽△☿ 10:10 pm

8 TUESDAY
☽△☿ **1:10 am**
☽☌♃ **4:11 am** 1:11 am
☽□☉ **6:28 am** 3:28 am
☽△♂ **10:46 am** 7:46 am
☽☌♅ **7:50 pm** 4:50 pm
☽□♀ **8:21 pm** 5:21 pm

9 WEDNESDAY
☽⚹♆ **4:00 am** 1:00 am
☽△♇ **6:39 am** 3:39 am
♀□♅ **7:08 am** 4:08 am
☽□♄ **6:45 pm** 3:45 pm
☿△♃ **8:47 pm** 5:47 pm

10 THURSDAY
☽⚺♃ **12:51 pm** 9:51 am
☽□☿ **2:02 pm** 11:02 am
☽⚹☉ **7:37 pm** 4:37 pm

☽□♂ **10:28 pm** 7:28 pm
☽⚹♀ 11:52 pm

11 FRIDAY
☽⚹♀ **2:52 am**
☽⚺♅ **5:03 am** 2:03 am
☽□♆ **1:27 pm** 10:27 am
☽⚻♇ **4:13 pm** 1:13 pm

12 SATURDAY
☽△♄ **4:37 am** 1:37 am
♀⚺♂ **8:15 pm** 5:15 pm
☽⚹♃ 9:06 pm

13 SUNDAY
☽⚹♃ **12:06 am**
☽⚹☿ **5:26 am** 2:26 am
☉☌♀ **7:16 am** 4:16 am
☽⚺♀ **11:17 am** 8:17 am
☽⚺☉ **11:51 am** 8:51 am
☽⚹♂ **12:56 pm** 9:56 am
☽⚹♅ **4:30 pm** 1:30 pm
☽△♆ 9:57 pm

14 MONDAY
☽△♆ **12:57 am**
☽☍♇ **3:46 am** 12:46 am
☽⚻♄ **4:12 pm** 1:12 pm
☉⚺♂ 10:10 pm

15 TUESDAY
☉⚺♂ **1:10 am**
☽□♃ **12:44 pm** 9:44 am
☿⚺♀ **1:04 pm** 10:04 am
☽☌♀ **8:44 pm** 5:44 pm

☽⚺☿ **9:34 pm** 6:34 pm
☉□♅ **10:35 pm** 7:35 pm

16 WEDNESDAY
☽⚺♂ **4:48 am** 1:48 am
☽□♅ **5:04 am** 2:04 am
☽☌☉ **5:38 am** 2:38 am
♂△♅ **9:53 am** 6:53 am
☽⚻♆ **1:26 pm** 10:26 am
☽⚻♇ **4:17 pm** 1:17 pm

17 THURSDAY
☽☍♄ **4:32 am** 1:32 am
☽△♃ 10:48 pm

18 FRIDAY
☽△♃ **1:48 am**
☽⚺♀ **6:35 am** 3:35 am
☽☌☿ **1:09 pm** 10:09 am
☽△♅ **5:51 pm** 2:51 pm
☽☌♂ **8:57 pm** 5:57 pm
☽⚺☉ **11:42 pm** 8:42 pm
☽☍♆ 11:01 pm

19 SATURDAY
☽☍♆ **2:01 am**
☽△♇ **4:51 am** 1:51 am
☽⚻♄ **4:43 pm** 1:43 pm

20 SUNDAY
☉⚻♆ **3:40 am** 12:40 am
☽⚻♃ **2:19 pm** 11:19 am
☽⚹♀ **4:07 pm** 1:07 pm
☽⚺☿ 11:50 pm

21 MONDAY
☽⚺☿ **2:50 am**
☽⚻♅ **5:47 am** 2:47 am
☽⚺♂ **12:02 pm** 9:02 am
☽⚻♆ **1:34 pm** 10:34 am
☉⚻♇ **2:07 pm** 11:07 am
☽□♇ **4:19 pm** 1:19 pm
☽⚹☉ **4:31 pm** 1:31 pm

22 TUESDAY
☽△♄ **3:33 am** 12:33 am
♀□♃ **8:16 am** 5:16 am
♂☍♆ **4:34 pm** 1:34 pm
☽□♀ 9:10 pm
☽☍♃ 9:48 pm

23 WEDNESDAY
☽□♀ **12:10 am**
☽☍♃ **12:48 am**
☽⚹☿ **1:03 pm** 10:03 am
☽☍♅ **3:19 pm** 12:19 pm
☽△♆ **10:33 pm** 7:33 pm
☽⚹♂ 9:09 pm
☽⚹♇ 10:10 pm

24 THURSDAY
☽⚹♂ **12:09 am**
☽⚹♇ **1:10 am**
☽□☉ **5:57 am** 2:57 am
☽□♄ **11:29 am** 8:29 am
♂△♇ **8:23 pm** 5:23 pm

25 FRIDAY
☽△♀ **5:27 am** 2:27 am
☽⚻♃ **7:49 am** 4:49 am

☽□☿ **6:43 pm** 3:43 pm
☽⚻♅ **9:12 pm** 6:12 pm

26 SATURDAY
☽□♆ **3:49 am** 12:49 am
☽⚺♇ **6:16 am** 3:16 am
☽□♂ **7:56 am** 4:56 am
☽△☉ **2:39 pm** 11:39 am
☽⚹♄ **3:39 pm** 12:39 pm

27 SUNDAY
☉☍♄ **4:28 am** 1:28 am
☽⚻♀ **7:28 am** 4:28 am
☽△♃ **10:58 am** 7:58 am
☽△☿ **8:00 pm** 5:00 pm
☽△♅ **11:22 pm** 8:22 pm

28 MONDAY
☽⚹♆ **5:29 am** 2:29 am
☽☌♇ **7:49 am** 4:49 am
☽△♂ **11:39 am** 8:39 am
☽⚺♄ **4:29 pm** 1:29 pm
☽⚻☉ **7:08 pm** 4:08 pm

29 TUESDAY
☽☍♀ **6:56 am** 3:56 am
☽□♃ **11:11 am** 8:11 am
☽⚻☿ **6:18 pm** 3:18 pm
☽□♅ **11:04 pm** 8:04 pm

30 WEDNESDAY
☽⚺♆ **4:56 am** 1:56 am
☽⚺♇ **7:14 am** 4:14 am
☽⚻♂ **1:07 pm** 10:07 am

☽☌♄ **3:33 pm** 12:33 pm
☽☍☉ **9:36 pm** 6:36 pm

31 THURSDAY
☽⚻♀ **5:33 am** 2:33 am
☽⚹♃ **10:25 am** 7:25 am
☽☍☿ **3:29 pm** 12:29 pm
☽⚹♅ **10:20 pm** 7:20 pm

AUGUST 2023

DATE	SID.TIME	SUN	MOON	NODE	MERCURY	VENUS	MARS	JUPITER	SATURN	URANUS	NEPTUNE	PLUTO	CERES	PALLAS	JUNO	VESTA	CHIRON
1 T	20 37 23	8♌ 31 31	27♑29	28♈32℞	4♍14	27♌01℞	13♍14	13♉41	5♓43℞	22♉45	27♓26℞	28♑54℞	12♎25	9♍56	22♋06	15♊38	19♈56℞
2 W	20 41 20	9 28 53	12♒45	28 21	5 31	26 39	13 51	13 47	5 39	22 46	27 25	28 52	12 47	10 23	22 38	16 00	19 55
3 Th	20 45 16	10 26 16	28 02	28 11	6 47	26 15	14 29	13 53	5 35	22 48	27 24	28 51	13 08	10 51	23 11	16 22	19 55
4 F	20 49 13	11 23 40	13♓10	28 04	8 00	25 49	15 06	13 59	5 31	22 49	27 23	28 49	13 30	11 18	23 43	16 45	19 54
5 Sa	20 53 9	12 21 05	27 59	27 59	9 11	25 20	15 44	14 05	5 27	22 50	27 22	28 48	13 51	11 46	24 15	17 07	19 54
6 Su	20 57 6	13 18 31	12♈23	27 56	10 20	24 50	16 21	14 11	5 23	22 51	27 21	28 47	14 13	12 13	24 47	17 29	19 53
7 M	21 1 2	14 15 59	26 21	27 55D	11 26	24 19	16 59	14 16	5 19	22 52	27 20	28 45	14 35	12 41	25 20	17 50	19 52
8 T	21 4 59	15 13 28	9♉52	27 55℞	12 30	23 46	17 36	14 21	5 15	22 53	27 19	28 44	14 57	13 08	25 52	18 12	19 52
9 W	21 8 56	16 10 58	23 00	27 55	13 31	23 11	18 14	14 26	5 11	22 54	27 18	28 43	15 19	13 36	26 24	18 34	19 51
10 Th	21 12 52	17 08 29	5♊47	27 54	14 30	22 36	18 52	14 31	5 07	22 55	27 17	28 41	15 41	14 04	26 56	18 55	19 50
11 F	21 16 49	18 06 02	18 17	27 50	15 25	22 00	19 29	14 36	5 03	22 56	27 15	28 40	16 03	14 31	27 28	19 17	19 49
12 Sa	21 20 45	19 03 36	0♋35	27 44	16 18	21 23	20 07	14 41	4 58	22 57	27 14	28 39	16 25	14 59	27 59	19 38	19 48
13 Su	21 24 42	20 01 12	12 42	27 35	17 08	20 46	20 45	14 45	4 54	22 58	27 13	28 37	16 48	15 26	28 31	19 59	19 47
14 M	21 28 38	20 58 49	24 43	27 24	17 54	20 08	21 23	14 49	4 50	22 59	27 12	28 36	17 10	15 54	29 03	20 20	19 46
15 T	21 32 35	21 56 27	6♌39	27 12	18 37	19 31	22 01	14 53	4 45	23 00	27 10	28 35	17 33	16 21	29 34	20 41	19 45
16 W	21 36 31	22 54 06	18 32	27 00	19 16	18 54	22 39	14 57	4 41	23 00	27 09	28 33	17 55	16 49	0♌06	21 02	19 44
17 Th	21 40 28	23 51 47	0♍23	26 49	19 51	18 18	23 17	15 01	4 37	23 01	27 08	28 32	18 18	17 17	0 37	21 22	19 42
18 F	21 44 25	24 49 29	12 13	26 39	20 22	17 43	23 55	15 05	4 32	23 01	27 07	28 31	18 41	17 44	1 09	21 43	19 41
19 Sa	21 48 21	25 47 12	24 06	26 32	20 49	17 08	24 33	15 08	4 28	23 02	27 05	28 30	19 04	18 12	1 40	22 03	19 40
20 Su	21 52 18	26 44 56	6♎02	26 27	21 12	16 35	25 11	15 11	4 23	23 02	27 04	28 28	19 27	18 39	2 11	22 24	19 39
21 M	21 56 14	27 42 42	18 06	26 25D	21 29	16 03	25 49	15 14	4 19	23 03	27 02	28 27	19 50	19 07	2 43	22 44	19 37
22 T	22 0 11	28 40 28	0♏19	26 25	21 42	15 33	26 27	15 17	4 14	23 03	27 01	28 26	20 13	19 35	3 14	23 04	19 36
23 W	22 4 7	29 38 16	12 48	26 26	21 49℞	15 04	27 05	15 19	4 10	23 04	27 00	28 25	20 36	20 02	3 45	23 24	19 34
24 Th	22 8 4	0♍36 05	25 35	26 27℞	21 51	14 38	27 44	15 22	4 05	23 04	26 58	28 24	20 59	20 30	4 16	23 43	19 33
25 F	22 12 0	1 33 55	8♐46	26 26	21 47	14 13	28 22	15 24	4 01	23 04	26 57	28 23	21 23	20 57	4 46	24 03	19 31
26 Sa	22 15 57	2 31 47	22 23	26 25	21 38	13 50	29 00	15 26	3 56	23 04	26 55	28 21	21 46	21 25	5 17	24 22	19 30
27 Su	22 19 54	3 29 40	6♑28	26 21	21 22	13 30	29 39	15 28	3 52	23 04	26 54	28 20	22 09	21 52	5 48	24 42	19 28
28 M	22 23 50	4 27 34	21 00	26 15	21 00	13 12	0♎17	15 29	3 47	23 04	26 52	28 19	22 33	22 20	6 19	25 01	19 26
29 T	22 27 47	5 25 29	5♒56	26 08	20 33	12 56	0 56	15 31	3 43	23 05℞	26 51	28 18	22 57	22 48	6 49	25 20	19 24
30 W	22 31 43	6 23 25	21 07	26 01	20 00	12 43	1 34	15 32	3 38	23 05	26 49	28 17	23 20	23 15	7 20	25 39	19 23
31 Th	22 35 40	7 21 23	6♓24	25 54	19 21	12 32	2 13	15 33	3 34	23 04	26 48	28 16	23 44	23 43	7 50	25 57	19 21

EPHEMERIS CALCULATED FOR 12 MIDNIGHT GREENWICH MEAN TIME. ALL OTHER DATA AND FACING ASPECTARIAN PAGE IN **EASTERN TIME (BOLD)** AND PACIFIC TIME (REGULAR).

SEPTEMBER 2023

☽ Last Aspect day	ET / hr:mn / PT		asp	☽ Ingress sign	day	ET / hr:mn / PT	
1	**6:36 am**	3:36 am	✶♇	♈	1	**9:25 am**	6:25 am
3	**7:57 am**	4:57 am	□♇	♉	3	**11:00 am**	8:00 am
5	**12:46 pm**	9:46 am	△♇	♊	5	**4:07 pm**	1:07 pm
7	**6:22 pm**	3:22 pm	□♆	♋	7		10:00 pm
7	**6:22 pm**	3:22 pm	□♆	♋	8	**1:00 am**	
10	**8:47 am**	5:47 am	☍♇	♌	10	**12:36 pm**	9:36 am
12	**11:06 am**	8:06 am	□♅	♍	12		10:18 pm
12	**11:06 am**	8:06 am	□♅	♍	13	**1:18 am**	
15	**9:49 am**	6:49 am	△♇	♎	15	**1:44 pm**	10:44 am
17	**9:06 pm**	6:06 pm	□♇	♏	17		9:58 pm
17	**9:06 pm**	6:06 pm	□♇	♏	18	**12:58 am**	
20	**6:21 am**	3:21 am	✶♇	♐	20	**10:06 am**	7:06 am
22	**3:32 pm**	12:32 pm	□☉	♑	22	**4:20 pm**	1:20 pm
24	**4:05 pm**	1:05 pm	☌♇	♒	24	**7:29 pm**	4:29 pm
26	**8:38 am**	5:38 am	□♅	♓	26	**8:18 pm**	5:18 pm
28	**4:58 pm**	1:58 pm	✶♇	♈	28	**8:17 pm**	5:17 pm
30	**5:50 pm**	2:50 pm	□♇	♉	30	**9:18 pm**	6:18 pm

☽ Phases & Eclipses phase	day	ET / hr:mn / PT	
4th Quarter	6	**6:21 pm**	3:21 pm
New Moon	14	**9:40 pm**	6:40 pm
2nd Quarter	22	**3:32 pm**	12:32 pm
Full Moon	29	**5:58 am**	2:58 am

Planet Ingress		day	ET / hr:mn / PT	
♀	♎	13	**12:38 pm**	9:38 am
⚵	♋	13	**7:28 pm**	4:28 pm
⚳	♏	15	**8:50 am**	5:50 am
☉	♎	22		11:50 pm
☉	♎	23	**2:50 am**	

Planetary Motion		day	ET / hr:mn / PT	
♀	D	3	**9:20 pm**	6:20 pm
♃	R	4	**10:10 am**	7:10 am
☿	D	15	**4:21 pm**	1:21 pm

1 FRIDAY
☽☌♆ **4:13 am** 1:13 am
☽✶♇ **6:36 am** 3:36 am
☽☍♂ **2:50 pm** 11:50 am
☽⊻♄ **2:56 pm** 11:56 am
♂⊼♄ **5:01 pm** 2:01 pm
☽⊼☉ 9:46 pm

2 SATURDAY
☽⊼☉ **12:46 am**
☽△♀ **5:19 am** 2:19 am
☽⊻♃ **10:47 am** 7:47 am
☽⊼☿ **1:25 pm** 10:25 am
☽⊻♅ **11:15 pm** 8:15 pm

3 SUNDAY
☽⊻♆ **5:24 am** 2:24 am
☽□♇ **7:57 am** 4:57 am
☽✶♄ **4:36 pm** 1:36 pm
☽⊼♂ **7:10 pm** 4:10 pm

4 MONDAY
☿△♃ **6:29 am** 3:29 am
☽△☉ **7:12 am** 4:12 am
☽□♀ **8:08 am** 5:08 am
☽△☿ **1:35 pm** 10:35 am
☽☌♃ **2:06 pm** 11:06 am
☉⊻♀ **8:42 pm** 5:42 pm

5 TUESDAY
☽☌♅ **3:28 am** 12:28 am
☽✶♆ **9:59 am** 6:59 am
☽△♇ **12:46 pm** 9:46 am
☽□♄ **9:50 pm** 6:50 pm

6 WEDNESDAY
☽△♂ **3:45 am** 12:45 am
☉☌☿ **7:09 am** 4:09 am
☽✶♀ **3:06 pm** 12:06 pm
☽□☿ **4:46 pm** 1:46 pm
☽□☉ **6:21 pm** 3:21 pm
☽⊻♃ **9:12 pm** 6:12 pm

7 THURSDAY
☽⊻♅ **11:30 am** 8:30 am
☿⊻♀ **12:18 pm** 9:18 am
☽□♆ **6:22 pm** 3:22 pm
☽⊼♇ **9:22 pm** 6:22 pm

8 FRIDAY
☽△♄ **6:43 am** 3:43 am
☉△♃ **7:13 am** 4:13 am
☽□♂ **4:34 pm** 1:34 pm
☽✶☿ **10:57 pm** 7:57 pm
☽⊻♀ 11:02 pm

9 SATURDAY
☽⊻♀ **2:02 am**
☽✶♃ **7:38 am** 4:38 am
☽✶☉ **9:49 am** 6:49 am
☽✶♅ **10:34 pm** 7:34 pm

10 SUNDAY
☽△♆ **5:36 am** 2:36 am
☽☍♇ **8:47 am** 5:47 am
☽⊼♄ **6:09 pm** 3:09 pm

11 MONDAY
☿⊻♂ **3:22 am** 12:22 am
☽⊻☿ **7:37 am** 4:37 am
☽✶♂ **8:06 am** 5:06 am
☽☌♀ **3:32 pm** 12:32 pm
☽□♃ **7:54 pm** 4:54 pm

12 TUESDAY
☽⊻☉ **3:37 am** 12:37 am
☽□♅ **11:06 am** 8:06 am
☽⊼♆ **6:07 pm** 3:07 pm
☽⊼♇ **9:24 pm** 6:24 pm

13 WEDNESDAY
☽☍♄ **6:31 am** 3:31 am
☽☌☿ **6:04 pm** 3:04 pm
☽⊻♂ 9:22 pm

14 THURSDAY
☽⊻♂ **12:22 am**
☽⊻♀ **5:56 am** 2:56 am
☽△♃ **8:27 am** 5:27 am
☽☌☉ **9:40 pm** 6:40 pm
☽△♅ **11:38 pm** 8:38 pm

15 FRIDAY
☽☍♆ **6:30 am** 3:30 am
☽△♇ **9:49 am** 6:49 am
☽⊼♄ **6:32 pm** 3:32 pm
☉△♅ **9:24 pm** 6:24 pm

16 SATURDAY
☽⊻☿ **5:45 am** 2:45 am
☽☌♂ **3:53 pm** 12:53 pm
☽✶♀ **7:57 pm** 4:57 pm
☽⊼♃ **8:12 pm** 5:12 pm
♀□♃ 11:10 pm

17 SUNDAY
♀□♃ **2:10 am**
☽⊼♅ **11:09 am** 8:09 am
☽⊻☉ **2:27 pm** 11:27 am
☽⊼♆ **5:47 pm** 2:47 pm
☽□♇ **9:06 pm** 6:06 pm

18 MONDAY
☽△♄ **5:19 am** 2:19 am
☽✶☿ **5:52 pm** 2:52 pm

19 TUESDAY
☽⊻♂ **5:31 am** 2:31 am
☽☍♃ **6:16 am** 3:16 am
☉☍♆ **7:17 am** 4:17 am
☽□♀ **8:29 am** 5:29 am
♂⊼♃ **6:48 pm** 3:48 pm
☽☍♅ **8:46 pm** 5:46 pm

20 WEDNESDAY
☽△♆ **3:06 am** 12:06 am
☽✶☉ **4:47 am** 1:47 am
☽✶♇ **6:21 am** 3:21 am
☽□♄ **1:58 pm** 10:58 am
☉△♇ 10:21 pm

21 THURSDAY
☉△♇ **1:21 am**
☽□☿ **5:13 am** 2:13 am
☽⊼♃ **1:47 pm** 10:47 am
☽✶♂ **4:12 pm** 1:12 pm
☽△♀ **6:25 pm** 3:25 pm

22 FRIDAY
☽⊼♅ **3:40 am** 12:40 am
☽□♆ **9:37 am** 6:37 am
☽⊻♇ **12:46 pm** 9:46 am
☽□☉ **3:32 pm** 12:32 pm
☽✶♄ **7:44 pm** 4:44 pm

23 SATURDAY
☽△☿ **2:24 pm** 11:24 am
☽△♃ **6:12 pm** 3:12 pm
☽□♂ **11:17 pm** 8:17 pm
☽□⚷ 9:07 pm
☽⊼♀ 10:04 pm

24 SUNDAY
☽⊼♀ **1:04 am**
☽△♅ **7:27 am** 4:27 am
☽✶♆ **1:03 pm** 10:03 am
☽☌♇ **4:05 pm** 1:05 pm
☽△☉ **10:26 pm** 7:26 pm
☽⊻♄ **10:29 pm** 7:29 pm
☉⊼♄ **11:10 pm** 8:10 pm

25 MONDAY
☿△♃ **8:10 am** 5:10 am
☽□♃ **7:49 pm** 4:49 pm
☽⊼☿ **9:02 pm** 6:02 pm

26 TUESDAY
☽△♂ **3:13 am** 12:13 am
☽☍♀ **4:47 am** 1:47 am
☽□♅ **8:38 am** 5:38 am
☽⊻♆ **2:00 pm** 11:00 am
☽⊻♇ **5:00 pm** 2:00 pm
☽☌♄ **11:01 pm** 8:01 pm
☽⊼☉ 11:33 pm

27 WEDNESDAY
☽⊼☉ **2:33 am**
☽✶♃ **7:46 pm** 4:46 pm
☽☍☿ 11:18 pm

28 THURSDAY
☽☍☿ **2:18 am**
☽⊼♂ **5:30 am** 2:30 am
☽⊼♀ **7:06 am** 4:06 am
☽✶♅ **8:35 am** 5:35 am
☽☌♆ **1:54 pm** 10:54 am
☽✶♇ **4:58 pm** 1:58 pm
☽⊻♄ **10:49 pm** 7:49 pm

29 FRIDAY
☽☍☉ **5:58 am** 2:58 am
♀□♅ **1:53 pm** 10:53 am
☽⊻♃ **7:46 pm** 4:46 pm

30 SATURDAY
☿⊻♂ **4:35 am** 1:35 am
☽☍♂ **8:20 am** 5:20 am
☽⊼☿ **8:36 am** 5:36 am
☽⊻♅ **9:06 am** 6:06 am
☽△♀ **10:08 am** 7:08 am
☿△♅ **12:55 pm** 9:55 am
☽⊻♆ **2:35 pm** 11:35 am
☽□♇ **5:50 pm** 2:50 pm
☽✶♄ **11:45 pm** 8:45 pm
♂⊼♅ 9:38 pm

Eastern time in bold type
Pacific time in medium type

SEPTEMBER 2023

DATE	SID.TIME	SUN	MOON	NODE	MERCURY	VENUS	MARS	JUPITER	SATURN	URANUS	NEPTUNE	PLUTO	CERES	PALLAS	JUNO	VESTA	CHIRON
1 F	22 39 36	8♍19 23	21♓36	25♈48℞	18♍37℞	12♌23℞	2♎51	15♉34	3♓29℞	23♉04℞	26♓46℞	28♑15℞	24♎08	24♍10	8♌20	26♊16	19♈19℞
2 Sa	22 43 33	9 17 24	6♈33	25 45	17 48	12 17	3 30	15 34	3 25	23 04	26 45	28 14	24 32	24 38	8 50	26 34	19 17
3 Su	22 47 29	10 15 27	21 07	25 43D	16 55	12 14	4 09	15 35	3 20	23 04	26 43	28 13	24 56	25 05	9 21	26 52	19 15
4 M	22 51 26	11 13 32	5♉15	25 43	16 00	12 12D	4 47	15 35℞	3 16	23 04	26 42	28 12	25 20	25 33	9 51	27 10	19 13
5 T	22 55 23	12 11 39	18 54	25 45	15 02	12 13	5 26	15 35	3 11	23 03	26 40	28 11	25 44	26 01	10 21	27 28	19 11
6 W	22 59 19	13 09 48	2♊07	25 46℞	14 04	12 17	6 05	15 35	3 07	23 03	26 38	28 10	26 08	26 28	10 50	27 46	19 09
7 Th	23 3 16	14 07 59	14 56	25 46	13 06	12 22	6 44	15 34	3 02	23 03	26 37	28 09	26 32	26 56	11 20	28 03	19 07
8 F	23 7 12	15 06 12	27 26	25 46	12 10	12 30	7 23	15 34	2 58	23 02	26 35	28 08	26 56	27 23	11 50	28 21	19 05
9 Sa	23 11 9	16 04 27	9♋41	25 43	11 16	12 40	8 02	15 33	2 53	23 02	26 34	28 08	27 20	27 51	12 20	28 38	19 03
10 Su	23 15 5	17 02 44	21 44	25 39	10 27	12 52	8 41	15 32	2 49	23 01	26 32	28 07	27 45	28 18	12 49	28 55	19 01
11 M	23 19 2	18 01 03	3♌40	25 33	9 44	13 07	9 20	15 31	2 45	23 00	26 30	28 06	28 09	28 46	13 18	29 11	18 58
12 T	23 22 58	18 59 24	15 32	25 26	9 07	13 23	9 59	15 29	2 40	23 00	26 29	28 05	28 33	29 13	13 48	29 28	18 56
13 W	23 26 55	19 57 47	27 23	25 20	8 37	13 41	10 38	15 28	2 36	22 59	26 27	28 04	28 58	29 41	14 17	29 44	18 54
14 Th	23 30 52	20 56 12	9♍15	25 13	8 16	14 01	11 17	15 26	2 32	22 58	26 25	28 04	29 22	0♎08	14 46	0♋00	18 51
15 F	23 34 48	21 54 39	21 09	25 08	8 04D	14 23	11 56	15 24	2 28	22 57	26 24	28 03	29 47	0 36	15 15	0 16	18 49
16 Sa	23 38 45	22 53 07	3♎08	25 05	8 00	14 47	12 36	15 22	2 24	22 57	26 22	28 02	0♏11	1 03	15 44	0 32	18 47
17 Su	23 42 41	23 51 38	15 13	25 03D	8 06	15 12	13 15	15 19	2 20	22 56	26 20	28 02	0 36	1 31	16 13	0 47	18 44
18 M	23 46 38	24 50 10	27 27	25 02	8 22	15 39	13 54	15 17	2 16	22 55	26 19	28 01	1 01	1 58	16 42	1 03	18 42
19 T	23 50 34	25 48 44	9♏51	25 03	8 47	16 08	14 34	15 14	2 12	22 54	26 17	28 00	1 26	2 26	17 10	1 18	18 39
20 W	23 54 31	26 47 20	22 28	25 05	9 21	16 38	15 13	15 11	2 08	22 53	26 15	28 00	1 50	2 53	17 39	1 33	18 37
21 Th	23 58 27	27 45 57	5♐21	25 06	10 04	17 09	15 53	15 08	2 04	22 52	26 14	27 59	2 15	3 21	18 07	1 47	18 34
22 F	0 2 24	28 44 36	18 33	25 07℞	10 55	17 42	16 32	15 05	2 00	22 50	26 12	27 59	2 40	3 48	18 36	2 01	18 32
23 Sa	0 6 21	29 43 17	2♑05	25 08	11 54	18 16	17 12	15 01	1 56	22 49	26 10	27 58	3 05	4 16	19 04	2 16	18 29
24 Su	0 10 17	0♎42 00	16 01	25 07	13 00	18 52	17 52	14 57	1 53	22 48	26 09	27 58	3 30	4 43	19 32	2 29	18 27
25 M	0 14 14	1 40 44	0♒18	25 05	14 12	19 29	18 31	14 53	1 49	22 47	26 07	27 57	3 55	5 11	20 00	2 43	18 24
26 T	0 18 10	2 39 30	14 56	25 03	15 31	20 07	19 11	14 49	1 45	22 45	26 05	27 57	4 20	5 38	20 28	2 56	18 22
27 W	0 22 7	3 38 18	29 49	25 00	16 54	20 46	19 51	14 45	1 42	22 44	26 04	27 56	4 45	6 06	20 56	3 09	18 19
28 Th	0 26 3	4 37 07	14♓49	24 57	18 22	21 27	20 31	14 40	1 38	22 43	26 02	27 56	5 10	6 33	21 23	3 22	18 17
29 F	0 30 0	5 35 58	29 49	24 55	19 54	22 09	21 10	14 36	1 35	22 41	26 01	27 56	5 35	7 00	21 51	3 35	18 14
30 Sa	0 33 56	6 34 51	14♈40	24 54D	21 30	22 51	21 50	14 31	1 32	22 40	25 59	27 55	6 00	7 28	22 18	3 47	18 11

EPHEMERIS CALCULATED FOR 12 MIDNIGHT GREENWICH MEAN TIME. ALL OTHER DATA AND FACING ASPECTARIAN PAGE IN **EASTERN TIME (BOLD)** AND PACIFIC TIME (REGULAR).

OCTOBER 2023

☽ Last Aspect day	ET / hr:mn / PT		asp	☽ Ingress sign	day	ET / hr:mn / PT	
2	**9:20 pm**	6:20 pm	△♇	♊	2		10:03 pm
2	**9:20 pm**	6:20 pm	△♇	♊	3	**1:03 am**	
4		11:34 pm	✶♀	♋	5	**8:32 am**	5:32 am
5	**2:34 am**		✶♀	♋	5	**8:32 am**	5:32 am
7	**3:12 pm**	12:12 pm	☍♇	♌	7	**7:24 pm**	4:24 pm
10	**5:37 am**	2:37 am	✶♂	♍	10	**8:02 am**	5:02 am
12	**4:10 pm**	1:10 pm	△♇	♎	12	**8:22 pm**	5:22 pm
15	**3:01 am**	12:01 am	□♇	♏	15	**7:04 am**	4:04 am
17	**11:44 am**	8:44 am	✶♇	♐	17	**3:36 pm**	12:36 pm
19	**3:02 pm**	12:02 pm	✶☉	♑	19	**9:55 pm**	6:55 pm

☽ Last Aspect day	ET / hr:mn / PT		asp	☽ Ingress sign	day	ET / hr:mn / PT	
21		11:00 pm	□☿	♒	21		11:06 pm
22	**2:00 am**		□☿	♒	22	**2:06 am**	
23	**3:04 pm**	12:04 pm	□♅	♓	24	**4:33 am**	1:33 am
25		11:39 pm	✶♇	♈	26	**6:02 am**	3:02 am
26	**2:39 am**		✶♇	♈	26	**6:02 am**	3:02 am
28	**4:20 am**	1:20 am	□♇	♉	28	**7:44 am**	4:44 am
30	**7:36 am**	4:36 am	△♇	♊	30	**11:08 am**	8:08 am

☽ Phases & Eclipses phase	day	ET / hr:mn / PT	
4th Quarter	6	**9:48 am**	6:48 am
New Moon	14	**1:55 pm**	10:55 am
	14	21° ♎ 08'	
2nd Quarter	21	**11:29 pm**	8:29 pm
Full Moon	28	**4:24 pm**	1:24 pm
	28	5° ♉ 09'	

Planet Ingress		day	ET / hr:mn / PT	
☿	♎	4	**8:09 pm**	5:09 pm
♀	♍	8	**9:11 pm**	6:11 pm
♂	♏	11		9:04 pm
♂	♏	12	**12:04 am**	
⚵	♍	17	**9:27 am**	6:27 am
☿	♏	21		11:49 pm
☿	♏	22	**2:49 am**	
☉	♏	23	**12:21 pm**	9:21 am

Planetary Motion		day	ET / hr:mn / PT	
♇	D	10	**9:10 pm**	6:10 pm

1 SUNDAY
♂⚻♅ **12:38 am**
☿⚺♀ **7:38 am** 4:38 am
☽⚻☉ **11:05 am** 8:05 am
☽☌♃ **9:37 pm** 6:37 pm

2 MONDAY
☿☍♆ **11:34 am** 8:34 am
☽☌♅ **11:57 am** 8:57 am
☽⚻♂ **1:50 pm** 10:50 am
☽□♀ **4:07 pm** 1:07 pm
☽✶♆ **5:47 pm** 2:47 pm
☽△☿ **6:41 pm** 3:41 pm
☽△♇ **9:20 pm** 6:20 pm

3 TUESDAY
☽□♄ **3:29 am** 12:29 am
☿△♇ **3:20 pm** 12:20 pm
☽△☉ **8:03 pm** 5:03 pm
♀⚻♆ **8:21 pm** 5:21 pm
☽⚺♃ 11:44 pm

4 WEDNESDAY
☽⚺♃ **2:44 am**
☽⚺♅ **6:22 pm** 3:22 pm
☽△♂ **11:33 pm** 8:33 pm
☽□♆ 9:37 pm
☽✶♀ 11:34 pm

5 THURSDAY
☽□♆ **12:37 am**
☽✶♀ **2:34 am**
☽⚻♇ **4:31 am** 1:31 am

☽□☿ **10:33 am** 7:33 am
☽△♄ **10:55 am** 7:55 am
☿⚻♄ **1:03 pm** 10:03 am
♂⚻♆ **7:09 pm** 4:09 pm

6 FRIDAY
♀⚻♇ **8:50 am** 5:50 am
☽□☉ **9:48 am** 6:48 am
☽✶♃ **11:30 am** 8:30 am

7 SATURDAY
☽✶♅ **4:22 am** 1:22 am
☉⚻♃ **5:04 am** 2:04 am
☽△♆ **10:58 am** 7:58 am
☽□♂ **1:25 pm** 10:25 am
☽☍♇ **3:12 pm** 12:12 pm
☽⚺♀ **5:27 pm** 2:27 pm
☽⚻♄ **9:41 pm** 6:41 pm

8 SUNDAY
☽✶☿ **7:47 am** 4:47 am
♂□♇ **9:05 pm** 6:05 pm
☽□♃ **10:55 pm** 7:55 pm

9 MONDAY
☽✶☉ **3:07 am** 12:07 am
☽□♅ **4:36 pm** 1:36 pm
☽⚻♆ **11:21 pm** 8:21 pm
♀☍♄ 11:11 pm

10 TUESDAY
♀☍♄ **2:11 am**
☽⚻♇ **3:45 am** 12:45 am
☽✶♂ **5:37 am** 2:37 am

☽☍♄ **10:06 am** 7:06 am
☽☌♀ **10:46 am** 7:46 am

11 WEDNESDAY
☽⚺☿ **7:08 am** 4:08 am
☽△♃ **11:06 am** 8:06 am
☽⚺☉ **9:18 pm** 6:18 pm

12 THURSDAY
☽△♅ **5:01 am** 2:01 am
☿⚻♃ **8:32 am** 5:32 am
☽☍♆ **11:42 am** 8:42 am
☽△♇ **4:10 pm** 1:10 pm
☽⚺♂ **9:34 pm** 6:34 pm
☽⚻♄ **10:13 pm** 7:13 pm

13 FRIDAY
☽⚺♀ **3:49 am** 12:49 am
♂△♄ **8:29 am** 5:29 am
☽⚻♃ **10:16 pm** 7:16 pm

14 SATURDAY
☽☌☿ **4:58 am** 1:58 am
☽☌☉ **1:55 pm** 10:55 am
☽⚻♅ **4:03 pm** 1:03 p
☽⚻♆ **10:34 pm** 7:34 pm

15 SUNDAY
☽□♇ **3:01 am** 12:01 am
☽△♄ **8:41 am** 5:41 am
☽☌♂ **11:35 am** 8:35 am
☉⚻♅ **3:44 pm** 12:44 pm
☽✶♀ **6:51 pm** 3:51 pm

16 MONDAY
☽☍♃ **7:31 am** 4:31 am
☽⚺☿ **11:29 pm** 8:29 pm
☽☍♅ 10:01 pm

17 TUESDAY
☽☍♅ **1:01 am**
☽⚺☉ **3:54 am** 12:54 am
☽△♆ **7:20 am** 4:20 am
☿⚻♅ **10:48 am** 7:48 am
☽✶♇ **11:44 am** 8:44 am
☽□♄ **5:02 pm** 2:02 pm
☽⚺♂ **11:03 pm** 8:03 pm

18 WEDNESDAY
☽□♀ **7:15 am** 4:15 am
☽⚻♃ **2:35 pm** 11:35 am
☉⚻♆ **11:40 pm** 8:40 pm

19 THURSDAY
☽⚻♅ **7:45 am** 4:45 am
☿⚻♆ **10:12 am** 7:12 am
☽□♆ **1:53 pm** 10:53 am
☽✶☿ **2:25 pm** 11:25 am
☽✶☉ **3:02 pm** 12:02 pm
☽⚺♇ **6:12 pm** 3:12 pm
☽✶♄ **11:10 pm** 8:10 pm
☉☌☿ 10:38 pm

20 FRIDAY
☉☌☿ **1:38 am**
☽✶♂ **7:54 am** 4:54 am
☽△♀ **4:59 pm** 1:59 pm
☽△♃ **7:30 pm** 4:30 pm
☿□♇ **8:51 pm** 5:51 pm

21 SATURDAY
☉□♇ **10:09 am** 7:09 am
☽△♅ **12:21 pm** 9:21 am
☽✶♆ **6:17 pm** 3:17 pm
☽☌♇ **10:33 pm** 7:33 pm
☽□☉ **11:29 pm** 8:29 pm
♀△♃ 9:32 pm
☽□☿ 11:00 pm

22 SUNDAY
♀△♃ **12:32 am**
☽□☿ **2:00 am**
☽⚺♄ **3:13 am** 12:13 am
☿△♄ **12:12 pm** 9:12 am
☽□♂ **2:21 pm** 11:21 am
☽□♃ **10:27 pm** 7:27 pm
☽⚻♀ 9:17 pm

23 MONDAY
☽⚻♀ **12:17 am**
☽□♅ **3:04 pm** 12:04 pm
☽⚺♆ **8:53 pm** 5:53 pm
☽⚺♇ 10:07 pm

24 TUESDAY
☽⚺♇ **1:07 am**
☉△♄ **3:14 am** 12:14 am
☽☌♄ **5:34 am** 2:34 am
☽△☉ **5:45 am** 2:45 am
☽△☿ **10:57 am** 7:57 am
☽△♂ **6:58 pm** 3:58 pm
☽✶♃ **11:57 pm** 8:57 pm

25 WEDNESDAY
☽☍♀ **5:52 am** 2:52 am
☽✶♅ **4:35 pm** 1:35 pm
☽☌♆ **10:22 pm** 7:22 pm
☽✶♇ 11:39 pm

26 THURSDAY
☽✶♇ **2:39 am**
☽⚺♄ **6:59 am** 3:59 am
☽⚻☉ **10:50 am** 7:50 am
☽⚻☿ **6:36 pm** 3:36 pm
☽⚻♂ **10:49 pm** 7:49 pm
☽⚺♃ 9:54 pm

27 FRIDAY
☽⚺♃ **12:54 am**
☽⚻♀ **11:00 am** 8:00 am
☽⚺♅ **5:57 pm** 2:57 pm
☽⚺♆ **11:53 pm** 8:53 pm

28 SATURDAY
☽□♇ **4:20 am** 1:20 am
☽✶♄ **8:40 am** 5:40 am
♂☍♃ **12:03 pm** 9:03 am
☽☍☉ **4:24 pm** 1:24 pm
☿☍♃ **11:44 pm** 8:44 pm
☽☌♃ 11:37 pm

29 SUNDAY
☽☌♃ **2:37 am**
☽☍☿ **3:00 am** 12:00 am
☽☍♂ **3:30 am** 12:30 am
☿☌♂ **10:22 am** 7:22 am

☽△♀ **5:33 pm** 2:33 pm
☽☌♅ **8:36 pm** 5:36 pm
☽✶♆ 11:51 pm

30 MONDAY
☽✶♆ **2:51 am**
☽△♇ **7:36 am** 4:36 am
☽□♄ **12:04 pm** 9:04 am
☽⚻☉ 9:22 pm

31 TUESDAY
☽⚻☉ **12:22 am**
☽⚺♃ **6:28 am** 3:28 am
♀△♅ **8:51 am** 5:51 am
☽⚻♂ **10:48 am** 7:48 am
☽⚻☿ **2:31 pm** 11:31 am
☽⚺♅ 10:53 pm

Eastern time in bold type
Pacific time in medium type

OCTOBER 2023

DATE	SID.TIME	SUN	MOON	NODE	MERCURY	VENUS	MARS	JUPITER	SATURN	URANUS	NEPTUNE	PLUTO	CERES	PALLAS	JUNO	VESTA	CHIRON
1 Su	0 37 53	7♎33 47	29♈13	24♈54	23♍08	23♌35	22♎30	14♉26℞	1♓29℞	22♉38℞	25♓57℞	27♑55℞	6♏25	7♎55	22♌46	3♋59	18♈09℞
2 M	0 41 50	8 32 44	13♉24	24 54	24 48	24 20	23 10	14 21	1 25	22 37	25 56	27 55	6 50	8 22	23 13	4 11	18 06
3 T	0 45 46	9 31 44	27 10	24 55	26 31	25 05	23 50	14 16	1 22	22 35	25 54	27 54	7 16	8 50	23 40	4 22	18 03
4 W	0 49 43	10 30 46	10♊29	24 57	28 15	25 52	24 30	14 10	1 19	22 34	25 53	27 54	7 41	9 17	24 07	4 34	18 01
5 Th	0 53 39	11 29 50	23 24	24 58	29 59	26 39	25 11	14 04	1 16	22 32	25 51	27 54	8 06	9 44	24 34	4 45	17 58
6 F	0 57 36	12 28 57	5♋58	24 58℞	1♎45	27 28	25 51	13 59	1 14	22 30	25 49	27 54	8 32	10 12	25 01	4 55	17 55
7 Sa	1 1 32	13 28 06	18 14	24 58	3 31	28 17	26 31	13 53	1 11	22 28	25 48	27 54	8 57	10 39	25 27	5 05	17 52
8 Su	1 5 29	14 27 17	0♌18	24 58	5 17	29 07	27 11	13 47	1 08	22 27	25 46	27 54	9 22	11 06	25 54	5 15	17 50
9 M	1 9 25	15 26 31	12 13	24 57	7 04	29 57	27 52	13 40	1 05	22 25	25 45	27 54	9 48	11 33	26 20	5 25	17 47
10 T	1 13 22	16 25 46	24 04	24 56	8 50	0♍49	28 32	13 34	1 03	22 23	25 43	27 54	10 13	12 01	26 46	5 34	17 44
11 W	1 17 19	17 25 04	5♍55	24 55	10 36	1 41	29 13	13 28	1 01	22 21	25 42	27 54D	10 38	12 28	27 12	5 43	17 41
12 Th	1 21 15	18 24 24	17 49	24 54	12 22	2 34	29 53	13 21	0 58	22 19	25 40	27 54	11 04	12 55	27 38	5 52	17 39
13 F	1 25 12	19 23 47	29 49	24 53	14 08	3 28	0♏34	13 14	0 56	22 17	25 39	27 54	11 29	13 22	28 04	6 00	17 36
14 Sa	1 29 8	20 23 11	11♎57	24 52	15 53	4 22	1 14	13 07	0 54	22 15	25 37	27 54	11 55	13 49	28 30	6 09	17 33
15 Su	1 33 5	21 22 38	24 16	24 52D	17 37	5 17	1 55	13 00	0 52	22 13	25 36	27 54	12 20	14 17	28 55	6 16	17 31
16 M	1 37 1	22 22 06	6♏45	24 52	19 21	6 12	2 36	12 53	0 50	22 11	25 34	27 54	12 46	14 44	29 21	6 24	17 28
17 T	1 40 58	23 21 37	19 28	24 53	21 04	7 08	3 16	12 46	0 48	22 09	25 33	27 54	13 12	15 11	29 46	6 30	17 25
18 W	1 44 54	24 21 10	2♐23	24 53℞	22 47	8 04	3 57	12 39	0 46	22 07	25 31	27 54	13 37	15 38	0♍11	6 37	17 22
19 Th	1 48 51	25 20 44	15 32	24 53	24 29	9 01	4 38	12 31	0 44	22 05	25 30	27 54	14 03	16 05	0 36	6 43	17 20
20 F	1 52 47	26 20 20	28 55	24 53	26 11	9 59	5 19	12 24	0 43	22 03	25 29	27 55	14 28	16 32	1 01	6 49	17 17
21 Sa	1 56 44	27 19 58	12♑33	24 52	27 51	10 57	6 00	12 16	0 41	22 01	25 27	27 55	14 54	16 59	1 25	6 55	17 14
22 Su	2 0 41	28 19 38	26 26	24 52D	29 32	11 56	6 41	12 08	0 40	21 58	25 26	27 55	15 20	17 26	1 50	7 00	17 12
23 M	2 4 37	29 19 20	10♒33	24 52	1♏11	12 55	7 22	12 01	0 39	21 56	25 25	27 56	15 45	17 53	2 14	7 05	17 09
24 T	2 8 34	0♏19 03	24 52	24 53	2 50	13 54	8 03	11 53	0 37	21 54	25 23	27 56	16 11	18 20	2 39	7 09	17 06
25 W	2 12 30	1 18 47	9♓20	24 53	4 29	14 54	8 44	11 45	0 36	21 52	25 22	27 56	16 37	18 47	3 03	7 13	17 04
26 Th	2 16 27	2 18 34	23 54	24 54	6 06	15 55	9 25	11 37	0 35	21 49	25 21	27 57	17 02	19 14	3 26	7 16	17 01
27 F	2 20 23	3 18 22	8♈29	24 54	7 44	16 55	10 07	11 29	0 34	21 47	25 20	27 57	17 28	19 41	3 50	7 20	16 59
28 Sa	2 24 20	4 18 12	22 59	24 55℞	9 20	17 57	10 48	11 21	0 34	21 45	25 18	27 58	17 54	20 07	4 14	7 22	16 56
29 Su	2 28 16	5 18 03	7♉17	24 54	10 57	18 58	11 29	11 13	0 33	21 42	25 17	27 58	18 19	20 34	4 37	7 25	16 53
30 M	2 32 13	6 17 57	21 19	24 54	12 32	20 00	12 11	11 05	0 32	21 40	25 16	27 59	18 45	21 01	5 00	7 27	16 51
31 T	2 36 10	7 17 53	5♊01	24 52	14 08	21 03	12 52	10 57	0 32	21 38	25 15	27 59	19 11	21 28	5 23	7 28	16 48

EPHEMERIS CALCULATED FOR 12 MIDNIGHT GREENWICH MEAN TIME. ALL OTHER DATA AND FACING ASPECTARIAN PAGE IN **EASTERN TIME (BOLD)** AND PACIFIC TIME (REGULAR).

NOVEMBER 2023

☽ Last Aspect				☽ Ingress			
day	ET / hr:mn / PT		asp	sign	day	ET / hr:mn / PT	
1	**8:36 am**	5:36 am	□♆	♋	1	**5:30 pm**	2:30 pm
3	**11:28 pm**	8:28 pm	☍♇	♌	4	**3:21 am**	12:21 am
5		11:25 pm	□☿	♍	6	**2:39 pm**	11:39 am
6	**2:25 am**		□☿	♍	6	**2:39 pm**	11:39 am
8	**11:55 pm**	8:55 pm	⚹☿	♎	9	**3:08 am**	12:08 am
11	**10:05 am**	7:05 am	□♇	♏	11	**1:39 pm**	10:39 am
13	**6:03 pm**	3:03 pm	⚹♇	♐	13	**9:23 pm**	6:23 pm
15	**5:57 pm**	2:57 pm	□♆	♑	15		11:41 pm
15	**5:57 pm**	2:57 pm	□♆	♑	16	**2:41 am**	
18	**3:27 am**	12:27 am	☌♇	♒	18	**6:28 am**	3:28 am
20	**5:50 am**	2:50 am	□☉	♓	20	**9:29 am**	6:29 am
22	**10:10 am**	7:10 am	△♂	♈	22	**12:19 pm**	9:19 am
24	**12:40 pm**	9:40 am	□♇	♉	24	**3:29 pm**	12:29 pm
26	**4:52 pm**	1:52 pm	△♇	♊	26	**7:40 pm**	4:40 pm
28	**8:03 pm**	5:03 pm	☍☿	♋	28		10:54 pm
28	**8:03 pm**	5:03 pm	☍☿	♋	29	**1:54 am**	

☽ Phases & Eclipses			
phase	day	ET / hr:mn / PT	
4th Quarter	5	**3:37 am**	1:37 am
New Moon	13	**4:27 am**	1:27 am
2nd Quarter	20	**5:50 am**	2:50 am
Full Moon	27	**4:16 am**	1:16 am

Planet Ingress			
	day	ET / hr:mn / PT	
♀ ♎	8	**4:30 am**	1:30 am
☿ ♐	9		10:25 pm
☿ ♐	10	**1:25 am**	
♀ ♏	19	**4:03 am**	1:03 am
☉ ♐	22	**9:03 am**	6:03 am
♂ ♐	24	**5:15 am**	2:15 am
⚳ ♐	24		9:14 pm
⚳ ♐	25	**12:14 am**	

Planetary Motion				
		day	ET / hr:mn / PT	
⚴	℞	2	**9:50 pm**	6:50 pm
♄	D	4	**3:03 am**	12:03 am

1 WEDNESDAY
☽ ⚺ ♅ **1:53 am**
☽ □ ♀ **3:26 am** 12:26 am
☽ □ ♆ **8:36 am** 5:36 am
☽ ⚻ ♇ **1:47 pm** 10:47 am
☽ △ ♄ **6:29 pm** 3:29 pm

2 THURSDAY
☽ △ ☉ **12:23 pm** 9:23 am
☽ ⚹ ♃ **1:31 pm** 10:31 am
☽ △ ♂ **10:01 pm** 7:01 pm
☉ ☍ ♃ 10:02 pm

3 FRIDAY
☉ ☍ ♃ **1:02 am**
☽ △ ☿ **6:49 am** 3:49 am
☽ ⚹ ♅ **10:36 am** 7:36 am
☽ ⚹ ♀ **5:49 pm** 2:49 pm
☽ △ ♆ **5:50 pm** 2:50 pm
♀ ☍ ♆ **6:06 pm** 3:06 pm
☽ ☍ ♇ **11:28 pm** 8:28 pm

4 SATURDAY
☽ ⚻ ♄ **4:22 am** 1:22 am
☿ ☍ ♅ **12:07 pm** 9:07 am
☽ □ ♃ **11:46 pm** 8:46 pm

5 SUNDAY
☽ □ ☉ **3:37 am** 1:37 am
☽ □ ♂ **12:00 pm** 9:00 am
☽ □ ♅ **9:11 pm** 6:11 pm
☽ □ ☿ 11:25 pm

6 MONDAY
☽ □ ☿ **2:25 am**
☽ ⚻ ♆ **4:48 am** 1:48 am
♀ △ ♇ **9:38 am** 6:38 am
☽ ⚻ ♇ **10:44 am** 7:44 am
☽ ⚺ ♀ **10:50 am** 7:50 am
☽ ☍ ♄ **3:42 pm** 12:42 pm
☿ △ ♆ **8:37 pm** 5:37 pm

7 TUESDAY
☽ △ ♃ **10:43 am** 7:43 am
☽ ⚹ ☉ **9:54 pm** 6:54 pm

8 WEDNESDAY
☽ ⚹ ♂ **4:29 am** 1:29 am
☽ △ ♅ **9:40 am** 6:40 am
♀ ⚻ ♄ **4:13 pm** 1:13 pm
☽ ☍ ♆ **5:20 pm** 2:20 pm
☿ ⚹ ♇ **7:17 pm** 4:17 pm
☽ △ ♇ **11:20 pm** 8:20 pm
☽ ⚹ ☿ **11:55 pm** 8:55 pm

9 THURSDAY
☽ ⚻ ♄ **4:12 am** 1:12 am
☽ ☌ ♀ **5:23 am** 2:23 am
☽ ⚻ ♃ **10:05 pm** 7:05 pm

10 FRIDAY
☿ □ ♄ **10:07 am** 7:07 am
☽ ⚺ ☉ **2:51 pm** 11:51 am
☽ ⚺ ♂ **7:29 pm** 4:29 pm
☽ ⚻ ♅ **8:43 pm** 5:43 pm

11 SATURDAY
☽ ⚻ ♆ **4:13 am** 1:13 am
☽ □ ♇ **10:05 am** 7:05 am
☽ △ ♄ **2:43 pm** 11:43 am
♂ ☍ ♅ **4:11 pm** 1:11 pm
☽ ⚺ ☿ **6:34 pm** 3:34 pm
☽ ⚺ ♀ **9:22 pm** 6:22 pm

12 SUNDAY
☽ ☍ ♃ **7:09 am** 4:09 am

13 MONDAY
☽ ☌ ☉ **4:27 am** 1:27 am
☽ ☍ ♅ **5:05 am** 2:05 am
☽ ☌ ♂ **7:18 am** 4:18 am
☽ △ ♆ **12:20 pm** 9:20 am
☉ ☍ ♅ **12:21 pm** 9:21 am
☽ ⚹ ♇ **6:03 pm** 3:03 pm
☽ □ ♄ **10:28 pm** 7:28 pm

14 TUESDAY
☽ ☌ ☿ **9:04 am** 6:04 am
☽ ⚹ ♀ **9:44 am** 6:44 am
☽ ⚻ ♃ **1:32 pm** 10:32 am

15 WEDNESDAY
☿ ⚹ ♀ **7:48 am** 4:48 am
☽ ⚻ ♅ **10:52 am** 7:52 am
☽ ⚺ ☉ **2:44 pm** 11:44 am
☽ ⚺ ♂ **4:05 pm** 1:05 pm
☽ □ ♆ **5:57 pm** 2:57 pm
☿ ⚻ ♃ **10:35 pm** 7:35 pm
☽ ⚺ ♇ **11:33 pm** 8:33 pm
♀ ⚻ ♃ 11:48 pm

16 THURSDAY
♀ ⚻ ♃ **2:48 am**
☽ ⚹ ♄ **3:49 am** 12:49 am
☽ △ ♃ **5:48 pm** 2:48 pm
☽ □ ♀ **7:16 pm** 4:16 pm
☽ ⚺ ☿ **8:17 pm** 5:17 pm

17 FRIDAY
♂ △ ♆ **3:36 am** 12:36 am
☉ △ ♆ **9:52 am** 6:52 am
☽ △ ♅ **2:51 pm** 11:51 am
☽ ⚹ ♆ **9:52 pm** 6:52 pm
☽ ⚹ ☉ **10:49 pm** 7:49 pm
☽ ⚹ ♂ **10:51 pm** 7:51 pm
☉ ☌ ♂ 9:42 pm

18 SATURDAY
☉ ☌ ♂ **12:42 am**
☽ ☌ ♇ **3:27 am** 12:27 am
☽ ⚺ ♄ **7:38 am** 4:38 am
☽ □ ♃ **8:50 pm** 5:50 pm

19 SUNDAY
☽ △ ♀ **3:12 am** 12:12 am
☽ ⚹ ☿ **5:39 am** 2:39 am
☽ □ ♅ **5:53 pm** 2:53 pm
☽ ⚺ ♆ 9:57 pm

20 MONDAY
☽ ⚺ ♆ **12:57 am**
☽ □ ♂ **4:38 am** 1:38 am
☽ □ ☉ **5:50 am** 2:50 am
☽ ⚺ ♇ **6:34 am** 3:34 am

☽ ☌ ♄ **10:45 am** 7:45 am
☉ ⚹ ♇ **4:26 pm** 1:26 pm
☽ ⚹ ♃ **11:20 pm** 8:20 pm

21 TUESDAY
☽ ⚻ ♀ **10:32 am** 7:32 am
☽ □ ☿ **2:16 pm** 11:16 am
♂ ⚹ ♇ **8:18 pm** 5:18 pm
☽ ⚹ ♅ **8:35 pm** 5:35 pm

22 WEDNESDAY
☽ ☌ ♆ **3:45 am** 12:45 am
☽ ⚹ ♇ **9:29 am** 6:29 am
☽ △ ♂ **10:10 am** 7:10 am
☽ △ ☉ **12:35 pm** 9:35 am
☽ ⚺ ♄ **1:42 pm** 10:42 am
☽ ⚺ ♃ 10:47 pm

23 THURSDAY
☽ ⚺ ♃ **1:47 am**
☉ □ ♄ **4:47 am** 1:47 am
☽ ☍ ♀ **5:57 pm** 2:57 pm
☽ △ ☿ **10:52 pm** 7:52 pm
☽ ⚺ ♅ **11:26 pm** 8:26 pm

24 FRIDAY
☿ ⚻ ♅ **4:27 am** 1:27 am
☽ ⚺ ♆ **6:47 am** 3:47 am
☽ □ ♇ **12:40 pm** 9:40 am
☽ ⚻ ♂ **4:02 pm** 1:02 pm
☽ ⚹ ♄ **5:00 pm** 2:00 pm
☽ ⚻ ☉ **7:43 pm** 4:43 pm

25 SATURDAY
☽ ☌ ♃ **4:43 am** 1:43 am
♂ □ ♄ **11:57 am** 8:57 am
☽ ⚻ ♀ 11:19 pm

26 SUNDAY
☽ ⚻ ♀ **2:19 am**
☽ ☌ ♅ **3:03 am** 12:03 am
☽ ⚻ ☿ **8:21 am** 5:21 am
☽ ⚹ ♆ **10:42 am** 7:42 am
♀ ⚻ ♅ **10:49 am** 7:49 am
☽ △ ♇ **4:52 pm** 1:52 pm
☽ □ ♄ **9:22 pm** 6:22 pm
☽ ☍ ♂ **11:08 pm** 8:08 pm

27 MONDAY
☽ ☍ ☉ **4:16 am** 1:16 am
☿ □ ♆ **8:27 am** 5:27 am
☽ ⚺ ♃ **8:54 am** 5:54 am

28 TUESDAY
☽ ⚺ ♅ **8:22 am** 5:22 am
☽ △ ♀ **12:54 pm** 9:54 am
☽ □ ♆ **4:30 pm** 1:30 pm
☽ ☍ ☿ **8:03 pm** 5:03 pm
☽ ⚻ ♇ **11:03 pm** 8:03 pm

29 WEDNESDAY
☽ △ ♄ **3:51 am** 12:51 am
☽ ⚻ ♂ **8:43 am** 5:43 am
☉ ⚻ ♃ **12:38 pm** 9:38 am
☽ ⚹ ♃ **3:21 pm** 12:21 pm
☽ ⚻ ☉ **3:37 pm** 12:37 pm

30 THURSDAY
☿ ⚺ ♇ **3:34 am** 12:34 am
♀ ⚻ ♆ **5:13 am** 2:13 am
☽ ⚹ ♅ **4:20 pm** 1:20 pm
☽ △ ♆ 10:05 pm

Eastern time in bold type
Pacific time in medium type

NOVEMBER 2023

DATE	SID.TIME	SUN	MOON	NODE	MERCURY	VENUS	MARS	JUPITER	SATURN	URANUS	NEPTUNE	PLUTO	CERES	PALLAS	JUNO	VESTA	CHIRON
1 W	2 40 6	8♏17 51	18♊22	24♈51℞	15♏42	22♍05	13♏34	10♉49℞	0♓31℞	21♉35℞	25♓14℞	28♑00	19♏37	21♎55	5♍46	7♋29	16♈46℞
2 Th	2 44 3	9 17 51	1♋20	24 49	17 17	23 09	14 15	10 40	0 31	21 33	25 13	28 01	20 02	22 21	6 09	7 30	16 43
3 F	2 47 59	10 17 53	13 57	24 47	18 50	24 12	14 57	10 32	0 31	21 30	25 12	28 01	20 28	22 48	6 31	7 30℞	16 41
4 Sa	2 51 56	11 17 58	26 17	24 45	20 24	25 16	15 38	10 24	0 31D	21 28	25 11	28 02	20 54	23 15	6 54	7 30	16 38
5 Su	2 55 52	12 18 04	8♌22	24 45D	21 57	26 20	16 20	10 16	0 31	21 25	25 10	28 03	21 20	23 41	7 16	7 29	16 36
6 M	2 59 49	13 18 12	20 18	24 45	23 29	27 24	17 02	10 08	0 31	21 23	25 09	28 03	21 45	24 08	7 38	7 28	16 34
7 T	3 3 45	14 18 23	2♍09	24 46	25 01	28 29	17 44	10 00	0 31	21 20	25 08	28 04	22 11	24 34	8 00	7 27	16 31
8 W	3 7 42	15 18 35	14 00	24 47	26 33	29 34	18 25	9 52	0 32	21 18	25 07	28 05	22 37	25 01	8 21	7 25	16 29
9 Th	3 11 39	16 18 50	25 56	24 49	28 05	0♎39	19 07	9 43	0 32	21 16	25 06	28 06	23 03	25 27	8 42	7 22	16 27
10 F	3 15 35	17 19 06	8♎00	24 50	29 36	1 45	19 49	9 35	0 33	21 13	25 05	28 07	23 29	25 54	9 04	7 20	16 24
11 Sa	3 19 32	18 19 24	20 17	24 51℞	1♐06	2 51	20 31	9 27	0 33	21 11	25 04	28 07	23 54	26 20	9 25	7 16	16 22
12 Su	3 23 28	19 19 44	2♏49	24 51	2 37	3 57	21 13	9 20	0 34	21 08	25 03	28 08	24 20	26 47	9 45	7 13	16 20
13 M	3 27 25	20 20 06	15 37	24 50	4 07	5 03	21 55	9 12	0 35	21 06	25 03	28 09	24 46	27 13	10 06	7 08	16 18
14 T	3 31 21	21 20 30	28 41	24 47	5 36	6 10	22 38	9 04	0 36	21 03	25 02	28 10	25 12	27 39	10 26	7 04	16 16
15 W	3 35 18	22 20 56	12♐02	24 43	7 05	7 17	23 20	8 56	0 37	21 01	25 01	28 11	25 37	28 06	10 46	6 59	16 14
16 Th	3 39 14	23 21 23	25 36	24 38	8 34	8 24	24 02	8 48	0 38	20 58	25 00	28 12	26 03	28 32	11 06	6 53	16 12
17 F	3 43 11	24 21 51	9♑23	24 34	10 02	9 31	24 44	8 41	0 39	20 56	25 00	28 13	26 29	28 58	11 26	6 47	16 10
18 Sa	3 47 8	25 22 21	23 19	24 30	11 30	10 39	25 27	8 33	0 41	20 53	24 59	28 14	26 55	29 24	11 45	6 41	16 08
19 Su	3 51 4	26 22 52	7♒21	24 27	12 58	11 47	26 09	8 26	0 42	20 51	24 58	28 15	27 20	29 50	12 05	6 34	16 06
20 M	3 55 1	27 23 25	21 28	24 25D	14 24	12 55	26 51	8 19	0 44	20 48	24 58	28 16	27 46	0♏16	12 24	6 27	16 04
21 T	3 58 57	28 23 58	5♓37	24 25	15 50	14 03	27 34	8 11	0 45	20 46	24 57	28 18	28 12	0 42	12 42	6 19	16 02
22 W	4 2 54	29 24 33	19 47	24 27	17 16	15 11	28 17	8 04	0 47	20 43	24 57	28 19	28 37	1 08	13 01	6 11	16 00
23 Th	4 6 50	0♐25 08	3♈56	24 28	18 41	16 20	28 59	7 57	0 49	20 41	24 56	28 20	29 03	1 34	13 19	6 02	15 58
24 F	4 10 47	1 25 45	18 02	24 29℞	20 05	17 28	29 42	7 51	0 51	20 38	24 56	28 21	29 29	2 00	13 37	5 53	15 57
25 Sa	4 14 44	2 26 23	2♉03	24 29	21 28	18 37	0♐24	7 44	0 53	20 36	24 56	28 22	29 54	2 26	13 55	5 44	15 55
26 Su	4 18 40	3 27 03	15 56	24 27	22 49	19 46	1 07	7 37	0 55	20 33	24 55	28 24	0♐20	2 51	14 12	5 34	15 53
27 M	4 22 37	4 27 43	29 37	24 23	24 10	20 55	1 50	7 31	0 58	20 31	24 55	28 25	0 46	3 17	14 30	5 24	15 52
28 T	4 26 33	5 28 26	13♊05	24 18	25 29	22 05	2 33	7 24	1 00	20 29	24 55	28 26	1 11	3 43	14 47	5 13	15 50
29 W	4 30 30	6 29 09	26 16	24 10	26 47	23 14	3 16	7 18	1 02	20 26	24 54	28 28	1 37	4 08	15 03	5 02	15 49
30 Th	4 34 26	7 29 54	9♋09	24 02	28 03	24 24	3 59	7 12	1 05	20 24	24 54	28 29	2 02	4 34	15 20	4 51	15 47

EPHEMERIS CALCULATED FOR 12 MIDNIGHT GREENWICH MEAN TIME. ALL OTHER DATA AND FACING ASPECTARIAN PAGE IN **EASTERN TIME (BOLD)** AND PACIFIC TIME (REGULAR).

DECEMBER 2023

☽ Last Aspect day	ET / hr:mn / PT		asp	☽ Ingress sign	day	ET / hr:mn / PT	
1	**8:07 am**	5:07 am	☍ ♇	♌	1	**11:00 am**	8:00 am
3	**9:11 pm**	6:11 pm	⚹ ♀	♍	3	**10:50 pm**	7:50 pm
6	**8:50 am**	5:50 am	△ ♇	♎	6	**11:35 am**	8:35 am
8	**8:05 pm**	5:05 pm	□ ♇	♏	8	**10:35 pm**	7:35 pm
11	**3:57 am**	12:57 am	⚹ ♇	♐	11	**6:11 am**	3:11 am
12		10:48 pm	□ ♆	♑	13	**10:31 am**	7:31 am
13	**1:48 am**		□ ♆	♑	13	**10:31 am**	7:31 am
15	**11:04 am**	8:04 am	☌ ♇	♒	15	**12:56 pm**	9:56 am
17	**7:04 am**	4:04 am	⚹ ☉	♓	17	**2:58 pm**	11:58 am
19	**4:03 pm**	1:03 pm	⚹ ♇	♈	19	**5:47 pm**	2:47 pm

☽ Last Aspect day	ET / hr:mn / PT		asp	☽ Ingress sign	day	ET / hr:mn / PT	
21	**9:47 pm**	6:47 pm	△ ☉	♉	21	**9:50 pm**	6:50 pm
23		10:40 pm	△ ♇	♊	24	**3:15 am**	12:15 am
24	**1:40 am**		△ ♇	♊	24	**3:15 am**	12:15 am
25		11:55 pm	☍ ☿	♋	26	**10:15 am**	7:15 am
26	**2:55 am**		☍ ☿	♋	26	**10:15 am**	7:15 am
28	**5:57 pm**	2:57 pm	☍ ♇	♌	28	**7:23 pm**	4:23 pm
30		9:18 pm	△ ♂	♍	31	**6:53 am**	3:53 am
31	**12:18 am**		△ ♂	♍	31	**6:53 am**	3:53 am

☽ Phases & Eclipses phase	day	ET / hr:mn / PT	
4th Quarter	4		9:49 pm
4th Quarter	5	**12:49 am**	
New Moon	12	**6:32 pm**	3:32 pm
2nd Quarter	19	**1:39 pm**	10:39 am
Full Moon	26	**7:33 pm**	4:33 pm

Planet Ingress		day	ET / hr:mn / PT	
☿	♑	1	**9:31 am**	6:31 am
♀	♏	4	**1:51 pm**	10:51 am
⚳	♊	20	**4:56 am**	1:56 am
☉	♑	21	**10:27 pm**	7:27 pm
☿	♐	22		10:18 pm
☿	♐	23	**1:18 am**	
♀	♐	29	**3:24 pm**	12:24 pm

Planetary Motion		day	ET / hr:mn / PT	
♆	D	6	**8:20 am**	5:20 am
☿	℞	12		11:09 pm
☿	℞	13	**2:09 am**	
⚷	D	26	**10:10 pm**	7:10 pm
♃	D	30	**9:40 pm**	6:40 pm

1 FRIDAY
☽ △ ♆ **1:05 am**
☽ □ ♀ **3:09 am** 12:09 am
☽ ☍ ♇ **8:07 am** 5:07 am
☽ ⚻ ☿ **11:10 am** 8:10 am
☽ ⚻ ♄ **1:17 pm** 10:17 am
☽ △ ♂ **9:48 pm** 6:48 pm
☽ □ ♃ 9:44 pm

2 SATURDAY
☽ □ ♃ **12:44 am**
☽ △ ☉ **6:45 am** 3:45 am
☿ ⚹ ♄ **10:27 am** 7:27 am

3 SUNDAY
☽ □ ♅ **3:13 am** 12:13 am
♀ □ ♇ **8:29 am** 5:29 am
☽ ⚻ ♆ **12:31 pm** 9:31 am
♂ ⚻ ♃ **6:20 pm** 3:20 pm
☽ ⚻ ♇ **7:57 pm** 4:57 pm
☽ ⚹ ♀ **9:11 pm** 6:11 pm
☽ ☍ ♄ 10:26 pm

4 MONDAY
☽ ☍ ♄ **1:26 am**
☽ △ ☿ **5:12 am** 2:12 am
☽ △ ♃ **12:33 pm** 9:33 am
☽ □ ♂ **1:52 pm** 10:52 am
☽ □ ☉ 9:49 pm

5 TUESDAY
☽ □ ☉ **12:49 am**
☽ △ ♅ **3:45 pm** 12:45 pm
♀ △ ♄ **5:51 pm** 2:51 pm
☽ ☍ ♆ 10:17 pm

6 WEDNESDAY
☽ ☍ ♆ **1:17 am**
☽ △ ♇ **8:50 am** 5:50 am
☽ ⚻ ♄ **2:26 pm** 11:26 am
☽ ⊻ ♀ **4:34 pm** 1:34 pm
☽ □ ☿ **11:00 pm** 8:00 pm
☽ ⚻ ♃ 9:42 pm

7 THURSDAY
☽ ⚻ ♃ **12:42 am**
☽ ⚹ ♂ **6:16 am** 3:16 am
☽ ⚹ ☉ **6:37 pm** 3:37 pm
☿ △ ♃ **11:09 pm** 8:09 pm

8 FRIDAY
☽ ⚻ ♅ **3:24 am** 12:24 am
☽ ⚻ ♆ **12:45 pm** 9:45 am
☽ □ ♇ **8:05 pm** 5:05 pm
☽ △ ♄ 10:33 pm

9 SATURDAY
☽ △ ♄ **1:33 am**
☽ ☌ ♀ **9:24 am** 6:24 am
☽ ☍ ♃ **10:41 am** 7:41 am
☽ ⚹ ☿ **12:46 pm** 9:46 am
☽ ⊻ ♂ **7:46 pm** 4:46 pm
♀ ☍ ♃ **10:35 pm** 7:35 pm

10 SUNDAY
☽ ⊻ ☉ **8:48 am** 5:48 am
☽ ☍ ♅ **12:03 pm** 9:03 am
☽ △ ♆ **8:58 pm** 5:58 pm

11 MONDAY
☽ ⚹ ♇ **3:57 am** 12:57 am
☽ □ ♄ **9:13 am** 6:13 am
☿ ⚹ ♀ **2:17 pm** 11:17 am
☽ ⚻ ♃ **5:15 pm** 2:15 pm
☽ ⊻ ☿ **9:03 pm** 6:03 pm
☽ ⊻ ♀ **9:35 pm** 6:35 pm
☉ ⚻ ♅ 10:21 pm

12 TUESDAY
☉ ⚻ ♅ **1:21 am**
☽ ☌ ♂ **5:05 am** 2:05 am
☽ ⚻ ♅ **5:14 pm** 2:14 pm
☽ ☌ ☉ **6:32 pm** 3:32 pm
☽ □ ♆ 10:48 pm

13 WEDNESDAY
☽ □ ♆ **1:48 am**
☽ ⊻ ♇ **8:31 am** 5:31 am
☽ ⚹ ♄ **1:39 pm** 10:39 am
☽ △ ♃ **8:51 pm** 5:51 pm
☽ ☌ ☿ 9:47 pm

14 THURSDAY
☽ ☌ ☿ **12:47 am**
☽ ⚹ ♀ **5:55 am** 2:55 am
☽ ⊻ ♂ **11:09 am** 8:09 am
☽ △ ♅ **8:00 pm** 5:00 pm
☽ ⊻ ☉ 10:15 pm

15 FRIDAY
☽ ⊻ ☉ **1:15 am**
☽ ⚹ ♆ **4:27 am** 1:27 am
☽ ☌ ♇ **11:04 am** 8:04 am
☽ ⊻ ♄ **4:13 pm** 1:13 pm
☽ □ ♃ **10:52 pm** 7:52 pm
☽ ⊻ ☿ 10:42 pm

16 SATURDAY
☽ ⊻ ☿ **1:42 am**
☽ □ ♀ **12:33 pm** 9:33 am
☽ ⚹ ♂ **3:52 pm** 12:52 pm
☽ □ ♅ **9:53 pm** 6:53 pm
☉ □ ♆ **10:43 pm** 7:43 pm

17 SUNDAY
☽ ⊻ ♆ **6:28 am** 3:28 am
☽ ⚹ ☉ **7:04 am** 4:04 am
☽ ⊻ ♇ **1:11 pm** 10:11 am
☽ ☌ ♄ **6:32 pm** 3:32 pm
☽ ⚹ ♃ 9:49 pm
☽ ⚹ ☿ 10:21 pm

18 MONDAY
☽ ⚹ ♃ **12:49 am**
☽ ⚹ ☿ **1:21 am**
☿ △ ♃ **9:28 am** 6:28 am
☽ △ ♀ **7:30 pm** 4:30 pm
☽ □ ♂ **8:58 pm** 5:58 pm
☽ ⚹ ♅ 9:14 pm

19 TUESDAY
☽ ⚹ ♅ **12:14 am**
☽ ☌ ♆ **9:07 am** 6:07 am
☽ □ ☉ **1:39 pm** 10:39 am
☽ ⚹ ♇ **4:03 pm** 1:03 pm
☽ ⊻ ♄ **9:41 pm** 6:41 pm
☽ □ ☿ 9:42 pm

20 WEDNESDAY
☽ □ ☿ **12:42 am**
☽ ⊻ ♃ **3:42 am** 12:42 am
♀ ⊻ ♂ **1:38 pm** 10:38 am
☉ ⊻ ♇ **11:39 pm** 8:39 pm
♀ ☍ ♅ 11:04 pm

21 THURSDAY
♀ ☍ ♅ **2:04 am**
☽ △ ♂ **3:23 am** 12:23 am
☽ ⊻ ♅ **3:44 am** 12:44 am
☽ ⚻ ♀ **3:54 am** 12:54 am
☿ ⚹ ♄ **7:33 am** 4:33 am
♂ ⚻ ♅ **9:44 am** 6:44 am
☽ ⊻ ♆ **12:59 pm** 9:59 am
☽ □ ♇ **8:11 pm** 5:11 pm
☽ △ ☉ **9:47 pm** 6:47 pm
☽ △ ☿ 9:21 pm
☽ ⚹ ♄ 11:08 pm

22 FRIDAY
☽ △ ☿ **12:21 am**
☽ ⚹ ♄ **2:08 am**
☽ ☌ ♃ **7:53 am** 4:53 am
☉ ☌ ☿ **1:54 pm** 10:54 am

23 SATURDAY
☽ ☌ ♅ **8:33 am** 5:33 am
☽ ⚻ ♂ **11:22 am** 8:22 am
☽ ☍ ♀ **2:04 pm** 11:04 am
☿ ⊻ ♇ **4:51 pm** 1:51 pm
☽ ⚹ ♆ **6:12 pm** 3:12 pm
☽ ⚻ ☿ 9:50 pm
☽ △ ♇ 10:40 pm

24 SUNDAY
☽ ⚻ ☿ **12:50 am**
☽ △ ♇ **1:40 am**
☽ ⚻ ☉ **7:38 am** 4:38 am
☽ □ ♄ **7:58 am** 4:58 am
☉ ⚹ ♄ **12:28 pm** 9:28 am
☽ ⊻ ♃ **1:28 pm** 10:28 am

25 MONDAY
♀ △ ♆ **12:15 pm** 9:15 am
☽ ⊻ ♅ **2:51 pm** 11:51 am
☽ ☍ ♂ **9:08 pm** 6:08 pm
☽ □ ♆ 9:57 pm
☽ ⚻ ♀ 11:15 pm
☽ ☍ ☿ 11:55 pm

26 TUESDAY
☽ □ ♆ **12:57 am**
☽ ⚻ ♀ **2:15 am**
☽ ☍ ☿ **2:55 am**
☿ ⊻ ♀ **6:18 am** 3:18 am
☽ ⚻ ♇ **8:45 am** 5:45 am
☽ △ ♄ **3:30 pm** 12:30 pm
☽ ☍ ☉ **7:33 pm** 4:33 pm
☽ ⚹ ♃ **8:45 pm** 5:45 pm
☿ □ ♆ 11:43 pm

27 WEDNESDAY
☿ □ ♆ **2:43 am**
☉ △ ♃ **10:28 am** 7:28 am
☿ ☌ ♂ **7:31 pm** 4:31 pm
☽ ⚹ ♅ **11:04 pm** 8:04 pm

28 THURSDAY
☽ ⚻ ☿ **7:40 am** 4:40 am
☽ ⚻ ♂ **9:17 am** 6:17 am
☽ △ ♆ **9:45 am** 6:45 am
☽ △ ♀ **5:12 pm** 2:12 pm
♂ □ ♆ **5:16 pm** 2:16 pm
☽ ☍ ♇ **5:57 pm** 2:57 pm
♀ ⚹ ♇ 10:01 pm
☽ ⚻ ♄ 10:15 pm

29 FRIDAY
♀ ⚹ ♇ **1:01 am**
☽ ⚻ ♄ **1:15 am**
☽ □ ♃ **6:18 am** 3:18 am
☽ ⚻ ☉ **10:19 am** 7:19 am

30 SATURDAY
☽ □ ♅ **9:39 am** 6:39 am
☽ △ ☿ **4:00 pm** 1:00 pm
☽ ⚻ ♆ **8:57 pm** 5:57 pm
☽ △ ♂ 9:18 pm

31 SUNDAY
☽ △ ♂ **12:18 am**
☽ ⚻ ♇ **5:34 am** 2:34 am
☽ □ ♀ **11:23 am** 8:23 am
☽ ☍ ♄ **1:24 pm** 10:24 am
☽ △ ♃ **6:10 pm** 3:10 pm

Eastern time in bold type
Pacific time in medium type

DECEMBER 2023

DATE	SID.TIME	SUN	MOON	NODE	MERCURY	VENUS	MARS	JUPITER	SATURN	URANUS	NEPTUNE	PLUTO	CERES	PALLAS	JUNO	VESTA	CHIRON
1 F	4 38 23	8♐30 40	21♋45	23♈54℞	29♐17	25♎34	4♐42	7♉06℞	1♓08	20♉22℞	24♓54℞	28♑30	2♐28	4♏59	15♍36	4♋39℞	15♈46℞
2 Sa	4 42 19	9 31 28	4♌05	23 48	0♑28	26 44	5 25	7 01	1 11	20 19	24 54	28 32	2 54	5 25	15 52	4 27	15 44
3 Su	4 46 16	10 32 17	16 10	23 42	1 36	27 54	6 08	6 55	1 13	20 17	24 54	28 33	3 19	5 50	16 08	4 15	15 43
4 M	4 50 13	11 33 07	28 06	23 39	2 42	29 05	6 51	6 50	1 16	20 15	24 53	28 34	3 45	6 15	16 23	4 02	15 42
5 T	4 54 9	12 33 59	9♍57	23 38D	3 44	0♏15	7 34	6 44	1 19	20 12	24 53	28 36	4 10	6 41	16 38	3 49	15 41
6 W	4 58 6	13 34 52	21 47	23 38	4 41	1 26	8 17	6 39	1 23	20 10	24 53D	28 37	4 36	7 06	16 53	3 36	15 39
7 Th	5 2 2	14 35 46	3♎42	23 39	5 34	2 36	9 01	6 34	1 26	20 08	24 53	28 39	5 01	7 31	17 07	3 22	15 38
8 F	5 5 59	15 36 41	15 48	23 41℞	6 21	3 47	9 44	6 30	1 29	20 06	24 53	28 40	5 26	7 56	17 22	3 08	15 37
9 Sa	5 9 55	16 37 38	28 08	23 41	7 02	4 58	10 27	6 25	1 33	20 04	24 53	28 42	5 52	8 21	17 36	2 54	15 36
10 Su	5 13 52	17 38 36	10♏47	23 39	7 37	6 09	11 11	6 21	1 36	20 01	24 53	28 43	6 17	8 46	17 49	2 40	15 35
11 M	5 17 48	18 39 35	23 48	23 35	8 03	7 21	11 54	6 17	1 40	19 59	24 54	28 45	6 42	9 11	18 02	2 25	15 34
12 T	5 21 45	19 40 36	7♐12	23 29	8 21	8 32	12 38	6 13	1 43	19 57	24 54	28 47	7 08	9 36	18 15	2 10	15 33
13 W	5 25 42	20 41 37	20 57	23 20	8 29℞	9 43	13 21	6 09	1 47	19 55	24 54	28 48	7 33	10 00	18 28	1 55	15 33
14 Th	5 29 38	21 42 39	4♑59	23 10	8 27	10 55	14 05	6 05	1 51	19 53	24 54	28 50	7 58	10 25	18 40	1 40	15 32
15 F	5 33 35	22 43 42	19 15	23 00	8 14	12 07	14 49	6 02	1 55	19 51	24 55	28 51	8 24	10 50	18 52	1 25	15 31
16 Sa	5 37 31	23 44 45	3♒39	22 51	7 49	13 18	15 33	5 59	1 59	19 49	24 55	28 53	8 49	11 14	19 04	1 09	15 31
17 Su	5 41 28	24 45 49	18 03	22 44	7 13	14 30	16 16	5 56	2 03	19 47	24 55	28 55	9 14	11 39	19 15	0 54	15 30
18 M	5 45 24	25 46 53	2♓24	22 39	6 25	15 42	17 00	5 53	2 07	19 45	24 56	28 56	9 39	12 03	19 26	0 38	15 29
19 T	5 49 21	26 47 57	16 38	22 36D	5 27	16 54	17 44	5 50	2 12	19 44	24 56	28 58	10 04	12 27	19 36	0 22	15 29
20 W	5 53 17	27 49 02	0♈43	22 36	4 19	18 06	18 28	5 48	2 16	19 42	24 56	29 00	10 29	12 51	19 46	0 07	15 29
21 Th	5 57 14	28 50 07	14 38	22 37℞	3 04	19 18	19 12	5 45	2 21	19 40	24 57	29 02	10 54	13 15	19 56	29♊51	15 28
22 F	6 1 11	29 51 12	28 23	22 37	1 44	20 30	19 56	5 43	2 25	19 38	24 57	29 03	11 19	13 39	20 06	29 35	15 28
23 Sa	6 5 7	0♑52 18	11♉59	22 35	0 22	21 43	20 40	5 42	2 30	19 37	24 58	29 05	11 44	14 03	20 15	29 19	15 28
24 Su	6 9 4	1 53 24	25 25	22 31	28♐59	22 55	21 24	5 40	2 34	19 35	24 59	29 07	12 09	14 27	20 23	29 03	15 27
25 M	6 13 0	2 54 30	8♊42	22 24	27 40	24 08	22 08	5 39	2 39	19 33	24 59	29 09	12 34	14 51	20 32	28 47	15 27
26 T	6 16 57	3 55 36	21 47	22 14	26 27	25 20	22 52	5 38	2 44	19 32	25 00	29 10	12 59	15 14	20 40	28 32	15 27
27 W	6 20 53	4 56 43	4♋40	22 01	25 20	26 33	23 37	5 37	2 49	19 30	25 01	29 12	13 23	15 38	20 47	28 16	15 27D
28 Th	6 24 50	5 57 50	17 21	21 48	24 23	27 45	24 21	5 36	2 54	19 29	25 01	29 14	13 48	16 01	20 54	28 00	15 27
29 F	6 28 47	6 58 57	29 48	21 35	23 36	28 58	25 05	5 35	2 59	19 27	25 02	29 16	14 13	16 25	21 01	27 45	15 27
30 Sa	6 32 43	8 00 04	12♌02	21 22	22 59	0♐11	25 50	5 35	3 04	19 26	25 03	29 18	14 37	16 48	21 08	27 30	15 27
31 Su	6 36 40	9 01 12	24 05	21 12	22 33	1 24	26 34	5 35D	3 09	19 24	25 04	29 20	15 02	17 11	21 14	27 15	15 28

EPHEMERIS CALCULATED FOR 12 MIDNIGHT GREENWICH MEAN TIME. ALL OTHER DATA AND FACING ASPECTARIAN PAGE IN **EASTERN TIME (BOLD)** AND PACIFIC TIME (REGULAR).

JANUARY 2024

☽ Last Aspect day	ET / hr:mn / PT		asp	☽ Ingress sign	day	ET / hr:mn / PT	
2	**6:36 pm**	3:36 pm	△♇	♎	2	**7:47 pm**	4:47 pm
5	**6:41 am**	3:41 am	□♇	♏	5	**7:39 am**	4:39 am
7	**3:22 pm**	12:22 pm	⚹♇	♐	7	**4:08 pm**	1:08 pm
9	**1:24 pm**	10:24 am	☌☿	♑	9	**8:33 pm**	5:33 pm
11	**9:33 pm**	6:33 pm	☌♇	♒	11	**10:01 pm**	7:01 pm
13	**4:59 am**	1:59 am	□♅	♓	13	**10:29 pm**	7:29 pm
15	**11:33 pm**	8:33 pm	⚹♇	♈	15	**11:49 pm**	8:49 pm
18	**3:03 am**	12:03 am	□♇	♉	18	**3:12 am**	12:12 am
20	**8:57 am**	5:57 am	△☉	♊	20	**8:58 am**	5:58 am
22	**3:40 pm**	12:40 pm	☍♀	♋	22	**4:51 pm**	1:51 pm

☽ Last Aspect day	ET / hr:mn / PT		asp	☽ Ingress sign	day	ET / hr:mn / PT	
24	**5:58 pm**	2:58 pm	△♆	♌	24		11:37 pm
24	**5:58 pm**	2:58 pm	△♆	♌	25	**2:37 am**	
26	**4:19 pm**	1:19 pm	□♅	♍	27	**2:11 pm**	11:11 am
29	**6:20 pm**	3:20 pm	☍♆	♎	30	**3:04 am**	12:04 am

☽ Phases & Eclipses phase	day	ET / hr:mn / PT	
4th Quarter	3	**10:30 pm**	7:30 pm
New Moon	11	**6:57 am**	3:57 am
2nd Quarter	17	**10:53 pm**	7:53 pm
Full Moon	25	**12:54 pm**	9:54 am

Planet Ingress		day	ET / hr:mn / PT	
♂	♑	4	**9:58 am**	6:58 am
☿	♑	13	**9:49 pm**	6:49 pm
☉	♒	20	**9:07 am**	6:07 am
♇	♒	20	**7:50 pm**	4:50 pm
♀	♑	23	**3:50 am**	12:50 am

Planetary Motion		day	ET / hr:mn / PT	
☿	D	1	**10:08 pm**	7:08 pm
✱	R	12	**11:55 pm**	8:55 pm
♅	D	26		11:35 pm
♅	D	27	**2:35 am**	

1 MONDAY
☽△☉ **3:59 am** 12:59 am
♀□♄ **8:26 am** 5:26 am
☽△♅ **10:09 pm** 7:09 pm

2 TUESDAY
☽□☿ **3:54 am** 12:54 am
☽☍♆ **9:50 am** 6:50 am
☽□♂ **5:13 pm** 2:13 pm
☽△♇ **6:36 pm** 3:36 pm
☽⚻♄ 11:47 pm

3 WEDNESDAY
☽⚻♄ **2:47 am**
♀⚻♃ **5:55 am** 2:55 am
☽⚻♃ **7:07 am** 4:07 am
☽⚹♀ **7:15 am** 4:15 am
♂⚺♇ **4:09 pm** 1:09 pm
☽□☉ **10:30 pm** 7:30 pm

4 THURSDAY
☽⚻♅ **10:37 am** 7:37 am
☽⚹☿ **5:25 pm** 2:25 pm
☽⚻♆ **10:08 pm** 7:08 pm

5 FRIDAY
☽□♇ **6:41 am** 3:41 am
☽⚹♂ **9:03 am** 6:03 am
☽△♄ **2:49 pm** 11:49 am
☽☍♃ **6:35 pm** 3:35 pm
☽⚺♀ 10:03 pm

6 SATURDAY
☽⚺♀ **1:03 am**
☽⚹☉ **2:12 pm** 11:12 am
☽☍♅ **8:24 pm** 5:24 pm

7 SUNDAY
☽⚺☿ **5:15 am** 2:15 am
☽△♆ **7:21 am** 4:21 am
☽⚹♇ **3:22 pm** 12:22 pm
☽⚺♂ **8:47 pm** 5:47 pm
☽□♄ **11:11 pm** 8:11 pm
☽⚻♃ 11:23 pm

8 MONDAY
☽⚻♃ **2:23 am**
☽☌♀ **1:44 pm** 10:44 am
☿□♆ **8:24 pm** 5:24 pm
☽⚺☉ 9:48 pm
☽⚻♅ 11:10 pm

9 TUESDAY
☽⚺☉ **12:48 am**
☽⚻♅ **2:10 am**
☽□♆ **12:27 pm** 9:27 am
☽☌☿ **1:24 pm** 10:24 am
☉△♅ **7:07 pm** 4:07 pm
☽⚺♇ **7:57 pm** 4:57 pm
♂⚹♄ **9:40 pm** 6:40 pm

10 WEDNESDAY
☽⚹♄ **3:29 am** 12:29 am
☽☌♂ **3:45 am** 12:45 am
☽△♃ **6:14 am** 3:14 am
☽⚺♀ **9:27 pm** 6:27 pm

11 THURSDAY
☽△♅ **4:26 am** 1:26 am
☽☌☉ **6:57 am** 3:57 am
☽⚹♆ **2:20 pm** 11:20 am
☽⚺☿ **6:27 pm** 3:27 pm
☽☌♇ **9:33 pm** 6:33 pm

12 FRIDAY
☽⚺♄ **5:01 am** 2:01 am
♂△♃ **5:42 am** 2:42 am
☽□♃ **7:29 am** 4:29 am
☽⚺♂ **7:34 am** 4:34 am
☽⚹♀ 11:32 pm

13 SATURDAY
☽⚹♀ **2:32 am**
☽□♅ **4:59 am** 1:59 am
☽⚺☉ **11:05 am** 8:05 am
☽⚺♆ **2:53 pm** 11:53 am
☿⚺♇ **4:39 pm** 1:39 pm
☽⚺♇ **10:07 pm** 7:07 pm
☽⚹☿ **10:32 pm** 7:32 pm

14 SUNDAY
☽☌♄ **5:50 am** 2:50 am
♀⚻♅ **8:03 am** 5:03 am
☽⚹♃ **8:08 am** 5:08 am
☽⚹♂ **10:40 am** 7:40 am

15 MONDAY
☽⚹♅ **5:47 am** 2:47 am
☽□♀ **7:48 am** 4:48 am
☽⚹☉ **3:47 pm** 12:47 pm
☽☌♆ **4:03 pm** 1:03 pm
☉⚹♆ **7:38 pm** 4:38 pm
☽⚹♇ **11:33 pm** 8:33 pm

16 TUESDAY
☽□☿ **4:05 am** 1:05 am
☽⚺♄ **7:47 am** 4:47 am
☽⚺♃ **9:59 am** 6:59 am
☽□♂ **3:14 pm** 12:14 pm

17 WEDNESDAY
☽⚺♅ **8:18 am** 5:18 am
☽△♀ **3:22 pm** 12:22 pm
☽⚺♆ **7:10 pm** 4:10 pm
☽□☉ **10:53 pm** 7:53 pm

18 THURSDAY
☽□♇ **3:03 am** 12:03 am
☿⚹♄ **3:49 am** 12:49 am
☽⚹♄ **11:57 am** 8:57 am
☽△☿ **12:42 pm** 9:42 am
☽☌♃ **2:05 pm** 11:05 am
☽△♂ **10:26 pm** 7:26 pm

19 FRIDAY
☿△♃ **4:31 am** 1:31 am
♀□♆ **10:49 am** 7:49 am
☽☌♅ **1:11 pm** 10:11 am
☽⚹♆ 9:40 pm
☽⚻♀ 11:04 pm

20 SATURDAY
☽⚹♆ **12:40 am**
☽⚻♀ **2:04 am**
☉☌♇ **8:46 am** 5:46 am
☽△♇ **8:56 am** 5:56 am
☽△☉ **8:57 am** 5:57 am
☽□♄ **6:32 pm** 3:32 pm
☽⚺♃ **8:36 pm** 5:36 pm
☽⚻☿ 9:45 pm

21 SUNDAY
☽⚻☿ **12:45 am**
☽⚻♂ **8:23 am** 5:23 am
☽⚺♅ **8:19 pm** 5:19 pm

22 MONDAY
☽□♆ **8:22 am** 5:22 am
☽☍♀ **3:40 pm** 12:40 pm
☽⚻♇ **4:58 pm** 1:58 pm
☽⚻☉ **9:43 pm** 6:43 pm

23 TUESDAY
☽△♄ **3:15 am** 12:15 am
☽⚹♃ **5:13 am** 2:13 am
♀⚺♇ **5:21 am** 2:21 am
☽☍☿ **3:53 pm** 12:53 pm
☽☍♂ **8:44 pm** 5:44 pm

24 WEDNESDAY
☽⚹♅ **5:24 am** 2:24 am
☽△♆ **5:58 pm** 2:58 pm
☽☍♇ 11:53 pm

25 THURSDAY
☽☍♇ **2:53 am**
☽⚻♀ **7:50 am** 4:50 am
☽☍☉ **12:54 pm** 9:54 am
☽⚻♄ **1:52 pm** 10:52 am
☽□♃ **3:46 pm** 12:46 pm
☉⚺♄ 10:52 pm

26 FRIDAY
☉⚺♄ **1:52 am**
☽⚻☿ **9:56 am** 6:56 am
☽⚻♂ **11:19 am** 8:19 am
☽□♅ **4:19 pm** 1:19 pm
☉□♃ 11:18 pm

27 SATURDAY
☉□♃ **2:18 am**
☽⚻♆ **5:25 am** 2:25 am
☿☌♂ **9:59 am** 6:59 am
☽⚻♇ **2:38 pm** 11:38 am
♀⚹♄ 10:03 pm
☽☍♄ 11:20 pm
☽△♀ 11:28 pm

28 SUNDAY
♀⚹♄ **1:03 am**
☽☍♄ **2:20 am**
☽△♀ **2:28 am**
☽△♃ **4:10 am** 1:10 am
☽⚻☉ **6:23 am** 3:23 am
☿△♅ **4:07 pm** 1:07 pm
♀△♃ **8:02 pm** 5:02 pm

29 MONDAY
☽△♂ **3:54 am** 12:54 am
☽△♅ **4:51 am** 1:51 am
☽△☿ **6:38 am** 3:38 am
☽☍♆ **6:20 pm** 3:20 pm
♂△♅ **6:41 pm** 3:41 pm

30 TUESDAY
☽△♇ **3:41 am** 12:41 am
☽⚻♄ **3:55 pm** 12:55 pm
☽⚻♃ **5:40 pm** 2:40 pm
☽□♀ **10:34 pm** 7:34 pm
☽△☉ 10:07 pm

31 WEDNESDAY
☽△☉ **1:07 am**
☽⚻♅ **5:48 pm** 2:48 pm
☽□♂ **9:00 pm** 6:00 pm

Eastern time in bold type
Pacific time in medium type

JANUARY 2024

DATE	SID.TIME	SUN	MOON	NODE	MERCURY	VENUS	MARS	JUPITER	SATURN	URANUS	NEPTUNE	PLUTO	CERES	PALLAS	JUNO	VESTA	CHIRON
1 M	6 40 36	10♑02 20	6♍00	21♈05R	22♐17R	2♐37	27♐19	5♉35	3♓15	19♉23R	25♓05	29♑21	15♐27	17♏34	21♍19	27♊00R	15♈28
2 T	6 44 33	11 03 29	17 49	21 00	22 11D	3 50	28 03	5 35	3 20	19 22	25 05	29 23	15 51	17 57	21 24	26 45	15 28
3 W	6 48 29	12 04 38	29 37	20 58	22 14	5 03	28 48	5 36	3 25	19 21	25 06	29 25	16 15	18 20	21 29	26 30	15 28
4 Th	6 52 26	13 05 47	11♎30	20 57	22 26	6 16	29 32	5 36	3 31	19 19	25 07	29 27	16 40	18 43	21 33	26 16	15 29
5 F	6 56 22	14 06 56	23 33	20 57	22 46	7 29	0♑17	5 37	3 36	19 18	25 08	29 29	17 04	19 05	21 37	26 02	15 29
6 Sa	7 0 19	15 08 06	5♏51	20 57	23 13	8 42	1 01	5 38	3 42	19 17	25 09	29 31	17 28	19 28	21 41	25 48	15 30
7 Su	7 4 16	16 09 16	18 31	20 54	23 46	9 56	1 46	5 40	3 48	19 16	25 10	29 33	17 53	19 50	21 44	25 34	15 30
8 M	7 8 12	17 10 26	1♐35	20 49	24 26	11 09	2 31	5 41	3 53	19 15	25 11	29 35	18 17	20 12	21 46	25 21	15 31
9 T	7 12 9	18 11 36	15 06	20 42	25 10	12 22	3 16	5 43	3 59	19 14	25 13	29 37	18 41	20 34	21 48	25 08	15 32
10 W	7 16 5	19 12 46	29 05	20 31	25 59	13 36	4 01	5 45	4 05	19 13	25 14	29 39	19 05	20 56	21 50	24 56	15 32
11 Th	7 20 2	20 13 57	13♑27	20 19	26 52	14 49	4 46	5 47	4 11	19 12	25 15	29 40	19 29	21 18	21 51	24 43	15 33
12 F	7 23 58	21 15 07	28 08	20 07	27 49	16 03	5 31	5 50	4 17	19 11	25 16	29 42	19 53	21 40	21 52	24 31	15 34
13 Sa	7 27 55	22 16 16	12♒59	19 55	28 49	17 16	6 16	5 52	4 23	19 11	25 17	29 44	20 17	22 02	21 52R	24 20	15 35
14 Su	7 31 51	23 17 25	27 51	19 46	29 52	18 30	7 01	5 55	4 29	19 10	25 19	29 46	20 41	22 23	21 52	24 08	15 36
15 M	7 35 48	24 18 33	12♓36	19 39	0♑58	19 43	7 46	5 58	4 35	19 09	25 20	29 48	21 04	22 45	21 51	23 58	15 37
16 T	7 39 45	25 19 41	27 07	19 36	2 06	20 57	8 31	6 01	4 41	19 09	25 21	29 50	21 28	23 06	21 50	23 47	15 38
17 W	7 43 41	26 20 48	11♈22	19 34D	3 17	22 10	9 16	6 04	4 48	19 08	25 23	29 52	21 52	23 27	21 49	23 37	15 39
18 Th	7 47 38	27 21 54	25 18	19 34R	4 29	23 24	10 01	6 08	4 54	19 08	25 24	29 54	22 15	23 48	21 47	23 27	15 40
19 F	7 51 34	28 23 00	8♉57	19 34	5 43	24 38	10 46	6 12	5 00	19 07	25 25	29 56	22 39	24 08	21 45	23 18	15 42
20 Sa	7 55 31	29 24 04	22 20	19 32	6 59	25 51	11 32	6 15	5 07	19 07	25 27	29 58	23 02	24 29	21 42	23 09	15 43
21 Su	7 59 27	0♒25 08	5♊28	19 28	8 16	27 05	12 17	6 20	5 13	19 06	25 28	0♒00	23 26	24 50	21 38	23 01	15 44
22 M	8 3 24	1 26 11	18 24	19 21	9 35	28 19	13 02	6 24	5 19	19 06	25 30	0 02	23 49	25 10	21 35	22 53	15 45
23 T	8 7 20	2 27 13	1♋08	19 10	10 55	29 33	13 48	6 28	5 26	19 06	25 31	0 04	24 12	25 30	21 30	22 45	15 47
24 W	8 11 17	3 28 14	13 42	18 58	12 16	0♑47	14 33	6 33	5 33	19 06	25 33	0 06	24 35	25 50	21 26	22 38	15 48
25 Th	8 15 14	4 29 14	26 06	18 44	13 38	2 01	15 18	6 38	5 39	19 05	25 34	0 08	24 58	26 10	21 21	22 31	15 50
26 F	8 19 10	5 30 14	8♌21	18 31	15 01	3 14	16 04	6 43	5 46	19 05	25 36	0 10	25 21	26 30	21 15	22 25	15 52
27 Sa	8 23 7	6 31 13	20 26	18 18	16 25	4 28	16 49	6 48	5 52	19 05D	25 38	0 12	25 44	26 49	21 09	22 19	15 53
28 Su	8 27 3	7 32 10	2♍23	18 07	17 50	5 42	17 35	6 54	5 59	19 05	25 39	0 14	26 07	27 08	21 03	22 14	15 55
29 M	8 31 0	8 33 08	14 15	17 59	19 16	6 56	18 20	6 59	6 06	19 05	25 41	0 16	26 29	27 28	20 56	22 09	15 57
30 T	8 34 56	9 34 04	26 02	17 54	20 43	8 10	19 06	7 05	6 13	19 05	25 43	0 17	26 52	27 47	20 48	22 05	15 58
31 W	8 38 53	10 34 59	7♎50	17 52D	22 10	9 24	19 52	7 11	6 20	19 06	25 44	0 19	27 15	28 05	20 41	22 01	16 00

EPHEMERIS CALCULATED FOR 12 MIDNIGHT GREENWICH MEAN TIME. ALL OTHER DATA AND FACING ASPECTARIAN PAGE IN **EASTERN TIME (BOLD)** AND PACIFIC TIME (REGULAR).

FEBRUARY 2024

☽ Last Aspect day	ET / hr:mn / PT		asp	☽ Ingress sign	day	ET / hr:mn / PT	
1	**4:03 am**	1:03 am	□☿	♏	1	**3:37 pm**	12:37 pm
3	**10:24 pm**	7:24 pm	⚹☿	♐	3		10:28 pm
3	**10:24 pm**	7:24 pm	⚹☿	♐	4	**1:28 am**	
5		9:06 pm	□♆	♑	6	**7:08 am**	4:08 am
6	**12:06 am**		□♆	♑	6	**7:08 am**	4:08 am
7		11:52 pm	☌♂	♒	8	**8:59 am**	5:59 am
8	**2:52 am**		☌♂	♒	8	**8:59 am**	5:59 am
9	**5:59 pm**	2:59 pm	☌☉	♓	10	**8:42 am**	5:42 am
12	**7:32 am**	4:32 am	⚹♂	♈	12	**8:26 am**	5:26 am
14	**5:21 am**	2:21 am	□♀	♉	14	**10:02 am**	7:02 am

☽ Last Aspect day	ET / hr:mn / PT		asp	☽ Ingress sign	day	ET / hr:mn / PT	
16	**10:01 am**	7:01 am	□☉	♊	16	**2:39 pm**	11:39 am
18	**10:21 pm**	7:21 pm	△☉	♋	18	**10:25 pm**	7:25 pm
20		10:38 pm	△♆	♌	21	**8:40 am**	5:40 am
21	**1:38 am**		△♆	♌	21	**8:40 am**	5:40 am
22	**11:18 pm**	8:18 pm	□♅	♍	23	**8:38 pm**	5:38 pm
25		11:35 pm	☍♆	♎	26	**9:29 am**	6:29 am
26	**2:35 am**		☍♆	♎	26	**9:29 am**	6:29 am
27	**1:22 pm**	10:22 am	△♀	♏	28	**10:09 pm**	7:09 pm

☽ Phases & Eclipses phase	day	ET / hr:mn / PT	
4th Quarter	2	**6:18 pm**	3:18 pm
New Moon	9	**5:59 pm**	2:59 pm
2nd Quarter	16	**10:01 am**	7:01 am
Full Moon	24	**7:30 am**	4:30 am

Planet Ingress		day	ET / hr:mn / PT	
☿	♒	4		9:10 pm
☿	♒	5	**12:10 am**	
⚴	♐	6	**3:09 am**	12:09 am
⚳	♑	7	**6:11 am**	3:11 am
♂	♒	12		10:05 pm
♂	♒	13	**1:05 am**	
♀	♒	16	**11:05 am**	8:05 am
☉	♓	18	**11:13 pm**	8:13 pm
☿	♓	22		11:29 pm
☿	♓	23	**2:29 am**	

Planetary Motion		day	ET / hr:mn / PT	
⚵	D	8	**4:41 am**	1:41 am

1 THURSDAY
☽□☿ **4:03 am** 1:03 am
☽⚻♆ **7:13 am** 4:13 am
☽□♇ **4:23 pm** 1:23 pm

2 FRIDAY
☽△♄ **4:39 am** 1:39 am
☿⚹♆ **5:55 am** 2:55 am
☽☍♃ **6:17 am** 3:17 am
☽⚹♀ **5:09 pm** 2:09 pm
☽□☉ **6:18 pm** 3:18 pm

3 SATURDAY
☽☍♅ **4:55 am** 1:55 am
☽⚹♂ **11:42 am** 8:42 am
☽△♆ **5:42 pm** 2:42 pm
☽⚹☿ **10:24 pm** 7:24 pm
☽⚹♇ 11:19 pm

4 SUNDAY
☽⚹♇ **2:19 am**
☽□♄ **2:10 pm** 11:10 am
☽⚻♃ **3:39 pm** 12:39 pm

5 MONDAY
☉⚺♀ **4:03 am** 1:03 am
☽⚹☉ **6:55 am** 3:55 am
☽⚺♀ **6:58 am** 3:58 am
☿☌♇ **7:58 am** 4:58 am
☽⚻♅ **12:11 pm** 9:11 am
☽⚺♂ **9:40 pm** 6:40 pm
☽□♆ 9:06 pm

6 TUESDAY
☽□♆ **12:06 am**
☽⚺♇ **8:03 am** 5:03 am
☽⚺☿ **10:59 am** 7:59 am
☽⚹♄ **7:18 pm** 4:18 pm
☽△♃ **8:41 pm** 5:41 pm

7 WEDNESDAY
☽⚺☉ **2:14 pm** 11:14 am
☽☌♀ **3:12 pm** 12:12 pm
☽△♅ **3:19 pm** 12:19 pm
♀△♅ **4:25 pm** 1:25 pm
♂⚹♆ **7:20 pm** 4:20 pm
☽⚹♆ 11:30 pm
☽☌♂ 11:52 pm

8 THURSDAY
☽⚹♆ **2:30 am**
☽☌♂ **2:52 am**
☉□♅ **5:46 am** 2:46 am
☽☌♇ **9:57 am** 6:57 am
☽☌☿ **6:25 pm** 3:25 pm
☽⚺♄ **8:51 pm** 5:51 pm
☽□♃ **10:10 pm** 7:10 pm

9 FRIDAY
☽□♅ **3:35 pm** 12:35 pm
☽☌☉ **5:59 pm** 2:59 pm
☿⚺♄ **6:59 pm** 3:59 pm
☽⚺♀ **7:44 pm** 4:44 pm
☽⚺♆ 11:29 pm

10 SATURDAY
☽⚺♆ **2:29 am**
☽⚺♂ **5:17 am** 2:17 am
☿□♃ **8:25 am** 5:25 am
☽⚺♇ **9:45 am** 6:45 am
☽☌♄ **8:45 pm** 5:45 pm
☽⚹♃ **10:05 pm** 7:05 pm
☽⚺☿ **11:34 pm** 8:34 pm

11 SUNDAY
☽⚹♅ **3:07 pm** 12:07 pm
☽⚺☉ **8:55 pm** 5:55 pm
☽⚹♀ **11:31 pm** 8:31 pm
☽☌♆ 11:11 pm

12 MONDAY
☽☌♆ **2:11 am**
☽⚹♂ **7:32 am** 4:32 am
☽⚹♇ **9:36 am** 6:36 am
☽⚺♄ **9:11 pm** 6:11 pm
☽⚺♃ **10:36 pm** 7:36 pm

13 TUESDAY
☽⚹☿ **5:44 am** 2:44 am
♀⚹♆ **8:36 am** 5:36 am
☽⚺♅ **3:55 pm** 12:55 pm
♂☌♇ 10:06 pm
☽⚹☉ 10:40 pm

14 WEDNESDAY
♂☌♇ **1:06 am**
☽⚹☉ **1:40 am**
☽⚺♆ **3:35 am** 12:35 am
☽□♀ **5:21 am** 2:21 am
☽□♇ **11:22 am** 8:22 am
☽□♂ **11:56 am** 8:56 am
☽⚹♄ **11:57 pm** 8:57 pm
☽☌♃ 10:31 pm

15 THURSDAY
☽☌♃ **1:31 am**
☉⚺♆ **5:28 am** 2:28 am
☽□☿ **3:36 pm** 12:36 pm
☽☌♅ **7:27 pm** 4:27 pm

16 FRIDAY
☽⚹♆ **7:55 am** 4:55 am
☽□☉ **10:01 am** 7:01 am
☽△♀ **3:02 pm** 12:02 pm
☽△♇ **4:11 pm** 1:11 pm
☽△♂ **7:56 pm** 4:56 pm
☿□♅ **10:53 pm** 7:53 pm

17 SATURDAY
♀☌♇ **3:48 am** 12:48 am
☽□♄ **5:57 am** 2:57 am
☽⚺♃ **7:42 am** 4:42 am
☽⚺♅ 11:12 pm

18 SUNDAY
☽⚺♅ **2:12 am**
☽△☿ **6:22 am** 3:22 am
☽□♆ **3:28 pm** 12:28 pm
☽△☉ **10:21 pm** 7:21 pm
☽⚻♇ 9:10 pm

19 MONDAY
☽⚻♇ **12:10 am**
☽⚻♀ **4:53 am** 1:53 am
☽⚻♂ **7:38 am** 4:38 am
☽△♄ **3:02 pm** 12:02 pm
☽⚹♃ **5:00 pm** 2:00 pm
☉⚺♇ **9:39 pm** 6:39 pm

20 TUESDAY
☽⚹♅ **11:45 am** 8:45 am
☽⚻☿ 10:32 pm
☽△♆ 10:38 pm
☿⚺♆ 11:10 pm

21 WEDNESDAY
☽⚻☿ **1:32 am**
☽△♆ **1:38 am**
☿⚺♆ **2:10 am**
☽☍♇ **10:37 am** 7:37 am
☽⚻☉ **1:53 pm** 10:53 am
☽☍♀ **10:03 pm** 7:03 pm
☽☍♂ **10:13 pm** 7:13 pm
♀☌♂ 11:14 pm
☽⚻♄ 11:28 pm

22 THURSDAY
♀☌♂ **2:14 am**
☽⚻♄ **2:28 am**
☽□♃ **4:39 am** 1:39 am
☽□♅ **11:18 pm** 8:18 pm

23 FRIDAY
☽⚻♆ **1:36 pm** 10:36 am
☿⚺♇ **4:31 pm** 1:31 pm
♀⚺♄ **9:26 pm** 6:26 pm
☽⚻♇ **10:46 pm** 7:46 pm
☽☍☿ **11:52 pm** 8:52 pm

24 SATURDAY
☽☍☉ **7:30 am** 4:30 am
☽⚻♂ **2:39 pm** 11:39 am
☽☍♄ **3:24 pm** 12:24 pm
☽⚻♀ **5:18 pm** 2:18 pm
☽△♃ **5:49 pm** 2:49 pm
♀□♃ **11:01 pm** 8:01 pm

25 SUNDAY
♂⚺♄ **4:20 am** 1:20 am
☽△♅ **12:04 pm** 9:04 am
☽☍♆ 11:35 pm

26 MONDAY
☽☍♆ **2:35 am**
☽△♇ **11:47 am** 8:47 am
☽⚻☿ **11:54 pm** 8:54 pm
☽⚻☉ 11:06 pm

27 TUESDAY
☽⚻☉ **2:06 am**
♂□♃ **3:30 am** 12:30 am
☽⚻♄ **4:59 am** 1:59 am
☽⚻♃ **7:38 am** 4:38 am
☽△♂ **7:51 am** 4:51 am
☽△♀ **1:22 pm** 10:22 am
☽⚻♅ 10:06 pm

28 WEDNESDAY
☽⚻♅ **1:06 am**
☉☌☿ **3:43 am** 12:43 am
☿☌♄ **10:08 am** 7:08 am
☽⚻♆ **3:32 pm** 12:32 pm
☉☌♄ **4:25 pm** 1:25 pm
☽□♇ 9:33 pm

29 THURSDAY
☽□♇ **12:33 am**
☿⚹♃ **4:53 am** 1:53 am
☽△♄ **5:52 pm** 2:52 pm
☽△☉ **7:53 pm** 4:53 pm
☽☍♃ **8:40 pm** 5:40 pm
☽△☿ **11:18 pm** 8:18 pm
☽□♂ 9:08 pm

Eastern time in bold type
Pacific time in medium type

FEBRUARY 2024

DATE	SID.TIME	SUN	MOON	NODE	MERCURY	VENUS	MARS	JUPITER	SATURN	URANUS	NEPTUNE	PLUTO	CERES	PALLAS	JUNO	VESTA	CHIRON
1 Th	8 42 49	11 ♒ 35 54	19 ♎ 42	17 ♈ 51	23 ♑ 39	10 ♑ 38	20 ♑ 37	7 ♉ 17	6 ♓ 26	19 ♉ 06	25 ♓ 46	0 ♒ 21	27 ♐ 37	28 ♏ 24	20 ♍ 33 R	21 ♊ 57 R	16 ♈ 02
2 F	8 46 46	12 36 48	1 ♏ 42	17 52 R	25 08	11 52	21 23	7 23	6 33	19 06	25 48	0 23	27 59	28 42	20 24	21 54	16 04
3 Sa	8 50 43	13 37 41	13 58	17 52	26 38	13 06	22 09	7 30	6 40	19 06	25 50	0 25	28 22	29 01	20 15	21 51	16 06
4 Su	8 54 39	14 38 34	26 33	17 51	28 09	14 20	22 55	7 36	6 47	19 07	25 51	0 27	28 44	29 19	20 06	21 49	16 08
5 M	8 58 36	15 39 26	9 ♐ 32	17 48	29 40	15 34	23 41	7 43	6 54	19 07	25 53	0 29	29 06	29 36	19 56	21 47	16 10
6 T	9 2 32	16 40 17	23 00	17 43	1 ♒ 13	16 49	24 26	7 50	7 01	19 08	25 55	0 31	29 28	29 54	19 46	21 46	16 12
7 W	9 6 29	17 41 07	6 ♑ 58	17 36	2 46	18 03	25 12	7 57	7 08	19 08	25 57	0 33	29 50	0 ♐ 11	19 35	21 45	16 14
8 Th	9 10 25	18 41 56	21 24	17 27	4 19	19 17	25 58	8 04	7 15	19 09	25 59	0 35	0 ♑ 12	0 29	19 24	21 45 D	16 16
9 F	9 14 22	19 42 44	6 ♒ 14	17 18	5 54	20 31	26 44	8 11	7 22	19 10	26 01	0 36	0 33	0 46	19 13	21 45	16 19
10 Sa	9 18 19	20 43 31	21 19	17 09	7 30	21 45	27 30	8 19	7 30	19 10	26 03	0 38	0 55	1 02	19 02	21 45	16 21
11 Su	9 22 15	21 44 16	6 ♓ 31	17 01	9 06	22 59	28 16	8 27	7 37	19 11	26 05	0 40	1 16	1 19	18 50	21 46	16 23
12 M	9 26 12	22 45 00	21 38	16 56	10 43	24 13	29 02	8 35	7 44	19 12	26 07	0 42	1 38	1 35	18 38	21 48	16 25
13 T	9 30 8	23 45 42	6 ♈ 31	16 54 D	12 21	25 28	29 48	8 42	7 51	19 13	26 09	0 44	1 59	1 51	18 25	21 49	16 28
14 W	9 34 5	24 46 23	21 05	16 53	13 59	26 42	0 ♒ 34	8 51	7 58	19 14	26 11	0 46	2 20	2 07	18 12	21 52	16 30
15 Th	9 38 1	25 47 02	5 ♉ 15	16 54	15 39	27 56	1 21	8 59	8 05	19 15	26 13	0 47	2 41	2 23	17 59	21 54	16 33
16 F	9 41 58	26 47 40	19 01	16 55 R	17 19	29 10	2 07	9 07	8 13	19 16	26 15	0 49	3 02	2 38	17 46	21 57	16 35
17 Sa	9 45 54	27 48 15	2 ♊ 24	16 55	19 00	0 ♒ 24	2 53	9 16	8 20	19 17	26 17	0 51	3 23	2 53	17 32	22 01	16 38
18 Su	9 49 51	28 48 49	15 27	16 54	20 42	1 39	3 39	9 25	8 27	19 18	26 19	0 53	3 44	3 08	17 18	22 05	16 40
19 M	9 53 48	29 49 22	28 12	16 50	22 25	2 53	4 25	9 33	8 34	19 19	26 21	0 55	4 04	3 23	17 04	22 09	16 43
20 T	9 57 44	0 ♓ 49 52	10 ♋ 44	16 45	24 09	4 07	5 11	9 42	8 42	19 20	26 23	0 56	4 25	3 37	16 50	22 14	16 46
21 W	10 1 41	1 50 21	23 03	16 37	25 54	5 21	5 58	9 51	8 49	19 21	26 25	0 58	4 45	3 51	16 36	22 19	16 48
22 Th	10 5 37	2 50 48	5 ♌ 13	16 29	27 40	6 36	6 44	10 01	8 56	19 23	26 27	1 00	5 05	4 05	16 21	22 24	16 51
23 F	10 9 34	3 51 13	17 15	16 20	29 27	7 50	7 30	10 10	9 04	19 24	26 29	1 01	5 25	4 18	16 06	22 30	16 54
24 Sa	10 13 30	4 51 36	29 12	16 12	1 ♓ 14	9 04	8 17	10 20	9 11	19 25	26 31	1 03	5 45	4 32	15 52	22 36	16 57
25 Su	10 17 27	5 51 58	11 ♍ 03	16 06	3 03	10 18	9 03	10 29	9 18	19 27	26 34	1 05	6 05	4 44	15 37	22 43	16 59
26 M	10 21 23	6 52 18	22 52	16 01	4 52	11 33	9 49	10 39	9 25	19 28	26 36	1 07	6 25	4 57	15 22	22 50	17 02
27 T	10 25 20	7 52 36	4 ♎ 41	15 59 D	6 43	12 47	10 36	10 49	9 33	19 30	26 38	1 08	6 44	5 09	15 07	22 57	17 05
28 W	10 29 16	8 52 53	16 31	15 58	8 34	14 01	11 22	10 59	9 40	19 31	26 40	1 10	7 04	5 22	14 51	23 05	17 08
29 Th	10 33 13	9 53 09	28 26	15 59	10 26	15 15	12 09	11 09	9 47	19 33	26 42	1 11	7 23	5 33	14 36	23 13	17 11

EPHEMERIS CALCULATED FOR 12 MIDNIGHT GREENWICH MEAN TIME. ALL OTHER DATA AND FACING ASPECTARIAN PAGE IN **EASTERN TIME (BOLD)** AND PACIFIC TIME (REGULAR).

MARCH 2024

☽ Last Aspect day	ET / hr:mn / PT		asp	☽ Ingress sign	day	ET / hr:mn / PT	
1		11:47 pm	△♆	♐	2	**8:56 am**	5:56 am
2	**2:47 am**		△♆	♐	2	**8:56 am**	5:56 am
4	**10:41 am**	7:41 am	□♆	♑	4	**4:15 pm**	1:15 pm
6	**2:35 pm**	11:35 am	⚹♆	♒	6	**7:38 pm**	4:38 pm
8	**1:56 pm**	10:56 am	☌♀	♓	8	**8:03 pm**	5:03 pm
10	**3:45 pm**	12:45 pm	☌♆	♈	10	**8:19 pm**	5:19 pm
12	**7:08 am**	4:08 am	⚹♂	♉	12	**8:28 pm**	5:28 pm
14	**6:29 pm**	3:29 pm	⚹♆	♊	14	**11:16 pm**	8:16 pm
16		9:43 pm	□♆	♋	17	**5:40 am**	2:40 am
17	**12:43 am**		□♆	♋	17	**5:40 am**	2:40 am
19	**2:52 pm**	11:52 am	△☉	♌	19	**3:33 pm**	12:33 pm
21		11:34 pm	☍♂	♍	22	**3:42 am**	12:42 am
22	**2:34 am**		☍♂	♍	22	**3:42 am**	12:42 am
24	**11:49 am**	8:49 am	☍♆	♎	24	**4:37 pm**	1:37 pm
26	**7:09 pm**	4:09 pm	☍☿	♏	27	**5:03 am**	2:03 am
29	**11:40 am**	8:40 am	△♆	♐	29	**3:52 pm**	12:52 pm
31	**8:16 pm**	5:16 pm	□♆	♑	31		9:05 pm
31	**8:16 pm**	5:16 pm	□♆	♑	4/1	**12:05 am**	

☽ Phases & Eclipses phase	day	ET / hr:mn / PT	
4th Quarter	3	**10:23 am**	7:23 am
New Moon	10	**5:00 am**	1:00 am
2nd Quarter	16		9:11 pm
2nd Quarter	17	**12:11 am**	
Full Moon	25	**3:00 am**	12:00 am
☍	25	5° ♎ 07'	

Planet Ingress		day	ET / hr:mn / PT	
☿	♈	9	**11:03 pm**	8:03 pm
♀	♓	11	**5:50 pm**	2:50 pm
☉	♈	19	**11:06 pm**	8:06 pm
♂	♓	22	**7:47 pm**	4:47 pm
⚶	♋	31	**7:02 am**	4:02 am

Planetary Motion		day	ET / hr:mn / PT	
♀	℞	29	**9:17 am**	6:17 am

1 FRIDAY
- ☽ □ ♂ 12:08 am
- ☉ ⚹ ♃ **7:15 am** 4:15 am
- ☿ ⚺ ♂ **7:41 am** 4:41 am
- ☽ □ ♀ **8:09 am** 5:09 am
- ☽ ☍ ♅ **12:53 pm** 9:53 am
- ☽ △ ♆ 11:47 pm

2 SATURDAY
- ☽ △ ♆ **2:47 am**
- ☽ ⚹ ♇ **11:20 am** 8:20 am

3 SUNDAY
- ☽ □ ♄ **4:12 am** 1:12 am
- ☽ ⚻ ♃ **7:04 am** 4:04 am
- ♀ □ ♅ **8:17 am** 5:17 am
- ☽ □ ☉ **10:23 am** 7:23 am
- ☽ ⚹ ♂ **1:11 pm** 10:11 am
- ☽ □ ☿ **6:39 pm** 3:39 pm
- ☽ ⚻ ♅ **9:39 pm** 6:39 pm
- ☽ ⚹ ♀ **11:01 pm** 8:01 pm

4 MONDAY
- ☽ □ ♆ **10:41 am** 7:41 am
- ☿ ⚹ ♅ **3:24 pm** 12:24 pm
- ☽ ⚺ ♇ **6:35 pm** 3:35 pm

5 TUESDAY
- ☽ ⚹ ♄ **10:38 am** 7:38 am
- ☽ △ ♃ **1:30 pm** 10:30 am
- ☽ ⚹ ☉ **8:01 pm** 5:01 pm
- ☽ ⚺ ♂ **9:37 pm** 6:37 pm
- ☽ △ ♅ 11:28 pm

6 WEDNESDAY
- ☽ △ ♅ **2:28 am**
- ☽ ⚹ ☿ **7:54 am** 4:54 am
- ☽ ⚺ ♀ **8:37 am** 5:37 am
- ☽ ⚹ ♆ **2:35 pm** 11:35 am
- ☿ ⚺ ♀ **9:00 pm** 6:00 pm
- ☽ ☌ ♇ **9:54 pm** 6:54 pm

7 THURSDAY
- ☽ ⚺ ♄ **1:14 pm** 10:14 am
- ☽ □ ♃ **4:08 pm** 1:08 pm
- ☽ ⚺ ☉ 10:12 pm
- ☽ ☌ ♂ 10:51 pm

8 FRIDAY
- ☽ ⚺ ☉ **1:12 am**
- ☽ ☌ ♂ **1:51 am**
- ☽ □ ♅ **3:50 am** 12:50 am
- ☿ ☌ ♆ **10:06 am** 7:06 am
- ☽ ☌ ♀ **1:56 pm** 10:56 am
- ☽ ⚺ ♆ **3:21 pm** 12:21 pm
- ☽ ⚺ ☿ **4:07 pm** 1:07 pm
- ☽ ⚺ ♇ **10:18 pm** 7:18 pm

9 SATURDAY
- ♀ ⚺ ♆ **7:49 am** 4:49 am
- ☽ ☌ ♄ **1:23 pm** 10:23 am
- ☽ ⚹ ♃ **4:24 pm** 1:24 pm
- ♂ □ ♅ **5:55 pm** 2:55 pm
- ☉ ⚹ ♅ **6:01 pm** 3:01 pm
- ☉ ⚺ ♂ **6:20 pm** 3:20 pm

10 SUNDAY
- ☽ ⚹ ♅ **4:22 am** 12:22 am
- ☽ ⚺ ♂ **4:52 am** 12:52 am
- ☽ ☌ ☉ **5:00 am** 1:00 am
- ☽ ☌ ♆ **3:45 pm** 12:45 pm
- ☿ ⚹ ♇ **6:21 pm** 3:21 pm
- ☽ ⚺ ♀ **6:25 pm** 3:25 pm
- ☽ ⚹ ♇ **10:38 pm** 7:38 pm
- ☽ ☌ ☿ **11:15 pm** 8:15 pm

11 MONDAY
- ☽ ⚺ ♄ **2:08 pm** 11:08 am
- ☽ ⚺ ♃ **5:24 pm** 2:24 pm

12 TUESDAY
- ☽ ⚺ ♅ **4:07 am** 1:07 am
- ☽ ⚹ ♂ **7:08 am** 4:08 am
- ☽ ⚺ ☉ **8:06 am** 5:06 am
- ☽ ⚺ ♆ **3:52 pm** 12:52 pm
- ☽ ⚹ ♀ **10:56 pm** 7:56 pm
- ☽ □ ♇ **10:57 pm** 7:57 pm
- ♀ ⚺ ♇ **11:11 pm** 8:11 pm

13 WEDNESDAY
- ☽ ⚺ ☿ **6:43 am** 3:43 am
- ☽ ⚹ ♄ **3:30 pm** 12:30 pm
- ☽ ☌ ♃ **7:13 pm** 4:13 pm

14 THURSDAY
- ☽ ☌ ♅ **6:00 am** 3:00 am
- ☽ □ ♂ **12:01 pm** 9:01 am
- ☽ ⚹ ☉ **1:57 pm** 10:57 am
- ☽ ⚹ ♆ **6:29 pm** 3:29 pm
- ☽ △ ♇ 11:00 pm

15 FRIDAY
- ☽ △ ♇ **2:00 am**
- ☽ □ ♀ **6:59 am** 3:59 am
- ☽ ⚹ ☿ **6:11 pm** 3:11 pm
- ☽ □ ♄ **8:06 pm** 5:06 pm
- ☽ ⚺ ♃ 9:22 pm

16 SATURDAY
- ☽ ⚺ ♃ **12:22 am**
- ☿ ⚺ ♄ **9:57 am** 6:57 am
- ☽ ⚺ ♅ **11:20 am** 8:20 am
- ☽ △ ♂ **9:02 pm** 6:02 pm
- ☽ □ ☉ 9:11 pm
- ☽ □ ♆ 9:43 pm

17 SUNDAY
- ☽ □ ☉ **12:11 am**
- ☽ □ ♆ **12:43 am**
- ☉ ☌ ♆ **7:22 am** 4:22 am
- ☽ ⚻ ♇ **8:42 am** 5:42 am
- ☽ △ ♀ **7:55 pm** 4:55 pm
- ☿ ⚺ ♃ 10:02 pm

18 MONDAY
- ☿ ⚺ ♃ **1:02 am**
- ☽ △ ♄ **4:29 am** 1:29 am
- ☽ ⚹ ♃ **9:24 am** 6:24 am
- ☽ □ ☿ **10:29 am** 7:29 am
- ☽ ⚹ ♅ **8:20 pm** 5:20 pm

19 TUESDAY
- ☽ ⚻ ♂ **10:20 am** 7:20 am
- ☽ △ ♆ **10:30 am** 7:30 am
- ♂ ⚺ ♆ **12:57 pm** 9:57 am
- ☽ △ ☉ **2:52 pm** 11:52 am
- ☽ ☍ ♇ **6:49 pm** 3:49 pm

20 WEDNESDAY
- ☽ ⚻ ♀ **1:13 pm** 10:13 am
- ☽ ⚻ ♄ **4:02 pm** 1:02 pm
- ☽ □ ♃ **9:35 pm** 6:35 pm

21 THURSDAY
- ☽ △ ☿ **5:57 am** 2:57 am
- ☽ □ ♅ **8:07 am** 5:07 am
- ☉ ⚹ ♇ **4:03 pm** 1:03 pm
- ♀ ☌ ♄ **7:09 pm** 4:09 pm
- ☽ ⚻ ♆ **10:42 pm** 7:42 pm
- ☿ ⚺ ♅ 11:27 pm
- ☽ ☍ ♂ 11:34 pm

22 FRIDAY
- ☿ ⚺ ♅ **2:27 am**
- ☽ ☍ ♂ **2:34 am**
- ☽ ⚻ ♇ **7:09 am** 4:09 am
- ☽ ⚻ ☉ **8:30 am** 5:30 am

23 SATURDAY
- ☽ ☍ ♄ **5:17 am** 2:17 am
- ☽ ☍ ♀ **8:54 am** 5:54 am
- ☽ △ ♃ **11:22 am** 8:22 am
- ☽ △ ♅ **9:10 pm** 6:10 pm
- ☽ ⚻ ☿ 10:37 pm

24 SUNDAY
- ☽ ⚻ ☿ **1:37 am**
- ☽ ☍ ♆ **11:49 am** 8:49 am
- ♀ ⚹ ♃ **12:37 pm** 9:37 am
- ☽ ⚻ ♂ **7:47 pm** 4:47 pm
- ☽ △ ♇ **8:11 pm** 5:11 pm
- ♂ ⚺ ♇ 10:58 pm

25 MONDAY
- ♂ ⚺ ♇ **1:58 am**
- ☽ ☍ ☉ **3:00 am** 12:00 am
- ☽ ⚻ ♄ **6:45 pm** 3:45 pm
- ☽ ⚻ ♃ 10:15 pm

26 TUESDAY
- ☽ ⚻ ♃ **1:15 am**
- ☽ ⚻ ♀ **4:47 am** 1:47 am
- ☽ ⚻ ♅ **10:06 am** 7:06 am
- ☽ ☍ ☿ **7:09 pm** 4:09 pm
- ☽ ⚻ ♆ 9:31 pm

27 WEDNESDAY
- ☽ ⚻ ♆ **12:31 am**
- ☽ □ ♇ **8:37 am** 5:37 am
- ☽ △ ♂ **12:18 pm** 9:18 am
- ☽ ⚻ ☉ **8:35 pm** 5:35 pm

28 THURSDAY
- ☽ △ ♄ **7:11 am** 4:11 am
- ♀ ⚹ ♅ **9:58 am** 6:58 am
- ☽ ☍ ♃ **1:59 pm** 10:59 am
- ☽ ☍ ♅ **9:46 pm** 6:46 pm
- ☽ △ ♀ **11:02 pm** 8:02 pm

29 FRIDAY
- ☽ ⚻ ☿ **9:10 am** 6:10 am
- ☽ △ ♆ **11:40 am** 8:40 am
- ☽ ⚹ ♇ **7:23 pm** 4:23 pm
- ☽ □ ♂ 11:43 pm

30 SATURDAY
- ☽ □ ♂ **2:43 am**
- ☽ △ ☉ **11:44 am** 8:44 am
- ☽ □ ♄ **5:29 pm** 2:29 pm
- ☽ ⚻ ♃ 9:26 pm

31 SUNDAY
- ☽ ⚻ ♃ **12:26 am**
- ☽ ⚻ ♅ **7:06 am** 4:06 am
- ☽ □ ♀ **2:06 pm** 11:06 am
- ☽ △ ☿ **6:54 pm** 3:54 pm
- ☽ □ ♆ **8:16 pm** 5:16 pm

Eastern time in bold type
Pacific time in medium type

MARCH 2024

DATE	SID.TIME	SUN	MOON	NODE	MERCURY	VENUS	MARS	JUPITER	SATURN	URANUS	NEPTUNE	PLUTO	CERES	PALLAS	JUNO	VESTA	CHIRON
1 F	10 37 10	10♓53 22	10♏29	16♈00	12♓19	16♒30	12♒55	11♉19	9♓55	19♉35	26♓44	1♒13	7♑42	5♐45	14♍21 R	23♊21	17♈14
2 Sa	10 41 6	11 53 35	22 45	16 02	14 13	17 44	13 42	11 29	10 02	19 36	26 47	1 15	8 01	5 56	14 06	23 30	17 17
3 Su	10 45 3	12 53 45	5♐18	16 03R	16 08	18 58	14 28	11 40	10 09	19 38	26 49	1 16	8 20	6 07	13 50	23 39	17 20
4 M	10 48 59	13 53 55	18 13	16 03	18 03	20 12	15 15	11 50	10 17	19 40	26 51	1 18	8 39	6 17	13 35	23 49	17 23
5 T	10 52 56	14 54 02	1♑33	16 02	19 59	21 27	16 01	12 01	10 24	19 42	26 53	1 19	8 57	6 27	13 20	23 58	17 26
6 W	10 56 52	15 54 09	15 21	16 00	21 55	22 41	16 48	12 11	10 31	19 44	26 56	1 21	9 16	6 37	13 05	24 09	17 29
7 Th	11 0 49	16 54 13	29 37	15 56	23 52	23 55	17 34	12 22	10 39	19 46	26 58	1 22	9 34	6 46	12 50	24 19	17 32
8 F	11 4 45	17 54 17	14♒18	15 52	25 48	25 10	18 21	12 33	10 46	19 48	27 00	1 24	9 52	6 56	12 35	24 30	17 36
9 Sa	11 8 42	18 54 18	29 20	15 48	27 45	26 24	19 07	12 44	10 53	19 50	27 02	1 25	10 10	7 04	12 20	24 41	17 39
10 Su	11 12 39	19 54 17	14♓33	15 45	29 41	27 38	19 54	12 55	11 01	19 52	27 05	1 26	10 28	7 13	12 05	24 52	17 42
11 M	11 16 35	20 54 15	29 48	15 43	1♈36	28 52	20 41	13 07	11 08	19 54	27 07	1 28	10 46	7 21	11 51	25 04	17 45
12 T	11 20 32	21 54 10	14♈54	15 42D	3 30	0♓07	21 27	13 18	11 15	19 56	27 09	1 29	11 03	7 28	11 37	25 16	17 48
13 W	11 24 28	22 54 04	29 43	15 43	5 23	1 21	22 14	13 29	11 22	19 58	27 11	1 31	11 20	7 36	11 22	25 28	17 52
14 Th	11 28 25	23 53 55	14♉09	15 44	7 13	2 35	23 00	13 41	11 30	20 01	27 14	1 32	11 37	7 42	11 08	25 40	17 55
15 F	11 32 21	24 53 44	28 08	15 45	9 02	3 49	23 47	13 52	11 37	20 03	27 16	1 33	11 54	7 49	10 55	25 53	17 58
16 Sa	11 36 18	25 53 31	11♊41	15 46	10 48	5 04	24 34	14 04	11 44	20 05	27 18	1 35	12 11	7 55	10 41	26 06	18 02
17 Su	11 40 14	26 53 16	24 49	15 47R	12 31	6 18	25 20	14 16	11 51	20 08	27 20	1 36	12 28	8 01	10 28	26 20	18 05
18 M	11 44 11	27 52 59	7♋35	15 47	14 10	7 32	26 07	14 28	11 58	20 10	27 23	1 37	12 44	8 06	10 15	26 33	18 08
19 T	11 48 8	28 52 39	20 02	15 46	15 45	8 46	26 54	14 40	12 05	20 12	27 25	1 38	13 00	8 11	10 02	26 47	18 12
20 W	11 52 4	29 52 17	2♌15	15 44	17 15	10 01	27 40	14 52	12 13	20 15	27 27	1 39	13 16	8 15	9 50	27 01	18 15
21 Th	11 56 1	0♈51 53	14 17	15 42	18 40	11 15	28 27	15 04	12 20	20 17	27 30	1 41	13 32	8 19	9 37	27 16	18 19
22 F	11 59 57	1 51 26	26 12	15 39	20 00	12 29	29 14	15 16	12 27	20 20	27 32	1 42	13 48	8 23	9 26	27 30	18 22
23 Sa	12 3 54	2 50 58	8♍02	15 37	21 14	13 43	0♓00	15 28	12 34	20 23	27 34	1 43	14 03	8 26	9 14	27 45	18 25
24 Su	12 7 50	3 50 27	19 51	15 36	22 22	14 58	0 47	15 40	12 41	20 25	27 36	1 44	14 18	8 29	9 03	28 00	18 29
25 M	12 11 47	4 49 54	1♎40	15 35	23 23	16 12	1 34	15 53	12 48	20 28	27 39	1 45	14 33	8 31	8 52	28 16	18 32
26 T	12 15 43	5 49 19	13 32	15 34D	24 17	17 26	2 20	16 05	12 55	20 30	27 41	1 46	14 48	8 33	8 41	28 31	18 36
27 W	12 19 40	6 48 42	25 28	15 34	25 04	18 40	3 07	16 18	13 02	20 33	27 43	1 47	15 03	8 34	8 31	28 47	18 39
28 Th	12 23 37	7 48 03	7♏32	15 35	25 44	19 54	3 54	16 30	13 09	20 36	27 45	1 48	15 17	8 35	8 21	29 03	18 43
29 F	12 27 33	8 47 22	19 45	15 36	26 17	21 08	4 41	16 43	13 16	20 39	27 48	1 49	15 31	8 36R	8 11	29 19	18 46
30 Sa	12 31 30	9 46 39	2♐09	15 36	26 42	22 23	5 27	16 56	13 22	20 41	27 50	1 50	15 45	8 36	8 02	29 36	18 50
31 Su	12 35 26	10 45 55	14 49	15 37	27 00	23 37	6 14	17 08	13 29	20 44	27 52	1 51	15 59	8 35	7 53	29 52	18 53

EPHEMERIS CALCULATED FOR 12 MIDNIGHT GREENWICH MEAN TIME. ALL OTHER DATA AND FACING ASPECTARIAN PAGE IN **EASTERN TIME (BOLD)** AND PACIFIC TIME (REGULAR).

APRIL 2024

☽ Last Aspect day	ET / hr:mn / PT		asp	☽ Ingress sign	day	ET / hr:mn / PT	
3/31	**8:16 pm**	5:16 pm	□♆	♑	3/31		9:05 pm
3/31	**8:16 pm**	5:16 pm	□♆	♑	1	**12:05 am**	
2		10:40 pm	⚹♆	♒	3	**5:08 am**	2:08 am
3	**1:40 am**		⚹♆	♒	3	**5:08 am**	2:08 am
4		10:40 pm	⚹☿	♓	5	**7:13 am**	4:13 am
5	**1:40 am**		⚹☿	♓	5	**7:13 am**	4:13 am
7	**4:27 am**	1:27 am	☌♆	♈	7	**7:25 am**	4:25 am
8	**10:39 pm**	7:39 pm	☌☿	♉	9	**7:23 am**	4:23 am
11	**6:04 am**	3:04 am	⚹♆	♊	11	**8:59 am**	5:59 am
13	**10:46 am**	7:46 am	□♆	♋	13	**1:45 pm**	10:45 am
15	**7:22 pm**	4:22 pm	△♆	♌	15	**10:24 pm**	7:24 pm
18	**8:02 am**	5:02 am	△☉	♍	18	**10:10 am**	7:10 am
20	**8:20 pm**	5:20 pm	☍♆	♎	20	**11:08 pm**	8:08 pm
22	**7:24 pm**	4:24 pm	☍♀	♏	23	**11:20 am**	8:20 am
25	**7:17 pm**	4:17 pm	△♆	♐	25	**9:37 pm**	6:37 pm
28	**3:31 am**	12:31 am	□♆	♑	28	**5:37 am**	2:37 am
30	**11:19 am**	8:19 am	⚹♂	♒	30	**11:20 am**	8:20 am

☽ Phases & Eclipses phase	day	ET / hr:mn / PT	
4th Quarter	1	**11:15 pm**	8:15 pm
New Moon	8	**2:21 pm**	11:21 am
●	8	19° ♈ 24'	
2nd Quarter	15	**3:13 pm**	12:13 pm
Full Moon	23	**7:49 pm**	4:49 pm

Planet Ingress		day	ET / hr:mn / PT	
♀	♈	4		9:00 pm
♀	♈	5	**12:00 am**	
☉	♉	19	**10:00 am**	7:00 am
♀	♉	29	**7:31 am**	4:31 am
♂	♈	30	**11:33 am**	8:33 am

Planetary Motion		day	ET / hr:mn / PT	
☿	℞	1	**6:14 pm**	3:14 pm
✷	D	21	**10:58 pm**	7:58 pm
☿	D	25	**8:54 am**	5:54 am

1 MONDAY
☽ ⚺ ♇ **3:29 am** 12:29 am
☽ ⚹ ♂ **1:49 pm** 10:49 am
☽ □ ☉ **11:15 pm** 8:15 pm
☽ ⚹ ♄ 9:46 pm

2 TUESDAY
☽ ⚹ ♄ **12:46 am**
☽ △ ♃ **7:44 am** 4:44 am
☽ △ ♅ **1:20 pm** 10:20 am
☿ ⚺ ♀ **4:58 pm** 1:58 pm
☉ ⚺ ♄ **10:42 pm** 7:42 pm
☽ □ ☿ 9:11 pm
☽ ⚹ ♀ 9:58 pm
☽ ⚹ ♆ 10:40 pm

3 WEDNESDAY
☽ □ ☿ **12:11 am**
☽ ⚹ ♀ **12:58 am**
☽ ⚹ ♆ **1:40 am**
☽ ☌ ♇ **8:23 am** 5:23 am
♀ ☌ ♆ **9:10 am** 6:10 am
☽ ⚺ ♂ **9:04 pm** 6:04 pm

4 THURSDAY
☽ ⚺ ♄ **4:47 am** 1:47 am
☽ ⚹ ☉ **6:45 am** 3:45 am
☽ □ ♃ **11:43 am** 8:43 am
☽ □ ♅ **4:24 pm** 1:24 pm
☽ ⚹ ☿ 10:40 pm

5 FRIDAY
☽ ⚹ ☿ **1:40 am**
☽ ⚺ ♆ **4:03 am** 1:03 am
☽ ⚺ ♀ **7:52 am** 4:52 am
☽ ⚺ ♇ **10:21 am** 7:21 am
☽ ☌ ♂ 10:08 pm

6 SATURDAY
☽ ☌ ♂ **1:08 am**
☽ ☌ ♄ **6:10 am** 3:10 am
☽ ⚺ ☉ **11:08 am** 8:08 am
☽ ⚹ ♃ **1:13 pm** 10:13 am
♀ ⚹ ♇ **1:46 pm** 10:46 am
☽ ⚹ ♅ **5:11 pm** 2:11 pm
☽ ⚺ ☿ 9:36 pm

7 SUNDAY
☽ ⚺ ☿ **12:36 am**
☽ ☌ ♆ **4:27 am** 1:27 am
☽ ⚹ ♇ **10:31 am** 7:31 am
☽ ☌ ♀ **12:22 pm** 9:22 am

8 MONDAY
☉ ⚺ ♃ **3:11 am** 12:11 am
☽ ⚺ ♂ **3:39 am** 12:39 am
☽ ⚺ ♄ **6:23 am** 3:23 am
☽ ⚺ ♃ **1:46 pm** 10:46 am
☽ ☌ ☉ **2:21 pm** 11:21 am
☽ ⚺ ♅ **5:12 pm** 2:12 pm
☽ ☌ ☿ **10:39 pm** 7:39 pm

9 TUESDAY
☽ ⚺ ♆ **4:30 am** 1:30 am
☽ □ ♇ **10:35 am** 7:35 am
☽ ⚺ ♀ **4:48 pm** 1:48 pm

10 WEDNESDAY
☽ ⚹ ♂ **6:49 am** 3:49 am
☽ ⚹ ♄ **7:16 am** 4:16 am
☉ ⚺ ♅ **12:00 pm** 9:00 am
☽ ☌ ♃ **3:19 pm** 12:19 pm
♂ ☌ ♄ **4:36 pm** 1:36 pm
☽ ☌ ♅ **6:18 pm** 3:18 pm
☽ ⚺ ☉ **6:44 pm** 3:44 pm
☽ ⚺ ☿ **9:31 pm** 6:31 pm

11 THURSDAY
☽ ⚹ ♆ **6:04 am** 3:04 am
☽ △ ♇ **12:23 pm** 9:23 am
☉ ☌ ☿ **7:03 pm** 4:03 pm
☽ ⚹ ♀ **11:47 pm** 8:47 pm

12 FRIDAY
☽ □ ♄ **10:39 am** 7:39 am
☽ □ ♂ **12:51 pm** 9:51 am
☽ ⚺ ♃ **7:43 pm** 4:43 pm
☽ ⚺ ♅ **10:13 pm** 7:13 pm
☽ ⚹ ☿ **10:43 pm** 7:43 pm
☽ ⚹ ☉ 11:35 pm

13 SATURDAY
☽ ⚹ ☉ **2:35 am**
☿ ⚺ ♅ **6:47 am** 3:47 am
☽ □ ♆ **10:46 am** 7:46 am
☽ ⚻ ♇ **5:26 pm** 2:26 pm

14 SUNDAY
☽ □ ♀ **11:24 am** 8:24 am
☿ ⚺ ♃ **3:38 pm** 12:38 pm
☽ △ ♄ **5:48 pm** 2:48 pm
☽ △ ♂ **11:17 pm** 8:17 pm

15 MONDAY
☽ □ ☿ **3:12 am** 12:12 am
☽ ⚹ ♃ **4:05 am** 1:05 am
☽ ⚹ ♅ **6:01 am** 3:01 am
☽ □ ☉ **3:13 pm** 12:13 pm
☽ △ ♆ **7:22 pm** 4:22 pm
☽ ☍ ♇ 11:23 pm

16 TUESDAY
☽ ☍ ♇ **2:23 am**
☿ ⚺ ♂ **10:46 am** 7:46 am

17 WEDNESDAY
☽ △ ♀ **4:03 am** 1:03 am
☽ ⚻ ♄ **4:42 am** 1:42 am
♀ ⚺ ♄ **10:53 am** 7:53 am
☽ △ ☿ **11:01 am** 8:01 am
☽ ⚻ ♂ **2:04 pm** 11:04 am
☽ □ ♃ **4:11 pm** 1:11 pm
☽ □ ♅ **5:20 pm** 2:20 pm
☉ ⚺ ♆ **9:31 pm** 6:31 pm

18 THURSDAY
☽ ⚻ ♆ **7:12 am** 4:12 am
☽ △ ☉ **8:02 am** 5:02 am
☽ ⚻ ♇ **2:20 pm** 11:20 am

19 FRIDAY
☿ ☌ ♀ **4:59 am** 1:59 am
♂ ⚹ ♃ **11:28 am** 8:28 am
☽ ☍ ♄ **5:53 pm** 2:53 pm
♂ ⚹ ♅ **7:56 pm** 4:56 pm
☽ ⚻ ☿ **9:10 pm** 6:10 pm
☽ ⚻ ♀ **11:47 pm** 8:47 pm

20 SATURDAY
☽ △ ♃ **6:14 am** 3:14 am
☽ △ ♅ **6:28 am** 3:28 am
☽ ☍ ♂ **7:09 am** 4:09 am
☽ ☍ ♆ **8:20 pm** 5:20 pm
♃ ☌ ♅ **10:27 pm** 7:27 pm
☽ ⚻ ☉ 11:28 pm

21 SUNDAY
☽ ⚻ ☉ **2:28 am**
☽ △ ♇ **3:20 am** 12:20 am
☉ □ ♇ **1:02 pm** 10:02 am

22 MONDAY
☽ ⚻ ♄ **7:08 am** 4:08 am
☽ ☍ ☿ **8:10 am** 5:10 am
♀ ⚺ ♅ **6:25 pm** 3:25 pm
☽ ⚻ ♅ **7:18 pm** 4:18 pm
☽ ☍ ♀ **7:24 pm** 4:24 pm
☽ ⚻ ♃ **7:58 pm** 4:58 pm
☽ ⚻ ♂ **11:51 pm** 8:51 pm
♀ ⚺ ♃ 11:04 pm

23 TUESDAY
♀ ⚺ ♃ **2:04 am**
☽ ⚻ ♆ **8:45 am** 5:45 am
☽ □ ♇ **3:27 pm** 12:27 pm
☽ ☍ ☉ **7:49 pm** 4:49 pm

24 WEDNESDAY
☿ ⚺ ♄ **5:14 am** 2:14 am
☽ ⚻ ☿ **6:41 pm** 3:41 pm
☽ △ ♄ **6:52 pm** 3:52 pm

25 THURSDAY
☽ ☍ ♅ **6:26 am** 3:26 am
☽ ☍ ♃ **7:55 am** 4:55 am
☽ ⚻ ♀ **12:42 pm** 9:42 am
☽ △ ♂ **2:25 pm** 11:25 am
☽ △ ♆ **7:17 pm** 4:17 pm
☽ ⚹ ♇ 10:36 pm

26 FRIDAY
☽ ⚹ ♇ **1:36 am**
☽ ⚻ ☉ **10:36 am** 7:36 am

27 SATURDAY
☽ △ ☿ **3:59 am** 12:59 am
☽ □ ♄ **4:21 am** 1:21 am
♀ ⚺ ♂ **8:36 am** 5:36 am
☽ ⚻ ♅ **3:18 pm** 12:18 pm
☽ ⚻ ♃ **5:30 pm** 2:30 pm
☽ □ ♂ 11:15 pm
☽ △ ♀ 11:56 pm

28 SUNDAY
☽ □ ♂ **2:15 am**
☽ △ ♀ **2:56 am**
☽ □ ♆ **3:31 am** 12:31 am
♀ ⚺ ♆ **9:13 am** 6:13 am
☽ ⚺ ♇ **9:27 am** 6:27 am
☿ ⚺ ♄ **6:49 pm** 3:49 pm
☽ △ ☉ **10:28 pm** 7:28 pm
♂ ☌ ♆ 9:31 pm

29 MONDAY
♂ ☌ ♆ **12:31 am**
☽ ⚹ ♄ **11:28 am** 8:28 am
☽ □ ☿ **11:45 am** 8:45 am
☽ △ ♅ **9:49 pm** 6:49 pm
☽ △ ♃ 9:39 pm

30 TUESDAY
☽ △ ♃ **12:39 am**
☽ ⚹ ♆ **9:25 am** 6:25 am
☽ ⚹ ♂ **11:19 am** 8:19 am
☽ □ ♀ **2:04 pm** 11:04 am
☽ ☌ ♇ **3:00 pm** 12:00 pm
♀ □ ♇ 9:30 pm

Eastern time in bold type
Pacific time in medium type

April 2024

DATE	SID.TIME	SUN	MOON	NODE	MERCURY	VENUS	MARS	JUPITER	SATURN	URANUS	NEPTUNE	PLUTO	CERES	PALLAS	JUNO	VESTA	CHIRON
1 M	12 39 23	11♈45 09	27♐46	15♈37	27♈10R	24♓51	7♓01	17♉21	13♓36	20♉47	27♓54	1♒52	16♑13	8♐34R	7♍45R	0♋09	18♈57
2 T	12 43 19	12 44 21	11♑03	15 37R	27 13	26 05	7 47	17 34	13 43	20 50	27 57	1 53	16 26	8 33	7 37	0 26	19 00
3 W	12 47 16	13 43 31	24 42	15 37	27 09	27 19	8 34	17 47	13 49	20 53	27 59	1 54	16 39	8 31	7 29	0 44	19 04
4 Th	12 51 12	14 42 40	8♒45	15 37D	26 58	28 33	9 21	18 00	13 56	20 56	28 01	1 55	16 52	8 29	7 22	1 01	19 07
5 F	12 55 9	15 41 47	23 09	15 37	26 41	29 48	10 07	18 13	14 03	20 59	28 03	1 55	17 04	8 26	7 15	1 19	19 11
6 Sa	12 59 6	16 40 52	7♓53	15 37	26 18	1♈02	10 54	18 26	14 09	21 02	28 05	1 56	17 17	8 23	7 08	1 37	19 15
7 Su	13 3 2	17 39 55	22 51	15 37	25 49	2 16	11 41	18 39	14 16	21 05	28 08	1 57	17 29	8 19	7 02	1 55	19 18
8 M	13 6 59	18 38 56	7♈54	15 38R	25 16	3 30	12 27	18 53	14 22	21 08	28 10	1 58	17 41	8 14	6 57	2 13	19 22
9 T	13 10 55	19 37 55	22 56	15 37	24 39	4 44	13 14	19 06	14 29	21 11	28 12	1 58	17 52	8 10	6 51	2 31	19 25
10 W	13 14 52	20 36 52	7♉46	15 37	23 58	5 58	14 01	19 19	14 35	21 14	28 14	1 59	18 04	8 04	6 46	2 50	19 29
11 Th	13 18 48	21 35 48	22 18	15 37	23 15	7 12	14 47	19 33	14 42	21 17	28 16	2 00	18 15	7 59	6 42	3 09	19 32
12 F	13 22 45	22 34 41	6♊27	15 36	22 31	8 26	15 34	19 46	14 48	21 20	28 18	2 00	18 25	7 52	6 38	3 28	19 36
13 Sa	13 26 41	23 33 32	20 09	15 35	21 45	9 41	16 21	19 59	14 54	21 24	28 20	2 01	18 36	7 45	6 34	3 47	19 39
14 Su	13 30 38	24 32 20	3♋25	15 34	21 00	10 55	17 07	20 13	15 01	21 27	28 23	2 01	18 46	7 38	6 31	4 06	19 43
15 M	13 34 35	25 31 07	16 16	15 34D	20 16	12 09	17 54	20 26	15 07	21 30	28 25	2 02	18 56	7 31	6 28	4 26	19 46
16 T	13 38 31	26 29 51	28 46	15 34	19 34	13 23	18 40	20 40	15 13	21 33	28 27	2 02	19 06	7 22	6 25	4 45	19 50
17 W	13 42 28	27 28 33	10♌59	15 34	18 54	14 37	19 27	20 54	15 19	21 36	28 29	2 03	19 15	7 14	6 23	5 05	19 53
18 Th	13 46 24	28 27 12	22 59	15 35	18 17	15 51	20 13	21 07	15 25	21 40	28 31	2 03	19 25	7 04	6 21	5 25	19 57
19 F	13 50 21	29 25 50	4♍51	15 36	17 44	17 05	21 00	21 21	15 31	21 43	28 33	2 04	19 33	6 55	6 20	5 45	20 01
20 Sa	13 54 17	0♉24 25	16 39	15 37	17 15	18 19	21 46	21 35	15 37	21 46	28 35	2 04	19 42	6 45	6 19	6 05	20 04
21 Su	13 58 14	1 22 58	28 27	15 39	16 50	19 33	22 33	21 48	15 43	21 49	28 37	2 04	19 50	6 34	6 18	6 26	20 08
22 M	14 2 10	2 21 29	10♎19	15 39R	16 30	20 47	23 19	22 02	15 49	21 53	28 39	2 05	19 58	6 23	6 18D	6 46	20 11
23 T	14 6 7	3 19 58	22 17	15 39	16 15	22 01	24 06	22 16	15 54	21 56	28 41	2 05	20 06	6 12	6 18	7 07	20 14
24 W	14 10 3	4 18 26	4♏24	15 38	16 05	23 15	24 52	22 30	16 00	21 59	28 43	2 05	20 13	6 00	6 19	7 27	20 18
25 Th	14 14 0	5 16 51	16 41	15 36	16 00D	24 29	25 38	22 44	16 06	22 03	28 45	2 05	20 21	5 48	6 19	7 48	20 21
26 F	14 17 57	6 15 15	29 09	15 34	15 59	25 43	26 25	22 58	16 11	22 06	28 47	2 06	20 27	5 35	6 21	8 09	20 25
27 Sa	14 21 53	7 13 36	11♐50	15 30	16 04	26 57	27 11	23 11	16 17	22 10	28 48	2 06	20 34	5 22	6 22	8 31	20 28
28 Su	14 25 50	8 11 57	24 45	15 27	16 14	28 11	27 57	23 25	16 22	22 13	28 50	2 06	20 40	5 08	6 24	8 52	20 32
29 M	14 29 46	9 10 15	7♑54	15 24	16 28	29 25	28 44	23 39	16 28	22 16	28 52	2 06	20 46	4 54	6 27	9 13	20 35
30 T	14 33 43	10 08 33	21 18	15 22	16 47	0♉38	29 30	23 53	16 33	22 20	28 54	2 06	20 51	4 40	6 29	9 35	20 39

EPHEMERIS CALCULATED FOR 12 MIDNIGHT GREENWICH MEAN TIME. ALL OTHER DATA AND FACING ASPECTARIAN PAGE IN **EASTERN TIME (BOLD)** AND PACIFIC TIME (REGULAR).

MAY 2024

☽ Last Aspect day	ET / hr:mn / PT	asp	☽ Ingress sign	day	ET / hr:mn / PT
2	**5:28 am** 2:28 am	□ ♃	♓	2	**2:52 pm** 11:52 am
4	**3:06 pm** 12:06 pm	☌ ♆	♈	4	**4:41 pm** 1:41 pm
5	10:57 pm	☌ ☿	♉	6	**5:42 pm** 2:42 pm
6	**1:57 am**	☌ ☿	♉	6	**5:42 pm** 2:42 pm
8	**5:55 pm** 2:55 pm	⚹ ♆	♊	8	**7:20 pm** 4:20 pm
10	**9:49 pm** 6:49 pm	□ ♆	♋	10	**11:13 pm** 8:13 pm
13	**5:13 am** 2:13 am	△ ♆	♌	13	**6:36 am** 3:36 am
15	**12:41 pm** 9:41 am	□ ♃	♍	15	**5:33 pm** 2:33 pm
18	**5:09 am** 2:09 am	☍ ♆	♎	18	**6:23 am** 3:23 am
19	**11:48 am** 8:48 am	☍ ♂	♏	20	**6:34 pm** 3:34 pm

☽ Last Aspect day	ET / hr:mn / PT	asp	☽ Ingress sign	day	ET / hr:mn / PT
23	**3:28 am** 12:28 am	△ ♆	♐	23	**4:24 am** 1:24 am
25	**10:47 am** 7:47 am	□ ♆	♑	25	**11:36 am** 8:36 am
27	**4:02 pm** 1:02 pm	⚹ ♆	♒	27	**4:45 pm** 1:45 pm
29	**10:20 am** 7:20 am	□ ♅	♓	29	**8:33 pm** 5:33 pm
31	**10:55 pm** 7:55 pm	☌ ♆	♈	31	**11:28 pm** 8:28 pm

☽ Phases & Eclipses phase	day	ET / hr:mn / PT
4th Quarter	1	**7:27 am** 4:27 am
New Moon	7	**11:22 pm** 8:22 pm
2nd Quarter	15	**7:48 am** 4:48 am
Full Moon	23	**9:53 am** 6:53 am
4th Quarter	30	**1:13 pm** 10:13 am

Planet Ingress		day	ET / hr:mn / PT
☿	♉	15	**1:05 pm** 10:05 am
♀	♏	16	**1:23 pm** 10:23 am
☉	♊	20	**8:59 am** 5:59 am
♀	♊	23	**4:30 pm** 1:30 pm
♃	♊	25	**7:15 pm** 4:15 pm

Planetary Motion		day	ET / hr:mn / PT
♇	℞	2	**1:46 pm** 10:46 am
⚷	℞	14	10:34 pm
⚷	℞	15	**1:34 am**

1 WEDNESDAY
♀ □ ♇ **12:30 am**
☽ □ ☉ **7:27 am** 4:27 am
☽ ⚺ ♄ **4:17 pm** 1:17 pm
☽ ⚹ ☿ **5:48 pm** 2:48 pm
☽ □ ♅ 11:06 pm

2 THURSDAY
☽ □ ♅ **2:06 am**
☽ □ ♃ **5:28 am** 2:28 am
☽ ⚺ ♆ **1:08 pm** 10:08 am
☽ ⚺ ♂ **5:48 pm** 2:48 pm
☽ ⚺ ♇ **6:24 pm** 3:24 pm
☽ ⚹ ♀ **10:21 pm** 7:21 pm

3 FRIDAY
♂ ⚹ ♇ **5:06 am** 2:06 am
☽ ⚹ ☉ **1:55 pm** 10:55 am
☽ ☌ ♄ **7:05 pm** 4:05 pm
☽ ⚺ ☿ **10:18 pm** 7:18 pm

4 SATURDAY
☽ ⚹ ♅ **4:28 am** 1:28 am
☽ ⚹ ♃ **8:22 am** 5:22 am
☽ ☌ ♆ **3:06 pm** 12:06 pm
☽ ⚹ ♇ **8:08 pm** 5:08 pm
☽ ☌ ♂ **10:17 pm** 7:17 pm

5 SUNDAY
☽ ⚺ ♀ **4:32 am** 1:32 am
☽ ⚺ ☉ **6:42 pm** 3:42 pm
☽ ⚺ ♄ **8:35 pm** 5:35 pm
☽ ☌ ☿ 10:57 pm

6 MONDAY
☽ ☌ ☿ **1:57 am**
☽ ⚺ ♅ **5:46 am** 2:46 am
☽ ⚺ ♃ **10:14 am** 7:14 am
☽ ⚺ ♆ **4:14 pm** 1:14 pm
☽ □ ♇ **9:08 pm** 6:08 pm
☉ ⚹ ♄ 10:42 pm
☽ ⚺ ♂ 11:01 pm

7 TUESDAY
☉ ⚹ ♄ **1:42 am**
☽ ⚺ ♂ **2:01 am**
☽ ☌ ♀ **10:05 am** 7:05 am
☽ ⚹ ♄ **10:02 pm** 7:02 pm
☽ ☌ ☉ **11:22 pm** 8:22 pm

8 WEDNESDAY
☽ ⚺ ☿ **6:14 am** 3:14 am
☽ ☌ ♅ **7:19 am** 4:19 am
☽ ☌ ♃ **12:30 pm** 9:30 am
☽ ⚹ ♆ **5:55 pm** 2:55 pm
☽ △ ♇ **10:52 pm** 7:52 pm
☿ ⚺ ♅ 9:17 pm

9 THURSDAY
☿ ⚺ ♅ **12:17 am**
☽ ⚹ ♂ **6:47 am** 3:47 am
☽ ⚺ ♀ **5:08 pm** 2:08 pm
☽ □ ♄ 10:03 pm

10 FRIDAY
☽ □ ♄ **1:03 am**
☽ ⚺ ☉ **6:00 am** 3:00 am

☽ ⚺ ♅ **10:44 am** 7:44 am
☽ ⚹ ☿ **1:13 pm** 10:13 am
☽ ⚺ ♃ **4:54 pm** 1:54 pm
☽ □ ♆ **9:49 pm** 6:49 pm
☽ ⚻ ♇ 11:57 pm

11 SATURDAY
☽ ⚻ ♇ **2:57 am**
☽ □ ♂ **2:36 pm** 11:36 am

12 SUNDAY
☽ ⚹ ♀ **3:57 am** 12:57 am
☽ △ ♄ **7:11 am** 4:11 am
☽ ⚹ ☉ **4:34 pm** 1:34 pm
☽ ⚹ ♅ **5:29 pm** 2:29 pm
☿ ⚺ ♃ 9:00 pm
☽ ⚹ ♃ 9:52 pm
☽ □ ☿ 9:56 pm

13 MONDAY
☿ ⚺ ♃ **12:00 am**
☽ ⚹ ♃ **12:52 am**
☽ □ ☿ **12:56 am**
☽ △ ♆ **5:13 am** 2:13 am
☉ ☌ ♅ **5:14 am** 2:14 am
☽ ☍ ♇ **10:35 am** 7:35 am
♀ ⚹ ♄ **3:45 pm** 12:45 pm
☽ △ ♂ 11:49 pm

14 TUESDAY
☽ △ ♂ **2:49 am**
☽ ⚻ ♄ **5:06 pm** 2:06 pm
☽ □ ♀ **7:47 pm** 4:47 pm
☿ ⚺ ♆ **11:45 pm** 8:45 pm

15 WEDNESDAY
☽ □ ♅ **3:58 am** 12:58 am
☽ □ ☉ **7:48 am** 4:48 am
☽ □ ♃ **12:41 pm** 9:41 am
☽ ⚻ ♆ **4:12 pm** 1:12 pm
☽ △ ☿ **6:04 pm** 3:04 pm
☽ ⚻ ♇ **9:42 pm** 6:42 pm

16 THURSDAY
☽ ⚻ ♂ **6:48 pm** 3:48 pm

17 FRIDAY
☿ □ ♇ **3:44 am** 12:44 am
☽ ☍ ♄ **5:48 am** 2:48 am
☽ △ ♀ **3:15 pm** 12:15 pm
☽ △ ♅ **4:53 pm** 1:53 pm
☽ △ ☉ 10:53 pm
☽ △ ♃ 11:42 pm

18 SATURDAY
☽ △ ☉ **1:53 am**
☽ △ ♃ **2:42 am**
☽ ☍ ♆ **5:09 am** 2:09 am
♀ ☌ ♅ **7:41 am** 4:41 am
☽ △ ♇ **10:32 am** 7:32 am
☽ ⚻ ☿ **2:29 pm** 11:29 am
☉ ☌ ♃ **2:45 pm** 11:45 am

19 SUNDAY
☽ ☍ ♂ **11:48 am** 8:48 am
☉ ⚹ ♆ **6:45 pm** 3:45 pm
☽ ⚻ ♄ **6:52 pm** 3:52 pm

20 MONDAY
☽ ⚻ ♅ **5:43 am** 2:43 am
☽ ⚻ ♀ **10:41 am** 7:41 am
☽ ⚻ ♃ **4:11 pm** 1:11 pm
☽ ⚻ ♆ **5:29 pm** 2:29 pm
☽ ⚻ ☉ **7:23 pm** 4:23 pm
☽ □ ♇ **10:34 pm** 7:34 pm

21 TUESDAY
☽ ☍ ☿ **10:18 am** 7:18 am
☽ ⚻ ♂ 11:49 pm

22 WEDNESDAY
☽ ⚻ ♂ **2:49 am**
☽ △ ♄ **6:03 am** 3:03 am
☉ △ ♇ **11:14 am** 8:14 am
☽ ☍ ♅ **4:24 pm** 1:24 pm

23 THURSDAY
☽ ☍ ♀ **3:07 am** 12:07 am
☽ ☍ ♃ **3:13 am** 12:13 am
☽ △ ♆ **3:28 am** 12:28 am
♀ ☌ ♃ **4:29 am** 1:29 am
♀ ⚹ ♆ **6:50 am** 3:50 am
☽ ⚹ ♇ **8:10 am** 5:10 am
☽ ☍ ☉ **9:53 am** 6:53 am
♃ ⚹ ♆ **5:44 pm** 2:44 pm

24 FRIDAY
☽ ⚻ ☿ **3:05 am** 12:05 am
♂ ⚺ ♄ **12:23 pm** 9:23 am
☽ □ ♄ **2:29 pm** 11:29 am
☽ △ ♂ **2:36 pm** 11:36 am
☽ ⚻ ♅ 9:21 pm

25 SATURDAY
☽ ⚻ ♅ **12:21 am**
♀ △ ♇ **7:16 am** 4:16 am
☽ □ ♆ **10:47 am** 7:47 am
☽ ⚻ ♃ **11:28 am** 8:28 am
☽ ⚺ ♇ **3:10 pm** 12:10 pm
☽ ⚻ ♀ **3:58 pm** 12:58 pm
☽ ⚻ ☉ **9:06 pm** 6:06 pm

26 SUNDAY
☽ △ ☿ **4:49 pm** 1:49 pm
☽ ⚹ ♄ **8:33 pm** 5:33 pm
☽ □ ♂ **11:37 pm** 8:37 pm

27 MONDAY
☽ △ ♅ **6:05 am** 3:05 am
☽ ⚹ ♆ **4:02 pm** 1:02 pm
☽ △ ♃ **5:32 pm** 2:32 pm
☽ ☌ ♇ **8:10 pm** 5:10 pm
☿ ⚹ ♄ **11:22 pm** 8:22 pm
☽ △ ♀ 11:10 pm

28 TUESDAY
☽ △ ♀ **2:10 am**
☽ △ ☉ **5:54 am** 2:54 am
☽ ⚺ ♄ 10:00 pm

29 WEDNESDAY
☽ ⚺ ♄ **1:00 am**
☽ □ ☿ **4:36 am** 1:36 am
☽ ⚹ ♂ **6:46 am** 3:46 am
☽ □ ♅ **10:20 am** 7:20 am
☽ ⚺ ♆ **7:55 pm** 4:55 pm

☽ □ ♃ **10:12 pm** 7:12 pm
☽ ⚺ ♇ **11:51 pm** 8:51 pm

30 THURSDAY
☿ ⚺ ♂ **7:54 am** 4:54 am
☽ □ ♀ **10:43 am** 7:43 am
☽ □ ☉ **1:13 pm** 10:13 am
☿ ☌ ♅ 10:54 pm

31 FRIDAY
☿ ☌ ♅ **1:54 am**
☽ ☌ ♄ **4:24 am** 1:24 am
☽ ⚺ ♂ **12:45 pm** 9:45 am
☽ ⚹ ♅ **1:36 pm** 10:36 am
☽ ⚹ ☿ **3:19 pm** 12:19 pm
☽ ☌ ♆ **10:55 pm** 7:55 pm
☽ ⚹ ♃ 10:57 pm
☽ ⚹ ♇ 11:41 pm

Eastern time in bold type
Pacific time in medium type

MAY 2024

DATE	SID.TIME	SUN	MOON	NODE	MERCURY	VENUS	MARS	JUPITER	SATURN	URANUS	NEPTUNE	PLUTO	CERES	PALLAS	JUNO	VESTA	CHIRON
1 W	14 37 39	11♉06 48	4♒58	15♈21 D	17♈11	1♉52	0♈16	24♉07	16♓38	22♉23	28♓56	2♒06	20♑56	4♐25 R	6♍32	9♋57	20♈42
2 Th	14 41 36	12 05 02	18 53	15 21	17 39	3 06	1 03	24 21	16 43	22 27	28 58	2 06 R	21 01	4 10	6 36	10 18	20 45
3 F	14 45 33	13 03 15	3♓03	15 22	18 11	4 20	1 49	24 35	16 49	22 30	28 59	2 06	21 06	3 55	6 39	10 40	20 49
4 Sa	14 49 29	14 01 26	17 27	15 23	18 47	5 34	2 35	24 49	16 54	22 34	29 01	2 06	21 10	3 39	6 43	11 02	20 52
5 Su	14 53 26	14 59 36	2♈02	15 24 R	19 26	6 48	3 21	25 04	16 59	22 37	29 03	2 06	21 14	3 23	6 48	11 25	20 55
6 M	14 57 22	15 57 44	16 43	15 25	20 10	8 02	4 07	25 18	17 04	22 41	29 04	2 06	21 17	3 07	6 52	11 47	20 59
7 T	15 1 19	16 55 51	1♉24	15 24	20 57	9 16	4 53	25 32	17 09	22 44	29 06	2 06	21 20	2 51	6 57	12 09	21 02
8 W	15 5 15	17 53 56	16 00	15 21	21 48	10 30	5 39	25 46	17 13	22 47	29 08	2 06	21 23	2 34	7 03	12 32	21 05
9 Th	15 9 12	18 52 00	0♊23	15 17	22 42	11 44	6 25	26 00	17 18	22 51	29 09	2 06	21 26	2 17	7 08	12 54	21 08
10 F	15 13 8	19 50 02	14 29	15 12	23 39	12 57	7 11	26 14	17 23	22 54	29 11	2 06	21 28	2 00	7 14	13 17	21 12
11 Sa	15 17 5	20 48 02	28 12	15 07	24 39	14 11	7 57	26 28	17 27	22 58	29 13	2 05	21 29	1 42	7 21	13 40	21 15
12 Su	15 21 2	21 46 00	11♋30	15 01	25 42	15 25	8 43	26 42	17 32	23 01	29 14	2 05	21 31	1 25	7 27	14 03	21 18
13 M	15 24 58	22 43 57	24 25	14 57	26 48	16 39	9 29	26 57	17 36	23 05	29 16	2 05	21 32	1 07	7 34	14 26	21 21
14 T	15 28 55	23 41 52	6♌58	14 54	27 56	17 53	10 15	27 11	17 41	23 08	29 17	2 04	21 32	0 49	7 41	14 49	21 24
15 W	15 32 51	24 39 45	19 12	14 53 D	29 08	19 07	11 01	27 25	17 45	23 12	29 19	2 04	21 33 R	0 31	7 49	15 12	21 27
16 Th	15 36 48	25 37 37	1♍13	14 53	0♉22	20 20	11 46	27 39	17 49	23 15	29 20	2 04	21 32	0 13	7 56	15 36	21 30
17 F	15 40 44	26 35 26	13 05	14 54	1 38	21 34	12 32	27 53	17 53	23 19	29 22	2 03	21 32	29♏55	8 04	15 59	21 33
18 Sa	15 44 41	27 33 14	24 54	14 55	2 57	22 48	13 18	28 07	17 57	23 22	29 23	2 03	21 31	29 37	8 13	16 23	21 36
19 Su	15 48 37	28 31 01	6♎43	14 56 R	4 19	24 02	14 03	28 21	18 01	23 26	29 24	2 03	21 30	29 19	8 21	16 46	21 39
20 M	15 52 34	29 28 45	18 39	14 57	5 43	25 16	14 49	28 36	18 05	23 29	29 26	2 02	21 28	29 00	8 30	17 10	21 42
21 T	15 56 31	0♊26 28	0♏44	14 55	7 09	26 29	15 35	28 50	18 09	23 33	29 27	2 02	21 27	28 42	8 39	17 34	21 45
22 W	16 0 27	1 24 10	13 01	14 52	8 38	27 43	16 20	29 04	18 12	23 36	29 28	2 01	21 24	28 24	8 48	17 58	21 48
23 Th	16 4 24	2 21 50	25 33	14 46	10 09	28 57	17 06	29 18	18 16	23 40	29 30	2 01	21 22	28 06	8 58	18 22	21 51
24 F	16 8 20	3 19 30	8♐21	14 39	11 42	0♊11	17 51	29 32	18 20	23 43	29 31	2 00	21 19	27 48	9 08	18 46	21 54
25 Sa	16 12 17	4 17 07	21 23	14 31	13 18	1 25	18 36	29 46	18 23	23 47	29 32	1 59	21 15	27 30	9 18	19 10	21 57
26 Su	16 16 13	5 14 44	4♑41	14 23	14 56	2 38	19 22	0♊00	18 26	23 50	29 33	1 59	21 11	27 13	9 28	19 34	22 00
27 M	16 20 10	6 12 20	18 11	14 15	16 36	3 52	20 07	0 15	18 30	23 53	29 35	1 58	21 07	26 55	9 39	19 58	22 02
28 T	16 24 6	7 09 55	1♒52	14 08	18 19	5 06	20 52	0 29	18 33	23 57	29 36	1 58	21 03	26 38	9 49	20 22	22 05
29 W	16 28 3	8 07 28	15 43	14 04	20 04	6 20	21 37	0 43	18 36	24 00	29 37	1 57	20 58	26 20	10 00	20 47	22 08
30 Th	16 32 0	9 05 01	29 41	14 02 D	21 51	7 33	22 23	0 57	18 39	24 04	29 38	1 56	20 53	26 03	10 11	21 11	22 11
31 F	16 35 56	10 02 33	13♓46	14 02	23 41	8 47	23 08	1 11	18 42	24 07	29 39	1 55	20 47	25 46	10 23	21 36	22 13

EPHEMERIS CALCULATED FOR 12 MIDNIGHT GREENWICH MEAN TIME. ALL OTHER DATA AND FACING ASPECTARIAN PAGE IN **EASTERN TIME (BOLD)** AND PACIFIC TIME (REGULAR).

JUNE 2024

☽ Last Aspect day	ET / hr:mn / PT	asp	☽ Ingress sign day	ET / hr:mn / PT
2	**6:04 pm** 3:04 pm	☌ ♂	♉ 2	10:55 pm
2	**6:04 pm** 3:04 pm	☌ ♂	♉ 3	**1:55 am**
5	**4:09 am** 1:09 am	⚹ ♆	♊ 5	**4:36 am** 1:36 am
7	**8:16 am** 5:16 am	□ ♆	♋ 7	**8:41 am** 5:41 am
9	**3:05 pm** 12:05 pm	△ ♆	♌ 9	**3:29 pm** 12:29 pm
11	**3:16 pm** 12:16 pm	□ ♅	♍ 11	10:39 pm
11	**3:16 pm** 12:16 pm	□ ♅	♍ 12	**1:39 am**
14	**1:54 pm** 10:54 am	☍ ♆	♎ 14	**2:12 pm** 11:12 am
16	11:05 pm	△ ☿	♏ 16	11:38 pm
17	**2:05 am**	△ ☿	♏ 17	**2:38 am**
19	**12:19 pm** 9:19 am	△ ♆	♐ 19	**12:32 pm** 9:32 am
21	**6:58 pm** 3:58 pm	□ ♆	♑ 21	**7:08 pm** 4:08 pm
23	**11:05 pm** 8:05 pm	⚹ ♆	♒ 23	**11:14 pm** 8:14 pm
25	**6:30 pm** 3:30 pm	□ ♅	♓ 25	11:08 pm
25	**6:30 pm** 3:30 pm	□ ♅	♓ 26	**2:08 am**
28	**4:45 am** 1:45 am	☌ ♆	♈ 28	**4:52 am** 1:52 am
29	9:56 pm	□ ☿	♉ 30	**8:00 am** 5:00 am
30	**12:56 am**	□ ☿	♉ 30	**8:00 am** 5:00 am

☽ Phases & Eclipses phase	day	ET / hr:mn / PT
New Moon	6	**8:38 am** 5:38 am
2nd Quarter	13	10:18 pm
2nd Quarter	14	**1:18 am**
Full Moon	21	**9:08 pm** 6:08 pm
4th Quarter	28	**5:53 pm** 2:53 pm

Planet Ingress	day	ET / hr:mn / PT
☿ ♊	3	**3:37 am** 12:37 am
♂ ♉	8	9:35 pm
♂ ♉	9	**12:35 am**
♀ ♋	16	11:20 pm
♀ ♋	17	**2:20 am**
☿ ♋	17	**5:07 am** 2:07 am
⚶ ♌	19	**6:11 pm** 3:11 pm
☉ ♋	20	**4:51 pm** 1:51 pm

Planetary Motion	day	ET / hr:mn / PT
♄ ℞	29	**3:07 pm** 12:07 pm

1 SATURDAY
☽ ⚹ ♃ **1:57 am**
☽ ⚹ ♇ **2:41 am**
♂ ⚺ ♅ **6:07 am** 3:07 am
☽ ⚹ ♀ **6:15 pm** 3:15 pm
☽ ⚹ ☉ **7:35 pm** 4:35 pm

2 SUNDAY
☽ ⚺ ♄ **7:08 am** 4:08 am
☽ ⚺ ♅ **4:18 pm** 1:18 pm
☽ ☌ ♂ **6:04 pm** 3:04 pm
♃ △ ♇ **8:13 pm** 5:13 pm
☿ ⚹ ♆ **11:57 pm** 8:57 pm
☽ ⚺ ♆ 10:25 pm
☽ ⚺ ☿ 10:39 pm

3 MONDAY
☽ ⚺ ♆ **1:25 am**
☽ ⚺ ☿ **1:39 am**
☽ □ ♇ **5:05 am** 2:05 am
☽ ⚺ ♃ **5:14 am** 2:14 am
☽ ⚺ ♀ 10:27 pm
☽ ⚺ ☉ 10:39 pm
☿ △ ♇ 11:12 pm

4 TUESDAY
☽ ⚺ ♀ **1:27 am**
☽ ⚺ ☉ **1:39 am**
☿ △ ♇ **2:12 am**
☿ ☌ ♃ **6:23 am** 3:23 am
☽ ⚹ ♄ **9:46 am** 6:46 am
☉ ☌ ♀ **11:32 am** 8:32 am
☽ ☌ ♅ **7:04 pm** 4:04 pm
☽ ⚺ ♂ **11:28 pm** 8:28 pm

5 WEDNESDAY
☽ ⚹ ♆ **4:09 am** 1:09 am
☽ △ ♇ **7:46 am** 4:46 am
☽ ☌ ♃ **8:49 am** 5:49 am
☽ ☌ ☿ **12:46 pm** 9:46 am

6 THURSDAY
☽ ☌ ☉ **8:38 am** 5:38 am
☽ ☌ ♀ **9:36 am** 6:36 am
☽ □ ♄ **1:19 pm** 10:19 am
☽ ⚺ ♅ **10:59 pm** 7:59 pm

7 FRIDAY
☽ ⚹ ♂ **6:22 am** 3:22 am
☽ □ ♆ **8:16 am** 5:16 am
☽ ⚻ ♇ **11:55 am** 8:55 am
☽ ⚺ ♃ **2:00 pm** 11:00 am
☽ ⚺ ☿ 11:55 pm

8 SATURDAY
☽ ⚺ ☿ **2:55 am**
♀ □ ♄ **4:25 am** 1:25 am
♂ ⚺ ♆ **5:33 pm** 2:33 pm
☽ ⚺ ☉ **6:15 pm** 3:15 pm
☽ △ ♄ **7:08 pm** 4:08 pm
☽ ⚺ ♀ **8:37 pm** 5:37 pm

9 SUNDAY
☽ ⚹ ♅ **5:26 am** 2:26 am
☉ □ ♄ **6:36 am** 3:36 am
☽ △ ♆ **3:05 pm** 12:05 pm
☽ □ ♂ **4:24 pm** 1:24 pm
☽ ☍ ♇ **6:50 pm** 3:50 pm
☽ ⚹ ♃ **10:09 pm** 7:09 pm

10 MONDAY
☽ ⚹ ☿ **10:35 pm** 7:35 pm

11 TUESDAY
☽ ⚻ ♄ **4:14 am** 1:14 am
☽ ⚹ ☉ **7:58 am** 4:58 am
♂ □ ♇ **9:21 am** 6:21 am
☽ ⚹ ♀ **12:02 pm** 9:02 am
☽ □ ♅ **3:16 pm** 12:16 pm
☽ ⚻ ♆ 10:17 pm

12 WEDNESDAY
☽ ⚻ ♆ **1:17 am**
☽ ⚻ ♇ **5:07 am** 2:07 am
☽ △ ♂ **6:26 am** 3:26 am
☿ □ ♄ **6:47 am** 3:47 am
☽ □ ♃ **9:49 am** 6:49 am
♀ ⚺ ♅ **9:24 pm** 6:24 pm

13 THURSDAY
☽ ☍ ♄ **4:18 pm** 1:18 pm
☽ □ ☿ **11:51 pm** 8:51 pm
☽ □ ☉ 10:18 pm

14 FRIDAY
☽ □ ☉ **1:18 am**
☽ △ ♅ **3:50 am** 12:50 am
☽ □ ♀ **7:13 am** 4:13 am
☉ ☌ ☿ **12:33 pm** 9:33 am
☽ ☍ ♆ **1:54 pm** 10:54 am
☽ △ ♇ **5:39 pm** 2:39 pm
☿ ⚺ ♅ **9:41 pm** 6:41 pm
☽ ⚻ ♂ **11:08 pm** 8:08 pm
☽ △ ♃ **11:44 pm** 8:44 pm

15 SATURDAY
☉ ⚺ ♅ **10:16 am** 7:16 am
♂ ⚺ ♃ **12:37 pm** 9:37 am

16 SUNDAY
☽ ⚻ ♄ **5:14 am** 2:14 am
☽ ⚻ ♅ **4:45 pm** 1:45 pm
☽ △ ☉ **7:14 pm** 4:14 pm
♀ □ ♆ **11:46 pm** 8:46 pm
☽ △ ☿ 11:05 pm
☽ ⚻ ♆ 11:22 pm
☽ △ ♀ 11:40 pm

17 MONDAY
☽ △ ☿ **2:05 am**
☽ ⚻ ♆ **2:22 am**
☽ △ ♀ **2:40 am**
☿ □ ♆ **3:41 am** 12:41 am
☽ □ ♇ **5:54 am** 2:54 am
☿ ☌ ♀ **8:43 am** 5:43 am
☽ ⚻ ♃ **1:02 pm** 10:02 am
☽ ☍ ♂ **3:10 pm** 12:10 pm
☿ ⚻ ♇ **11:13 pm** 8:13 pm

18 TUESDAY
♀ ⚻ ♇ **10:12 am** 7:12 am
☽ △ ♄ **4:19 pm** 1:19 pm

19 WEDNESDAY
☽ ☍ ♅ **3:24 am** 12:24 am
☽ ⚻ ☉ **10:15 am** 7:15 am
☽ △ ♆ **12:19 pm** 9:19 am
☽ ⚹ ♇ **3:32 pm** 12:32 pm
☽ ⚻ ♀ **6:41 pm** 3:41 pm
☿ ⚺ ♃ **9:40 pm** 6:40 pm
☽ ☍ ♃ **11:22 pm** 8:22 pm
☽ ⚻ ☿ **11:40 pm** 8:40 pm

20 THURSDAY
☽ ⚻ ♂ **3:47 am** 12:47 am
☉ □ ♆ **2:12 pm** 11:12 am
☽ □ ♄ 9:08 pm

21 FRIDAY
☽ □ ♄ **12:08 am**
☽ ⚻ ♅ **10:44 am** 7:44 am
☿ ⚹ ♂ **12:23 pm** 9:23 am
☽ □ ♆ **6:58 pm** 3:58 pm
☽ ☍ ☉ **9:08 pm** 6:08 pm
☽ ⚺ ♇ **9:55 pm** 6:55 pm

22 SATURDAY
♀ ⚺ ♃ **5:56 am** 2:56 am
☽ ⚻ ♃ **6:18 am** 3:18 am
☽ ☍ ♀ **6:20 am** 3:20 am
☉ ⚻ ♇ **8:01 am** 5:01 am
☽ △ ♂ **12:37 pm** 9:37 am
☽ ☍ ☿ **3:25 pm** 12:25 pm

23 SUNDAY
☽ ⚹ ♄ **5:02 am** 2:02 am
☽ △ ♅ **3:20 pm** 12:20 pm
☽ ⚹ ♆ **11:05 pm** 8:05 pm
☽ ☌ ♇ 10:50 pm

24 MONDAY
☽ ☌ ♇ **1:50 am**
☽ ⚻ ☉ **4:57 am** 1:57 am
☽ △ ♃ **10:52 am** 7:52 am
☽ ⚻ ♀ **3:00 pm** 12:00 pm
☽ □ ♂ **6:58 pm** 3:58 pm

25 TUESDAY
☽ ⚻ ☿ **3:27 am** 12:27 am
☽ ⚺ ♄ **8:14 am** 5:14 am
☽ □ ♅ **6:30 pm** 3:30 pm
☽ ⚺ ♆ 11:00 pm

26 WEDNESDAY
☽ ⚺ ♆ **2:00 am**
☽ ⚺ ♇ **4:37 am** 1:37 am
☽ △ ☉ **11:26 am** 8:26 am
☿ △ ♄ **2:10 pm** 11:10 am
☽ □ ♃ **2:27 pm** 11:27 am
☽ △ ♀ **10:33 pm** 7:33 pm
☽ ⚹ ♂ 9:26 pm

27 THURSDAY
☽ ⚹ ♂ **12:26 am**
☽ ☌ ♄ **10:57 am** 7:57 am
☽ △ ☿ **2:11 pm** 11:11 am
☽ ⚹ ♅ **9:23 pm** 6:23 pm

28 FRIDAY
☽ ☌ ♆ **4:45 am** 1:45 am
☽ ⚹ ♇ **7:18 am** 4:18 am
☽ □ ☉ **5:53 pm** 2:53 pm
☽ ⚹ ♃ **6:03 pm** 3:03 pm
☉ ⚺ ♃ **8:54 pm** 5:54 pm
♀ ⚹ ♂ 9:49 pm

29 SATURDAY
♀ ⚹ ♂ **12:49 am**
☽ ⚺ ♂ **6:04 am** 3:04 am
☽ □ ♀ **6:16 am** 3:16 am
☽ ⚺ ♄ **1:55 pm** 10:55 am
☿ ⚹ ♅ **10:20 pm** 7:20 pm
☽ ⚺ ♅ 9:37 pm
☽ □ ☿ 9:56 pm

30 SUNDAY
☽ ⚺ ♅ **12:37 am**
☽ □ ☿ **12:56 am**
☽ ⚺ ♆ **7:53 am** 4:53 am
☽ □ ♇ **10:23 am** 7:23 am
☽ ⚺ ♃ **10:09 pm** 7:09 pm
☽ ⚹ ☉ 9:57 pm

Eastern time in bold type
Pacific time in medium type

JUNE 2024

DATE	SID.TIME	SUN	MOON	NODE	MERCURY	VENUS	MARS	JUPITER	SATURN	URANUS	NEPTUNE	PLUTO	CERES	PALLAS	JUNO	VESTA	CHIRON
1 Sa	16 39 53	11♊00 04	27♓57	14♈02	25♉32	10♊01	23♈53	1♊25	18♓45	24♉10	29♓40	1♒55R	20♑41R	25♏30R	10♍34	22♋01	22♈16
2 Su	16 43 49	11 57 35	12♈11	14 03R	27 26	11 15	24 38	1 39	18 48	24 14	29 41	1 54	20 35	25 13	10 46	22 25	22 18
3 M	16 47 46	12 55 05	26 29	14 02	29 23	12 28	25 23	1 53	18 50	24 17	29 42	1 53	20 28	24 57	10 58	22 50	22 21
4 T	16 51 42	13 52 34	10♉45	14 00	1♊21	13 42	26 08	2 07	18 53	24 20	29 43	1 52	20 22	24 41	11 11	23 15	22 23
5 W	16 55 39	14 50 02	24 57	13 55	3 22	14 56	26 53	2 21	18 55	24 24	29 44	1 51	20 14	24 26	11 23	23 40	22 26
6 Th	16 59 35	15 47 29	8♊59	13 47	5 24	16 10	27 37	2 35	18 58	24 27	29 45	1 51	20 07	24 11	11 36	24 05	22 28
7 F	17 3 32	16 44 56	22 49	13 37	7 28	17 23	28 22	2 49	19 00	24 30	29 45	1 50	19 59	23 56	11 49	24 30	22 31
8 Sa	17 7 29	17 42 22	6♋21	13 27	9 34	18 37	29 07	3 03	19 02	24 34	29 46	1 49	19 50	23 42	12 02	24 55	22 33
9 Su	17 11 25	18 39 47	19 32	13 17	11 42	19 51	29 51	3 17	19 04	24 37	29 47	1 48	19 42	23 27	12 15	25 21	22 35
10 M	17 15 22	19 37 10	2♌24	13 07	13 51	21 04	0♉36	3 30	19 06	24 40	29 48	1 47	19 33	23 14	12 28	25 46	22 37
11 T	17 19 18	20 34 33	14 55	13 00	16 01	22 18	1 21	3 44	19 08	24 43	29 48	1 46	19 24	23 00	12 42	26 11	22 40
12 W	17 23 15	21 31 55	27 09	12 55	18 12	23 32	2 05	3 58	19 10	24 47	29 49	1 45	19 14	22 47	12 56	26 37	22 42
13 Th	17 27 11	22 29 16	9♍10	12 52	20 23	24 46	2 49	4 12	19 12	24 50	29 50	1 44	19 04	22 35	13 09	27 02	22 44
14 F	17 31 8	23 26 35	21 02	12 51D	22 35	25 59	3 34	4 25	19 13	24 53	29 50	1 43	18 54	22 23	13 24	27 28	22 46
15 Sa	17 35 4	24 23 54	2♎51	12 52R	24 47	27 13	4 18	4 39	19 15	24 56	29 51	1 42	18 44	22 11	13 38	27 53	22 48
16 Su	17 39 1	25 21 12	14 42	12 52	26 59	28 27	5 02	4 53	19 16	24 59	29 52	1 41	18 34	22 00	13 52	28 19	22 50
17 M	17 42 58	26 18 29	26 40	12 51	29 10	29 41	5 46	5 06	19 18	25 02	29 52	1 40	18 23	21 49	14 07	28 45	22 52
18 T	17 46 54	27 15 46	8♏50	12 48	1♋21	0♋54	6 30	5 20	19 19	25 05	29 53	1 39	18 12	21 38	14 22	29 10	22 54
19 W	17 50 51	28 13 01	21 16	12 43	3 31	2 08	7 14	5 34	19 20	25 08	29 53	1 37	18 00	21 29	14 37	29 36	22 56
20 Th	17 54 47	29 10 16	4♐00	12 36	5 39	3 22	7 58	5 47	19 21	25 12	29 53	1 36	17 49	21 19	14 52	0♌02	22 58
21 F	17 58 44	0♋07 31	17 05	12 26	7 46	4 35	8 42	6 01	19 22	25 15	29 54	1 35	17 37	21 10	15 07	0 28	23 00
22 Sa	18 2 40	1 04 45	0♑29	12 14	9 52	5 49	9 26	6 14	19 23	25 18	29 54	1 34	17 25	21 01	15 22	0 54	23 01
23 Su	18 6 37	2 01 58	14 11	12 03	11 56	7 03	10 10	6 27	19 23	25 20	29 54	1 33	17 13	20 53	15 38	1 20	23 03
24 M	18 10 34	2 59 12	28 06	11 52	13 58	8 17	10 54	6 41	19 24	25 23	29 55	1 32	17 01	20 46	15 53	1 46	23 05
25 T	18 14 30	3 56 25	12♒12	11 43	15 59	9 30	11 37	6 54	19 25	25 26	29 55	1 30	16 49	20 38	16 09	2 12	23 06
26 W	18 18 27	4 53 37	26 22	11 36	17 57	10 44	12 21	7 07	19 25	25 29	29 55	1 29	16 36	20 32	16 25	2 38	23 08
27 Th	18 22 23	5 50 50	10♓35	11 32	19 53	11 58	13 04	7 21	19 25	25 32	29 55	1 28	16 24	20 26	16 41	3 05	23 09
28 F	18 26 20	6 48 03	24 46	11 31D	21 48	13 11	13 48	7 34	19 26	25 35	29 56	1 27	16 11	20 20	16 57	3 31	23 11
29 Sa	18 30 16	7 45 15	8♈55	11 31R	23 40	14 25	14 31	7 47	19 26R	25 38	29 56	1 25	15 58	20 14	17 13	3 57	23 12
30 Su	18 34 13	8 42 28	22 59	11 30	25 30	15 39	15 14	8 00	19 26	25 40	29 56	1 24	15 45	20 10	17 30	4 24	23 14

EPHEMERIS CALCULATED FOR 12 MIDNIGHT GREENWICH MEAN TIME. ALL OTHER DATA AND FACING ASPECTARIAN PAGE IN **EASTERN TIME (BOLD)** AND PACIFIC TIME (REGULAR).

JULY 2024

☽ Last Aspect day	ET / hr:mn	PT	asp	☽ Ingress sign	day	ET / hr:mn	PT
2	**11:43 am**	8:43 am	✶♆	♊	2	**11:50 am**	8:50 am
4	**4:44 pm**	1:44 pm	□♆	♋	4	**4:51 pm**	1:51 pm
6	**11:47 pm**	8:47 pm	△♆	♌	6	**11:56 pm**	8:56 pm
8		11:04 pm	□♅	♍	9	**9:48 am**	6:48 am
9	**2:04 am**		□♅	♍	9	**9:48 am**	6:48 am
11	**9:55 pm**	6:55 pm	☍♆	♎	11	**10:06 pm**	7:06 pm
13	**6:49 pm**	3:49 pm	□☉	♏	14	**10:53 am**	7:53 am
16	**9:10 pm**	6:10 pm	△♆	♐	16	**9:25 pm**	6:25 pm
19	**3:58 am**	12:58 am	□♆	♑	19	**4:14 am**	1:14 am
21	**7:26 am**	4:26 am	✶♆	♒	21	**7:43 am**	4:43 am
23	**5:58 am**	2:58 am	☍☿	♓	23	**9:23 am**	6:23 am
25	**10:31 am**	7:31 am	☌♆	♈	25	**10:52 am**	7:52 am
26	**6:14 pm**	3:14 pm	△♀	♉	27	**1:23 pm**	10:23 am
29	**4:59 pm**	1:59 pm	✶♆	♊	29	**5:28 pm**	2:28 pm
31	**10:46 pm**	7:46 pm	□♆	♋	31	**11:19 pm**	8:19 pm

☽ Phases & Eclipses phase	day	ET / hr:mn	PT
New Moon	5	**6:57 pm**	3:57 pm
2nd Quarter	13	**6:49 pm**	3:49 pm
Full Moon	21	**6:17 am**	3:17 am
4th Quarter	27	**10:52 pm**	7:52 pm

Planet Ingress		day	ET / hr:mn	PT
☿	♌	2	**8:50 am**	5:50 am
♀	♌	11	**12:19 pm**	9:19 am
♂	♊	20	**4:43 pm**	1:43 pm
☉	♌	22	**3:44 am**	12:44 am
☿	♍	25	**6:42 pm**	3:42 pm

Planetary Motion		day	ET / hr:mn	PT
♆	℞	2	**6:40 am**	3:40 am
♀	D	9	**10:46 pm**	7:46 pm
⚷	℞	26	**9:59 am**	6:59 am

1 MONDAY
☽ ✶ ☉ **12:57 am**
☽ ☌ ♂ **12:19 pm** 9:19 am
☽ ✶ ♀ **2:42 pm** 11:42 am
☽ ✶ ♄ **5:28 pm** 2:28 pm

2 TUESDAY
☽ ☌ ♅ **4:29 am** 1:29 am
☿ △ ♆ **7:53 am** 4:53 am
☽ ✶ ♆ **11:43 am** 8:43 am
☽ ✶ ☿ **12:16 pm** 9:16 am
☽ △ ♇ **2:11 pm** 11:11 am
♀ △ ♄ **9:41 pm** 6:41 pm

3 WEDNESDAY
☽ ☌ ♃ **3:05 am** 12:05 am
☿ ☍ ♇ **3:27 am** 12:27 am
☽ ⚺ ☉ **9:01 am** 6:01 am
☽ ⚺ ♂ **7:38 pm** 4:38 pm
☽ □ ♄ **9:58 pm** 6:58 pm
☽ ⚺ ♀ 9:24 pm

4 THURSDAY
☽ ⚺ ♀ **12:24 am**
☽ ⚺ ♅ **9:28 am** 6:28 am
☽ □ ♆ **4:44 pm** 1:44 pm
☽ ⚻ ♇ **7:11 pm** 4:11 pm
☽ ⚺ ☿ 9:57 pm

5 FRIDAY
☽ ⚺ ☿ **12:57 am**
☽ ⚺ ♃ **9:29 am** 6:29 am
♂ ✶ ♄ **3:02 pm** 12:02 pm
☽ ☌ ☉ **6:57 pm** 3:57 pm

6 SATURDAY
☽ △ ♄ **4:10 am** 1:10 am
☽ ✶ ♂ **4:56 am** 1:56 am
☽ ☌ ♀ **12:27 pm** 9:27 am
☽ ✶ ♅ **4:24 pm** 1:24 pm
☽ △ ♆ **11:47 pm** 8:47 pm
☽ ☍ ♇ 11:16 pm

7 SUNDAY
☽ ☍ ♇ **2:16 am**
☽ ☌ ☿ **4:23 pm** 1:23 pm
☽ ✶ ♃ **6:19 pm** 3:19 pm

8 MONDAY
♀ ✶ ♅ **7:04 am** 4:04 am
☽ ⚺ ☉ **8:00 am** 5:00 am
☿ ✶ ♃ **10:26 am** 7:26 am
☽ ⚻ ♄ **12:57 pm** 9:57 am
☽ □ ♂ **5:18 pm** 2:18 pm
☽ □ ♅ 11:04 pm

9 TUESDAY
☽ □ ♅ **2:04 am**
☽ ⚺ ♀ **4:07 am** 1:07 am
☽ ⚻ ♆ **9:38 am** 6:38 am
☽ ⚻ ♇ **12:08 pm** 9:08 am

10 WEDNESDAY
☽ □ ♃ **6:07 am** 3:07 am
☽ ⚺ ☿ **11:24 am** 8:24 am
☉ △ ♄ **11:05 pm** 8:05 pm
☽ ☍ ♄ 9:27 pm
☽ ✶ ☉ 9:34 pm

11 THURSDAY
☽ ☍ ♄ **12:27 am**
☽ ✶ ☉ **12:34 am**
☽ △ ♂ **8:51 am** 5:51 am
♀ △ ♆ **10:32 am** 7:32 am
☽ △ ♅ **2:20 pm** 11:20 am
☽ ☍ ♆ **9:55 pm** 6:55 pm
☽ ✶ ♀ **11:15 pm** 8:15 pm
☽ △ ♇ 9:24 pm

12 FRIDAY
☽ △ ♇ **12:24 am**
♀ ☍ ♇ **10:12 am** 7:12 am
☽ △ ♃ **7:58 pm** 4:58 pm

13 SATURDAY
☽ ✶ ☿ **8:18 am** 5:18 am
☽ ⚻ ♄ **1:16 pm** 10:16 am
☽ □ ☉ **6:49 pm** 3:49 pm
☽ ⚻ ♂ 10:35 pm

14 SUNDAY
☽ ⚻ ♂ **1:35 am**
☽ ⚻ ♅ **3:24 am** 12:24 am
☽ ⚻ ♆ **10:40 am** 7:40 am
☽ □ ♇ **1:01 pm** 10:01 am
☽ □ ♀ **6:55 pm** 3:55 pm

15 MONDAY
☿ ⚻ ♄ **4:57 am** 1:57 am
☽ ⚻ ♃ **9:15 am** 6:15 am
♂ ☌ ♅ **10:05 am** 7:05 am
☽ △ ♄ 9:45 pm
☽ □ ☿ 11:59 pm

16 TUESDAY
☽ △ ♄ **12:45 am**
☽ □ ☿ **2:59 am**
☽ △ ☉ **11:04 am** 8:04 am
☽ ☍ ♅ **2:31 pm** 11:31 am
☽ ☍ ♂ **4:06 pm** 1:06 pm
☽ △ ♆ **9:10 pm** 6:10 pm
☽ ✶ ♇ **11:20 pm** 8:20 pm

17 WEDNESDAY
☽ △ ♀ **11:08 am** 8:08 am
☽ ☍ ♃ **7:20 pm** 4:20 pm

18 THURSDAY
☽ □ ♄ **8:49 am** 5:49 am
☉ ✶ ♅ **10:00 am** 7:00 am
☽ △ ☿ **4:24 pm** 1:24 pm
☽ ⚻ ♅ **9:56 pm** 6:56 pm
☽ ⚻ ☉ **10:49 pm** 7:49 pm
☽ ⚻ ♂ 11:16 pm

19 FRIDAY
☽ ⚻ ♂ **2:16 am**
☽ □ ♆ **3:58 am** 12:58 am
☽ ⚺ ♇ **5:55 am** 2:55 am
☽ ⚻ ♀ **10:17 pm** 7:17 pm
☽ ⚻ ♃ 10:29 pm

20 SATURDAY
☽ ⚻ ♃ **1:29 am**
♂ ✶ ♆ **11:17 am** 8:17 am
☽ ✶ ♄ **1:15 pm** 10:15 am
☽ ⚻ ☿ 9:42 pm
☽ △ ♅ 10:53 pm

21 SUNDAY
☽ ⚻ ☿ **12:42 am**
☽ △ ♅ **1:53 am**
☽ ☍ ☉ **6:17 am** 3:17 am
☽ ✶ ♆ **7:26 am** 4:26 am
☽ △ ♂ **8:29 am** 5:29 am
☽ ☌ ♇ **9:14 am** 6:14 am
♀ ✶ ♃ **4:43 pm** 1:43 pm
☿ □ ♅ **6:21 pm** 3:21 pm
☉ △ ♆ **11:25 pm** 8:25 pm
♂ △ ♇ **11:48 pm** 8:48 pm

22 MONDAY
☽ △ ♃ **4:43 am** 1:43 am
☽ ☍ ♀ **5:39 am** 2:39 am
☽ ⚺ ♄ **3:16 pm** 12:16 pm
☉ ☍ ♇ 10:38 pm

23 TUESDAY
☉ ☍ ♇ **1:38 am**
☽ □ ♅ **3:47 am** 12:47 am
☽ ☍ ☿ **5:58 am** 2:58 am
☽ ⚺ ♆ **9:05 am** 6:05 am
☽ ⚺ ♇ **10:48 am** 7:48 am
☽ ⚻ ☉ **11:27 am** 8:27 am
☽ □ ♂ **12:36 pm** 9:36 am

24 WEDNESDAY
☽ □ ♃ **6:47 am** 3:47 am
☽ ⚻ ♀ **11:36 am** 8:36 am
☽ ☌ ♄ **4:31 pm** 1:31 pm

25 THURSDAY
☽ ✶ ♅ **5:19 am** 2:19 am
☽ ⚻ ☿ **10:26 am** 7:26 am
☽ ☌ ♆ **10:31 am** 7:31 am
☿ ⚻ ♆ **12:00 pm** 9:00 am
☽ ✶ ♇ **12:13 pm** 9:13 am
☽ △ ☉ **4:29 pm** 1:29 pm
☽ ✶ ♂ **4:36 pm** 1:36 pm
☉ ✶ ♂ **10:32 pm** 7:32 pm

26 FRIDAY
☽ ✶ ♃ **9:16 am** 6:16 am
☽ △ ♀ **6:14 pm** 3:14 pm
☽ ⚺ ♄ **6:24 pm** 3:24 pm
♀ ⚻ ♄ **8:07 pm** 5:07 pm
☿ ⚻ ♇ **8:49 pm** 5:49 pm

27 SATURDAY
☽ ⚺ ♅ **7:47 am** 4:47 am
☽ ⚺ ♆ **12:58 pm** 9:58 am
☽ □ ♇ **2:41 pm** 11:41 am
☽ △ ☿ **3:36 pm** 12:36 pm
☽ ⚺ ♂ **9:52 pm** 6:52 pm
☽ □ ☉ **10:52 pm** 7:52 pm

28 SUNDAY
☽ ⚺ ♃ **1:08 pm** 10:08 am
☽ ✶ ♄ **9:42 pm** 6:42 pm
☽ □ ♀ 11:45 pm

29 Monday
☽ □ ♀ **2:45 am**
☽ ☌ ♅ **11:47 am** 8:47 am
☽ ✶ ♆ **4:59 pm** 1:59 pm
☽ △ ♇ **6:43 pm** 3:43 pm
☽ □ ☿ **10:00 pm** 7:00 pm

30 TUESDAY
☽ ☌ ♂ **5:01 am** 2:01 am
☽ ✶ ☉ **7:15 am** 4:15 am
☽ ☌ ♃ **6:45 pm** 3:45 pm
☽ □ ♄ 11:42 pm

31 WEDNESDAY
☽ □ ♄ **2:42 am**
☽ ✶ ♀ **1:33 pm** 10:33 am
☽ ⚺ ♅ **5:33 pm** 2:33 pm
☽ □ ♆ **10:46 pm** 7:46 pm
☽ ⚻ ♇ 9:31 pm

Eastern time in bold type
Pacific time in medium type

JULY 2024

DATE	SID.TIME	SUN	MOON	NODE	MERCURY	VENUS	MARS	JUPITER	SATURN	URANUS	NEPTUNE	PLUTO	CERES	PALLAS	JUNO	VESTA	CHIRON
1 M	18 38 9	9♋39 41	6♉59	11♈29R	27♋18	16♋53	15♉58	8♊13	19♓26R	25♉43	29♓56	1♒23R	15♑32R	20♏05R	17♍46	4♌50	23♈15
2 T	18 42 6	10 36 55	20 53	11 25	29 04	18 06	16 41	8 26	19 25	25 46	29 56R	1 22	15 19	20 01	18 03	5 16	23 16
3 W	18 46 3	11 34 08	4♊41	11 19	0♌48	19 20	17 24	8 39	19 25	25 49	29 56	1 20	15 06	19 58	18 20	5 43	23 18
4 Th	18 49 59	12 31 22	18 18	11 10	2 30	20 34	18 07	8 52	19 25	25 51	29 56	1 19	14 52	19 55	18 37	6 10	23 19
5 F	18 53 56	13 28 35	1♋45	10 59	4 09	21 47	18 50	9 05	19 24	25 54	29 56	1 18	14 39	19 52	18 54	6 36	23 20
6 Sa	18 57 52	14 25 49	14 57	10 46	5 47	23 01	19 33	9 17	19 24	25 56	29 56	1 16	14 26	19 50	19 11	7 03	23 21
7 Su	19 1 49	15 23 03	27 54	10 34	7 22	24 15	20 16	9 30	19 23	25 59	29 56	1 15	14 13	19 49	19 28	7 30	23 22
8 M	19 5 45	16 20 17	10♌35	10 22	8 55	25 29	20 58	9 43	19 22	26 02	29 55	1 14	13 59	19 47	19 45	7 56	23 23
9 T	19 9 42	17 17 30	22 59	10 13	10 26	26 42	21 41	9 55	19 21	26 04	29 55	1 12	13 46	19 47	20 03	8 23	23 24
10 W	19 13 38	18 14 44	5♍09	10 06	11 55	27 56	22 23	10 08	19 21	26 06	29 55	1 11	13 33	19 46D	20 20	8 50	23 25
11 Th	19 17 35	19 11 58	17 07	10 02	13 22	29 10	23 06	10 20	19 19	26 09	29 55	1 09	13 20	19 47	20 38	9 17	23 26
12 F	19 21 32	20 09 11	28 58	10 00D	14 46	0♌24	23 48	10 33	19 18	26 11	29 54	1 08	13 07	19 47	20 56	9 44	23 26
13 Sa	19 25 28	21 06 24	10♎46	10 00R	16 08	1 37	24 30	10 45	19 17	26 14	29 54	1 07	12 54	19 48	21 14	10 11	23 27
14 Su	19 29 25	22 03 38	22 36	10 00	17 28	2 51	25 13	10 57	19 16	26 16	29 54	1 05	12 41	19 50	21 32	10 38	23 28
15 M	19 33 21	23 00 51	4♏34	10 00	18 45	4 05	25 55	11 09	19 14	26 18	29 53	1 04	12 29	19 52	21 50	11 05	23 29
16 T	19 37 18	23 58 05	16 46	9 58	20 00	5 19	26 37	11 21	19 13	26 20	29 53	1 02	12 16	19 54	22 08	11 32	23 29
17 W	19 41 14	24 55 19	29 15	9 53	21 13	6 32	27 19	11 33	19 11	26 23	29 52	1 01	12 04	19 57	22 26	11 59	23 30
18 Th	19 45 11	25 52 33	12♐07	9 47	22 23	7 46	28 01	11 45	19 09	26 25	29 52	1 00	11 52	20 00	22 44	12 26	23 30
19 F	19 49 7	26 49 47	25 22	9 38	23 31	9 00	28 42	11 57	19 08	26 27	29 51	0 58	11 40	20 03	23 03	12 53	23 31
20 Sa	19 53 4	27 47 02	9♑01	9 27	24 36	10 13	29 24	12 09	19 06	26 29	29 51	0 57	11 28	20 07	23 21	13 21	23 31
21 Su	19 57 1	28 44 17	23 03	9 17	25 38	11 27	0♊06	12 21	19 04	26 31	29 50	0 55	11 16	20 11	23 40	13 48	23 31
22 M	20 0 57	29 41 32	7♒21	9 07	26 37	12 41	0 47	12 32	19 02	26 33	29 50	0 54	11 04	20 16	23 58	14 15	23 32
23 T	20 4 54	0♌38 48	21 52	8 58	27 33	13 55	1 29	12 44	18 59	26 35	29 49	0 53	10 53	20 21	24 17	14 42	23 32
24 W	20 8 50	1 36 04	6♓27	8 52	28 26	15 08	2 10	12 55	18 57	26 37	29 48	0 51	10 42	20 27	24 36	15 10	23 32
25 Th	20 12 47	2 33 22	21 01	8 49	29 16	16 22	2 51	13 07	18 55	26 39	29 48	0 50	10 31	20 32	24 55	15 37	23 32
26 F	20 16 43	3 30 40	5♈29	8 48D	0♍02	17 36	3 32	13 18	18 52	26 40	29 47	0 48	10 21	20 39	25 14	16 05	23 32R
27 Sa	20 20 40	4 27 59	19 46	8 48	0 45	18 49	4 13	13 29	18 50	26 42	29 46	0 47	10 10	20 45	25 33	16 32	23 32
28 Su	20 24 36	5 25 19	3♉52	8 48R	1 25	20 03	4 54	13 40	18 47	26 44	29 46	0 45	10 00	20 52	25 52	17 00	23 32
29 M	20 28 33	6 22 40	17 45	8 48	2 00	21 17	5 35	13 51	18 44	26 46	29 45	0 44	9 51	20 59	26 11	17 27	23 32
30 T	20 32 30	7 20 03	1♊26	8 46	2 32	22 30	6 16	14 02	18 42	26 47	29 44	0 43	9 41	21 07	26 30	17 55	23 32
31 W	20 36 26	8 17 26	14 55	8 41	2 59	23 44	6 57	14 13	18 39	26 49	29 43	0 41	9 32	21 15	26 50	18 22	23 32

EPHEMERIS CALCULATED FOR 12 MIDNIGHT GREENWICH MEAN TIME. ALL OTHER DATA AND FACING ASPECTARIAN PAGE IN **EASTERN TIME (BOLD)** AND PACIFIC TIME (REGULAR).

AUGUST 2024

☽ Last Aspect				☽ Ingress			
day	ET / hr:mn / PT		asp	sign	day	ET / hr:mn / PT	
3	**6:31 am**	3:31 am	△♆	♌	3	**7:10 am**	4:10 am
5	**11:16 am**	8:16 am	□♅	♍	5	**5:17 pm**	2:17 pm
8	**4:40 am**	1:40 am	☍♆	♎	8	**5:31 am**	2:31 am
9	**5:45 pm**	2:45 pm	⚹☉	♏	10	**6:34 pm**	3:34 pm
13	**5:01 am**	2:01 am	△♆	♐	13	**6:01 am**	3:01 am
15	**12:52 pm**	9:52 am	△☿	♑	15	**1:51 pm**	10:51 am
17	**4:43 pm**	1:43 pm	⚹♆	♒	17	**5:45 pm**	2:45 pm
19	**2:26 pm**	11:26 am	☍☉	♓	19	**6:52 pm**	3:52 pm
21	**5:54 pm**	2:54 pm	☌♆	♈	21	**7:02 pm**	4:02 pm
23	**8:44 am**	5:44 am	△☿	♉	23	**8:00 pm**	5:00 pm

☽ Last Aspect				☽ Ingress			
day	ET / hr:mn / PT		asp	sign	day	ET / hr:mn / PT	
25	**9:40 pm**	6:40 pm	⚹♆	♊	25	**11:04 pm**	8:04 pm
28	**3:14 am**	12:14 am	□♆	♋	28	**4:47 am**	1:47 am
30	**11:24 am**	8:24 am	△♆	♌	30	**1:09 pm**	10:09 am

☽ Phases & Eclipses			
phase	day	ET / hr:mn / PT	
New Moon	4	**7:13 am**	4:13 am
2nd Quarter	12	**11:19 am**	8:19 am
Full Moon	19	**2:26 pm**	11:26 am
4th Quarter	26	**5:26 am**	2:26 am

Planet Ingress				
		day	ET / hr:mn / PT	
♀	♍	4	**10:23 pm**	7:23 pm
⚵	♎	9	**12:35 pm**	9:35 am
☿	♌	14	**8:16 pm**	5:16 pm
☉	♍	22	**10:55 am**	7:55 am
⚶	♍	24	**7:38 pm**	4:38 pm
♀	♎	29	**9:23 am**	6:23 am

Planetary Motion				
		day	ET / hr:mn / PT	
☿	℞	4		9:56 pm
☿	℞	5	**12:56 am**	
⚳	D	26	**3:37 am**	12:37 am
☿	D	28	**5:14 pm**	2:14 pm

1 THURSDAY
☽ ⚻ ♇ **12:31 am**
☽ ⚹ ☿ **5:43 am** 2:43 am
☽ ⚺ ♂ **2:15 pm** 11:15 am
☽ ⚺ ☉ **5:55 pm** 2:55 pm
☽ ⚺ ♃ 11:16 pm

2 FRIDAY
☽ ⚺ ♃ **2:16 am**
♀ □ ♅ **9:27 am** 6:27 am
☽ △ ♄ **9:32 am** 6:32 am
☽ ⚹ ♅ 10:17 pm
☽ ⚺ ♀ 11:57 pm

3 SATURDAY
☽ ⚹ ♅ **1:17 am**
☽ ⚺ ♀ **2:57 am**
☽ △ ♆ **6:31 am** 3:31 am
☽ ☍ ♇ **8:19 am** 5:19 am
☽ ⚺ ☿ **2:48 pm** 11:48 am
☽ ⚹ ♂ 10:54 pm

4 SUNDAY
☽ ⚹ ♂ **1:54 am**
☽ ☌ ☉ **7:13 am** 4:13 am
☽ ⚹ ♃ **12:01 pm** 9:01 am
♀ ⚻ ♆ **3:24 pm** 12:24 pm
☽ ⚻ ♄ **6:31 pm** 3:31 pm

5 MONDAY
♀ ⚻ ♇ **9:18 am** 6:18 am
☽ □ ♅ **11:16 am** 8:16 am
☽ ⚻ ♆ **4:32 pm** 1:32 pm
☽ ⚻ ♇ **6:22 pm** 3:22 pm
☽ ☌ ♀ **7:24 pm** 4:24 pm
☽ ☌ ☿ 10:19 pm

6 TUESDAY
☽ ☌ ☿ **1:19 am**
☽ □ ♂ **4:15 pm** 1:15 pm
☽ ⚺ ☉ **11:27 pm** 8:27 pm
☽ □ ♃ 9:08 pm

7 WEDNESDAY
☽ □ ♃ **12:08 am**
☽ ☍ ♄ **5:44 am** 2:44 am
☉ ⚹ ♃ **9:37 am** 6:37 am
☿ ☌ ♀ **11:12 pm** 8:12 pm
☽ △ ♅ **11:27 pm** 8:27 pm

8 THURSDAY
☽ ☍ ♆ **4:40 am** 1:40 am
☽ △ ♇ **6:32 am** 3:32 am
☽ ⚺ ☿ **12:47 pm** 9:47 am
☽ ⚺ ♀ **2:43 pm** 11:43 am

9 FRIDAY
☽ △ ♂ **8:40 am** 5:40 am
☽ △ ♃ **1:55 pm** 10:55 am
☽ ⚹ ☉ **5:45 pm** 2:45 pm
☽ ⚻ ♄ **6:24 pm** 3:24 pm
☉ ⚻ ♄ 10:26 pm

10 SATURDAY
☉ ⚻ ♄ **1:26 am**
☽ ⚻ ♅ **12:36 pm** 9:36 am
☽ ⚻ ♆ **5:37 pm** 2:37 pm
☽ □ ♇ **7:27 pm** 4:27 pm
☽ ⚹ ☿ **11:42 pm** 8:42 pm

11 SUNDAY
☽ ⚹ ♀ **10:40 am** 7:40 am
☽ ⚻ ♂ 9:48 pm

12 MONDAY
☽ ⚻ ♂ **12:48 am**
☽ ⚻ ♃ **3:14 am** 12:14 am
☽ △ ♄ **6:29 am** 3:29 am
☽ □ ☉ **11:19 am** 8:19 am
☽ ☍ ♅ 9:24 pm

13 TUESDAY
☽ ☍ ♅ **12:24 am**
☽ △ ♆ **5:01 am** 2:01 am
☽ ⚹ ♇ **6:45 am** 3:45 am
☽ □ ☿ **8:09 am** 5:09 am

14 WEDNESDAY
☽ □ ♀ **3:33 am** 12:33 am
☿ ⚻ ♇ **9:03 am** 6:03 am
♂ ☌ ♃ **11:22 am** 8:22 am
☽ ☍ ♃ **1:35 pm** 10:35 am
☽ ☍ ♂ **1:40 pm** 10:40 am
☽ □ ♄ **3:38 pm** 12:38 pm
☽ △ ☉ 9:57 pm

15 THURSDAY
☽ △ ☉ **12:57 am**
☽ ⚻ ♅ **8:42 am** 5:42 am
☽ □ ♆ **12:50 pm** 9:50 am
☽ △ ☿ **12:52 pm** 9:52 am
☿ ⚻ ♆ **1:19 pm** 10:19 am
☽ ⚺ ♇ **2:27 pm** 11:27 am
♂ □ ♄ 10:30 pm

16 FRIDAY
♂ □ ♄ **1:30 am**
☽ △ ♀ **3:08 pm** 12:08 pm
☽ ⚻ ♃ **7:45 pm** 4:45 pm
☽ ⚹ ♄ **8:49 pm** 5:49 pm
☽ ⚻ ♂ **9:51 pm** 6:51 pm

17 SATURDAY
☽ ⚻ ☉ **9:33 am** 6:33 am
☽ △ ♅ **12:59 pm** 9:59 am
☽ ⚻ ☿ **1:57 pm** 10:57 am
☽ ⚹ ♆ **4:43 pm** 1:43 pm
☽ ☌ ♇ **6:13 pm** 3:13 pm

18 SUNDAY
☿ □ ♅ **5:47 am** 2:47 am
☉ ☌ ☿ **9:58 pm** 6:58 pm
☽ ⚻ ♀ **10:05 pm** 7:05 pm
☽ △ ♃ **10:22 pm** 7:22 pm
☽ ⚺ ♄ **10:38 pm** 7:38 pm
♀ □ ♃ 10:53 pm
☽ △ ♂ 11:08 pm

19 MONDAY
♀ □ ♃ **1:53 am**
☽ △ ♂ **2:08 am**
♀ ☍ ♄ **4:30 am** 1:30 am
☽ ☍ ☿ **12:32 pm** 9:32 am
☉ □ ♅ **12:45 pm** 9:45 am
☽ □ ♅ **2:19 pm** 11:19 am
☽ ☍ ☉ **2:26 pm** 11:26 am
♃ □ ♄ **5:46 pm** 2:46 pm
☽ ⚺ ♆ **5:48 pm** 2:48 pm
☽ ⚺ ♇ **7:15 pm** 4:15 pm

20 TUESDAY
☽ ☌ ♄ **10:45 pm** 7:45 pm
☽ □ ♃ **11:10 pm** 8:10 pm
☽ ☍ ♀ 11:44 pm

21 WEDNESDAY
☽ ☍ ♀ **2:44 am**
☽ □ ♂ **4:34 am** 1:34 am
☽ ⚻ ☿ **10:15 am** 7:15 am
☽ ⚹ ♅ **2:32 pm** 11:32 am
☉ ⚻ ♆ **5:29 pm** 2:29 pm
☽ ☌ ♆ **5:54 pm** 2:54 pm
☽ ⚻ ☉ **5:56 pm** 2:56 pm
☽ ⚹ ♇ **7:21 pm** 4:21 pm

22 THURSDAY
☉ ⚻ ♇ **3:34 pm** 12:34 pm
☽ ⚺ ♄ **10:58 pm** 7:58 pm
♀ □ ♂ **11:20 pm** 8:20 pm
☽ ⚹ ♃ 9:05 pm

23 FRIDAY
☽ ⚹ ♃ **12:05 am**
☽ ⚹ ♂ **7:21 am** 4:21 am
☽ ⚻ ♀ **7:43 am** 4:43 am
☽ △ ☿ **8:44 am** 5:44 am
☽ ⚺ ♅ **3:24 pm** 12:24 pm
☿ ⚺ ♀ **4:15 pm** 1:15 pm
☽ ⚺ ♆ **6:46 pm** 3:46 pm
☽ □ ♇ **8:17 pm** 5:17 pm
☽ △ ☉ **10:22 pm** 7:22 pm
☿ ⚹ ♂ 9:31 pm

24 SATURDAY
☿ ⚹ ♂ **12:31 am**
☽ ⚹ ♄ 9:46 pm
☽ ⚺ ♃ 11:40 pm

25 SUNDAY
☽ ⚹ ♄ **12:46 am**
☽ ⚺ ♃ **2:40 am**
☽ □ ☿ **9:25 am** 6:25 am
☽ ⚺ ♂ **12:12 pm** 9:12 am
☽ △ ♀ **3:03 pm** 12:03 pm
☽ ☌ ♅ **6:15 pm** 3:15 pm
☽ ⚹ ♆ **9:40 pm** 6:40 pm
☽ △ ♇ **11:17 pm** 8:17 pm

26 MONDAY
☽ □ ☉ **5:26 am** 2:26 am

27 TUESDAY
♀ △ ♅ **3:24 am** 12:24 am
☽ □ ♄ **5:02 am** 2:02 am
☽ ☌ ♃ **7:50 am** 4:50 am
☽ ⚹ ☿ **1:17 pm** 10:17 am
☽ ☌ ♂ **8:00 pm** 5:00 pm
☽ ⚺ ♅ **11:45 pm** 8:45 pm
☽ □ ♀ 10:50 pm

28 WEDNESDAY
☽ □ ♀ **1:50 am**
☽ □ ♆ **3:14 am** 12:14 am
☽ ⚻ ♇ **4:56 am** 1:56 am
☽ ⚹ ☉ **3:50 pm** 12:50 pm
♀ ☍ ♆ **4:25 pm** 1:25 pm

29 THURSDAY
♀ △ ♇ **10:32 am** 7:32 am
☽ △ ♄ **11:57 am** 8:57 am
☽ ⚺ ♃ **3:46 pm** 12:46 pm
☽ ⚺ ☿ **8:56 pm** 5:56 pm

30 FRIDAY
☽ ⚺ ♂ **6:52 am** 3:52 am
☽ ⚹ ♅ **7:54 am** 4:54 am
☽ △ ♆ **11:24 am** 8:24 am
☽ ☍ ♇ **1:14 pm** 10:14 am
☽ ⚹ ♀ **4:10 pm** 1:10 pm

31 SATURDAY
♂ ⚺ ♅ **3:52 am** 12:52 am
☽ ⚺ ☉ **5:30 am** 2:30 am
☽ ⚻ ♄ **9:18 pm** 6:18 pm
☽ ⚹ ♃ 11:10 pm

Eastern time in bold type
Pacific time in medium type

AUGUST 2024

DATE	SID.TIME	SUN	MOON	NODE	MERCURY	VENUS	MARS	JUPITER	SATURN	URANUS	NEPTUNE	PLUTO	CERES	PALLAS	JUNO	VESTA	CHIRON
1 Th	20 40 23	9♌ 14 51	28♊ 11	8♈ 34 R	3♍ 22	24♌ 58	7♊ 37	14♊ 24	18♓ 36 R	26♉ 51	29♓ 42 R	0♒ 40 R	9♑ 23 R	21♏ 23	27♍ 09	18♌ 50	23♈ 31 R
2 F	20 44 19	10 12 16	11♋ 15	8 25	3 40	26 12	8 18	14 35	18 33	26 52	29 41	0 38	9 14	21 31	27 28	19 18	23 31
3 Sa	20 48 16	11 09 43	24 06	8 15	3 54	27 25	8 58	14 45	18 30	26 54	29 40	0 37	9 06	21 40	27 48	19 45	23 31
4 Su	20 52 12	12 07 10	6♌ 44	8 05	4 03	28 39	9 39	14 56	18 27	26 55	29 39	0 36	8 58	21 49	28 07	20 13	23 30
5 M	20 56 9	13 04 38	19 09	7 56	4 06 R	29 53	10 19	15 06	18 23	26 56	29 38	0 34	8 50	21 59	28 27	20 41	23 30
6 T	21 0 6	14 02 08	1♍ 23	7 48	4 05	1♍ 06	10 59	15 16	18 20	26 58	29 37	0 33	8 43	22 09	28 47	21 08	23 29
7 W	21 4 2	14 59 38	13 25	7 43	3 58	2 20	11 39	15 27	18 17	26 59	29 36	0 32	8 36	22 19	29 07	21 36	23 29
8 Th	21 7 59	15 57 09	25 19	7 40	3 46	3 34	12 19	15 37	18 13	27 00	29 35	0 30	8 29	22 29	29 26	22 04	23 28
9 F	21 11 55	16 54 41	7♎ 07	7 39 D	3 28	4 47	12 58	15 47	18 10	27 01	29 34	0 29	8 23	22 40	29 46	22 32	23 27
10 Sa	21 15 52	17 52 14	18 53	7 40	3 05	6 01	13 38	15 56	18 06	27 03	29 33	0 27	8 17	22 51	0♎ 06	23 00	23 27
11 Su	21 19 48	18 49 47	0♏ 43	7 41	2 37	7 15	14 18	16 06	18 02	27 04	29 32	0 26	8 11	23 02	0 26	23 28	23 26
12 M	21 23 45	19 47 22	12 40	7 42 R	2 05	8 28	14 57	16 16	17 59	27 05	29 31	0 25	8 06	23 14	0 46	23 56	23 25
13 T	21 27 41	20 44 58	24 50	7 42	1 27	9 42	15 36	16 25	17 55	27 06	29 29	0 23	8 01	23 26	1 06	24 23	23 24
14 W	21 31 38	21 42 34	7♐ 19	7 41	0 46	10 56	16 15	16 35	17 51	27 07	29 28	0 22	7 56	23 38	1 26	24 51	23 23
15 Th	21 35 35	22 40 12	20 10	7 38	0 01	12 09	16 55	16 44	17 47	27 08	29 27	0 21	7 52	23 50	1 47	25 19	23 22
16 F	21 39 31	23 37 50	3♑ 27	7 33	29♌ 13	13 23	17 33	16 53	17 43	27 08	29 26	0 20	7 48	24 03	2 07	25 47	23 21
17 Sa	21 43 28	24 35 30	17 11	7 27	28 23	14 37	18 12	17 02	17 39	27 09	29 25	0 18	7 45	24 15	2 27	26 15	23 20
18 Su	21 47 24	25 33 10	1♒ 21	7 20	27 31	15 50	18 51	17 11	17 35	27 10	29 23	0 17	7 42	24 28	2 47	26 44	23 19
19 M	21 51 21	26 30 52	15 54	7 14	26 40	17 04	19 30	17 20	17 31	27 11	29 22	0 16	7 39	24 42	3 08	27 12	23 18
20 T	21 55 17	27 28 35	0♓ 43	7 09	25 49	18 17	20 08	17 28	17 27	27 11	29 21	0 15	7 36	24 55	3 28	27 40	23 17
21 W	21 59 14	28 26 19	15 40	7 06	25 00	19 31	20 47	17 37	17 23	27 12	29 19	0 13	7 34	25 09	3 49	28 08	23 15
22 Th	22 3 10	29 24 05	0♈ 36	7 04 D	24 14	20 44	21 25	17 45	17 19	27 13	29 18	0 12	7 33	25 23	4 09	28 36	23 14
23 F	22 7 7	0♍ 21 52	15 25	7 04	23 32	21 58	22 03	17 53	17 14	27 13	29 16	0 11	7 31	25 37	4 30	29 04	23 13
24 Sa	22 11 3	1 19 42	0♉ 00	7 05	22 54	23 11	22 41	18 02	17 10	27 14	29 15	0 10	7 30	25 52	4 50	29 32	23 11
25 Su	22 15 0	2 17 32	14 17	7 07	22 23	24 25	23 19	18 10	17 06	27 14	29 14	0 09	7 30	26 06	5 11	0♍ 00	23 10
26 M	22 18 57	3 15 25	28 14	7 08 R	21 57	25 39	23 56	18 17	17 01	27 14	29 12	0 08	7 29 D	26 21	5 31	0 29	23 08
27 T	22 22 53	4 13 20	11♊ 52	7 08	21 39	26 52	24 34	18 25	16 57	27 15	29 11	0 06	7 29	26 36	5 52	0 57	23 07
28 W	22 26 50	5 11 16	25 12	7 06	21 28 D	28 06	25 12	18 33	16 53	27 15	29 09	0 05	7 30	26 52	6 13	1 25	23 05
29 Th	22 30 46	6 09 14	8♋ 14	7 03	21 25	29 19	25 49	18 40	16 48	27 15	29 08	0 04	7 31	27 07	6 34	1 53	23 04
30 F	22 34 43	7 07 14	21 00	6 59	21 30	0♎ 33	26 26	18 47	16 44	27 15	29 06	0 03	7 32	27 23	6 54	2 22	23 02
31 Sa	22 38 39	8 05 16	3♌ 33	6 54	21 43	1 46	27 03	18 54	16 39	27 15	29 05	0 02	7 33	27 39	7 15	2 50	23 00

EPHEMERIS CALCULATED FOR 12 MIDNIGHT GREENWICH MEAN TIME. ALL OTHER DATA AND FACING ASPECTARIAN PAGE IN **EASTERN TIME (BOLD)** AND PACIFIC TIME (REGULAR).

SEPTEMBER 2024

☽ Last Aspect day	ET / hr:mn / PT		asp	☽ Ingress sign	day	ET / hr:mn / PT	
1	**8:25 pm**	5:25 pm	⚹♂	♍	1	**11:48 pm**	8:48 pm
4	**12:06 pm**	9:06 am	△♇	♎	4	**12:12 pm**	9:12 am
6		10:08 pm	□♇	♏	6		10:18 pm
7	**1:08 am**		□♇	♏	7	**1:18 am**	
9	**1:11 pm**	10:11 am	⚹♇	♐	9	**1:26 pm**	10:26 am
11	**8:21 pm**	5:21 pm	□♆	♑	11	**10:38 pm**	7:38 pm
14	**3:35 am**	12:35 am	☌♇	♒	14	**3:53 am**	12:53 am
15		10:04 pm	□♅	♓	16	**5:39 am**	2:39 am
16	**1:04 am**		□♅	♓	16	**5:39 am**	2:39 am
18	**5:02 am**	2:02 am	⚹♇	♈	18	**5:24 am**	2:24 am

☽ Last Aspect day	ET / hr:mn / PT		asp	☽ Ingress sign	day	ET / hr:mn / PT	
20	**4:39 am**	1:39 am	□♇	♉	20	**5:03 am**	2:03 am
22	**6:14 am**	3:14 am	△⊙	♊	22	**6:24 am**	3:24 am
24	**7:59 am**	4:59 am	□♆	♋	24	**10:50 am**	7:50 am
26	**6:12 pm**	3:12 pm	☍♇	♌	26	**6:47 pm**	3:47 pm
28	**11:36 pm**	8:36 pm	□♅	♍	29	**5:42 am**	2:42 am

☽ Phases & Eclipses phase	day	ET / hr:mn / PT	
New Moon	2	**9:56 pm**	6:56 pm
2nd Quarter	10		11:06 pm
2nd Quarter	11	**2:06 am**	
Full Moon	17	**10:34 pm**	7:34 pm
☊	17	25° ♓ 41'	
4th Quarter	24	**2:50 pm**	11:50 am

Planet Ingress		day	ET / hr:mn / PT	
♇	♑	1	**8:10 pm**	5:10 pm
♂	♋	4	**3:46 pm**	12:46 pm
♀	♐	8	**6:29 am**	3:29 am
☿	♍	8		11:50 pm
☿	♍	9	**2:50 am**	
⊙	♎	22	**8:44 am**	5:44 am
♀	♏	22	**10:36 pm**	7:36 pm
☿	♎	26	**4:09 am**	1:09 am

Planetary Motion		day	ET / hr:mn / PT	
♅	℞	1	**11:18 am**	8:18 am

1 SUNDAY
☽ ⚹ ♃ **2:10 am**
☽ ☌ ☿ **8:36 am** 5:36 am
☽ □ ♅ **6:22 pm** 3:22 pm
☽ ⚹ ♂ **8:25 pm** 5:25 pm
☽ ⚻ ♆ **9:52 pm** 6:52 pm
☽ ⚻ ♇ **11:48 pm** 8:48 pm

2 MONDAY
☽ ⚺ ♀ **9:35 am** 6:35 am
☽ ☌ ⊙ **9:56 pm** 6:56 pm
♂ □ ♆ 9:10 pm

3 TUESDAY
♂ □ ♆ **12:10 am**
☽ ☍ ♄ **8:37 am** 5:37 am
☽ □ ♃ **2:34 pm** 11:34 am
☽ ⚺ ☿ 9:17 pm

4 WEDNESDAY
☽ ⚺ ☿ **12:17 am**
☽ △ ♅ **6:37 am** 3:37 am
☽ ☍ ♆ **10:05 am** 7:05 am
☽ □ ♂ **12:00 pm** 9:00 am
☽ △ ♇ **12:06 pm** 9:06 am
♂ ⚻ ♇ **1:59 pm** 10:59 am

5 Thursday
☽ ☌ ♀ **5:12 am** 2:12 am
☽ ⚺ ⊙ **4:12 pm** 1:12 pm
☽ ⚻ ♄ **9:11 pm** 6:11 pm

6 FRIDAY
☽ △ ♃ **4:08 am** 1:08 am
☽ ⚹ ☿ **7:11 pm** 4:11 pm
☽ ⚻ ♅ **7:42 pm** 4:42 pm
☽ ⚻ ♆ **11:04 pm** 8:04 pm
☿ □ ♅ 9:21 pm
☽ □ ♇ 10:08 pm

7 SATURDAY
☿ □ ♅ **12:21 am**
☽ □ ♇ **1:08 am**
☽ △ ♂ **4:24 am** 1:24 am
⊙ ☍ ♄ 9:35 pm
☽ ⚺ ♀ 10:14 pm

8 SUNDAY
⊙ ☍ ♄ **12:35 am**
☽ ⚺ ♀ **1:14 am**
☿ ⚻ ♆ **6:52 am** 3:52 am
☽ △ ♄ **9:37 am** 6:37 am
☽ ⚹ ⊙ **10:29 am** 7:29 am
☽ ⚻ ♃ **5:20 pm** 2:20 pm
☿ ⚻ ♇ 9:55 pm

9 MONDAY
☿ ⚻ ♇ **12:55 am**
☽ ☍ ♅ **7:58 am** 4:58 am
☽ △ ♆ **11:07 am** 8:07 am
☽ ⚹ ♇ **1:11 pm** 10:11 am
☽ □ ☿ **2:50 pm** 11:50 am
☽ ⚻ ♂ **7:28 pm** 4:28 pm

10 TUESDAY
☽ ⚹ ♀ **6:48 pm** 3:48 pm
☽ □ ♄ **8:02 pm** 5:02 pm
☽ □ ⊙ 11:06 pm

11 WEDNESDAY
☽ □ ⊙ **2:06 am**
☽ ☍ ♃ **4:07 am** 1:07 am
♀ ⚻ ♄ **6:52 am** 3:52 am
☽ ⚻ ♅ **5:28 pm** 2:28 pm
☽ □ ♆ **8:21 pm** 5:21 pm
☽ ⚺ ♇ **10:21 pm** 7:21 pm
☿ ⚹ ♂ **11:42 pm** 8:42 pm

12 THURSDAY
⊙ □ ♃ **6:53 am** 3:53 am
☽ ☍ ♂ **6:56 am** 3:56 am
☽ △ ☿ **7:36 am** 4:36 am
☽ ⚹ ♄ 11:53 pm

13 FRIDAY
☽ ⚹ ♄ **2:53 am**
☽ □ ♀ **7:30 am** 4:30 am
☽ ⚻ ♃ **11:02 am** 8:02 am
☽ △ ⊙ **1:01 pm** 10:01 am
☽ △ ♅ **11:04 pm** 8:04 pm
☽ ⚹ ♆ 10:40 pm

14 SATURDAY
☽ ⚹ ♆ **1:40 am**
☽ ☌ ♇ **3:35 am** 12:35 am
☽ ⚻ ♂ **1:52 pm** 10:52 am
☽ ⚻ ☿ **7:21 pm** 4:21 pm
♀ △ ♃ 10:34 pm

15 SUNDAY
♀ △ ♃ **1:34 am**
☽ ⚺ ♄ **5:55 am** 2:55 am
☽ △ ♃ **2:05 pm** 11:05 am
☽ △ ♀ **3:09 pm** 12:09 pm
☽ ⚻ ⊙ **7:15 pm** 4:15 pm
☽ □ ♅ 10:04 pm

16 MONDAY
☽ □ ♅ **1:04 am**
☽ ⚺ ♆ **3:27 am** 12:27 am
☽ ⚺ ♇ **5:19 am** 2:19 am
☽ △ ♂ **5:03 pm** 2:03 pm
☽ ☍ ☿ 11:55 pm

17 TUESDAY
☽ ☍ ☿ **2:55 am**
☽ ☌ ♄ **6:11 am** 3:11 am
☽ □ ♃ **2:30 pm** 11:30 am
☽ ⚻ ♀ **7:31 pm** 4:31 pm
☽ ☍ ⊙ **10:34 pm** 7:34 pm
☽ ⚹ ♅ 9:53 pm

18 WEDNESDAY
☽ ⚹ ♅ **12:53 am**
☽ ☌ ♆ **3:10 am** 12:10 am
☿ ☍ ♄ **4:50 am** 1:50 am
☽ ⚹ ♇ **5:02 am** 2:02 am
☽ □ ♂ **6:27 pm** 3:27 pm

19 THURSDAY
☽ ⚺ ♄ **5:24 am** 2:24 am
☽ ⚻ ☿ **8:57 am** 5:57 am
⊙ △ ♅ **10:04 am** 7:04 am
☽ ⚹ ♃ **2:11 pm** 11:11 am
☽ ☍ ♀ **11:14 pm** 8:14 pm
☽ ⚺ ♅ 9:25 pm
☽ ⚻ ⊙ 10:26 pm
☽ ⚺ ♆ 11:41 pm

20 FRIDAY
☽ ⚺ ♅ **12:25 am**
☽ ⚻ ⊙ **1:26 am**
☽ ⚺ ♆ **2:41 am**
☽ □ ♇ **4:39 am** 1:39 am
♀ ⚻ ♅ **1:36 pm** 10:36 am
⊙ ☍ ♆ **8:17 pm** 5:17 pm
☽ ⚹ ♂ **8:18 pm** 5:18 pm

21 SATURDAY
☿ □ ♃ **4:50 am** 1:50 am
☽ ⚹ ♄ **5:28 am** 2:28 am
☽ ⚺ ♃ **3:03 pm** 12:03 pm
☽ △ ☿ **4:30 pm** 1:30 pm
♀ ⚻ ♆ **4:53 pm** 1:53 pm
☽ ☌ ♅ 10:29 pm
⊙ △ ♇ 11:12 pm

22 SUNDAY
☽ ☌ ♅ **1:29 am**
⊙ △ ♇ **2:12 am**
☽ ⚹ ♆ **3:50 am** 12:50 am
☽ ⚻ ♀ **4:53 am** 1:53 am
☽ △ ♇ **5:57 am** 2:57 am
☽ △ ⊙ **6:14 am** 3:14 am
♀ □ ♇ **5:15 pm** 2:15 pm
☽ ⚺ ♂ 9:37 pm

23 MONDAY
☽ ⚺ ♂ **12:37 am**
☽ □ ♄ **7:58 am** 4:58 am
☽ ☌ ♃ **6:39 pm** 3:39 pm

24 TUESDAY
☽ □ ☿ **4:13 am** 1:13 am
☽ ⚺ ♅ **5:31 am** 2:31 am
☽ □ ♆ **7:59 am** 4:59 am
☽ ⚻ ♇ **10:19 am** 7:19 am
☿ △ ♅ **1:27 pm** 10:27 am
☽ △ ♀ **2:30 pm** 11:30 am
☽ □ ⊙ **2:50 pm** 11:50 am

25 WEDNESDAY
☿ ☍ ♆ **7:07 am** 4:07 am
⊙ ⚺ ♀ **7:27 am** 4:27 am
☽ ☌ ♂ **8:40 am** 5:40 am
☽ △ ♄ **1:52 pm** 10:52 am
☿ △ ♇ 9:14 pm
☽ ⚺ ♃ 10:45 pm

26 THURSDAY
☿ △ ♇ **12:14 am**
☽ ⚺ ♃ **1:45 am**
☽ ⚹ ♅ **1:02 pm** 10:02 am
☽ △ ♆ **3:38 pm** 12:38 pm
☽ ☍ ♇ **6:12 pm** 3:12 pm
☽ ⚹ ☿ **9:18 pm** 6:18 pm

27 FRIDAY
☽ ⚹ ⊙ **3:51 am** 12:51 am
☽ □ ♀ **4:47 am** 1:47 am
☽ ⚺ ♂ **8:33 pm** 5:33 pm
☽ ⚻ ♄ **11:04 pm** 8:04 pm

28 SATURDAY
☽ ⚹ ♃ **12:05 pm** 9:05 am
☽ □ ♅ **11:36 pm** 8:36 pm
☽ ⚻ ♆ 11:16 pm

29 SUNDAY
☽ ⚻ ♆ **2:16 am**
☽ ⚻ ♇ **5:03 am** 2:03 am
☽ ⚺ ☿ **6:48 am** 3:48 am
☽ ⚺ ⊙ **8:25 pm** 5:25 pm
☽ ⚹ ♀ **10:49 pm** 7:49 pm
♂ △ ♄ 9:06 pm

30 MONDAY
♂ △ ♄ **12:06 am**
☽ ☍ ♄ **10:38 am** 7:38 am
☽ ⚹ ♂ **11:11 am** 8:11 am
⊙ ☌ ☿ **5:09 pm** 2:09 pm
☽ □ ♃ 9:30 pm

Eastern time in bold type
Pacific time in medium type

SEPTEMBER 2024

DATE	SID.TIME	SUN	MOON	NODE	MERCURY	VENUS	MARS	JUPITER	SATURN	URANUS	NEPTUNE	PLUTO	CERES	PALLAS	JUNO	VESTA	CHIRON
1 Su	22 42 36	9♍03 20	15♌54	6♈50R	22♌05	2♎59	27♊40	19♊01	16♓35R	27♉15R	29♓03R	0♒01R	7♑35	27♏55	7♎36	3♍18	22♈58R
2 M	22 46 33	10 01 25	28 05	6 45	22 35	4 13	28 17	19 08	16 30	27 15	29 02	0 00	7 37	28 11	7 57	3 47	22 57
3 T	22 50 29	10 59 32	10♍07	6 42	23 13	5 26	28 54	19 15	16 25	27 15	29 00	29♑59	7 40	28 28	8 18	4 15	22 55
4 W	22 54 26	11 57 40	22 01	6 40	23 59	6 40	29 30	19 21	16 21	27 15	28 59	29 58	7 43	28 44	8 39	4 43	22 53
5 Th	22 58 22	12 55 51	3♎50	6 39D	24 53	7 53	0♋06	19 28	16 16	27 15	28 57	29 57	7 46	29 01	9 00	5 12	22 51
6 F	23 2 19	13 54 02	15 37	6 39	25 54	9 07	0 43	19 34	16 12	27 15	28 55	29 56	7 49	29 18	9 21	5 40	22 49
7 Sa	23 6 15	14 52 16	27 23	6 40	27 02	10 20	1 19	19 40	16 07	27 15	28 54	29 55	7 53	29 35	9 42	6 09	22 47
8 Su	23 10 12	15 50 31	9♏14	6 42	28 16	11 33	1 54	19 46	16 03	27 14	28 52	29 54	7 57	29 52	10 03	6 37	22 45
9 M	23 14 8	16 48 47	21 12	6 43	29 36	12 47	2 30	19 52	15 58	27 14	28 51	29 53	8 02	0♐10	10 24	7 05	22 43
10 T	23 18 5	17 47 06	3♐21	6 45	1♍02	14 00	3 06	19 57	15 53	27 14	28 49	29 53	8 07	0 28	10 45	7 34	22 41
11 W	23 22 1	18 45 25	15 48	6 45R	2 32	15 13	3 41	20 03	15 49	27 13	28 47	29 52	8 12	0 45	11 06	8 02	22 39
12 Th	23 25 58	19 43 47	28 35	6 45	4 07	16 27	4 16	20 08	15 44	27 13	28 46	29 51	8 17	1 03	11 27	8 31	22 37
13 F	23 29 55	20 42 10	11♑46	6 44	5 45	17 40	4 51	20 13	15 40	27 12	28 44	29 50	8 23	1 21	11 48	8 59	22 34
14 Sa	23 33 51	21 40 34	25 25	6 43	7 27	18 53	5 26	20 18	15 35	27 12	28 43	29 49	8 29	1 40	12 09	9 28	22 32
15 Su	23 37 48	22 39 00	9♒31	6 41	9 11	20 07	6 01	20 23	15 30	27 11	28 41	29 49	8 36	1 58	12 31	9 56	22 30
16 M	23 41 44	23 37 28	24 03	6 39	10 57	21 20	6 35	20 27	15 26	27 10	28 39	29 48	8 42	2 17	12 52	10 25	22 28
17 T	23 45 41	24 35 57	8♓56	6 38	12 45	22 33	7 10	20 32	15 21	27 09	28 38	29 47	8 49	2 35	13 13	10 53	22 25
18 W	23 49 37	25 34 28	24 03	6 37D	14 35	23 46	7 44	20 36	15 17	27 09	28 36	29 47	8 57	2 54	13 34	11 22	22 23
19 Th	23 53 34	26 33 01	9♈15	6 37	16 25	25 00	8 18	20 40	15 12	27 08	28 34	29 46	9 04	3 13	13 55	11 50	22 20
20 F	23 57 30	27 31 36	24 21	6 37	18 16	26 13	8 52	20 44	15 08	27 07	28 33	29 45	9 12	3 32	14 17	12 19	22 18
21 Sa	0 1 27	28 30 13	9♉15	6 38	20 07	27 26	9 26	20 47	15 04	27 06	28 31	29 45	9 20	3 51	14 38	12 47	22 16
22 Su	0 5 24	29 28 53	23 49	6 38	21 59	28 39	9 59	20 51	14 59	27 05	28 29	29 44	9 29	4 10	14 59	13 16	22 13
23 M	0 9 20	0♎27 34	7♊58	6 39	23 50	29 52	10 32	20 54	14 55	27 04	28 28	29 44	9 37	4 30	15 21	13 44	22 11
24 T	0 13 17	1 26 18	21 43	6 39R	25 42	1♏05	11 05	20 57	14 51	27 03	28 26	29 43	9 46	4 50	15 42	14 13	22 08
25 W	0 17 13	2 25 05	5♋03	6 39	27 32	2 18	11 38	21 00	14 46	27 02	28 24	29 43	9 56	5 09	16 03	14 41	22 06
26 Th	0 21 10	3 23 53	18 00	6 39	29 23	3 31	12 11	21 03	14 42	27 01	28 23	29 42	10 05	5 29	16 24	15 10	22 03
27 F	0 25 6	4 22 44	0♌38	6 39	1♎12	4 44	12 43	21 05	14 38	27 00	28 21	29 42	10 15	5 49	16 46	15 38	22 00
28 Sa	0 29 3	5 21 37	13 00	6 39	3 01	5 57	13 16	21 08	14 34	26 58	28 19	29 41	10 25	6 09	17 07	16 07	21 58
29 Su	0 32 59	6 20 32	25 08	6 39D	4 50	7 10	13 48	21 10	14 30	26 57	28 18	29 41	10 35	6 29	17 29	16 35	21 55
30 M	0 36 56	7 19 29	7♍08	6 39	6 37	8 23	14 19	21 12	14 26	26 56	28 16	29 41	10 46	6 49	17 50	17 04	21 53

EPHEMERIS CALCULATED FOR 12 MIDNIGHT GREENWICH MEAN TIME. ALL OTHER DATA AND FACING ASPECTARIAN PAGE IN **EASTERN TIME (BOLD)** AND PACIFIC TIME (REGULAR).

OCTOBER 2024

☽ Last Aspect day	ET / hr:mn	PT	asp	☽ Ingress sign	day	ET / hr:mn	PT
1	**5:39 pm**	2:39 pm	△♇	♎	1	**6:20 pm**	3:20 pm
4	**6:40 am**	3:40 am	□♇	♏	4	**7:22 am**	4:22 am
6	**6:52 pm**	3:52 pm	⚹♇	♐	6	**7:34 pm**	4:34 pm
8		10:54 pm	□♆	♑	9	**5:38 am**	2:38 am
9	**1:54 am**		□♆	♑	9	**5:38 am**	2:38 am
11	**11:53 am**	8:53 am	☌♇	♒	11	**12:31 pm**	9:31 am
13	**10:11 am**	7:11 am	□♅	♓	13	**3:55 pm**	12:55 pm
15	**4:00 pm**	1:00 pm	⚹♇	♈	15	**4:34 pm**	1:34 pm
17	**3:26 pm**	12:26 pm	□♇	♉	17	**4:00 pm**	1:00 pm
19	**3:33 pm**	12:33 pm	△♇	♊	19	**4:07 pm**	1:07 pm
21	**5:00 pm**	2:00 pm	△☉	♋	21	**6:50 pm**	3:50 pm
23		9:47 pm	☍♇	♌	23		10:24 pm
24	**12:47 am**		☍♇	♌	24	**1:24 am**	
26	**4:04 am**	1:04 am	□♅	♍	26	**11:47 am**	8:47 am
28	**11:54 pm**	8:54 pm	△♇	♎	28		9:30 pm
28	**11:54 pm**	8:54 pm	△♇	♎	29	**12:30 am**	
31	**12:57 pm**	9:57 am	□♇	♏	31	**1:29 pm**	10:29 am

☽ Phases & Eclipses phase	day	ET / hr:mn	PT
New Moon	2	**2:49 pm**	11:49 am
●	2	10° ♎ 04'	
2nd Quarter	10	**2:55 pm**	11:55 am
Full Moon	17	**7:26 am**	4:26 am
4th Quarter	24	**4:03 am**	1:03 am

Planet Ingress	day	ET / hr:mn	PT
☿ ♏	13	**3:23 pm**	12:23 pm
♀ ♐	17	**3:28 pm**	12:28 pm
☉ ♏	22	**6:15 pm**	3:15 pm
⚶ ♎	26		11:35 pm
⚶ ♎	27	**2:35 am**	

Planetary Motion	day	ET / hr:mn	PT
♃ ℞	9	**3:05 am**	12:05 am
♇ D	11	**8:34 pm**	5:34 pm

1 TUESDAY
☽ □ ♃ **12:30 am**
☽ △ ♅ **12:00 pm** 9:00 am
☽ ☍ ♆ **2:42 pm** 11:42 am
☽ △ ♇ **5:39 pm** 2:39 pm

2 WEDNESDAY
☽ ☌ ☉ **2:49 pm** 11:49 am
☽ ☌ ☿ **6:22 pm** 3:22 pm
☽ ⚺ ♀ **6:43 pm** 3:43 pm
☽ ⚻ ♄ **11:17 pm** 8:17 pm
☿ ⚺ ♀ 10:26 pm

3 THURSDAY
☿ ⚺ ♀ **1:26 am**
☽ □ ♂ **3:00 am** 12:00 am
☽ △ ♃ **1:40 pm** 10:40 am
☽ ⚻ ♅ 9:56 pm
☿ ⚻ ♄ 11:46 pm

4 FRIDAY
☽ ⚻ ♅ **12:56 am**
☿ ⚻ ♄ **2:46 am**
☽ ⚻ ♆ **3:37 am** 12:37 am
☽ □ ♇ **6:40 am** 3:40 am
♀ △ ♄ **1:04 pm** 10:04 am

5 SATURDAY
☽ ⚺ ☉ **9:13 am** 6:13 am
☽ △ ♄ **11:46 am** 8:46 am
☽ ☌ ♀ **2:28 pm** 11:28 am
☽ ⚺ ☿ **5:30 pm** 2:30 pm

☽ △ ♂ **6:27 pm** 3:27 pm
☽ ⚻ ♃ 11:19 pm
☿ □ ♂ 11:37 pm

6 SUNDAY
☽ ⚻ ♃ **2:19 am**
☿ □ ♂ **2:37 am**
☽ ☍ ♅ **1:09 pm** 10:09 am
☉ ⚻ ♄ **2:28 pm** 11:28 am
☽ △ ♆ **3:47 pm** 12:47 pm
☽ ⚹ ♇ **6:52 pm** 3:52 pm

7 MONDAY
☽ □ ♄ **10:50 pm** 7:50 pm
☽ ⚹ ☉ 10:49 pm

8 TUESDAY
☽ ⚹ ☉ **1:49 am**
♀ △ ♂ **6:22 am** 3:22 am
☽ ⚻ ♂ **8:02 am** 5:02 am
☽ ⚺ ♀ **8:09 am** 5:09 am
☿ △ ♃ **8:23 am** 5:23 am
☽ ☍ ♃ **1:10 pm** 10:10 am
☽ ⚹ ☿ **1:54 pm** 10:54 am
☽ ⚻ ♅ **11:23 pm** 8:23 pm
☽ □ ♆ 10:54 pm

9 WEDNESDAY
☽ □ ♆ **1:54 am**
☽ ⚺ ♇ **4:58 am** 1:58 am

10 THURSDAY
☽ ⚹ ♄ **7:16 am** 4:16 am
♀ ⚻ ♃ **11:44 am** 8:44 am

☽ □ ☉ **2:55 pm** 11:55 am
☽ ☍ ♂ **6:22 pm** 3:22 pm
☽ ⚻ ♃ **9:02 pm** 6:02 pm
☽ ⚹ ♀ **9:58 pm** 6:58 pm

11 FRIDAY
☽ □ ☿ **5:35 am** 2:35 am
☽ △ ♅ **6:31 am** 3:31 am
☽ ⚹ ♆ **8:54 am** 5:54 am
☽ ☌ ♇ **11:53 am** 8:53 am
☿ ⚻ ♅ **1:11 pm** 10:11 am

12 SATURDAY
☿ ⚻ ♆ **8:41 am** 5:41 am
☽ ⚺ ♄ **12:19 pm** 9:19 am
☽ △ ☉ **11:39 pm** 8:39 pm
☽ ⚻ ♂ 9:44 pm
☽ △ ♃ 10:22 pm

13 SUNDAY
☽ ⚻ ♂ **12:44 am**
☽ △ ♃ **1:22 am**
☽ □ ♀ **7:08 am** 4:08 am
☿ □ ♇ **10:03 am** 7:03 am
☽ □ ♅ **10:11 am** 7:11 am
☽ ⚺ ♆ **12:26 pm** 9:26 am
☽ ⚺ ♇ **3:19 pm** 12:19 pm
☽ △ ☿ **3:59 pm** 12:59 pm
♂ ⚺ ♃ **7:08 pm** 4:08 pm
☉ △ ♃ **11:52 pm** 8:52 pm

14 MONDAY
☉ □ ♂ **4:15 am** 1:15 am
☽ ☌ ♄ **2:09 pm** 11:09 am

♀ ☍ ♅ **6:22 pm** 3:22 pm
☽ □ ♃ 11:38 pm

15 TUESDAY
☽ □ ♃ **2:38 am**
☽ △ ♂ **3:41 am** 12:41 am
☽ ⚻ ☉ **4:34 am** 1:34 am
☽ ⚹ ♅ **10:59 am** 7:59 am
☽ △ ♀ **12:28 pm** 9:28 am
☽ ☌ ♆ **1:09 pm** 10:09 am
☽ ⚹ ♇ **4:00 pm** 1:00 pm
♀ △ ♆ **8:49 pm** 5:49 pm
☽ ⚻ ☿ **10:22 pm** 7:22 pm

16 WEDNESDAY
☽ ⚺ ♄ **1:52 pm** 10:52 am
☽ ⚹ ♃ 11:09 pm

17 THURSDAY
☽ ⚹ ♃ **2:09 am**
☽ □ ♂ **4:44 am** 1:44 am
☽ ☍ ☉ **7:26 am** 4:26 am
♀ ⚹ ♇ **8:30 am** 5:30 am
☽ ⚺ ♅ **10:21 am** 7:21 am
☽ ⚺ ♆ **12:32 pm** 9:32 am
☽ □ ♇ **3:26 pm** 12:26 pm
☽ ⚻ ♀ **4:02 pm** 1:02 pm

18 FRIDAY
☽ ☍ ☿ **3:15 am** 12:15 am
☽ ⚹ ♄ **1:13 pm** 10:13 am
☽ ⚺ ♃ 10:46 pm
☉ ⚻ ♅ 11:40 pm

19 SATURDAY
☽ ⚺ ♃ **1:46 am**
☉ ⚻ ♅ **2:40 am**
☽ ⚹ ♂ **6:00 am** 3:00 am
☽ ☌ ♅ **10:11 am** 7:11 am
☽ ⚻ ☉ **10:44 am** 7:44 am
☽ ⚹ ♆ **12:28 pm** 9:28 am
☽ △ ♇ **3:33 pm** 12:33 pm
☽ ☍ ♀ **8:30 pm** 5:30 pm

20 SUNDAY
☽ ⚻ ☿ **9:39 am** 6:39 am
☉ ⚻ ♆ **11:44 am** 8:44 am
☽ □ ♄ **2:07 pm** 11:07 am

21 MONDAY
☽ ☌ ♃ **3:25 am** 12:25 am
☽ ⚺ ♂ **9:39 am** 6:39 am
☽ ⚺ ♅ **12:22 pm** 9:22 am
☽ □ ♆ **2:50 pm** 11:50 am
☽ △ ☉ **5:00 pm** 2:00 pm
☽ ⚻ ♇ **6:15 pm** 3:15 pm
☿ △ ♄ 11:35 pm

22 TUESDAY
☿ △ ♄ **2:35 am**
☽ ⚻ ♀ **4:30 am** 1:30 am
☉ □ ♇ **10:15 am** 7:15 am
☽ △ ♄ **6:17 pm** 3:17 pm
☽ △ ☿ **8:22 pm** 5:22 pm

23 WEDNESDAY
☽ ⚺ ♃ **8:36 am** 5:36 am
☽ ☌ ♂ **5:20 pm** 2:20 pm
☽ ⚹ ♅ **6:16 pm** 3:16 pm

☽ △ ♆ **9:00 pm** 6:00 pm
☽ ☍ ♇ 9:47 pm

24 THURSDAY
☽ ☍ ♇ **12:47 am**
☽ □ ☉ **4:03 am** 1:03 am
☽ △ ♀ **5:43 pm** 2:43 pm
♂ ⚹ ♅ **8:13 pm** 5:13 pm
☽ ⚻ ♄ 11:27 pm

25 FRIDAY
☽ ⚻ ♄ **2:27 am**
☽ □ ☿ **12:41 pm** 9:41 am
☽ ⚹ ♃ **5:42 pm** 2:42 pm

26 SATURDAY
☽ □ ♅ **4:04 am** 1:04 am
☽ ⚺ ♂ **5:16 am** 2:16 am
☽ ⚻ ♆ **7:02 am** 4:02 am
☽ ⚻ ♇ **11:11 am** 8:11 am
☽ ⚹ ☉ **7:54 pm** 4:54 pm

27 SUNDAY
☿ ⚻ ♃ **4:50 am** 1:50 am
☽ □ ♀ **11:39 am** 8:39 am
☽ ☍ ♄ **1:56 pm** 10:56 am

28 MONDAY
☽ □ ♃ **5:37 am** 2:37 am
♂ △ ♆ **8:31 am** 5:31 am
☽ ⚹ ☿ **9:16 am** 6:16 am
♀ □ ♄ **9:35 am** 6:35 am
☽ △ ♅ **4:23 pm** 1:23 pm
☽ ☍ ♆ **7:31 pm** 4:31 pm

☽ ⚹ ♂ **7:55 pm** 4:55 pm
☽ △ ♇ **11:54 pm** 8:54 pm

29 TUESDAY
☽ ⚺ ☉ **2:24 pm** 11:24 am
☽ ⚻ ♄ 11:50 pm

30 WEDNESDAY
☽ ⚻ ♄ **2:50 am**
☽ ⚹ ♀ **7:39 am** 4:39 am
☿ ☍ ♅ **6:15 pm** 3:15 pm
☽ △ ♃ **6:22 pm** 3:22 pm

31 THURSDAY
☽ ⚻ ♅ **5:15 am** 2:15 am
☽ ⚺ ☿ **6:47 am** 3:47 am
☽ ⚻ ♆ **8:27 am** 5:27 am
☽ □ ♂ **10:57 am** 7:57 am
☽ □ ♇ **12:57 pm** 9:57 am
☿ △ ♆ **8:33 pm** 5:33 pm

Eastern time in bold type
Pacific time in medium type

OCTOBER 2024

DATE	SID.TIME	SUN	MOON	NODE	MERCURY	VENUS	MARS	JUPITER	SATURN	URANUS	NEPTUNE	PLUTO	CERES	PALLAS	JUNO	VESTA	CHIRON
1 T	0 40 53	8♎18 28	19♍01	6♈39	8♎24	9♏36	14♋51	21♊13	14♓22R	26♉54R	28♓14R	29♑40R	10♑57	7♐10	18♎11	17♍33	21♈50R
2 W	0 44 49	9 17 30	0♎49	6 39R	10 10	10 49	15 22	21 15	14 18	26 53	28 13	29 40	11 08	7 30	18 33	18 01	21 47
3 Th	0 48 46	10 16 33	12 36	6 39	11 55	12 02	15 53	21 16	14 14	26 51	28 11	29 40	11 19	7 51	18 54	18 30	21 45
4 F	0 52 42	11 15 39	24 24	6 39	13 39	13 15	16 24	21 17	14 10	26 50	28 10	29 39	11 31	8 11	19 15	18 58	21 42
5 Sa	0 56 39	12 14 46	6♏14	6 38	15 23	14 28	16 55	21 18	14 06	26 48	28 08	29 39	11 42	8 32	19 37	19 27	21 39
6 Su	1 0 35	13 13 56	18 10	6 37	17 06	15 41	17 25	21 19	14 02	26 47	28 06	29 39	11 54	8 53	19 58	19 55	21 37
7 M	1 4 32	14 13 07	0♐13	6 36	18 47	16 54	17 56	21 20	13 59	26 45	28 05	29 39	12 07	9 14	20 19	20 24	21 34
8 T	1 8 28	15 12 21	12 27	6 35	20 28	18 07	18 25	21 20	13 55	26 43	28 03	29 39	12 19	9 35	20 41	20 52	21 31
9 W	1 12 25	16 11 36	24 55	6 34	22 09	19 20	18 55	21 20R	13 52	26 42	28 02	29 39	12 32	9 56	21 02	21 21	21 28
10 Th	1 16 22	17 10 53	7♑40	6 34D	23 48	20 32	19 24	21 20	13 48	26 40	28 00	29 39	12 45	10 17	21 24	21 49	21 26
11 F	1 20 18	18 10 12	20 46	6 34	25 27	21 45	19 53	21 20	13 45	26 38	27 59	29 39	12 58	10 39	21 45	22 18	21 23
12 Sa	1 24 15	19 09 32	4♒15	6 34	27 05	22 58	20 22	21 20	13 41	26 36	27 57	29 39D	13 11	11 00	22 06	22 46	21 20
13 Su	1 28 11	20 08 54	18 09	6 35	28 42	24 11	20 51	21 19	13 38	26 35	27 56	29 39	13 25	11 22	22 28	23 15	21 17
14 M	1 32 8	21 08 18	2♓28	6 36	0♏18	25 23	21 19	21 18	13 35	26 33	27 54	29 39	13 38	11 43	22 49	23 43	21 15
15 T	1 36 4	22 07 44	17 10	6 37	1 54	26 36	21 47	21 17	13 32	26 31	27 53	29 39	13 52	12 05	23 10	24 12	21 12
16 W	1 40 1	23 07 11	2♈09	6 38R	3 29	27 49	22 15	21 16	13 29	26 29	27 51	29 39	14 07	12 26	23 32	24 40	21 09
17 Th	1 43 57	24 06 41	17 20	6 37	5 04	29 01	22 42	21 14	13 26	26 27	27 50	29 39	14 21	12 48	23 53	25 09	21 06
18 F	1 47 54	25 06 12	2♉32	6 36	6 38	0♐14	23 09	21 13	13 23	26 25	27 48	29 39	14 35	13 10	24 14	25 37	21 04
19 Sa	1 51 51	26 05 46	17 35	6 34	8 11	1 26	23 36	21 11	13 20	26 23	27 47	29 39	14 50	13 32	24 35	26 05	21 01
20 Su	1 55 47	27 05 21	2♊22	6 32	9 44	2 39	24 02	21 09	13 18	26 21	27 45	29 39	15 05	13 54	24 57	26 34	20 58
21 M	1 59 44	28 04 59	16 45	6 29	11 16	3 51	24 29	21 07	13 15	26 19	27 44	29 40	15 20	14 16	25 18	27 02	20 56
22 T	2 3 40	29 04 40	0♋40	6 26	12 47	5 04	24 54	21 04	13 13	26 17	27 43	29 40	15 35	14 38	25 39	27 31	20 53
23 W	2 7 37	0♏04 22	14 07	6 24	14 18	6 16	25 20	21 01	13 10	26 14	27 41	29 40	15 51	15 00	26 00	27 59	20 50
24 Th	2 11 33	1 04 07	27 08	6 23D	15 48	7 28	25 45	20 59	13 08	26 12	27 40	29 41	16 06	15 22	26 22	28 27	20 47
25 F	2 15 30	2 03 54	9♌45	6 23	17 18	8 41	26 10	20 56	13 06	26 10	27 39	29 41	16 22	15 45	26 43	28 56	20 45
26 Sa	2 19 26	3 03 43	22 03	6 24	18 47	9 53	26 34	20 52	13 04	26 08	27 37	29 41	16 38	16 07	27 04	29 24	20 42
27 Su	2 23 23	4 03 34	4♍06	6 26	20 15	11 05	26 58	20 49	13 01	26 06	27 36	29 42	16 54	16 30	27 25	29 52	20 39
28 M	2 27 20	5 03 28	16 00	6 28	21 43	12 18	27 22	20 45	13 00	26 03	27 35	29 42	17 11	16 52	27 46	0♎21	20 37
29 T	2 31 16	6 03 23	27 48	6 29R	23 10	13 30	27 45	20 42	12 58	26 01	27 34	29 43	17 27	17 15	28 07	0 49	20 34
30 W	2 35 13	7 03 21	9♎34	6 30	24 37	14 42	28 08	20 38	12 56	25 59	27 32	29 43	17 44	17 37	28 28	1 17	20 31
31 Th	2 39 9	8 03 20	21 22	6 28	26 03	15 54	28 31	20 33	12 54	25 56	27 31	29 44	18 01	18 00	28 49	1 45	20 29

EPHEMERIS CALCULATED FOR 12 MIDNIGHT GREENWICH MEAN TIME. ALL OTHER DATA AND FACING ASPECTARIAN PAGE IN **EASTERN TIME (BOLD)** AND PACIFIC TIME (REGULAR).

NOVEMBER 2024

☽ Last Aspect day	ET / hr:mn / PT		asp	☽ Ingress sign	day	ET / hr:mn / PT	
2		9:51 pm	⚹♇	♐	2		10:19 pm
3	**12:51 am**		⚹♇	♐	3	**1:19 am**	
5	**5:23 am**	2:23 am	□♆	♑	5	**10:17 am**	7:17 am
7	**5:38 pm**	2:38 pm	☌♇	♒	7	**5:58 pm**	2:58 pm
9	**7:23 pm**	4:23 pm	⚹♀	♓	9	**11:00 pm**	8:00 pm
11		10:13 pm	⚹♇	♈	11		10:26 pm
12	**1:13 am**		⚹♇	♈	12	**1:26 am**	
13		10:50 pm	□♇	♉	13		10:59 pm
14	**1:50 am**		□♇	♉	14	**1:59 am**	
15		11:03 pm	△♇	♊	15		11:09 pm
16	**2:03 am**		△♇	♊	16	**2:09 am**	
17	**11:09 pm**	8:09 pm	□♆	♋	18	**3:50 am**	12:50 am
20	**6:20 am**	3:20 am	△☉	♌	20	**8:51 am**	5:51 am
22	**8:15 am**	5:15 am	□♅	♍	22	**6:01 pm**	3:01 pm
24		9:35 pm	☍♆	♎	25	**6:20 am**	3:20 am
25	**12:35 am**		☍♆	♎	25	**6:20 am**	3:20 am
27	**4:14 am**	1:14 am	⚹☿	♏	27	**7:21 pm**	4:21 pm
29		10:19 pm	△♆	♐	30	**6:53 am**	3:53 am
30	**1:19 am**		△♆	♐	30	**6:53 am**	3:53 am

☽ Phases & Eclipses phase	day	ET / hr:mn / PT	
New Moon	1	**8:47 am**	5:47 am
2nd Quarter	8		9:55 pm
2nd Quarter	9	**12:55 am**	
Full Moon	15	**4:28 pm**	1:28 pm
4th Quarter	22	**8:28 pm**	5:28 pm
New Moon	30		10:21 pm
New Moon	12/1	**1:21 am**	

Planet Ingress		day	ET / hr:mn / PT	
☿	♐	2	**3:18 pm**	12:18 pm
⚵	♏	3	**3:35 am**	1:35 am
♂	♌	3	**11:10 pm**	8:10 pm
♀	♑	11	**1:26 pm**	10:26 am
♇	♒	19	**3:29 pm**	12:29 pm
☉	♐	21	**2:56 pm**	11:56 am
♀	♑	30	**5:37 pm**	2:37 pm

Planetary Motion		day	ET / hr:mn / PT	
♄	D	15	**9:20 am**	6:20 am
☿	℞	25	**9:42 pm**	6:42 pm

1 FRIDAY
☽ ☌ ☉ **8:47 am** 5:47 am
☽ △ ♄ **3:20 pm** 12:20 pm
☽ ⚺ ♀ 11:53 pm

2 SATURDAY
☽ ⚺ ♀ **2:53 am**
☿ △ ♂ **4:21 am** 1:21 am
☽ ⚻ ♃ **6:18 am** 3:18 am
☿ ⚹ ♇ **11:03 am** 8:03 am
☽ ☍ ♅ **5:06 pm** 2:06 pm
☽ △ ♆ **8:20 pm** 5:20 pm
☽ △ ♂ 9:40 pm
☽ ⚹ ♇ 9:51 pm
☽ ☌ ☿ 11:37 pm

3 SUNDAY
☽ △ ♂ **12:40 am**
☽ ⚹ ♇ **12:51 am**
☽ ☌ ☿ **1:37 am**
♂ ☍ ♇ **6:37 am** 3:37 am
♀ ☍ ♃ **10:25 am** 7:25 am
☽ ⚺ ☉ 9:18 pm
☽ □ ♄ 10:19 pm

4 MONDAY
☽ ⚺ ☉ **12:18 am**
☽ □ ♄ **1:19 am**
☉ △ ♄ **12:36 pm** 9:36 am
☽ ☍ ♃ **3:32 pm** 12:32 pm
☽ ☌ ♀ **6:51 pm** 3:51 pm
☽ ⚻ ♅ 11:10 pm

5 TUESDAY
☽ ⚻ ♅ **2:10 am**
☽ □ ♆ **5:23 am** 2:23 am
☽ ⚺ ♇ **9:53 am** 6:53 am
☽ ⚻ ♂ **11:15 am** 8:15 am
☽ ⚺ ☿ **6:30 pm** 3:30 pm

6 WEDNESDAY
☽ ⚹ ♄ **10:17 am** 7:17 am
☽ ⚹ ☉ **2:11 pm** 11:11 am
☽ ⚻ ♃ **11:38 pm** 8:38 pm

7 THURSDAY
☽ ⚺ ♀ **8:51 am** 5:51 am
☽ △ ♅ **10:01 am** 7:01 am
☽ ⚹ ♆ **1:12 pm** 10:12 am
☽ ☌ ♇ **5:38 pm** 2:38 pm
☽ ☍ ♂ **8:15 pm** 5:15 pm
♀ ⚻ ♅ **9:20 pm** 6:20 pm

8 FRIDAY
☽ ⚹ ☿ **7:52 am** 4:52 am
☽ ⚺ ♄ **4:48 pm** 1:48 pm
☽ □ ☉ 9:55 pm

9 SATURDAY
☽ □ ☉ **12:55 am**
☽ △ ♃ **5:12 am** 2:12 am
♀ □ ♆ **8:15 am** 5:15 am
☽ □ ♅ **3:17 pm** 12:17 pm
☽ ⚺ ♆ **6:25 pm** 3:25 pm
☽ ⚹ ♀ **7:23 pm** 4:23 pm
☽ ⚺ ♇ **10:44 pm** 7:44 pm
☽ ⚻ ♂ 11:21 pm

10 SUNDAY
☽ ⚻ ♂ **2:21 am**
☽ □ ☿ **5:20 pm** 2:20 pm
☽ ☌ ♄ **8:39 pm** 5:39 pm

11 MONDAY
☉ ⚻ ♃ **6:08 am** 3:08 am
☽ □ ♃ **8:07 am** 5:07 am
☽ △ ☉ **8:17 am** 5:17 am
♀ ⚺ ♇ **10:44 am** 7:44 am
☽ ⚹ ♅ **5:56 pm** 2:56 pm
☽ ☌ ♆ **9:01 pm** 6:01 pm
☽ ⚹ ♇ 10:13 pm
☽ □ ♀ 11:29 pm

12 TUESDAY
☽ ⚹ ♇ **1:13 am**
☽ □ ♀ **2:29 am**
☽ △ ♂ **5:37 am** 2:37 am
☿ □ ♄ **8:22 am** 5:22 am
☽ ⚺ ♄ **10:08 pm** 7:08 pm
☽ △ ☿ **11:19 pm** 8:19 pm

13 WEDNESDAY
☽ ⚹ ♃ **8:51 am** 5:51 am
☽ ⚻ ☉ **12:54 pm** 9:54 am
☽ ⚺ ♅ **6:34 pm** 3:34 pm
☽ ⚺ ♆ **9:38 pm** 6:38 pm
☽ □ ♇ 10:50 pm

14 THURSDAY
☽ □ ♇ **1:50 am**
♀ ⚻ ♂ **3:02 am** 12:02 am
☽ □ ♂ **6:57 am** 3:57 am
☽ △ ♀ **7:13 am** 4:13 am
☽ ⚹ ♄ **10:18 pm** 7:18 pm

15 FRIDAY
☽ ⚻ ☿ **3:20 am** 12:20 am
☽ ⚺ ♃ **8:36 am** 5:36 am
☽ ☍ ☉ **4:28 pm** 1:28 pm
☽ ☌ ♅ **6:32 pm** 3:32 pm
☽ ⚹ ♆ **9:43 pm** 6:43 pm
☽ △ ♇ 11:03 pm

16 SATURDAY
☽ △ ♇ **2:03 am**
☽ ⚹ ♂ **8:00 am** 5:00 am
☽ ⚻ ♀ **11:41 am** 8:41 am
☉ ☍ ♅ **9:45 pm** 6:45 pm
☽ □ ♄ **10:52 pm** 7:52 pm

17 SUNDAY
☽ ☍ ☿ **7:41 am** 4:41 am
☽ ☌ ♃ **9:07 am** 6:07 am
☽ ⚺ ♅ **7:42 pm** 4:42 pm
☽ ⚻ ☉ **9:27 pm** 6:27 pm
☽ □ ♆ **11:09 pm** 8:09 pm

18 MONDAY
☽ ⚻ ♇ **3:47 am** 12:47 am
☿ ☍ ♃ **3:55 am** 12:55 am
☽ ⚺ ♂ **10:49 am** 7:49 am
☽ ☍ ♀ **6:35 pm** 3:35 pm
☉ △ ♆ **9:07 pm** 6:07 pm
☽ △ ♄ 10:48 pm

19 TUESDAY
☽ △ ♄ **1:48 am**
☽ ⚺ ♃ **12:17 pm** 9:17 am
☽ ⚻ ☿ **2:43 pm** 11:43 am
☽ ⚹ ♅ **11:56 pm** 8:56 pm

20 WEDNESDAY
☽ △ ♆ **3:46 am** 12:46 am
☽ △ ☉ **6:20 am** 3:20 am
☽ ☍ ♇ **8:52 am** 5:52 am
☽ ☌ ♂ **5:15 pm** 2:15 pm

21 THURSDAY
☽ ⚻ ♀ **6:20 am** 3:20 am
☽ ⚻ ♄ **8:36 am** 5:36 am
☉ ⚹ ♇ **3:49 pm** 12:49 pm
☽ ⚹ ♃ **7:21 pm** 4:21 pm
☽ △ ☿ 10:36 pm

22 FRIDAY
☽ △ ☿ **1:36 am**
♀ ⚹ ♄ **6:55 am** 3:55 am
☽ □ ♅ **8:15 am** 5:15 am
☽ ⚻ ♆ **12:31 pm** 9:31 am
☽ ⚻ ♇ **6:08 pm** 3:08 pm
☽ □ ☉ **8:28 pm** 5:28 pm

23 SATURDAY
☽ ⚺ ♂ **3:53 am** 12:53 am
☽ ☍ ♄ **7:24 pm** 4:24 pm
☽ △ ♀ **11:21 pm** 8:21 pm

24 SUNDAY
☽ □ ♃ **6:04 am** 3:04 am
☽ □ ☿ **3:10 pm** 12:10 pm
☽ △ ♅ **7:59 pm** 4:59 pm
☽ ☍ ♆ 9:35 pm

25 MONDAY
☽ ☍ ♆ **12:35 am**
☽ △ ♇ **6:33 am** 3:33 am
☽ ⚹ ☉ **2:32 pm** 11:32 am
☽ ⚹ ♂ **5:18 pm** 2:18 pm

26 TUESDAY
☽ ⚻ ♄ **8:25 am** 5:25 am
♀ ⚻ ♃ **1:08 pm** 10:08 am
☽ △ ♃ **6:27 pm** 3:27 pm
☽ □ ♀ **7:06 pm** 4:06 pm

27 WEDNESDAY
☉ △ ♂ **3:06 am** 12:06 am
☽ ⚹ ☿ **4:14 am** 1:14 am
☽ ⚻ ♅ **8:51 am** 5:51 am
☽ ⚻ ♆ **1:36 pm** 10:36 am
☽ □ ♇ **7:40 pm** 4:40 pm

28 THURSDAY
☽ □ ♂ **6:49 am** 3:49 am
☽ ⚺ ☉ **9:05 am** 6:05 am
☽ △ ♄ **9:07 pm** 6:07 pm

29 FRIDAY
☽ ⚻ ♃ **6:08 am** 3:08 am
☽ ⚹ ♀ **1:51 pm** 10:51 am
☽ ⚺ ☿ **2:13 pm** 11:13 am
☿ ⚺ ♀ **4:26 pm** 1:26 pm
☽ ☍ ♅ **8:32 pm** 5:32 pm
☽ △ ♆ 10:19 pm

30 SATURDAY
☽ △ ♆ **1:19 am**
☽ ⚹ ♇ **7:18 am** 4:18 am
☽ △ ♂ **6:23 pm** 3:23 pm
☽ ☌ ☉ 10:21 pm

Eastern time in bold type
Pacific time in medium type

NOVEMBER 2024

DATE	SID.TIME	SUN	MOON	NODE	MERCURY	VENUS	MARS	JUPITER	SATURN	URANUS	NEPTUNE	PLUTO	CERES	PALLAS	JUNO	VESTA	CHIRON
1 F	2 43 6	9♏03 22	3♏14	6♈26R	27♏28	17♐06	28♋53	20♊29R	12♓53R	25♉54R	27♓30R	29♑44	18♑18	18♐23	29♎10	2♎13	20♈26R
2 Sa	2 47 2	10 03 26	15 12	6 21	28 53	18 18	29 14	20 24	12 51	25 52	27 29	29 45	18 35	18 45	29 32	2 41	20 24
3 Su	2 50 59	11 03 31	27 18	6 15	0♐16	19 30	29 36	20 20	12 50	25 49	27 28	29 45	18 52	19 08	29 53	3 10	20 21
4 M	2 54 55	12 03 39	9♐33	6 09	1 39	20 42	29 56	20 15	12 49	25 47	27 27	29 46	19 09	19 31	0♏13	3 38	20 19
5 T	2 58 52	13 03 48	21 59	6 02	3 01	21 54	0♌17	20 10	12 47	25 44	27 26	29 47	19 27	19 54	0 34	4 06	20 16
6 W	3 2 49	14 03 58	4♑37	5 56	4 22	23 06	0 37	20 05	12 46	25 42	27 25	29 47	19 45	20 17	0 55	4 34	20 14
7 Th	3 6 45	15 04 11	17 28	5 51	5 42	24 18	0 56	19 59	12 45	25 40	27 24	29 48	20 02	20 40	1 16	5 02	20 11
8 F	3 10 42	16 04 25	0♒34	5 48	7 01	25 30	1 15	19 54	12 45	25 37	27 23	29 49	20 20	21 03	1 37	5 30	20 09
9 Sa	3 14 38	17 04 40	13 58	5 47D	8 19	26 42	1 34	19 48	12 44	25 35	27 22	29 50	20 38	21 26	1 58	5 58	20 07
10 Su	3 18 35	18 04 57	27 41	5 47	9 35	27 53	1 51	19 42	12 43	25 32	27 21	29 51	20 57	21 49	2 19	6 26	20 04
11 M	3 22 31	19 05 15	11♓44	5 48	10 50	29 05	2 09	19 36	12 43	25 30	27 20	29 51	21 15	22 12	2 39	6 53	20 02
12 T	3 26 28	20 05 34	26 06	5 50R	12 02	0♑17	2 26	19 30	12 42	25 27	27 19	29 52	21 34	22 35	3 00	7 21	20 00
13 W	3 30 24	21 05 55	10♈46	5 50	13 13	1 28	2 42	19 24	12 42	25 25	27 18	29 53	21 52	22 59	3 21	7 49	19 57
14 Th	3 34 21	22 06 17	25 39	5 48	14 22	2 40	2 58	19 17	12 42	25 22	27 18	29 54	22 11	23 22	3 41	8 17	19 55
15 F	3 38 18	23 06 41	10♉38	5 44	15 28	3 51	3 14	19 11	12 42D	25 20	27 17	29 55	22 30	23 45	4 02	8 44	19 53
16 Sa	3 42 14	24 07 07	25 35	5 38	16 31	5 02	3 28	19 04	12 42	25 17	27 16	29 56	22 49	24 09	4 22	9 12	19 51
17 Su	3 46 11	25 07 34	10♊21	5 31	17 31	6 14	3 43	18 57	12 42	25 15	27 15	29 57	23 08	24 32	4 43	9 40	19 49
18 M	3 50 7	26 08 03	24 47	5 22	18 28	7 25	3 56	18 50	12 42	25 12	27 15	29 58	23 27	24 55	5 03	10 07	19 46
19 T	3 54 4	27 08 33	8♋49	5 14	19 20	8 36	4 10	18 43	12 42	25 10	27 14	29 59	23 46	25 19	5 24	10 35	19 44
20 W	3 58 0	28 09 05	22 23	5 07	20 08	9 47	4 22	18 36	12 43	25 07	27 13	0♒00	24 06	25 42	5 44	11 02	19 42
21 Th	4 1 57	29 09 39	5♌29	5 02	20 50	10 58	4 34	18 29	12 43	25 05	27 13	0 01	24 25	26 06	6 04	11 30	19 40
22 F	4 5 53	0♐10 15	18 10	4 59	21 27	12 09	4 45	18 21	12 44	25 02	27 12	0 02	24 45	26 29	6 25	11 57	19 38
23 Sa	4 9 50	1 10 52	0♍30	4 59D	21 57	13 20	4 56	18 14	12 44	25 00	27 12	0 04	25 05	26 53	6 45	12 24	19 37
24 Su	4 13 47	2 11 31	12 33	4 59	22 20	14 30	5 06	18 06	12 45	24 57	27 11	0 05	25 25	27 16	7 05	12 52	19 35
25 M	4 17 43	3 12 12	24 26	5 00R	22 34	15 41	5 15	17 59	12 46	24 55	27 11	0 06	25 45	27 40	7 25	13 19	19 33
26 T	4 21 40	4 12 54	6♎13	5 00	22 40R	16 52	5 24	17 51	12 47	24 52	27 10	0 07	26 05	28 03	7 45	13 46	19 31
27 W	4 25 36	5 13 38	17 59	4 59	22 36	18 02	5 32	17 43	12 48	24 50	27 10	0 08	26 25	28 27	8 05	14 13	19 29
28 Th	4 29 33	6 14 23	29 50	4 56	22 22	19 13	5 39	17 35	12 50	24 47	27 10	0 10	26 45	28 50	8 25	14 40	19 28
29 F	4 33 29	7 15 10	11♏48	4 50	21 57	20 23	5 45	17 27	12 51	24 45	27 09	0 11	27 06	29 14	8 45	15 07	19 26
30 Sa	4 37 26	8 15 58	23 55	4 42	21 21	21 33	5 51	17 19	12 53	24 43	27 09	0 12	27 26	29 38	9 05	15 34	19 24

EPHEMERIS CALCULATED FOR 12 MIDNIGHT GREENWICH MEAN TIME. ALL OTHER DATA AND FACING ASPECTARIAN PAGE IN **EASTERN TIME (BOLD)** AND PACIFIC TIME (REGULAR).

DECEMBER 2024

☽ Last Aspect day	ET / hr:mn / PT		asp	☽ Ingress sign	day	ET / hr:mn / PT	
2	**10:47 am**	7:47 am	□♆	♑	2	**4:09 pm**	1:09 pm
4	**6:34 pm**	3:34 pm	☌♀	♒	4	**11:21 pm**	8:21 pm
6	**7:01 pm**	4:01 pm	□♅	♓	7	**4:49 am**	1:49 am
9	**3:45 am**	12:45 am	☌♆	♈	9	**8:38 am**	5:38 am
10	**5:13 pm**	2:13 pm	△☉	♉	11	**10:55 am**	7:55 am
13	**7:39 am**	4:39 am	✶♆	♊	13	**12:22 pm**	9:22 am
15	**9:32 am**	6:32 am	□♆	♋	15	**2:21 pm**	11:21 am
17	**1:33 pm**	10:33 am	△♆	♌	17	**6:39 pm**	3:39 pm
19		9:19 pm	△☉	♍	19		11:37 pm
20	**12:19 am**		△☉	♍	20	**2:37 am**	
22	**8:27 am**	5:27 am	☍♆	♎	22	**2:08 pm**	11:08 am
24	**5:44 am**	2:44 am	△♀	♏	25	**3:06 am**	12:06 am
27	**9:24 am**	6:24 am	△♆	♐	27	**2:46 pm**	11:46 am
29	**6:34 pm**	3:34 pm	□♆	♑	29	**11:37 pm**	8:37 pm
31		10:02 pm	✶♆	♒	1/1	**5:50 am**	2:50 am
1/1	**1:02 am**		✶♆	♒	1/1	**5:50 am**	2:50 am

☽ Phases & Eclipses phase	day	ET / hr:mn / PT	
New Moon	11/30		10:21 pm
New Moon	1	**1:21 am**	
2nd Quarter	8	**10:27 am**	7:27 am
Full Moon	15	**4:02 am**	1:02 am
4th Quarter	22	**5:18 pm**	2:18 pm
New Moon	30	**5:27 pm**	2:27 pm

Planet Ingress		day	ET / hr:mn / PT	
♀	♒	6		10:13 pm
♀	♒	7	**1:13 am**	
⚳	♒	7	**4:16 am**	1:16 am
☉	♑	21	**4:21 am**	1:21 am

Planetary Motion		day	ET / hr:mn / PT	
♂	℞	6	**6:33 pm**	3:33 pm
♆	D	7	**6:43 pm**	3:43 pm
☿	D	15	**3:56 am**	12:56 pm
⚷	D	29	**4:13 pm**	1:13 pm

1 SUNDAY
☽ ☌ ☉ **1:21 am**
☽ □ ♄ **7:49 am** 4:49 am
☽ ☍ ♃ **3:45 pm** 12:45 pm
☽ ☌ ☿ **8:29 pm** 5:29 pm

2 MONDAY
☽ ⚺ ♀ **5:39 am** 2:39 am
☽ ⚻ ♅ **6:02 am** 3:02 am
♀ △ ♅ **9:43 am** 6:43 am
☽ □ ♆ **10:47 am** 7:47 am
☽ ⚺ ♇ **4:39 pm** 1:39 pm

3 TUESDAY
☽ ⚻ ♂ **3:30 am** 12:30 am
☽ ⚺ ☉ **2:43 pm** 11:43 am
☽ ✶ ♄ **4:17 pm** 1:17 pm
☽ ⚻ ♃ **11:13 pm** 8:13 pm
☽ ⚺ ☿ **11:43 pm** 8:43 pm

4 WEDNESDAY
☿ ☍ ♃ **5:16 am** 2:16 am
☉ □ ♄ **11:18 am** 8:18 am
☽ △ ♅ **1:24 pm** 10:24 am
♀ ✶ ♆ **1:52 pm** 10:52 am
☽ ✶ ♆ **6:09 pm** 3:09 pm
☽ ☌ ♀ **6:34 pm** 3:34 pm
☽ ☌ ♇ **11:56 pm** 8:56 pm

5 THURSDAY
☽ ☍ ♂ **10:28 am** 7:28 am
☉ ☌ ☿ **9:18 pm** 6:18 pm
☽ ⚺ ♄ **10:50 pm** 7:50 pm
☽ ✶ ☿ 9:56 pm
☽ ✶ ☉ 10:38 pm

6 FRIDAY
☽ ✶ ☿ **12:56 am**
☽ ✶ ☉ **1:38 am**
☽ △ ♃ **4:53 am** 1:53 am
☽ □ ♅ **7:01 pm** 4:01 pm
☿ □ ♄ **8:53 pm** 5:53 pm
☽ ⚺ ♆ **11:46 pm** 8:46 pm

7 SATURDAY
☽ ⚺ ♀ **5:09 am** 2:09 am
☽ ⚺ ♇ **5:29 am** 2:29 am
♀ ☌ ♇ **9:08 am** 6:08 am
☽ ⚻ ♂ **3:36 pm** 12:36 pm
☉ ☍ ♃ **3:58 pm** 12:58 pm
☽ □ ☿ 9:58 pm

8 SUNDAY
☽ □ ☿ **12:58 am**
☽ ☌ ♄ **3:43 am** 12:43 am
☽ □ ♃ **8:56 am** 5:56 am
☽ □ ☉ **10:27 am** 7:27 am
☽ ✶ ♅ **11:00 pm** 8:00 pm

9 MONDAY
☽ ☌ ♆ **3:45 am** 12:45 am
☽ ✶ ♇ **9:22 am** 6:22 am
☽ ✶ ♀ **1:33 pm** 10:33 am
☽ △ ♂ **6:59 pm** 3:59 pm
☽ △ ☿ 9:19 pm

10 TUESDAY
☽ △ ☿ **12:19 am**
☽ ⚺ ♄ **6:59 am** 3:59 am
☽ ✶ ♃ **11:24 am** 8:24 am
☽ △ ☉ **5:13 pm** 2:13 pm
☽ ⚺ ♅ 10:25 pm

11 WEDNESDAY
☽ ⚺ ♅ **1:25 am**
☽ ⚺ ♆ **6:10 am** 3:10 am
☽ □ ♇ **11:43 am** 8:43 am
☽ □ ♀ **8:01 pm** 5:01 pm
☽ □ ♂ **8:50 pm** 5:50 pm
☽ ⚻ ☿ **11:29 pm** 8:29 pm

12 THURSDAY
♀ ☍ ♂ **5:46 am** 2:46 am
☽ ✶ ♄ **8:55 am** 5:55 am
☽ ⚺ ♃ **12:39 pm** 9:39 am
☽ ⚻ ☉ **10:34 pm** 7:34 pm
☿ ✶ ♀ 11:45 pm
☽ ☌ ♅ 11:49 pm

13 FRIDAY
☿ ✶ ♀ **2:45 am**
☽ ☌ ♅ **2:49 am**
☽ ✶ ♆ **7:39 am** 4:39 am
☽ △ ♇ **1:15 pm** 10:15 am
☽ ✶ ♂ **9:58 pm** 6:58 pm
☽ ☍ ☿ **11:20 pm** 8:20 pm
☽ △ ♀ 10:40 pm

14 SATURDAY
☽ △ ♀ **1:40 am**
☽ □ ♄ **10:34 am** 7:34 am
☽ ☌ ♃ **1:43 pm** 10:43 am

15 SUNDAY
☽ ☍ ☉ **4:02 am** 1:02 am
☽ ⚺ ♅ **4:27 am** 1:27 am
☽ □ ♆ **9:32 am** 6:32 am
☉ ⚻ ♅ **9:44 am** 6:44 am
☽ ⚻ ♇ **3:22 pm** 12:22 pm
☽ ⚺ ♂ **11:52 pm** 8:52 pm
☽ ⚻ ☿ 10:16 pm

16 MONDAY
☽ ⚻ ☿ **1:16 am**
☽ ⚻ ♀ **8:34 am** 5:34 am
☽ △ ♄ **1:34 pm** 10:34 am
☽ ⚺ ♃ **4:11 pm** 1:11 pm

17 TUESDAY
☽ ✶ ♅ **8:02 am** 5:02 am
☽ ⚻ ☉ **11:56 am** 8:56 am
☽ △ ♆ **1:33 pm** 10:33 am
☽ ☍ ♇ **7:50 pm** 4:50 pm

18 WEDNESDAY
☽ ☌ ♂ **4:13 am** 1:13 am
☽ △ ☿ **7:15 am** 4:15 am
☉ □ ♆ **9:29 am** 6:29 am
☽ ☍ ♀ **7:10 pm** 4:10 pm
☽ ⚻ ♄ **7:39 pm** 4:39 pm
☽ ✶ ♃ **9:40 pm** 6:40 pm
♀ ⚺ ♄ 9:52 pm

19 THURSDAY
♀ ⚺ ♄ **12:52 am**
☽ □ ♅ **3:04 pm** 12:04 pm
☽ ⚻ ♆ **9:10 pm** 6:10 pm
♀ △ ♃ **9:11 pm** 6:11 pm
☽ △ ☉ 9:19 pm

20 FRIDAY
☽ △ ☉ **12:19 am**
☽ ⚻ ♇ **4:01 am** 1:01 am
☽ ⚺ ♂ **12:05 pm** 9:05 am
☽ □ ☿ **6:46 pm** 3:46 pm

21 SATURDAY
☽ ☍ ♄ **5:39 am** 2:39 am
☽ □ ♃ **6:55 am** 3:55 am
☽ ⚻ ♀ **10:45 am** 7:45 am
☉ ⚺ ♇ **10:32 pm** 7:32 pm
☽ △ ♅ 10:50 pm

22 SUNDAY
☽ △ ♅ **1:50 am**
☽ ☍ ♆ **8:27 am** 5:27 am
☽ △ ♇ **3:44 pm** 12:44 pm
☽ □ ☉ **5:18 pm** 2:18 pm
☽ ✶ ♂ **10:59 pm** 7:59 pm

23 Monday
☽ ✶ ☿ **11:22 am** 8:22 am
☽ ⚻ ♄ **6:30 pm** 3:30 pm
☽ △ ♃ **6:51 pm** 3:51 pm

24 TUESDAY
☽ △ ♀ **5:44 am** 2:44 am
☽ ⚻ ♅ **2:35 pm** 11:35 am
♃ □ ♄ **4:59 pm** 1:59 pm
☽ ⚻ ♆ **9:28 pm** 6:28 pm
☉ ⚻ ♂ 9:00 pm

25 WEDNESDAY
☉ ⚻ ♂ **12:00 am**
☽ □ ♇ **4:51 am** 1:51 am
☽ □ ♂ **10:44 am** 7:44 am
☽ ✶ ☉ **12:00 pm** 9:00 am

26 THURSDAY
☽ ⚺ ☿ **5:43 am** 2:43 am
☽ ⚻ ♃ **6:55 am** 3:55 am
☽ △ ♄ **7:31 am** 4:31 am
☿ ☍ ♃ **5:48 pm** 2:48 pm
☽ □ ♀ 9:08 pm
☿ □ ♄ 11:29 pm
☽ ☍ ♅ 11:34 pm

27 FRIDAY
☽ □ ♀ **12:08 am**
☿ □ ♄ **2:29 am**
☽ ☍ ♅ **2:34 am**
☽ △ ♆ **9:24 am** 6:24 am
☽ ✶ ♇ **4:36 pm** 1:36 pm
☽ △ ♂ **8:50 pm** 5:50 pm
♀ □ ♅ 11:42 pm

28 SATURDAY
♀ □ ♅ **2:42 am**
☽ ⚺ ☉ **4:35 am** 1:35 am
☽ ☍ ♃ **4:50 pm** 1:50 pm
☽ □ ♄ **6:15 pm** 3:15 pm
☽ ☌ ☿ **10:01 pm** 7:01 pm

29 SUNDAY
☽ ⚻ ♅ **11:55 am** 8:55 am
☽ ✶ ♀ **3:03 pm** 12:03 pm
☽ □ ♆ **6:34 pm** 3:34 pm
☽ ⚺ ♇ 10:29 pm

30 MONDAY
☽ ⚺ ♇ **1:29 am**
☽ ⚻ ♂ **4:07 am** 1:07 am
☽ ☌ ☉ **5:27 pm** 2:27 pm
☽ ⚻ ♃ **11:56 pm** 8:56 pm
☽ ✶ ♄ 11:03 pm

31 TUESDAY
☽ ✶ ♄ **2:03 am**
♀ ⚺ ♆ **9:38 am** 6:38 am
☽ ⚺ ☿ **11:00 am** 8:00 am
☽ △ ♅ **6:30 pm** 3:30 pm
☽ ✶ ♆ 10:02 pm
☽ ⚺ ♀ 11:21 pm

Eastern time in bold type
Pacific time in medium type

DECEMBER 2024

DATE	SID.TIME	SUN	MOON	NODE	MERCURY	VENUS	MARS	JUPITER	SATURN	URANUS	NEPTUNE	PLUTO	CERES	PALLAS	JUNO	VESTA	CHIRON
1 Su	4 41 22	9♐16 48	6♐15	4♈31 R	20♐35 R	22♑43	5♌56	17♊11 R	12♓54	24♉40 R	27♓09 R	0♒14	27♑47	0♑01	9♏25	16♎01	19♈23 R
2 M	4 45 19	10 17 39	18 47	4 18	19 37	23 53	6 00	17 03	12 56	24 38	27 08	0 15	28 07	0 25	9 44	16 28	19 21
3 T	4 49 16	11 18 31	1♑31	4 06	18 31	25 03	6 04	16 55	12 58	24 35	27 08	0 16	28 28	0 49	10 04	16 55	19 20
4 W	4 53 12	12 19 24	14 28	3 54	17 17	26 13	6 07	16 47	12 59	24 33	27 08	0 18	28 49	1 12	10 24	17 21	19 18
5 Th	4 57 9	13 20 18	27 36	3 44	15 57	27 23	6 09	16 39	13 01	24 31	27 08	0 19	29 10	1 36	10 43	17 43	19 17
6 F	5 1 5	14 21 12	10♒55	3 37	14 35	28 33	6 10 R	16 31	13 04	24 28	27 08	0 21	29 31	2 00	11 03	18 15	19 16
7 Sa	5 5 2	15 22 08	24 25	3 33	13 12	29 42	6 10	16 23	13 06	24 26	27 08 D	0 22	29 52	2 24	11 22	18 41	19 15
8 Su	5 8 58	16 23 04	8♓07	3 31 D	11 52	0♒51	6 10	16 14	13 08	24 24	27 08	0 23	0♒13	2 47	11 41	19 07	19 13
9 M	5 12 55	17 24 01	22 01	3 31 R	10 37	2 01	6 09	16 06	13 10	24 22	27 08	0 25	0 34	3 11	12 01	19 34	19 12
10 T	5 16 51	18 24 58	6♈07	3 31	9 30	3 10	6 07	15 58	13 13	24 19	27 08	0 26	0 56	3 35	12 20	20 00	19 11
11 W	5 20 48	19 25 56	20 25	3 30	8 32	4 19	6 04	15 50	13 15	24 17	27 08	0 28	1 17	3 59	12 39	20 26	19 10
12 Th	5 24 45	20 26 54	4♉53	3 27	7 44	5 27	6 00	15 42	13 18	24 15	27 08	0 30	1 38	4 22	12 58	20 52	19 09
13 F	5 28 41	21 27 54	19 27	3 21	7 08	6 36	5 56	15 34	13 21	24 13	27 08	0 31	2 00	4 46	13 17	21 18	19 08
14 Sa	5 32 38	22 28 54	4♊01	3 12	6 42	7 44	5 50	15 26	13 24	24 11	27 08	0 33	2 21	5 10	13 36	21 44	19 07
15 Su	5 36 34	23 29 54	18 29	3 01	6 28 D	8 53	5 44	15 18	13 27	24 09	27 09	0 34	2 43	5 34	13 54	22 10	19 06
16 M	5 40 31	24 30 56	2♋44	2 49	6 24	10 01	5 37	15 10	13 30	24 07	27 09	0 36	3 05	5 57	14 13	22 36	19 05
17 T	5 44 27	25 31 58	16 39	2 36	6 30	11 09	5 29	15 02	13 33	24 05	27 09	0 38	3 27	6 21	14 32	23 01	19 05
18 W	5 48 24	26 33 00	0♌12	2 25	6 45	12 16	5 20	14 54	13 36	24 03	27 10	0 39	3 49	6 45	14 50	23 27	19 04
19 Th	5 52 21	27 34 04	13 19	2 16	7 09	13 24	5 11	14 46	13 40	24 01	27 10	0 41	4 10	7 09	15 09	23 52	19 03
20 F	5 56 17	28 35 08	26 02	2 10	7 40	14 31	5 01	14 38	13 43	23 59	27 10	0 43	4 32	7 32	15 27	24 18	19 03
21 Sa	6 0 14	29 36 13	8♍25	2 07	8 18	15 39	4 49	14 31	13 47	23 57	27 11	0 44	4 55	7 56	15 45	24 43	19 02
22 Su	6 4 10	0♑37 19	20 30	2 06	9 02	16 46	4 37	14 23	13 50	23 55	27 11	0 46	5 17	8 20	16 03	25 08	19 02
23 M	6 8 7	1 38 25	2♎24	2 06	9 51	17 52	4 25	14 15	13 54	23 53	27 12	0 48	5 39	8 43	16 21	25 33	19 01
24 T	6 12 3	2 39 33	14 12	2 05	10 45	18 59	4 11	14 08	13 58	23 51	27 12	0 50	6 01	9 07	16 39	25 58	19 01
25 W	6 16 0	3 40 40	26 00	2 04	11 43	20 05	3 57	14 01	14 02	23 49	27 13	0 51	6 23	9 31	16 57	26 23	19 01
26 Th	6 19 56	4 41 49	7♏53	2 00	12 45	21 11	3 41	13 54	14 06	23 48	27 14	0 53	6 46	9 54	17 15	26 47	19 00
27 F	6 23 53	5 42 58	19 55	1 54	13 50	22 17	3 25	13 47	14 10	23 46	27 14	0 55	7 08	10 18	17 33	27 12	19 00
28 Sa	6 27 50	6 44 07	2♐11	1 45	14 58	23 23	3 09	13 40	14 14	23 44	27 15	0 57	7 30	10 42	17 50	27 37	19 00
29 Su	6 31 46	7 45 17	14 42	1 33	16 09	24 28	2 51	13 33	14 18	23 43	27 16	0 58	7 53	11 05	18 08	28 01	19 00 D
30 M	6 35 43	8 46 28	27 30	1 19	17 21	25 33	2 33	13 26	14 23	23 41	27 16	1 00	8 16	11 29	18 25	28 25	19 00
31 T	6 39 39	9 47 38	10♑35	1 06	18 36	26 38	2 14	13 19	14 27	23 40	27 17	1 02	8 38	11 53	18 42	28 49	19 00

EPHEMERIS CALCULATED FOR 12 MIDNIGHT GREENWICH MEAN TIME. ALL OTHER DATA AND FACING ASPECTARIAN PAGE IN **EASTERN TIME (BOLD)** AND PACIFIC TIME (REGULAR).

Notes